Computing and Language Variation

Edited by John Nerbonne, Charlotte Gooskens, Sebastian
Kürschner and Renée van Bezooijen

A special issue of International Journal of Humanities and
Arts Computing

Volume 2
(Numbers 1–2 2008)

EDITORS
David J. Bodenhamer and Paul S. Ell

Published by Edinburgh University Press
for the
Association for History and Computing

Subscription rates for 2009

Two issues per year, published in March and October

		UK	RoW	N. America
Institutions	Print	£70.00	£76.00	$153.00
	Online	£63.00	£63.00	$126.00
	Print and online	£87.50	£95.00	$191.00
Individuals	Print	£31.00	£34.00	$68.00
	Online	£28.00	£28.00	$56.00
	Print and online	£39.00	£42.00	$84.00
Back issues/ single copies		£27.00	£31.00	$62.00

How to order

Subscriptions can be accepted for complete volumes only. Print prices include packing and airmail for subscribers in North America and surface postage for subscribers in the Rest of the World. Volumes back to the year 2000 (where applicable) are included in online prices. Print back volumes will be charged at the current volume subscription rate.

All orders must be accompanied by the correct payment. You can pay by cheque, bank transfer, UNESCO coupons, or Visa/Mastercard. The individual rate applies only when a subscription is paid for with a personal cheque, credit card or bank transfer.

To order using the online subscription form, please visit www.eupjournals.com/ihhac/page/subscribe

Alternatively you may place your order by telephone on +44 (0)131 650 6207, fax on +44 (0)131 662 0053 or email to journals@eup.ed.ac.uk using your Visa or Mastercard credit card. Don't forget to include the expiry date of your card, the security number (three digits on the reverse of the card) and the address that the card is registered to.

Please make your cheque payable to Edinburgh University Press Ltd. Sterling cheques must be drawn on a UK bank account.

If you would like to pay by bank transfer, contact us at journals@eup.ed.ac.uk and we will send you instructions.

Advertising

Advertisements are welcomed and rates are available on request, or by consulting our website at www.eupjournals.com. Advertisers should send their enquiries to the Journals Marketing Manager at the address above.

CONTENTS

iii

Contents

FROM THE EDITORS

We are pleased to launch the first of several special issues designed to highlight cutting-edge research, methods, applications, literature, and websites in key fields of humanities and arts computing. The current double issue on variationist linguistics and computational humanities is an exemplar of what we hope to accomplish, especially in shortening the time it takes for important papers to move from initial presentation to publication. Under the guest editorship of John Nerbonne, Professor of Humanities Computing, Charlotte Gooskens, Associate Professor of Scandinavian Languages and Literature, both at the University of Groningen, The Netherlands, Sebastian Kürschner, Tenure track position ('Juniorprofessur') in variationist linguistics and language contact at the University of Erlangen-Nürnberg, Germany, and Renée van Bezooijen, Researcher at the University of Groningen, The Netherlands. This issue also introduces a roundtable discussion that we intend to become a regular feature of these special editions. The aim of the forum is to assess contributions to the field and link them to the broader interests of humanities and arts computing, as well as to highlight opportunities for connection and research within and among disciplines.

Over the next year, we will publish two additional thematic issues. Volume 3.1 will focus on humanities GIS. The past decade has witnessed an explosion of interest in the application of geo-spatial technologies to history, literature, and other arts and humanities disciplines. The special issue will highlight leading presentations from an August 2008 conference at the University of Essex and will include two new features – book reviews and website/tool reviews. Volume 3.2, to be published in spring 2010, will focus on important new research presented at the Digital Resources in Humanities and Arts Conference to be held at Queens University of Belfast in early September 2009.

Our goal is to make the *International Journal of Humanities and Arts Computing* a leading outlet for the interdisciplinary presentation and discussion of new ideas and innovative applications in how technology can be used to create and disseminate knowledge within and among humanities and arts disciplines. Our disciplines have been slow to adopt newer technologies, sometimes with good

International Journal of Humanities and Arts Computing 2 (1–2) 2008, v–vi
DOI: 10.3366/E1753854809000263

reason, but increasingly we find ourselves foundering with problems that can only be tackled through computational strategies, broadly defined. We also are influenced (and challenged) continually by new technological applications, such as the increasing use of volunteered information made possible by Google APIs. The issue we confront often is not the lack of interest or energy but the need for forums to put these developments in a broader perspective, make them more accessible to non-specialists, and offer instructive examples. Embracing technology for its own sake will never be a suitable answer, but neither will shunning it for reasons of complexity, cost, or inconvenience. The digital deluge, still in its early stages, makes it necessary for us to grapple with the challenges it poses to our craft. Our hope is that *IJHAC* becomes one avenue for engaging these problems creatively. For this purpose, we always seek essays that provide conceptual frameworks, advance new methods, review developments in the application of digital technologies to the various humanities disciplines, and, of course, use computing in its various forms to create new scholarship.

DJB and PSE
May 2009

CONTRIBUTORS

Karin Beijering studied Scandinavian Languages and Cultures (BA) and Linguistics (Research MA) at the University of Groningen. She wrote her MA thesis on the role of phonetic and lexical distances in the intelligibility and perception of Scandinavian language varieties. Currently she is a doctoral candidate at the Centre for Language and Cognition Groningen, working on a comparative study of epistemic modality in the Mainland Scandinavian languages. E-mail: K.Beijering@rug.nl

Andy Castro has researched the dialects of Hongshuihe Zhuang in Guangxi and various Yi languages in Western Yunnan. He lives in Kunming, China, and currently works as sociolinguistics coordinator for SIL, East Asia Group. E-mail: andy_castro@sil.org

Koenraad De Smedt is professor of computational linguistics at the University of Bergen. He has done research on computational psycholinguistic models of language production and on language technology. His current interests are in research infrastructures for language, in particular treebanks. He has coordinated European projects in education and researcher training. Email: desmedt@uib.no

Folkert de Vriend studied General Linguistics at the Radboud University in Nijmegen. He has worked on language policy and preservation and validation of language resources. Currently, he is working towards a Ph.D. in Linguistics. His current research is in language variation and research infrastructures. E-mail: f.devriend@let.ru.nl

Dirk Geeraerts teaches theoretical linguistics at the University of Leuven. He is the director of the research team *Quantitative Lexicology and*

International Journal of Humanities and Arts Computing 2 (1–2) 2008, vii–xi
10.3366/E1753854809000275
© Edinburgh University Press and the Association for History and Computing 2009

Variational Linguistics. His main research interests involve the overlapping fields of lexical semantics and lexicology, from the theoretical point of view of Cognitive Linguistics, with a specific descriptive interest in social variation and a strong methodological commitment to corpus analysis. E-mail: dirk.geeraerts@arts.kuleuven.be

Charlotte Giesbers studied German Language and Literature at the Radboud University in Nijmegen. She has worked on the dialect dictionary project *Woordenboek van de Gelderse Dialecten* (WGD) and has a Ph.D. in Linguistics. In her Ph.D. project she researched the Kleverlandish dialect continuum. E-mail: c.reijngoudt-giesbers@gelderserfgoed.nl

Charlotte Gooskens is associate professor of Scandinavian linguistics at the University of Groningen. Her interests lie in the field of sociophonetics and perceptual dialectology. Her current research focuses on the relationship between the mutual intelligibility of closely related languages and linguistic factors. E-mail: c.s.gooskens@rug.nl

Wilbert Heeringa works as a postdoc at the Meertens Institute in Amsterdam. He is especially interested in (techniques for measuring) diachronic and synchronic language variation. Currently he works on a project which focuses on 80 dialect and language varieties in the Netherlands and Flanders. The goal of the project is to show and explain dialect change, and to determine which linguistic level – lexical, phonological or phonetic – has been affected most strongly. E-mail: wilbert.heeringa@meertens.knaw.nl

Paul Heggarty is an expert on the Quechua language family, and also works on Romance and Germanic, studying both synchronic variation and diachronic developments, where he is one of a growing number of researchers applying phylogenetic inference (and software developed in biology for this purpose) to historical linguistics. He is at Cambridge. E-mail: pah1003@cam.ac.uk

Saara Hyvönen holds a Ph.D. in mathematics from Helsinki University of Technology. Her research is concentrated on theoretical and applied problems in data analysis, including applications in fields such as dialectology and atmospheric sciences. Currently she works on search problems at Fonecta Ltd. E-mail: Saara.Hyvonen@iki.fi

Leen Impe holds a four-year doctoral scholarship at the University of Leuven and is involved in a VNC research project on mutual intelligibility in the Low Countries, in cooperation with the universities of Nijmegen and Groningen. E-mail: leen.impe@arts.kuleuven.be

Sebastian Kürschner holds a tenure track position ('Juniorprofessur') in variational linguistics and language contact at the University of Erlangen-Nürnberg. He received the doctoral degree from the University of Freiburg in 2007. Until 2009, he was a postdoc at the University of Groningen. His main research topics include mutual intelligibility, contrastive Germanic linguistics, and historical morphology. E-mail: Sebastian.Kuerschner@ger.phil.uni-erlangen.de

Antti Leino is a university lecturer in computer science waiting to return to a linguistic research institute, whose research interests include data mining, onomastics, dialectology and combinations of these. Since 2008 Leino is a member of the Board of Directors of the International Council of Onomastic Sciences. E-mail: antti.leino@cs.helsinki.fi

Therese Leinonen studied Scandinavian Languages and Literature at the University of Helsinki. After finishing her Masters degree in 2001 she has worked as a book editor and as researcher at the Research Institute for the Languages of Finland. Since 2006 she is a Ph.D.-student at the University of Groningen in the project Determinants of Dialectal Variation. E-mail: t.leinonen@rug.nl

Warren Maguire is a lecturer in English Language at the University of Edinburgh. His research interests include methods in dialectology, phonetic and phonological variation and change, phonological mergers and their reversal, dialect levelling, varieties of English and Scots, and electronic corpora of non-standard speech. E-mail: w.maguire@ed.ac.uk

Simonetta Montemagni is Senior Researcher at the Institute of Computational Linguistics in Pisa. Her research interests range from Natural Language Processing and Information Extraction to Computational Dialectology. As a member of the Editorial Board of the Lexical Atlas of Tuscany since 1986, she was responsible for the design and development of its on-line version, ALT-Web (http://serverdbt.ilc.cnr.it/altweb/). Current work in the area includes advanced methods and techniques for modelling diatopic language variation. E-mail: simonetta.montemagni@ilc.cnr.it

John Nerbonne is professor of Computational Linguistics and head of Humanities Computing at the University of Groningen. He served as president of the Association for Computational Linguistics in 2002 and is a member of the Royal Netherlands Academy of Sciences (KNAW). His current research concerns language variation and interference in language contact phenomena. E-mail: j.nerbonne@rug.nl

Jelena Prokić is a PhD student at the Humanities Computing department at the University of Groningen. She works in the field of dialectometry and her main research interest is application of dialectometric and other statistical methods in the investigation of language contact and language change. E-mail: j.prokic@rug.nl

David Robey was until recently Professor of Italian at Reading and Director of the ICT in Arts and Humanities Research Programme of the (British) Arts and Humanities Research Council. He is currently Arts and Humanities Consultant at the Oxford e-Research Centre and is also President of the Association for Literary and Linguistic Computing. E-mail: d.j.b.robey@reading.ac.uk

Dirk Speelman teaches ICT for language students and corpus linguistics at the University of Leuven. His main research interest lies in the fields of corpus linguistics, computational lexicology and variationist linguistics in general. Much of his work focuses on methodology and on the application of quantitative methods to the study of language. He also is author of several software tools in support of linguistic research. E-mail: dirk.speelman@arts.kuleuven.be

Benedikt Szmrecsanyi is a Fellow at the Freiburg Institute for Advanced Studies, and affiliated with the English Department at the University of Freiburg. His current research interests lie with dialectology and dialectometry, variationist and cognitive sociolinguistics, language typology, and psycholinguistics. E-mail: bszm@frias.uni-freiburg.de

Louis ten Bosch has a background in mathematics. He has a PhD in Phonetics/Linguistics and has been working in the area of Automatic Speech Recognition. Currently he is a researcher at the department of Language and Speech at the Radboud University in Nijmegen. His current interest is in computational modelling of language acquisition. E-mail: l.tenbosch@let.ru.nl

Renée van Bezooijen has been working as a sociophonetician and dialectologist at the University of Nijmegen. She is currently working at the University of Groningen, where she is involved in the research programme of Charlotte Gooskens on the mutual intelligibility of closely related northern and western European languages. E-mail: r.vanbezooijen@let.ru.nl

Vincent J. van Heuven is professor of Experimental Linguistics and Phonetics at the Leiden University Centre for Linguistics, and former director of the institute. He is a member of the Royal Netherlands Academy of Arts and Sciences, secretary of the Permanent Council of the IPA, and associate editor of *Phonetica*. E-mail: V.J.J.P.van.Heuven@hum.leidenuniv.nl

Roeland van Hout is a linguist working on language variation, applied linguistics, and methodology of linguistic research. He has done research on geographical and social variation in Dutch dialects and in Standard Dutch. He also researched the acquisition of Dutch by Moroccans and Turks in the Netherlands and is the author of *Statistics in Language Research* (with Toni Rietveld, for De Gruyter). E-mail: hout@let.ru.nl

Cathryn Yang has lived and worked in Yunnan, China, for four years, focusing on dialect studies of minority languages such as Southern Zhuang, Nisu, and Lalo. She is currently working towards her Ph.D. at La Trobe University in Melbourne, Australia. E-mail: cathryn_yang@sil.org

LANGUAGE VARIATION STUDIES AND COMPUTATIONAL HUMANITIES

JOHN NERBONNE, CHARLOTTE GOOSKENS, SEBASTIAN KÜRSCHNER AND RENÉE VAN BEZOOIJEN

The volume we are introducing here contains a selection of the papers presented at a special track on computational techniques for studying language variation held at *The Thirteenth International Conference on Methods in Dialectology* in Leeds on 4–5 August 2008. We are grateful to the conference organisers, Nigel Armstrong, Joan Beal, Fiona Douglas, Barry Heselwood, Susan Lacey, Ann Thompson, and Clive Upton for their cooperation in our organisation of the event. We likewise owe thanks to the referees of the present volume, who we are pleased to acknowledge explicitly: Agnes de Bie, Roberto Bolognesi, David Britain, Cynthia Clopper, Ken Decker, Anders Eriksson, Hans Goebl, Stefan Grondelaers, Carlos Gussenhoven, Nynke de Haas, Frans Hinskens, Angela Kluge, Gitte Kristiansen, Alexandra Lenz, Maarten Mous, Hermann Niebaum, Lisa Lena Opas-Hänninen, Petya Osenova, John Paolillo, Louis Pols, Helge Sandøy, Bob Shackleton, Felix Schaeffler, Marco Spruit, Rint Sybesma, Nathan Vaillette, Gunther de Vogelaer, and Esteve Valls.

The conference track consisted of 24 papers and posters, including a keynote address by Vincent van Heuven on phonetic techniques for studying variation and comprehensibility. Fourteen contributions were selected for publication in this special issue of the *International Journal for Humanities and Arts Computing*, including van Heuven's. In addition the conference track featured a panel session reflecting on the introduction of computational techniques to the study of language variation and more generally, on computing and the humanities. We have prepared a report on the panel session for publication here as well.

International Journal of Humanities and Arts Computing 2 (1–2) 2008, 1–18
DOI: 10.3366/E1753854809000287

In the remainder of this article we sketch variationist linguistics as a subfield within the discipline of linguistics and relate how we see the path that led to computational studies occupying a modest place in this branch of linguistics. Our intention is that the present introduction provides a context within which the more specialised contributions can be better appreciated.

More importantly for those especially interested in humanities computing, we sketch the contributions of this volume collectively as an example of what we might refer to as an ENGAGED HUMANITIES COMPUTING, which we intend as a contribution to the ongoing debate about how computational work can best be integrated into the humanities disciplines (Nerbonne, 2005; McCarty, 2005). We shall elaborate on this further below, but we mean in particular that it has been the strategy of computationalists working in language variation that they primarily address existing questions from this sub-discipline, that they attempt to solve existing analytical problems, that they compare their results to those of non-computational scholars, and that they examine their methods and results critically from the perspective of the sub-discipline. The goal is to have computational techniques accepted into the toolbox that the sub-discipline normally recommends.

VARIATIONIST LINGUISTICS

Linguistics is the scientific study of language, and VARIATIONIST LINGUISTICS studies the variation found within languages, especially variation that is geographically or socially conditioned. DIALECTOLOGY is one of the oldest branches of linguistics, focusing especially on the way language varies geographically. SOCIOLINGUISTICS focuses on the social conditioning of variation. Linguistic variation was studied early on for the clues it suggested for the manner in which language changes diffuse geographically, but it is clearly fascinating to a large number of people, judging by the interest it inspires in learned and lay audiences. In the 1960s Labov demonstrated that variation not only existed along social lines (as well as along the above mentioned geographic lines), but also that these same social lines likewise demarcated the path of change for some linguistic innovations (see Chambers and Trudgill, 1998: Chap. 4). In this way the study of dialectology was expanded to include not only geographic, but also social variation. Indeed, some date the birth of sociolinguistics from this period (although there was clearly interest in issues involving language and social structure earlier, as well). Contemporary linguists who work on dialectology are normally interested in social variation as well, justifying our referring to this subfield as variationist linguistics.

Variationist linguistics sees dialects and sociolects as elements of culture, and has long been interested in the degree to which linguistic culture follows the same paths as technical, political, and aesthetic culture. Gilliéron, one of the earliest French dialectologists, linked variation in French (*langue d'oc* vs. *langue d'oil*) to differences in architecture, agricultural practice and legal institutions (Chambers and Trudgill, 1998: 95–103). This makes language variation study interesting from the point of view of more general studies in human culture, the humanities.

DATA COLLECTIONS

A major achievement of dialectology has been the compiling of substantial data collections in structured form, normally referred to as DIALECT ATLASES. Although no one rivals Georg Wenker (1881), who collected questionnaires from over 48,500 German towns and villages on the pronunciation of words in some 40 different sentences at the end of the nineteenth century (Niebaum and Macha, 2006: 58ff), still dialectologists have always been concerned to base their work on large collections of comparable data. (See the *Deutscher Sprachatlas*, 1927–1956, published by Ferdinand Wrede and others, for 128 of the maps resulting from Wenker's survey, and see http://www.diwa.info/ for an internet presentation of the whole atlas.) By 'comparable' we mean, e.g., that the pronunciations of the same words are collected at a range of sites, or the words for a given concept, or the syntactic means of expressing something more abstract. Many of the papers in this volume are based on substantial samples culled from dialect atlases, and it is easy to imagine how attractive it is to apply computational techniques to such large bodies of data, and conversely, how difficult and frustrating it is to attempt to analyse such large data sets without the benefit of extensive computation.

SÉGUY AND GOEBL

The early pioneers in the application of computing to problems in dialectology were Jean Séguy (1973) and Hans Goebl (1982), who knew of each other's work, but appear to have developed their ideas independently. Their emphases lay in the measurement of dialect differences, which explains their preference for the term 'dialectometry'. Goebl also emphasised the application of novel statistical techniques, which at that time had only recently been developed for the analysis of categorical data. They pioneered not only the use of the computer in dialectology for the purpose of managing and analysing large volumes of data, but Séguy was (and Goebl is) still very much a dialectologist himself. So computational dialectology began auspiciously, initiated by practicing dialectologists, very much familiar with problems in the field, such as the failure to develop a methodology for the selection of which linguistic material to use for samples, the lack of a theoretical foundation for commonly used notions such as 'dialect area', and the relative inattention to more abstract questions, e.g. about how geography influenced language variation and how it might be related to other issues in the diffusion of cultural innovations. All of these issues have been addressed in more detail thanks to the deployment of computational techniques in dialectology. See Nerbonne (2009) for a review of the advantages of an aggregate perspective in analysing linguistic variation and Nerbonne and Heeringa (to appear) for a review of techniques suitable for measuring linguistic variation.

THE COMPUTATIONAL ISSUES

The basic computational issues facing the researcher who would like to contribute to dialectology have been addressed, but in the interest of potentially stimulating improvements, perhaps from other humanities disciplines, and in the interest of indicating where solutions in dialectology might be useful to others, we shall review the issues here briefly. To begin there are serious problems in choosing a format suitable for processing and storing research data. Modern dialectological collections should include the original recordings of fieldworkers, meaning the audio and perhaps even video recordings of linguistic data, and this needs to adhere to standards only now emerging for such multimedia data. Two projects are worth special note for their efforts in promoting standards and good practices for recording and archiving linguistic material: first, the Max Planck Institute's Dobes project (*Dokumentation Bedrohter Sprachen*, http://www.mpi.nl/DOBES/), and second, the E-MELD project, sponsored by the U.S. National Science Foundation and endorsed by the Linguist List. E-MELD stands for the "Electronic Metastructure for Endangered Languages Data" (http://emeld.org/). In addition to issues concerning multimedia data, the dialectologist often faces issues concerning multilingual data, data in various writing systems, and data in phonetic transcription. We refer to the project sites above for advice on these matters as well.

Naturally, the problems in representing and storing data are preliminaries with respect to the questions of how one should analyse dialectological data. We can usefully distinguish the basic measurement of similarity (or dissimilarity) from further steps in the analysis. Since we view similarity and dissimilarity as each other's converse, we will normally mention only one from now on, assuming we can always derive the other via the application of a suitable inverse. If we view a dialectological survey as producing an array of categorical responses $\mathbf{a}$, then the bulk of work has been done using HAMMING DISTANCE as a measure of site distance $d(\mathbf{a}, \mathbf{b}) = \sum_i \mathbf{a}_i \neq \mathbf{b}_i$, i.e. the number of survey items for which $\mathbf{a}$ and $\mathbf{b}$ differ. Goebl (1982) adds an inverse frequency weighting to this, reasoning that common infrequent responses are especially reliable indicators of dialect affinity. Naturally, this sort of measure is appropriate for categorical data of non-linguistic origin – preference for first names, styles of clothing or architecture,

4

religious affiliation, or any number of other cultural markers. It would therefore be an excellent candidate for measurement in other areas (see above) where one wished to gauge cultural overlap. Speelman and Geeraerts's paper in the present volume suggests that this simple Hamming measure of dialectological affinity ought to be normalised with respect to the heterogeneity one should expect on the basis of conceptual grounds.

Language is also highly structured, so more recent developments have emphasised measures of difference that are sensitive to linguistic structure. Nerbonne and Heeringa's (to appear) survey article reviews a substantial body of work applying variants of EDIT DISTANCE (also known as string distance, or Levenshtein distance) to pronunciation data. Edit distance counts the number of edit operations – insertions, deletions or substitutions – needed to transform one sequence to another. It is sensitive to linear order, and thus introduces a first level of structural sensitivity into the measurements. Several articles in the present volume use edit distance, and one (Yang and Castro) explores a refinement for detail with languages with tonal distinctions. This sort of measure might be interesting for the analysis of other material with linear structure, e.g. folk melodies or sequences of ritual actions. But linguistic structure is much deeper than sequence comparison might detect, so it is not surprising to see other attempts at structurally sensitive comparison. Resonant frequencies (FORMANTS) are well-established phonetic characterisations of vowels, which have resisted automatic extraction, but Leinonen (this volume) applies techniques to detect these with no manual intervention, paving the way to more sensitive large-scale comparisons. Maguire (this volume) proposes techniques sensitive to PHONEMIC structure (the system of sounds capable of marking differences in meaning), and Van Heuven (this volume) explores the degree to which comprehensibility can serve as a basis for studies in language variation. Gooskens, Heeringa and Beijering's and Kürschner, Gooskens and van Bezooijen's papers examine the relation between comprehensibility and other measures of linguistic distance. Montemagni's paper investigates the relation between pronunciation and vocabulary and Szmrecsanyi's uses data from MORPHOLOGY (word forms) and SYNTAX (the structure of phrases and sentences).

If the basic measurements of distance or similarity have been fairly simple throughout the history of dialectometry, the further analysis of differences has been quite varied. Clustering has been popular, as has been a range of dimension reduction techniques, including especially multidimensional scaling, principal component analysis and factor analysis. Prokić and Nerbonne (this volume) and Leino and Hyvönen (this volume) continue investigation into these areas. This line of investigation is important for several reasons: first, as means of probing how geography influences cultural variation; second, in order to explore the linguistic space with an eye toward detecting co-varying linguistic elements, perhaps with an eye toward investigating structural effects; third, for the opportunity it affords to compare the computational work with earlier, non-computational work, most of which presented its results in the form of maps showing areas of relative coherence.

An exciting aspect of work reported on in the current volume is the degree to which it engages other, non-computational aspects of variationist linguistics. This is interesting in itself, offering opportunities to examine more fundamental issues in how language varieties differ, but it also illustrates one strategy for computational studies in the humanities, that of seeking close engagement with non-computational studies. Computational dialectology has regularly asked whether its techniques make sense from the perspective of the larger discipline (see McMahon and McMahon (2005) and the review by Nerbonne (2007) for an example of a dispute on whether computational techniques make sense linguistically). This is a primary point of engagement, and several papers focus on techniques that are presented and presumably evaluated on the basis of what they show about the geographic distributions of linguistic variation. Yang and Castro's paper on incorporating lexical tone differences into sequence distance measures, Prokić and Nerbonne's paper on clustering, Leino and Hyvönen's paper on statistical dimension reduction techniques, Leinonen's paper on extracting vowel system profiles from acoustic data, and Speelman and Geeraerts's paper on compensating for inherent conceptual tendencies influencing variation all fall into this category.

But naturally we are also interested in how computational results shed light not on how to detect variation and the influence geography has on it, but rather on further central questions of the sub-discipline, and this sort of question forms a second point of engagement.

One line of work which illustrates the strategy of engaged computational work is illustrated by the studies on comprehensibility, for example, Gooskens, Heeringa and Beijering's paper. The interesting added dimension in their work is the functional perspective it adopts. Linguistic variation signals social and geographic provenance, but it is overlaid on a system whose primary purpose is undoubtedly communication. If variation is too extreme, communication deteriorates. Gooskens et al. contrast computational measures of pronunciation and vocabulary difference in how well they predict difficulties in comprehension, showing that the pronunciation differences present the more serious problems (at least in this material). Maguire's paper on the lexical distribution of variation has a similar strategic aim, that of tracking which changes result in differing distributions of phonemes, i.e. sounds capable of distinguishing meaning. Maguire's work is similar to Moberg et al.'s (2007) study, but he uses a measure which allows symmetrical comparison of varieties, and applies it to a range of English accents, while Moberg and his colleagues studied the asymmetric case of 'semi-communication' among Scandinavian languages.

Montemagni's paper illustrates an avenue from variationist study into historical linguistics. The paper examines the degree to which pronunciation and vocabulary co-vary and it closes with an interesting historical conjecture. Most explanations of linguistic diffusion assume that the avenues of diffusion should be similar (Bloomfield, 1933: 18.12; Trudgill, 1974), and most earlier studies have shown similar distributions of differences in the different linguistic levels (Spruit, Heeringa and Nerbonne, 2009). Montemagni shows, however, that vocabulary differences correlate better with geography in Tuscany than pronunciation differences do, and conjectures that relatively recent pronunciation changes spreading radially from Florence lie behind the current patterns. The changes have not yet reached peripheral areas which are therefore more like each other than like immediately adjacent areas that have already been affected by the changes.

Heeringa, Gooskens, and De Smedt's paper superficially present a methodological correction to a problem in the validation of linguistic distance measures concerning the role of preconceived opinion in the perception of linguistic distance but it also opens deeper questions concerning the relation between the perception of distance and attitudes and opinions about distance that may be the result of mere hearsay. Are our perceptions influenced by our attitudes and prejudices concerning linguistic variation?

PAPERS IN THE PRESENT VOLUME

We briefly discuss each of the papers in turn in this special issue. We discuss first papers which examine varietal differences via their impact on intelligibility, i.e. the point where signalling social and geographic provenance begins to impede communication. Since signalling one's provenance is surely less important than communication, we appear to be dealing with a secondary function that begins to encroach on the primary one.

In his keynote speech, 'Making Sense of Strange Sounds: (Mutual) Intelligibility of Related Language Varieties. A Review', Vincent van Heuven advances mutual intelligibility as a functional operationalisation of a one-dimensional notion of remoteness between closely related language varieties. The greater the intelligibility of speaker A to listener B, the smaller the distance between variety A and B. A one-dimensional yardstick for linguistic distance is invaluable if we aim to come up with computational models of linguistic distance in which the contribution of lexical, phonological and syntactic differences between language varieties are to be weighed against each other in a comparison of symbolic input (i.e. distance measures derived from comparisons of transcriptions of vocabularies, grammars and texts). Moreover, Van Heuven notes that intelligibility is asymmetrical: speaker A may be more intelligible to listener B than vice versa. Van Heuven explicitly ignores the role of experience with the non-native variety. When the aim is to exploit intelligibility as a yardstick for linguistic distance between two varieties, the listeners should have no familiarity with the non-native variety. Intelligibility should be measured before any learning effects may have taken place. Given this simplification, listening to speech in a closely related language variety is quite like listening to noisy speech. The remainder of his review deals with possibilities of measuring intelligibility and considers how low-level deviations affect the process of word recognition – which he considers to be the central skill involved in understanding input speech in a closely related language variety. The contributions of deviations at the level of vowels, consonants and of word prosody (stress, tone) are considered. Van Heuven makes a convincing claim that much insight can be gained from related fields of inquiry, specifically from the study of the effects of foreign accent on the intelligibility of second-language speakers, and from computational models predicting intelligibility from mismatches between the non-native input language system on the one hand and the sound categories and lexical structures of the target language on the other. Models of perceptual assimilation of non-native sounds to the native categories, and of word recognition are reviewed. Although it is still impossible to predict the intelligibility of deviant input speech (for instance speech in a closely related variety), the problem seems soluble in principle: the development of adequate computational models predicting the intelligibility of deviant speech – such as speech in a closely related language variety – is mainly a matter of investing time and effort.

In 'Phonetic and Lexical Predictors of Intelligibility', Charlotte Gooskens, Wilbert Heeringa and Karin Beijering proceed from the strength of dialectometric methods such as the Levenshtein algorithm, which allows the researcher to measure objective aggregate distances between language varieties. These distances can be used for dialectometric purposes and have proved to be a powerful tool for the classification of dialects. Recent research has shown that Levenshtein distance is also a good predictor of intelligibility of closely related language varieties. However, since only aggregate distance measures have been applied so far, no conclusions could be drawn about the nature of the phonetic differences that contribute most to intelligibility. In their paper, Gooskens, Heeringa and Beijering measure distances between Standard Danish and each of 17 Scandinavian language varieties at the lexical level and at various phonetic levels. In addition, they conducted a listening experiment to assess the intelligibility of the 17 varieties to young Danes from Copenhagen. In order to determine how well the linguistic levels can predict intelligibility, they correlated the intelligibility scores with the linguistic distances and carried out a number of regression analyses. The results show that for this particular set of closely related language varieties phonetic distance is a better predictor of intelligibility than lexical distance. Consonant substitutions, vowel insertions and vowel shortenings contribute significantly to the prediction of intelligibility. Knowledge about the linguistic determinants of mutual intelligibility is useful for language planning at the national and European levels. If the less frequently spoken languages are to survive in a European context, it is important to gain knowledge about the mechanisms involved in using one's own language for communication with speakers of other, closely related European languages. Knowledge of the role of different linguistic levels for mutual intelligibility is also useful for didactic purposes. It will make it easier to give specific instructions to people trying to gain the necessary passive knowledge needed to understand a language.

A further study on intelligibility is presented by Sebastian Kürschner, Charlotte Gooskens and Renée van Bezooijen, 'Linguistic Determinants of the Intelligibility of Swedish Words among Danes'. They asked how one can predict which Swedish words will and will not be understood when spoken to Danes. Many Scandinavians have the interesting custom of speaking in their own languages in conversations with those who speak other Scandinavians languages natively. So a Dane and a Swede may carry on a conversation, each speaking his own native language. It would be natural to assume that the success of such 'semi-communication' (Haugen, 1966) depends on an individual's experience with the non-native language, but probably also on the degree to which native comprehension procedures may be applied to the foreign material. In fact, the authors cite earlier work noting that experience is a relatively poor predictor of comprehensibility. Kürschner et al. focus on the comprehension of isolated spoken words in contrast to most earlier work which concentrates on textual understanding, and they examine a wide variety of potential linguistic predictors, including first and foremost how similar the Swedish pronunciation of the word is to the corresponding Danish word's pronunciation. But Danish has a conservative orthography that reflects the historical relation to Swedish rather more faithfully than pronunciation, and this might aid comprehension in the relevant cases, so this was also examined, as was the number of syllables, the density of the neighbourhood of words competing to be understood, and the frequency with which the words are heard in everyday speech. The extensive literature on spoken word recognition had shown the last two factors to be important in the understanding of words by natives. A particularly interesting aspect of Kürschner et al.'s work from the perspective of more general opportunities in humanities computing is their use of an internet experiment to gather data from a geographically distant group of test persons.

Two papers examine in particular national borders that may play a role in the linguistic differences. Naturally these may be relevant in the Scandinavian case noted above, but that was not the focus of the study. In the first paper, intelligibility is again the behavioural crux, while judgements of similarity are used in the second.

In 'Mutual Intelligibility of Standard and Regional Dutch Language Varieties', Leen Impe, Dirk Geeraerts and Dirk Speelman investigate the mutual word intelligibility among ten Dutch language varieties, both Belgian and Netherlandic. No local dialects are included, only regional and standard varieties. Word intelligibility was tested by means of a computer-controlled lexical decision task, in which subjects had to decide as quickly as possible whether the auditorily presented word was an existing or non-existing word, and a multiple choice task, in which subjects had to select from two alternatives the one which best reflected the meaning of the stimulus word. Subjects were 641 secondary school pupils in Dutch-speaking Belgium and 404 secondary school pupils in the Netherlands. At the national level, an asymmetry was found in the sense that subjects from Belgium experienced fewer intelligibility problems with words from the Netherlands, both phonetically and lexically, than the other way around. The asymmetry is explained by the (historical) language-political situation in the Dutch language area, in which the language spoken in the Netherlands figured and still figures to some extent as a model for the language spoken in Belgium. At the regional level, intelligibility differences between standard and regional varieties were found to be larger in Belgium than in the Netherlands. The experimental techniques employed in this study are very sensitive (especially the response times obtained with the lexical decision task), and they are new to the field of dialectology, where the quantification of intelligibility has been neglected. The measurement method is not only relevant to the study of the intelligibility of related languages and language varieties, but more generally also to other fields, such as speech pathology, second language acquisition and speech technology.

Of course, intelligibility is also affected by processes which impede the 'density' of communication (the term is Bloomfield's). One such process is the establishment of a national border. In their paper 'The Dutch-German Border: Relating Linguistic, Geographic and Perceptual Distances', Folkert de Vriendt, Charlotte Giesbers, Roeland van Hout and Louis ten Bosch examine a dialect region which straddles a national border, a particularly interesting case. Their data were collected in a sub-area of the Kleverland dialect region, extending from Duisburg in Germany to Nijmegen in the Netherlands. The dialects spoken there used to constitute a dialect continuum, marked by a direct relationship between geographic and linguistic distance. However, there is strong evidence that the Dutch-German state border established in 1830 has given rise to a linguistic gap. De Vriendt et al. try to establish the impact of the border on linguistic distance, using multidimensional scaling and correlation techniques. They compare three models to explain linguistic distance. Their first and simplest model is one where linguistic distance is a monotonic function of geographic distance. The second model is expanded by including a constant representing the state border gap. The third model is based on perceptual distances. The perceptual data were collected by means of a questionnaire in which informants were asked to indicate the linguistic similarity between neighbouring locations and the intensity of contacts with friends, relatives, and shops. The study reveals that a model based on perceptual distance, including both perceptual linguistic distance and perceptual socio-geographic contact distances, explains linguistic distance much better than a continuum or gap model based on geographic distance. The method applied and the results obtained are relevant not only for the study of linguistic variation in other dialect areas intersected by state borders but more generally for the investigation of the role of state borders for the variation and transmission of cultural products in a rapidly globalising world.

We now turn to a wider range of topics, including a historical conjecture about an unusual divergence in geographical diffusion between two levels of linguistics, several examinations of dimension-reducing techniques for their utility in the study of variation, and a proposal for incorporating the tone in languages such as Chinese into existing measures of pronunciation difference.

It is clear that de Vriendt et al. examine a well-documented historical situation with respect to its linguistic consequences. Simonetta Montemagni examines a curiously divergent pattern in Tuscany and suggests that there may be a historical explanation. She examines the relation between two different levels of linguistic variation in 'The Space of Tuscan Dialectal Variation. A Correlation Study'. Using L04, software developed in Groningen, as well as VDM, developed in Salzburg, she measures on the one hand the degree to which pronunciation differs from town to town in Tuscany, and on the other the degree to which vocabulary (the lexicon) varies, i.e. the degree to which different words are used for the same concepts. By measuring phonetic and lexical differences at the same set of sites, she is able to calculate the degree of correlation between the two. Further, she measures the degree to which geographic distance can predict phonetic and lexical distances. The linguistic assumptions behind these questions are definitely of interest to students of cultural transmission in general. We assume in linguistics that variation in both pronunciation and vocabulary is diffused through social contact. Linguists have also observed that the lexicon is quite easily changed: words come and go in languages in large numbers. If we regard proper names as words as well, which is justified, then it is clear that individuals adopt new words quite easily as well. Pronunciations are less volatile, perhaps for cognitive reasons having to do with the way first languages are imprinted in the mind, or perhaps for social reasons having to do with guaranteeing enough comprehensibility for communication. Whatever the reason, we expect a less than perfect correlation between pronunciation and the lexicon, and we expect lexical variation to be the more variable of the two, *inter alia* as it is the more sensitive indicator of social contact. It is simply easier to change one's vocabulary than one's pronunciation. If we operationalise the chance of social contact via simple geographic distance, then we expect the greater variability of lexical differences to translate to a correlation between geography and lexical differences that is weaker than the correlation between geography and pronunciation differences, and this expectation has been borne out in the past (see references in Montemagni's paper). Montemagni notes that correlations between linguistic variation and geography may be complicated by Tuscany's hilly terrain, which is difficult for travel, but this does not explain the difference between pronunciation and vocabulary. She closes with a speculation that ongoing pronunciation changes spreading radially from Florence, which moreover have not reached the various borders, may have left a ring of linguistic similarity. This might result in a large number of similar sites which are quite distant from one another.

In 'Recognising Groups among Dialects', Jelena Prokić and John Nerbonne review clustering as a means of recognising groups in data, in particular groups of language varieties that might be said to constitute a common dialect. As the authors note, finding groups among data is a problem linguistics shares with other humanities disciplines, at least with history, musicology and archaeology. Focusing on pronunciation data from Bulgarian, and noting the embarrassment of riches in the form of different clustering algorithms, and the problem of clustering's instability with respect to small differences in input data, they review various means of comparing clustering results. These results may be visualised as DENDROGRAMS, trees which group more similar varieties more closely, and which display reconstructed (clustered) distance in the branch length between varieties, i.e. COPHENETIC DISTANCE. They compare the results of clustering to those of the more stable multi-dimensional scaling, and they examine COPHENETIC CORRELATION, i.e. the degree to which input distances and the distances in dendrograms coincide, a comparison, and the information-theoretic measures of purity and entropy as "internal comparisons" that give a sense of the quality of clustering solutions independent of external information. They note, however, that there is a substantial literature on the dialect landscapes of many modern European (and Asian) languages, and there are formal measures with allow one to gauge how well one classification coincides with another. Prokić and Nerbonne settle on the MODIFIED RAND INDEX, which assigns a score between zero and one indicating how well one partition (due to clustering) overlaps with another (due to independent scholarship). As the humanities disciplines focus even more on the history of scholarship than other sciences, this is a useful measure for other purposes, as well. Methodologically, the paper concludes that the determination of groups is easily confounded by unclear borders, even when these are only sparsely instantiated, which means that some judgment is always sensible. The study also draws surprising conclusions about

Bulgarian dialects, seeing only two very distinct and internally coherent groups and a third, Rupskian group which is extremely diverse. Earlier scholarship had distinguished six groups where Prokić and Nerbonne see two.

Antti Leino and Saara Hyvönen's paper 'Comparison of Component Models in Analysing the Distribution of Dialect Features' may be understood as an exploration into alternatives to the clustering techniques explored in Prokić and Nerbonne's contribution. Instead of searching for groups in the sample sites, Leino and Hyvönen examine dialect variation more generally as a range of distributions of linguistic material not necessarily organised neatly into groups or areas. It is a technical paper comparing various statistical techniques with respect to their success in uncovering linguistic structure in large atlases (or other collections of linguistically varying material). The statistical techniques all attempt to identify the linguistic 'components' or factors in the atlas material, and they are all applied to two Finnish databases, one phonetic and one lexical. They authors conclude that factor analysis is the most robust of the techniques, that non-negative matrix factorisation and aspect Bernoulli are most sensitive to possible flaws in the data, that independent component analysis is most likely to provide new insights, and, finally that principal component analysis is most capable of providing a 'layered' view of dialect structure. The focus of this paper is the methodological comparison of the various statistical techniques, but the argument is carried out using the dialect atlas material. Given the abstract level of the presentation, it is to be expected that the discussion could be of interest to other areas of scholarship, and, in fact the authors are interested not only in dialects but also in 'similar cultural aggregates'.

The 'Factor Analysis of Vowel Pronunciation in Swedish Dialects' by Therese Leinonen attempts to secure insight into linguistic details even while retaining the advantages of aggregate analyses. Dialectometric research avoids the problem of having to choose which linguistic factors to use as the basis for dialect areas by aggregating over large data sets. These methods have mostly been based on pair-wise distances between dialects, obtained by aggregating over large amounts of linguistic material, but the aggregation step has made it difficult to trace the underlying linguistic features determining the dialect division. This paper expands the horizons of dialectometry by acoustic measurements of vowel pronunciations in Swedish dialects. Vowel spectra were analysed by means of principal component analysis. Two principal components were extracted explaining more than three quarters of the total variance in the vowel spectra. Plotting vowels in the PC1–PC2 plane showed a solution with strong resemblance to vowels in a formant plane. For the analysis of dialectal variation factor analysis was used. Nine factors were extracted showing different geographical distribution patterns in the data, without, however, suggesting distinct dialect areas. Results are visualised using coloured maps showing the Swedish dialect area as a continuum. The study is based on acoustic measurements of the vowels of more than 1,014 speakers: 91 sites spread over 6 traditional Swedish dialect regions, 12 speakers per site (3 elderly and 3 younger women, 3 elderly and 3 younger men). Per speaker 18 words repeated 3–5 times were recorded. The approach taken is valuable for other high-dimensional data involving computers and the humanities. It may be important not only for the analysis of language, but also in the larger context of cultural history and the analysis of other human activities as investigated by disciplines like archaeology, ethnology and musicology.

Cathryn Yang and Andy Castro examine pronunciation differences in so-called TONE LANGUAGES in 'Representing tone in Levenshtein distance'. Linguists distinguish SEGMENTAL components of pronunciation, i.e. what is represented in a good alphabet, from so-called SUPRASEGMENTAL components, which include in particular tone (or pitch) and duration. All languages, including English, use pitch at a phrasal or sentential level to distinguish different structures, but many other languages, including Chinese, but also Bai and Zhuang, which Yang and Castro study, also use tone extensively as a means of distinguishing words. LEVENSHTEIN DISTANCE has come to be accepted as a computational means of measuring pronunciation distance between words, but it is limited to processing sequences of symbols, i.e. segmental information. Yang and Castro focus on Bai and Zhuang, in which different atomic tonal elements are always associated with single syllables. Their proposal is essentially to measure tonal differences separately from segmental differences. For both levels they measure differences in sequences, so they in addition compare several different tonal representations including e.g. sequences of pitches, or alternatively initial pitches plus contours (melodies). They report on a series of measurements of pronunciation differences which they validate via a comparison to intelligibility measured behaviourally. They are able to demonstrate in two in-depth studies first, that tone is in one case just as important and in a second case even *more* important than segmental aspects of pronunciation in determining intelligibility, a definitely surprising result, and second, that the representation of tone using initial tone level and contour is most informative. A natural next step in this research line would be to verify that the segmental and suprasegmental levels complement each other in assaying linguistic distance (perhaps using the same intelligibility tests), and then examine means of combining the segmental and suprasegmental levels, e.g. by simply adding the two.

A final group of four papers examines alternatives and corrections to existing methodologies, including normalising for the effect of inherent variability in some concepts, the potential effect of second-hand opinions on the perception of linguistic differentiation, a proposal on how to analyse differing sound systems (rather than simply different sounds), and a proposal for obtaining and analysing data that reflects language use more directly than questionnaires.

Dirk Speelman and Dirk Geeraerts's paper, 'The Role of Concept Characteristics and Lexical Dialectometry', proceeds from the suspicion that genuine geographic influence may be signalled better by some concepts than by others. The idea behind their essay is that some concepts lend themselves to heterogeneous expression and that this second, conceptual source of variation may confound the measures of geographic variation currently used in dialectology. If there were attempts to measure cultural affinity on non-linguistic material, then one would expect similar sorts of issues to arise. Just as concepts such as 'money' are lexically variable in many languages and dialects, and thus seems to be inherently heterogeneous in expression, others, e.g. 'eyebrow', are not (usually). But if we were to examine the physical realisations of the same concept ('money'), any attempt to gauge the affinity of one settlement with another based on the concept's physical realisation would likewise run the risk of being confounded by the variability of the physical realisations. It is clear that linguistic concepts need to be a bit heterogeneous for their variability to signal geographic provenance, but extremely heterogeneous concepts also do not function well if the subdialectal variation is likewise large. Speelman and Geeraerts examine several factors which contribute to conceptual heterogeneity, including the unfamiliarity of concepts, their tendency not to be verbalised (and therefore to be missing from surveys at many locations), their tendency to multi-word expression, their sheer variety of lexicalisations, and whether the concept is negatively 'charged.' They examine a substantial sample of words with respect to these properties asking whether they contribute to the concept's heterogeneity as reflected in the diversity of words used to lexicalise the concept, how limited the use of the words are geographically and finally, how compact the region is in which a given word is used. Speelman and Geeraerts test their ideas on dialect atlas material from Limburg.

In 'What Role does Dialect Knowledge Play in the Perception of Linguistic Distances?', Wilbert Heeringa, Charlotte Gooskens, and Koenraad De Smedt raise the question whether naive listeners base their judgments of linguistic distances between their own dialect and other dialects of the same language solely on what they hear during an experiment or whether they also generalise from the knowledge that they have from previous experience with the dialects. In order to answer this question the authors first performed an experiment among Norwegian dialect listeners in order to measure perceptual linguistic distances between 15 Norwegian dialects. These perceptual distances were correlated with objective phonetic distances measured on the basis of the transcriptions of the recordings used in the perception experiment. In addition, they correlated the perceptual distances with objective distances between the same dialects but based on other datasets. On the basis of the correlation results and multiple regression analyses they conclude that the listeners did *not* base their judgments solely on information that they heard during the experiments but also on their general knowledge of the dialects. This conclusion is confirmed by the fact that the effect is stronger for the group of listeners who recognised the dialects on tape than for listeners who did not. This dialectometric study is of interest to (computational) dialectologists, sociolinguists and psycholinguists. The results are important to scholars who want to understand how dialect speakers perceive dialect pronunciation differences and may give more insight in the mechanisms behind the way in which linguistic variation is experienced.

'Quantifying Dialect Similarity by Comparison of the Lexical Distribution of Phonemes' by Warren Maguire introduces a method for quantifying the similarity of the lexical distribution of phonemes in different language varieties exemplified by standard and dialectal varieties of English. He takes dialectometry beyond lexicostatistic comparison and a purely phonetic comparison of words by considering lexical distributions (i.e. which cognate pairs have the same phone in a given position and which have a different phone). He integrates the lexical distribution of phonemes in the varieties in the measurements by examining the vowel correspondences that result when one aligns the 1,000 most frequent English words phonemically. Similarity is calculated by taking the most frequent correspondence per phoneme into account, and dividing the frequency by the number of comparisons made (i.e. including all correspondences with less frequent corresponding items). The method assesses to what degree dialects have differentiated from each other in the course of history and provides a means of examining historical connections between language varieties which are not obvious from surface inspection. Since this method is aimed at uncovering historical connections between varieties, it has implications for the interaction between dialects and historical factors of all kinds, including migration, standardisation, language death/replacement, historical boundaries, etc. Methods of this sort should add to our understanding of history. In addition, it allows for correlations between geography and linguistic variation, and may well allow us to look into recent changes in languages which are the result of wider societal pressures.

Benedikt Szmrecsanyi's contribution to this volume is noteworthy in several ways. First, while the great majority of studies in variation both in this volume and in more general scholarship focuses on pronunciation and vocabulary, Szmrecsanyi's piece 'Corpus-based Dialectometry: Aggregate Morphosyntactic Variability in British English Dialects' concentrates rather on morphology and syntax. Second, while most variation studies draw their data from the responses to the carefully designed questionnaires, Szmrecsanyi looks rather to naturally recorded collections of material, so-called CORPORA. It is certain that naturally occurring data reflect genuine speech habits more faithfully than do the responses to questionnaires, so the attempt to use this sort of data is worthwhile, but it is also more difficult to control the sorts of material one collects. Third, Szmrecsanyi also compares his findings to those in earlier literature which relied on selected features rather than larger aggregates. A first question is whether this naturalistic data will submit profitably to the usual sorts of analyses, and this question is answered in the positive (but see below). Even though there have been earlier aggregate studies of syntactic variation (see Szmrecsanyi's paper for references), there have not been many, making the fundamental question of geographical structuring of the data a very interesting second question. In particular typologists and syntactic theorists have been sceptical about the role of geography as an influence on linguistic variation, conjecturing that structural constraints would prove to be the more influential elements in explaining syntactic variation. And indeed, Szmrecsanyi's analysis displays rather less geographic conditioning than we are accustomed to in the study of linguistic variation, in particular in a rather weak correlation between geographic and linguistic (syntactic) distance ($r = 0.22$). It remains therefore to be seen whether this reflects a difficulty with the use of the naturalistic data or whether it reflects the typologist's conjecture that syntax offers less affordance for the expression of affinity.

CONSPECTUS AND PROSPECTUS

What does the present collection contain in the way of indications for humanities computing more generally? We select two prominent elements, namely the need for statistics on the one hand, and the virtues of deeper engagement with noncomputational work on the other.

The present volume presents a range of papers applying computational, and almost always statistical techniques to topics in the study of language variation. We suspect that the extensive and serious use of statistics is a benefit not only to our computational humanities discipline, but to others as well. Since one of the greatest advantages of the computer is its ability to process very large amounts of material, and since that material is usually empirical for most humanities disciplines, excepting perhaps philosophy, it is also variable. We simply do not see clean categorical generalisations in the data. Statistics allow us to wean lawful regularities from the complexity of noise, error and counterindicating factors. We suspect that the computational turn in the humanities will be accompanied by a statistical turn as well.

In addition to this technical reflection we return to the theme of 'engaged computational humanities' we mentioned in the introduction. Our goal is to have computational techniques accepted beside the range of techniques already available to the researcher in language variation, and the papers in this volume illustrate some of the consequences of this choice. As we noted at the beginning of this introduction, this entails our addressing questions from this sub-discipline, attempting to solve existing analytical problems, and comparing our results to those of non-computational scholars, and examining our methods and results critically from a variationist perspective. The papers in this volume illustrate these consequences abundantly, e.g. in the large number of papers, including the paper arising from Van Heuven's keynote, exploring how to validate computational techniques using alternatives known from non-computational studies, including in particular behavioural studies. Leinonen's paper, developing a computational technique for automatically comparing large numbers of vowel pronunciations, is also careful to show how the innovative technique relates to well-established techniques which require manual intervention.

One way to summarise the strategy of engaged computational humanities is to note that computational humanities scholarship remains humanities scholarship, meaning in particular that it must be compared to non-computational scholarship and that apparently conflicting results always stimulate reflection.

REFERENCES

L. Bloomfield (1933), *Language* (New York).

J. K. Chambers and P. Trudgill (1998), *Dialectology*, 2nd Ed (Cambridge).

Deutscher Sprachatlas (DSA) (1927–1956), Auf Grund des Sprachatlas des deutschen Reichs von Georg Wenker, begonnen von Ferdinand Wrede, fortgesetzt von Walther Mitzka und Bernhard Martin (Marburg).

H. Goebl (1982), *Dialektometrie: Prinzipien und Methoden des Einsatzes der numerischen Taxonomie im Bereich der Dialektgeographie*. Vol. 157 of *Philosophisch-Historische Klasse Denkschriften* (Vienna).

E. Haugen (1966), 'Semi-communication: The language gap in Scandinavia', *Sociological Inquiry*, 36 (2), 280–297.

W. McCarty (2005), *Humanities Computing* (New York).

A. McMahon and R. McMahon (2005), *Language Classification by Numbers* (Oxford).

J. Moberg, C. Gooskens, J. Nerbonne and N. Vaillette (2007), 'Conditional entropy measures intelligibility among related languages', in P. Dirix, I. Schuurman, V. Vandeghinste and F. Van Eynde, eds, *Computational Linguistics in the Netherlands 2006* (Utrecht), 51–66.

J. Nerbonne (2005), 'Computational contributions to humanities', *Linguistic and Literary Computing* 20(1), 25–40.

J. Nerbonne (2007), 'Review of McMahon and McMahon (2005)', *Linguistic Typology* 11, 425–436.

J. Nerbonne (2009), 'Data-driven dialectology', *Language and Linguistics Compass* 3(1), 175–198. doi: 10.1111/j.1749–818×2008.00114.x

J. Nerbonne and W. Heeringa (to appear), 'Measuring dialect differences', in J. E. Schmidt and P. Auer, eds, *Theories and Methods* Vol. in series *Language and Space* (Berlin).

H. Niebaum and J. Macha (2006), *Einführung in die Dialektologie des Deutschen* (Tübingen).

J. Séguy (1973), 'La dialectométrie dans l'Atlas linguistique de la Gascogne', *Revue de linguistique romane*, 37, 1–24.

M. Spruit, W. Heeringa and J. Nerbonne (2009), 'Associations among linguistic levels', *Lingua*. To appear. doi:10.1016/j.lingua.2009.02.001

P. Trudgill (1974), 'Linguistic change and diffusion: Description and explanation in sociolinguistic dialect geography', *Language in Society*, 2, 215–246.

G. Wenker (1881), *Sprachatlas von Nord- und Mitteldeutschland. Auf Grund von systematisch mit Hülfe der Volksschullehrer gesammeltem Material aus circa 30000 Orten. Abtheilung I Lieferung 1 (6 Karten und Textheft)* (Strasbourg/London).

PANEL DISCUSSION ON COMPUTING AND THE HUMANITIES

JOHN NERBONNE, PAUL HEGGARTY, ROELAND VAN HOUT AND DAVID ROBEY

This is the report of a panel discussion held in connection with the special session on computational methods in dialectology at *Methods XIII: Methods in Dialectology* on 5 August, 2008 at the University of Leeds. We scheduled this panel discussion in order to reflect on what the introduction of computational methods has meant to our subfield of linguistics, dialectology (in alternative divisions of linguistic subfields also known as variationist linguistics), and whether the dialectologists' experience is typical of such introductions in other humanities studies. Let's emphasise that we approach the question as working scientists and scholars in the humanities rather than as methodology experts or as historians or philosophers of science, i.e. we wished to reflect on how the introduction of computational methods has gone in our own field in order to conduct our own future research more effectively, or alternatively, to suggest to colleagues in neighbouring disciplines which aspects of computational studies have been successful, which have not been, and which might have been introduced more effectively. Since we explicitly wished to reflect not only on how things have gone in dialectology, but also to compare our experiences to others, we invited panellists with broad experience in linguistics and other fields.

We introduce the chair and panellists briefly.

John Nerbonne chaired the panel discussion. He works on dialectology, but also on grammar, and on applications such as language learning and information extraction and information access. He works in Groningen, and is past president of the *Association for Computational Linguistics* (2002).

International Journal of Humanities and Arts Computing 2 (1–2) 2008, 19–37
DOI: 10.3366/E1753854809000299

David Robey is an expert on medieval Italian literature, professor at Reading, and Programme Director of the *ICT in Arts and Humanities* Research Programme of the (British) Arts and Humanities Research Council. He is also president of the *Association for Literary and Linguistic Computing*.

Paul Heggarty is an expert on the Quechua language family, and also works on Romance and Germanic, studying both synchronic variation and diachronic developments, where he's one of a growing number of researchers applying phylogenetic inference (and software developed in biology for this purpose) to historical linguistics. He's at Cambridge.

Roeland van Hout is an expert on sociolinguistics, phonetics and second language acquisition. He is co-author (with Toni Rietveld) of the world's best book on applying statistics to linguistics, (Harald Baayen has just come out (2008) with a contender, but 15 years at #1 is impressive). He's at Nijmegen, and he's served on the Dutch research council's Humanities board for the last five years.

We suggested in inviting the panellists that they deliver some introductory remarks structured in a way that responds *inter alia* to two questions:

Are there elements of the computational work in language variation that should be made known to other scholars in the humanities?

Are there other computational lines of work in the humanities that are not used in studying language variation but which should be of interest? Is the primary common interest the computational tools or are there research issues which might benefit from a plurality of perspectives?

We emphasised, however, that the panel speakers should feel free to respond to the question of how the disciplines might interact in more creative ways, especially if they feel that the questions above are put too narrowly.

Each panellist presented some ideas before the discussion started.

Paul Heggarty *summarised some basic methodological issues in applying computational techniques to language data, reviewing typical criticisms – and how best to answer them.*

A burgeoning interest in the use of computational techniques is certainly something that linguistics holds in common with other fields in the humanities. But what might the various disciplines learn from each other in this? Here I offer a perspective from the experience of attempts to apply such techniques to comparative and historical linguistics, to be taken here as an illustrative 'humanities data-type'. Not that this experience has always been plain sailing, so some of the 'lessons' turn out to be more in how *not* to go about things.

An important aside to begin with is to clarify that what the disciplines learn from each other is hardly limited just to the methods, but extends also to the *results* from applying them. Computational approaches can have a particularly powerful impact when they turn out to challenge traditional views which, while entrenched, have hitherto remained unquantified and essentially impressionistic. Such is the case with Gray and Atkinson's (2003) article in *Nature*: while much disputed, to be sure, it has undoubtedly forced open again the question of the dating and origins of Indo-European, and a possible link with agriculture as a driving force. The relevance of this particular application of computational techniques to language data, then, transcends linguistics into several other branches of the humanities and beyond, not least archaeology, (pre-)history and genetics.

To focus on methods, though, we need to consider not only which tools to use, but more general issues of methodology, two in particular. Firstly, how freely transferable are computational methods between disciplines? And secondly, it is not just about which methods to use, but also what one does with them, how imaginative one has to be in order to make the best use of them.

A good illustration of transferability is provided by phylogenetic analysis algorithms for reconstructing 'family trees' of descent. While initially devised for applications in the life sciences, particularly speciation, genetics and population studies, these methods are now increasingly applied in historical linguistics and dialectology, while further examples from across the humanities include comparative studies of the histories of manuscripts, cultural artefacts and religions.

From these illustrations there might appear to be no limit to the potential uses of such methods across disciplines. Indeed, one widespread view is that computational methods are *per se* generic, and as such 'discipline-neutral' and therefore applicable in principle to any field. Yet for other scholars the whole enterprise of applying computational methods in the humanities is undermined by too automatic an assumption of transferability. This school argues that one cannot just take existing computational methods 'off the peg', for especially if they were originally designed for the data in the natural sciences, they simply may not be meaningfully applicable to the forms of data proper to the humanities, such as language variation data.

There is, however, a sense in which it is possible for both views to be valid, albeit at two quite different stages. To understand how this can be so, one must distinguish component stages within the process of applying computational techniques to data from another discipline, as follows.

Stage 1: Encoding: getting from 'raw' real-world data to expressions of them in numerical or state data format, suitable for computational analysis.

Stage 2: Processing: further 'number crunching' on the now encoded data, typically statistical or phylogenetic analyses.

Stage 3: Interpretation of what the results from such processing mean, back in the real world: e.g. for the divergence histories of languages.

For our question of transferability, what matters is that by the end of stage 1, once the data have been converted into state or numerical format, then the link has been broken with whatever original 'real-world' form those data take in any particular discipline. So from then on, any further mathematical processing, of what are now effectively just numbers, is indeed intrinsically field-neutral. It follows that for stage 2 processing it generally is safe to take computational techniques 'off-the-peg', even if originally developed for applications in other disciplines.

Not so for methods for the preceding stage, however, during which the original raw data – such as language data on sounds, vocabulary or grammatical structures – are first encoded into state or numerical format. For, in marked contrast to the natural sciences, social science data generally do not lend themselves to straightforward expression either in numerical terms or as a set of state values all equally different to each other. Long-standing objections to lexicostatistics, for instance, question whether relationships and entities in natural languages really are discrete enough for the method's 'straightjacket' of all-or-nothing yes/no data-points to constitute valid encodings of a complex linguistic reality, rather than doing violence to it.

A poor stage 1 method, then, is open to the charge that it positively misrepresents the linguistic reality. Indeed, much of the scepticism towards attempts to apply computational methods in linguistics boils down to a widespread perception that (to paraphrase the typical refrain) simply 'bandying numbers about' is rather 'too easy a game to play'.

Representations need to be grounded from the outset in a sound and principled methodological approach to the whole enterprise of encoding. Particularly in a context where one needs to inspire greater confidence among sceptics, computational methods are best accompanied by a frank and explicit recognition that no particular encoding can claim necessarily to represent the definitive, absolute numerical expression of linguistic facts. To be realistic, we can aspire to no more than a best approximation, as meaningful a mathematical interpretation of linguistic concepts as can reasonably be achieved. As an illustration, take the task of measuring distance between languages on the level of sound: naturally, any solution must be 'phonetics-led', with weightings based upon and reflecting the true relative significance of the various types of difference in phonetics, as per the principles and architecture of phonetic analysis. An off-the-peg computational method, by contrast, with no particular relation to the sounds of human language, is unlikely to convince sceptics that the numbers it churns out are valid approximations to linguistic reality.

Furthermore, it turns out that there are even some limits to the universal applicability of stage 2 processing methods too. One type of further processing, increasingly popular in recent years, is phylogenetic analysis. As applied in historical linguistics, at the simplest level this can be seen as attempting to reconstruct from data on the divergence of related languages the 'family tree' by which they most plausibly 'evolved' into the particular relationships now observed between them. Some of these very terms, however, are ones with which many sceptical linguists are uncomfortable, and it is here that the question of transferability can resurface, if in another form, even for stage 2 techniques. For each of the various phylogenetic analysis methods embodies some particular *model* of 'evolution' (of character states); but do these models necessarily match how the entities in any particular humanities discipline (e.g. languages, or their words and sounds) 'evolve' in reality? Most phylogenetic analysis packages were originally developed for applications in the biological sciences; but do speciation, genetic or population evolution represent realistic models also for the change and divergence processes in any given humanities discipline?

To close, I venture a few tips that might serve other disciplines, drawn from the experience of attempts to apply computational techniques to language, and the typical responses from sceptical critics.

Response 1: 'Publish and be damned!'. Certainly, computational and especially phylogenetic analyses appear to offer a rare opportunity for work in humanities disciplines such as historical linguistics to break into the leading world journals for the natural sciences, such as *Nature*, *Science* or *PNAS*. Yet while this may be a way to acquire a reputation, it by no means guarantees that it will be a glowing one within the humanities discipline in question. Linguists, for instance, have frequently taken a dim view of such approaches to language data – often applied by non-linguists, and 'computation-led' rather than linguistics-led.

Response 2: 'Lies, damned lies, and statistics'. The objection here is that it is all too easy to churn out *some* numbers, and then to make claims for what they 'demonstrate', when in fact the numbers can equally well be interpreted in quite different ways. Witness for instance Nichols' (1990) claim of linguistic support for an *early* date for the population of the Americas, to which Nettle (1999) ripostes that Nichols' own figures are in fact just as compatible with a *late* date, and really say nothing either way. One must clearly be honest and realistic in one's claims, and mindful of how heavily they may rest on any debatable assumptions. Another cautionary tale is that of glottochronology, widely discredited for its base assumption of a 'clockwork' rate of change over time, observable in practice to be quite false.

Response 3: 'So what?' This final form of reaction is reflected in how, as already observed, sceptics frequently object that the numbers and graphics produced in computational studies are, for specialists in that field, neither useful nor informative, and represent little more than another way of portraying what we already know, without saying anything new.

How can one go about countering all these objections, particularly the third, to 'sell' the utility of computational techniques to a sceptical discipline?

One approach is to target as directly as possible particular research questions as yet unresolved, especially where debate has continued to rage between unquantified, impressionistic and thus potentially subjective positions. It is particularly in such cases that computational methods can be shown to offer a valuable new perspective and objectivity. Gray and Atkinson (2003), for instance, squarely addressed the age-old problem of the time-depth of the Indo-European language dispersal, recruiting for this specific purpose an approach to dating never previously applied to the question. Or, closer to home for the purposes of this issue, a study in preparation by Warren Maguire and colleagues devises statistical tests of subset diversity to investigate whether two particular topical claims in English dialectology are actually borne out in reality: is 'dialect levelling' really going on, and is there such a thing as a coherent 'Northern Englishes' dialect grouping?

Where quantitative and further processing methods really come into their own, offering undeniable advantages over impressionistic and unquantified judgements, is in handling great masses of data. Large datasets on variation typically encompass multiple complex and conflicting signals which cannot all be weighed up against each other simply by 'eyeballing' them; indeed attempting this usually tempts us towards unduly simple analyses easier to 'get our heads around'.

In any case, to convince sceptics of the utility of computational methods in the humanities, it is not just a question of *which* method(s) to use. Rather, much hangs also on precisely *how* they are put to use: it pays to be as imaginative as possible in order to get the very most out of all these techniques. Above all, a key alternative approach for cutting through masses of complex variation data is not to look only at overall results for a database as a whole, but to home in on particular research questions by isolating multiple independent sub-sets of data within it, and then comparing and contrasting them.

Many such inventive applications are pursued in this volume, which together attest to the growing enthusiasm for computational techniques, both in dialectology and in linguistics more generally. It is hoped that their successes and teething troubles alike, as reviewed here, might serve to help other disciplines to harness the undoubted potential of such methods – when carefully applied – far more widely across the humanities.

Roeland van Hout *calls for more reflection on the choice of computational methods and more attention to work in closely related fields.*

It is very sensible to consider the relation of computational techniques in the study of language variation to their use in other humanities disciplines although it is only a small field compared to humanities in general. Nevertheless, the application of all kinds of computational tools is common in the area of language variation research. What can we learn from each other as we continue to expand the remit of computational work in the humanities?

It should be clear that the role of the computer is not only central to the study of language variation but also that it has expanded enormously in different parts of the humanities over the past five or ten years. The computer provides access to data, which we see reflected in the much larger datasets that are now routinely analysed, and we have seen good examples of the benefits of broader access at this workshop. The computer most obviously improves the opportunities for sophisticated access, data analysis and visualisation, especially visualisation based on statistical analysis, again, an improvement we have benefited from in the past two days. In the earlier days of dialect geography straightforward symbol maps or maps with isoglosses were the main visualisation instrument. Nowadays, we have all sorts of maps and graphical representations, and we know better how different data sources can be combined, recombined and integrated in language variation studies. The opportunities to open up, combine and integrate various rich data sources (e.g. historical, geographical, social, political, linguistic), again and again, opens new vistas for doing research in the humanities. It will be a main trigger in developing e-humanities.

Finally we suspect that simulation will play an increasing and decisive role in scholarly thinking and argumentation, including the field of language variation, and simulation is naturally completely dependent on computers. Computer simulations are more than a play, they give the researcher in humanities the possibility to develop and test theoretical claims, as we can observe in many other scientific fields nowadays, in different disciplines. There is no reason to assume that this way of scholarly thinking would not pervade the humanities. I note all of this as a background to a criticism, and, in particular to emphasise that my criticism appreciates the enormous advantages computational techniques have brought to the study of language variation.

Let me take the opportunity to note a couple of points in the study of language variation and its use of computers where I think more progress might be expected and where therefore more attention might be paid. First, many of the computational techniques probe language and dialect differences at a fairly high level of aggregation, while most linguistic theory concerns smaller units of language, say, words, sounds, features and constraints. So it looks as if there is an opportunity to pay more attention to the role of individual items of variation in these larger scale analyses. This might be important as we attempt to link the study of language variation to the study of variation in other aspects of culture. Second, we see different lines of research using different sorts of data, some proceeding from abstract, theoretically motivated linguistic features and others proceeding from more concrete, intuitively accessible material. Naturally this stimulates the question of how these relate to each other. Third, we have also seen linguistic variety approached from a large number of perspectives using a variety of measures, including acoustic measures, pronunciation distance using Levenshtein distance, lexical heterogeneity, and even measures involving the

25

informed opinions of lay dialect speakers. What intrigues me about this variety linguistically is the varied inroads that might open to understand linguistic structure and linguistic systems. Fourth, let me segue to more general issues by noting that even while we acknowledge the multi-dimensionality of linguistic variation, many successful approaches to its study focus on the lexicon where these many dimensions are reflected. This leads me to speculate that lexical studies may also serve as the most important bridge to other disciplines, as well.

I wish to turn then to the more general issues of how we might learn from each other in the different humanities disciplines. When I consider how we might present the results of our work to fellow scholars in the humanities, then several remarks are appropriate. First, we need to distinguish the development of a measure of difference from an account of all that a difference might entail. Levenshtein distance appears to be an effective technique for getting at pronunciation differences, but this in not the same as an account of the production or perception of these differences in the individual. Perhaps the intelligence test might be an appropriate analogy. The intelligence test measures intelligence, most agree, but that doesn't mean that it sheds light on the cognitive operations required for intelligent behaviour. I think it is useful to keep this in mind as we present our work to neighbouring disciplines.

Second, it is my impression that the use of computational techniques in the study of language variation is still young and exploratory, and that a period of reflection about the appropriate techniques would be useful. There is a large range of computational techniques we might choose from, which calls for reflection about that choice. We need not only to apply techniques, but also to justify the choice of technique, in order to develop a sound and transparent methodology.

Third, and finally, and quite within the spirit of considering interdisciplinary work, I would like to remind the linguists and dialectologists here that we are dealing with space at nearly every turn. This suggests that we should examine and consider how other disciplines have analysed spatial relations, e.g. human geography. Human behaviour produces spatial consequences and constructs. We ought to examine the techniques applied there with an eye on opportunities for learning from each other.

David Robey *asked what scholars using computational techniques in the various Humanities disciplines may learn from each other. His remarks follow.*

My focus here is on the institutional and strategic context of humanities computing in the UK, and particularly on the recent changes in that context. The focus on the UK will also be of interest to researchers in other countries, I hope, because we have recently moved from a position in the digital humanities that was exceptional, in international terms, to one that presents much the same kind of problems as that of other countries.

Until 2008 the UK had the strongest system of support services for ICT use in arts and humanities (A&H) research in the world. This was made up of, first, the Arts and Humanities Data Service (AHDS), joint-funded by the Arts and Humanities Research Council (AHRC) and the Joint Information Systems Committee (JISC), to serve as a national repository for data outputs in the A&H, and as a source of advice on data creation, curation and preservation. This was divided into a number of Centres, of which the most relevant for linguistics was AHDS Literature and Linguistics, associated with the Oxford Text Archive at Oxford University Computing Services. Funding for the AHDS was terminated at the end of March 2008, largely as a result of financial exigencies at the AHRC. The AHRC also argued that the use of the AHDS's resources did not justify the considerable cost of maintaining it, and that much of the expertise that it provided was now widely available in UK universities.

A second major source of support was the AHRC Resource Enhancement Scheme, the last grants from which were made in 2006. This funded mostly digital resource outputs, overall a total of some 175, to a total value of almost £40m. Some examples in the area of linguistics and dialectology are: Yaron Matras (University of Manchester), *Morphosyntactic typology of Romani*; Karen Corrigan (University of Hertfordshire), *The Newcastle Electronic Corpus of Tyneside English*; Justin Watkins (University of London), *Wa dictionary and internet database for minority languages of Burma*; and databases of the Scots, Irish and Welsh languages. To see the AHRC's review of the Resource Enhancement Scheme, visit http://www.ahrc.ac.uk/FundedResearch/Pages/ResourceEnhancementSchemeReview.aspx

The third and most recent source of support was the AHRC ICT in Arts and Humanities Research Programme, funded to a total of £3.8m from October 2003 to December 2008: for details see http://www.ahrc.ac.uk/ict. Its aims were to build national capacity in the use of ICT for arts and humanities research and to advise the AHRC on matters of ICT strategy. Its largest single project was the AHRC ICT Methods Network, a forum for the exchange and dissemination of advanced expertise on the use of ICT for A&H Research, which ran for three years to the end of March 2008. It also funded a set of ICT Strategy Projects, a mix of survey and tools development work, of which two are particularly relevant to linguistics: Alan Marsden (Lancaster) and John Coleman (Oxford), *Strategies, Requirements and Tools for the Analysis of Time-based Media*; and Jeremy Smith (Glasgow), *Lexical Searches for the Arts and Humanities*, which developed a new user interface for the Glasgow Historical Thesaurus of English. Its other major activity is the Arts and Humanities e-Science Initiative, funded jointly with JISC and the Engineering and Physical Sciences Research Council, which has extended to the A&H the e-Science agenda for the development of advanced technologies for collaboration and resource-sharing across the Internet. While it may seem oxymoronic, at least in English, to speak of e-Science in the A&H,

27

the e-Science agenda is important for the A&H above all in its approach to the problem of data dispersal: a major problem that confronts the humanities researcher is not the lack of relevant electronic data so much as the fact that so much of it is dispersed in self-contained databases and archives that do not communicate with each other; yet it is a truism that the more data can be connected with other data, the more it tends to be useful. For more details on the joint Initiative, see http://www.ahrc.ac.uk/e-science.

What then are the problems that confront us now that we have come to the end of this period of exceptionally strong support for ICT in A&H research? The first is that of finding secure repositories for the publicly-funded data outputs that would previously have found homes in the AHDS. While the former AHDS Centres still remain in existence, supported by their host universities, and still maintain access to the collections that have been deposited with them in the past, it is far from clear how much longer they will continue to do so, nor are they in a position to receive new deposits without some form of special funding. In the longer term a national system of institutional repositories (IRs) in universities may provide a solution to the data preservation problem. There is a strong public agenda to develop such a system, largely driven by JISC, but for the moment the IRs that exist serve mainly to preserve open-access e-prints of journal articles, and very few are capable of handling other types of data. A publicly-funded study is also currently under way on the feasibility of establishing a UK Research Data Service (see http://www.ukrds.ac.uk/), which may eventually provide a solution to the data storage problem, but whatever the outcome of this study is, it is unlikely that the solution will be effective in the short-to-medium term. In the meantime a good proportion of the Resource Enhancement projects funded by the AHRC have serious concerns about the long-term sustainability of their outputs: see the recent review at http://www.ahrcict.rdg.ac.uk/activities/review/sustainability.htm.

But the most urgent issue is to maintain the knowledge and expertise that was built up over the years by the AHDS and, more recently, by the AHRC ICT Methods Network; and together with this to keep in existence and develop the communities of practitioners that built up around the two organisations. The Methods Network in particular, through a series of some 50 expert seminars, workshops and similar meetings, was remarkably successful in bringing together advanced practitioners of digital methods in the A&H, many of whom were previously unaware of each other's existence, and most of whom had previously had little direct contact with one another. It is vital, if we are to maintain the current quality and volume of UK activities in the digital arts and humanities, to keep these communities in existence – a point particularly relevant to the topic of this session.

Support continues to be provided in a limited number of areas. The AHRC still funds the former Archaeology Centre of the AHDS, on the grounds that the use of digital resources is more firmly embedded in Archaeology than in other A&H disciplines. JISC continues to provide direct support for e-Science activities, now broadened to include all advanced ICT-based methodologies in the A&H, through its A&H e-Science Support Centre; for details see http://www.ahessc.ac.uk/. It also needs to be emphasised that provision of generic ICT infrastructures for research remains strong, mainly through JISC, but it is not part of JISC's mission to provide for individual discipline domains such as the A&H. Support for research projects using ICT in the A&H also continues to be strong: a high proportion of the standard research grants made by the AHRC under its responsive-mode schemes continues to include the production of digital outputs of one kind or another. The important issue is not the provision of the generic e-Infrastructure, or the support of ICT-based research projects, but ICT support services, resources and infrastructure specifically for A&H research: the A&H e-research infrastructure.

In current circumstances, and pending a possible solution of the data repository issue, the best immediate prospect is to develop support in virtual mode. With the help of transitional funding from JISC, considerable effort is currently going into the development of a set of on-line resources for the use of ICT for Arts and Humanities research, based at the Centre for e-Research at King's College London. These will maintain a knowledge base of training and methodological materials, and at the same time support virtual communities of practitioners, including a network of expert centres in data creation, preservation and use. The knowledge base will support the virtual communities, who in turn, it is hoped, will feed material into the knowledge base: see http://www.arts-humanities.net. By these means we hope to maintain and build on part of the legacy of what, with hindsight, was a quite exceptional period of public funding for digital A&H support services. But it is hard to see how, without further public investment, we can maintain the current volume and quality of activity in the longer term.

DISCUSSION

John Nerbonne: Thanks to our panellists for their opening remarks. I'd now like to open the general discussion by asking if the panellists have points of discussion or questions for each other. For example, David addressed one of the things that Paul had said earlier, namely that the value of the long-term preservation of digital resources for the humanities is still unsure.

David Robey: Paul, you didn't quite explain the value of the resources in historical linguistics, did you? Of course, you did explain what you are doing and why.

Paul Heggarty: The value for others in the discipline is certainly clear in the case I described, but how it's perceived depends in general on the orientation of the other people in the discipline. Most disciplines will have a divide between the computationally inclined and the non-computationally inclined.

John Nerbonne: Maybe a question then with respect to the point about the perceived value of the computational work: you opened your presentation, David, with the pessimistic view, or at least pessimistic report, that the very good level of funding in the UK will not be continued, while we have heard from both Paul and Roeland van Hout that they see that the computational work in the Humanities, the interdisciplinary work involving Computing Science on the one hand and Humanities on the other, and sometimes disciplines outside the Humanities as well, has been really quite successful. Has there been a final verdict in the UK then, that the time when you needed to fund very special computational efforts in the Humanities has passed, and that it now should become a more normal way of working in the Arts and Humanities, one that requires no special attention and no special funding? I didn't know about the report, and your presentation surprised me.

Roeland van Hout: In the Netherlands we see a version of the funding problem that is particularly frustrating. Everyone is looking to one another, asking who is responsible. Everyone knows that money needs to be invested, but whose budget should it come out of? For example, the money in the Netherlands from our National Science Foundation needs to be invested in projects. So long-term grants are not given at all, and projects requiring long-term budgets should be taken over by some other institution. Alternatively, the results of the projects become the responsibility of some institution, and that is also a problem in the Netherlands. When working with short-term (3–4 yr.) projects, it means that at a specific moment there is a lot of money, and suddenly later the money is gone, and you have to look for other funds, making the sustainability of the whole enterprise a problem. Not only in the Humanities, by the way, but also in other branches of science, too, where there is actually more money than in Linguistics and the Humanities (but that's another problem).

John Nerbonne: Linguistic searches and frequency counts look like quick and easy results that need no special funding. Maybe we've been too successful in showing how much benefit accrues to even modest computational efforts.

David Robey: Research councils are fond of quick results.

Paul Heggarty: I wonder also whether there's a cross-disciplinary divide in how these things are perceived. So if you look at publications on Linguistics in the big natural sciences journals – *Science*, *Nature* or the *Proceedings of the National Academy of Sciences* (PNAS) – they are quite reasonably seen as important because they have been reviewed and accepted in these very selective journals, even though colleagues in the Humanities have often been very critical about their content. There's also the attitude reported by some colleagues who work with natural scientists, that the latter, the natural scientists, feel a sort of frustration with the computer literacy of people in the Humanities. The responses to the PNAS article I mentioned involved some terrible mud-slinging across the disciplinary gorge, where Forster and Toth were really slammed for not doing linguistics properly. It was said that they really did it very badly, while Forster's response in an interview was along the lines of: 'Well they [i.e. linguists] just don't understand what we are doing'. There are a lot of traditional people in the Humanities who don't see the value of computational work. Unfortunately, they often don't know what's going on; for example, they understand the statistics so poorly that they're very suspicious about its value. I just wonder if this distrust came through in the debate about funding.

David Robey: This is quite interesting. Much of the funding from my research council has computational aspects, and in the latest, most recent rounds of research grant applications about half of the projects involved some kind of digital output. In many cases the applications were not required or even encouraged to plan digital outputs, but the community submits applications with digital aspects anyway. There are other indications as well that information technology is actually a fairly fundamental part of the way in which about half the community works. There is quite a lot going on, I think. I think the real problem is for it to be done more effectively. That's the thing that worries me, that it's not always done nearly as effectively as it should be.

Roeland van Hout: John, don't you want to take comments from the audience, as well?

John Nerbonne: It sounds like a very good time to get our audience involved. If you wouldn't mind using the microphone, that would help. I need to record you because I want to make this available later.

Eric Wheeler, Toronto: My comment concerns our talking about sustainability, and how you have to go after follow-up grants after your first grant is up. I'm worried what happens about 100 years from now, when I may be retired and not able to go after grants. I still want the work I am doing to survive. If we look back 100 years or 200 years ago, the tradition was that you wrote a book, and it was put on the library shelf. Now that library will be there forever, but when you create a database, you put in on the shelf, and you hope that your software isn't obsolete before the first colleague asks you for a copy of it.

John Nerbonne: And it's not only that your software becomes obsolete, the entire environment is changing all the time.

Eric Wheeler: Well, it's the environment changing, and the demands, and the directions, and there are lots of things, but we don't have this institutional sense of how to preserve, use, support, maintain, and distribute what we are producing digitally. This is related to a second problem that I'd like to mention, namely that we are still very much pioneers in this, even though we may be jumping on a band-wagon that started long ago. I have worked across disciplines I guess for my whole career, and I have always been put down for not being in the right discipline. I am always at the margin of something, and when the margin is

31

information technology, and you see everybody using it, you say 'This isn't right somehow, how can my work be viewed as marginal?' I mean they should come begging me to do this work, and they don't. And that is another fundamental problem we have, I think. How do we make it a priority to solve these problems? They are huge, long term problems that need big money and big thinking and more than just one individual coming up with one individual solution. But the rest of the Humanities depends on us because everything you discover sooner or later you are going to want it put in digital form and so that we keep it.

John Nerbonne: Paul, want to pick up on that?

Paul Heggarty: As an anecdote on preservation problems, the 2003 article in *Nature* by Gray and Atkinson was based on a database by Dyen, Kruskal and Black of 90-odd Indo-European languages that had originally been entered on punch cards, I think. Dyen and his co-authors later re-entered it, making it available at a website at a university in Australia where one of them [Paul Black] worked. But as of two years ago, the site was gone. I've done searches at the university, and you just can't find it anymore. I happen to have a copy, but I don't know where it's available anywhere on the internet. That was a huge dataset of 93 languages, 200 words per language, used for a big article in *Nature*, that caused a huge amount of fuss. Now nobody knows where it is. [Update: after the debate a member of the audience suggested I contact Paul Black directly about this. I did so and eventually another site was found that is now hosting the database.]

John Nerbonne: Bill Kretzschmar, who makes lot of data available to people, wishes to contribute.

Bill Kretzschmar, Georgia: I try. Well, one piece of good news on this front. My university librarian tells me that it is a big topic in conversation among the librarians in America. I've actually made an agreement with my university library to store my archive, which is, well, large. It is in the range of 20 terabytes of material that they are going to store and maintain as part of their digital media, multimedia archive, and what I contribute is only a tiny piece of it. I want to store TV, movies and all sort of things that are very space-intensive, and so I think that this is maybe a movement we need to take interest in, which means that we need to be talking to our university librarians. To me it always seemed odd that the university was willing to take indirect costs for research grants but was unwilling to archive the results of those grants. I think now is the time for us to be active on that front.

David Robey: I think that's absolutely right. Libraries are the obvious place to look, even if librarians sometimes need quite a lot of persuasion. That's also a key solution, since the money isn't coming from anywhere else.

John Nerbonne: Are there further discussion points?

Fiona Douglas, Leeds: A question really, I suppose for David, involving the same point I made when there was the recent consultation process on whether we should have a national repository or not, and what it should look like. It seems to me that having a Humanities-wide approach might mean that we avoid the current problem where we have lots and lots of data that might be really useful to other people who might use it in entirely different ways. Maybe the way to market the more general approach is to note that the data might be useful to other people. So, for example, you know, I have worked with newspaper texts, but all the newspaper resources are designed for journalists. They are not designed for linguists and yet lots and lots of researchers use newspapers as, you know, examples of standard English around the world. It seems to me crazy that we spend all this money setting up resources for only one very specific niche market when with very little effort we could extend that and make it much more available and more generally useful to other researchers with very different interests. I mean many of you might be interested in oral histories not because you are oral historians but because you are interested in the language that is used. So, especially if the research money is increasingly limited, so that we have to kind of make the resources we have go further, one way of doing it would be to stimulate resource builders to make their resources more generally accessible and more generally useful.

David Robey: Well, I think Fiona has put her finger on a very important point. In this country we are probably not going to have enough funding for a specialised Arts and Humanities data service again. I would guess that it is not going to happen. So what we have to do is to find some kind of infrastructure that can deliver that data at lower cost, working as a default with the university libraries and such. I think that's the agenda for the future.

Roeland van Hout: There's also another point here where I think we researchers also can do things. 10 years ago when one was collecting data, the data were personal data, and there was no intention to ultimately make the data more generally available. I think that nowadays we should not accept, for instance, articles written on the basis of a database if the database is not available. Further, making the database available means that it has an open structure, so not an idiosyncratic, unstructured form. Here I think that researchers themselves can make the information more effectively available so that databases have much better chance to survive. And that was the point of your argument.

David Robey: I think people need to think about publishing databases in the same way they think about publishing books.

Patrick McConvell, Australian National University: Can't the research councils make it an obligation when they fund a grant hosted by a university, that the university has to look after the results and provide access to the data. Wouldn't that be possible?

David Robey: In real life I think probably not. I mean at the moment my research council requires three years' maintenance after the end of the grant period, and there is a question about whether that can be extended. But of course we don't ever have much control because the money has been spent, and then influence is over.

Paul Heggarty: On that cross-disciplinary point I remember something that Russell Gray said. He was trying to get hold of language data to compare genetic and linguistic groups. He found it incredibly difficult to obtain the linguistic data as opposed to the data from genetics. The human genome project has resulted in databases with world-wide standardisations for genetic information, and he just couldn't believe how bad linguistics was when it came to reliable standards.

Eric Wheeler: It is as much our fault because we do it in craftsmen-like, small-scale ways, and we need to do it on a larger scale. I mean the fact that we have these databases and they have names is wonderful, I mean that's a vast improvement over what was there 10 years ago. But it's not quite the same as the Human Genome Project, and we wonder why we don't get funding: it's because we look like poor cousins when we come in with our projects, the poor cousin projects that get poor-cousin funding.

Bill Kretzschmar: Part of the reason for that is that we are a diverse field in language studies, that we are not all doing the same thing or close to the same thing, and that the datasets don't look the same. We have radically different datasets and radically different uses we make of them, and I just don't believe that we can have one style of encoding that works for all of us. SGML tried to do this, and TEI has made a stab at language, too, and failed, as far as I'm concerned, but I think that's just because it's an impossible task. We will always have divisions. We have to accept that.

David Robey: But you can add degrees and degrees of reusability to that. You can improve reusability, but you can't have total reusability.

Bill Kretzschmar: We can't throw things away just because we have different encodings. We have to preserve the metadata so that people can use our encodings.

John Nerbonne: Right, I also see an enormous reuse of the data that is available. I don't know how many articles have been written about the Wall Street Journal (Penn) Treebank and the different sorts of syntactic analysis that have been applied to it. One group at Penn took the time to syntactically annotate it, and surely there have been 80 or 90 articles on it, it's really enormous. There is hunger for data. And for comparable analyses, using the same dataset. Reusing data is not merely efficient, it often allows you to say a lot more.

David Robey: Actually I think it's relatively easy for you guys to demonstrate evidence of value compared to history and literature studies where that's so much more difficult.

John Nerbonne: It's a good point that you brought that up because actually we look at the computational side of things most of the time. Perhaps that's what gets the imagination going here. What about the cross-disciplinary aspects, one of the perspectives we wished to address in this discussion? Paul most explicitly addressed interdisciplinary issues. Historians, archaeologists, geneticists are all interested in some of the same questions, and therefore interested in collaboration. What about the other Humanities disciplines? What about History and Religion? Anthropology? Are we witnessing increased collaboration through computational studies in these other areas of the Humanities?

David Robey: There's a lot of use going on of geographical information systems, spread across a surprising number of Humanities disciplines. Among the fields you see using GIS are History, Archaeology (obviously), and Literature studies, sometimes.

Eric Wheeler: I think again one of the concerns is that GIS systems were designed for geography and are being adapted piecemeal to other things. If we really got the experts in geography to come and look at what our problems were, I think they would design the systems differently. Our personal experience in that was thinking that when we developed our dialect software, the mapping was going to be hard, but it turned out to be very easy. What was hard was the interface to access the data because we asked different questions than you would typically ask in geography or anywhere else. And I think that is going to happen all across the Humanities. It is understanding what my data is all about and what the interesting questions to ask are about a dialect or a language or whatever, that will drive that the developments. But there is still a need for people who have expertise to develop systems. They can help a great deal. A meeting ground for these groups would be useful.

David Robey: I think there is a larger sustainability problem with interface software. Online data is much easier to preserve. – Just keeping online searchable interfaces sustainable is a real problem, not to mention creating them.

Eric Wheeler: And even having a standard for what they should look like. I mean much as we curse Windows, we now have a point where we can talk to files and systems in a fairly standard way. Wouldn't it be nice if you could ask your dialect questions in some kind of standard ways?

John Nerbonne: Generic tools?

Eric Wheeler: Generic tools.

Bill Kretzschmar: I don't believe that they're feasible, at least not beyond very simple programs.

Eric Wheeler: I agree that it is difficult.

Bill Kretzschmar: The point is, we have to steal everything possible from other people who already made them. But the creation of generic Humanistic tools is something that people always talk about in the digital Humanities, and that I'm never been convinced of buying into.

Roeland van Hout: No, but, it's my experience that there is a lot of information around nowadays about all kinds of cultural and historical things, which can be related to the development of dialects for instance. It is admittedly sometimes problematic to get this data. For example, all the institutional borders, political borders, etc. It's not very simple but it has become easier to combine the linguistic data with many other types of data, and that's maybe a message we can have for the Humanities. We can use all these different resources now!

David Robey: That's why we got excited by e-science. Because that's exactly what e-sciences are about: about integrating data. – But they, too, have a long way to go.

Roeland van Hout: Maybe not that long, but OK.

Bill Kretzschmar: One good thing about this is that in a long period of time seeking research funds, I've never yet been successful in getting money to build a tool. I think that funding organisations are resistant to people who want to build tools, and they would rather have data collections or innovative methods. Don't set out to build a generic tool, but look instead for a breakthrough in analysis.

Patrick McConvell: We just had a one-year experience in Australia with money that was given out for research in the Humanities, precisely to build tools. But it lasted for one year maybe, and then, ... then, the money ran out.

David Robey: I mean if there's a problem with the sustainability of data resources, then probably the sustainability of tools is of a different order, isn't it?

John Nerbonne: It's true but there are examples, well known in the community of variationist linguists. The VARBRULE package, which was built when one could only use 4 K on a PDP 7 somewhere. It has been around for 30 years, which is amazing. People are still using it. David Sankoff really deserves credit for this.

Eli Johanne Ellingsve, Oslo: I am one of the editors of the Norwegian dictionary in Norway, planned to be finished around 2014. We have started discussing connecting with historical databases, Archaeology, Geology, sites of interest for nature research, including petro-geology (oil), and recently the ordnance service. (Is that what you call it in English? – Yes.) – The mapping authorities hold a key position. Most importantly, they organise a great deal. In Norway they are well organised, and we plan to connect to their structure and their data system. We have started discussions with them, and there is interest. They are state funded, i.e., officially funded. So they have money, and they would like us to connect to build up the linguistic databases, to provide more information, including linguistic and historical linguistic information as well. So the ordnance service in different countries may be as interesting as it is in Norway. You may try that.

John Nerbonne: Thank you. I'm going to make a round of the panellists now, because we have a plenary talk at 16.45 and that'll give you just about enough time to get there. But maybe we'll go in reverse order this time. David, do you have any final remarks?

David Robey: I'll pass, as I've talked quite a lot, thanks.

John: Ok, then Roeland.

Roeland van Hout: My final remark concerns the state of databases, but again especially the interaction between institutions and the producers of the databases. So I would like to repeat: if you are creating databases, try to make these databases available and take responsibility for your own data, because that may be helpful to convince the larger parties to take part in our enterprise.

Franz Manni, *Musée de l'Homme*, Paris: May it also be useful to print them sometimes? If they are printable.

John Nerbonne: OK, and let's give Paul the final word, then.

Paul Heggarty: Sometimes I think, maybe I should put my data on Wikipedia or something. It's the best place I know of – because no one else is doing it – to get Swadesh lists for hundreds of languages. It's not on Wikipedia itself, it's one of its sub-branches [the Wiktionary Appendix system], but the lists are pretty much standardised. I use Google for my language mapping as well. These are things that are becoming *de facto* standards. And it seems like linguists may be forced to work via Wikipedia just because academic organisations are not doing it anywhere. It's a bit of a shame that we have to wait for 'Google Lingo' or some such to come out... But at least the Wikipedia sites use some sort of standardisation. Maybe solutions are arising through the web and through organisations like Google or Wikipedia.

John Nerbonne: OK so we close the session with a word on the web. We thank in particular our panellists!

MAKING SENSE OF STRANGE SOUNDS: (MUTUAL) INTELLIGIBILITY OF RELATED LANGUAGE VARIETIES. A REVIEW

VINCENT J. VAN HEUVEN

I. INTRODUCTION

1.1 Two basic questions

In this paper we ask two questions, which superficially seem to ask the same thing but in actual fact do not. First, we ask to what degree two languages (or language varieties) A and B resemble each other. The second question is how well a listener of variety B understands a speaker of variety A.

When we ask to what degree two language varieties resemble one another, or how different they are (which is basically the same question), it should be clear that the answer cannot be expressed in a single number. Languages differ from each other not in just one dimension but in a great many respects. They may differ in their sound inventories, in the details of the sounds in the inventory, in their stress, tone and intonation systems, in their vocabularies, and in the way they build words from morphemes and sentences from words. Last, but not least, they may differ in the meanings they attach to the forms in the language, in so far as the forms in two languages may be related to each other. In order to express the distance between two languages, we need a weighted average of the component distances along each of the dimensions identified (and probably many more). So, linguistic distance is a multidimensional phenomenon and we have no a priori way of weighing the dimensions.[1]

The answer to the question how well listener B understands speaker A can be expressed as a single number. If listener B does not understand speaker A at all, the number would be zero. If listener B gets every detail of speaker A's intentions, the score would be maximal.

The primary goal of human language is to communicate intentions from speaker to listener. When listener B does not know the structural details of

International Journal of Humanities and Arts Computing 2 (1–2) 2008, 39–62
DOI: 10.3366/E1753854809000305

speaker A's language, communication will be less than optimal, and if the difference between speaker A's and listener B's linguistic codes is larger than some critical amount, communication will fail altogether. Intelligibility between languages may serve as the ultimate criterion to decide how structural dimensions should be weighed against each other in the computation of linguistic distance. Suppose, for instance, that differences in word order hardly compromise the communication between A and B, but that even small discrepancies between sound systems cause a complete communication breakdown. Then, phonology should be weighted much more in the computation of linguistic distance than syntax.

So, the two basic questions have a mutual feeding relationship. On the one hand, we would like to be able to predict from differences and similarities between two languages A and B how well listener B will understand speaker A. Here we need a detailed survey of structural similarities and differences along all of the dimensions along which languages may differ, and we need to know how to weigh the dimensions against each other in order to make the prediction. On the other hand, we need to know how well listener B understands speaker A. The intelligibility score is the only criterion against which the relative importance of linguistic dimensions can be gauged. It is the only reasonable criterion if we subscribe to the communicative principle underlying linguistic structure. In this article our initial focus will be on the second question because we want to use intelligibility as a criterion for weighing the different dimensions of linguistic distance. In later sections we will also consider factors that influence intelligibility.

1.2 Defining the problem

The problem that we wish to address is the following. Given two related language varieties A and B, where A and B share a substantial part of their lexicon and linguistic structure, by what mechanism is listener B able to understand speaker A? That is to say, we are interested in the *psycholinguistic mechanism* that enables communication between speakers and listeners of related language varieties – such as dialects of a language of related languages within a language family.

A human language processor, i.e. a listener, may have at his disposal adaptive strategies to cope with deviant speech input. For instance, a Dutch listener B when confronted with English input A may realise that the sound shape /haʊs/ refers to the same concept 'house' as the obviously cognate Dutch form /hœys/. Once the Dutch listener has discovered this relationship he may apply this sound transformation to other English forms, such as /laʊs, maʊs, laʊd, snaʊt/ 'louse, mouse, loud, snout', which all transform regularly to Dutch /lœys, mœys, lœyt, snœyt/. In this case, the listener has discovered a rule that relates the English sound shapes to their equivalents in Dutch. The transformation is not as simple as it seems, however. The phonology of Dutch distinguishes between two rounded low diphthongs /ɑʊ and /œy/, where English has only one. Not only does the Dutch listener of English have to learn that Dutch /œy/ maps onto a different vowel in English, viz. /ɣʊ/ but also that Dutch /ɑʊ/ as in /ɣɑʊt/ 'gold' or /hɑʊt/ 'hold' maps onto the English sound combination /əʊl/, and so on. To keep the problem within manageable bounds, therefore, I will exclude such learning strategies from our problem. I will assume that the listener's linguistic knowledge is static and that no rules are being developed to cope with the deviant input speech. In other words, I explicitly limit the problem of understanding deviant speech to first confrontation, assuming that listener B has no previous experience with the kind of aberrations that are characteristic of language A.

To simplify matters further, I will assume a laboratory setting for the testing of intelligibility of deviant speech. The input speech will be sound only, presented out of context. No visual or situational cues will be present in the stimulus.

Languages may also differ in their syntax. Differences in word order may determine the meaning of sentences. If the default word order in the language is Subject-Verb-Object (SVO) then the sentence *X kills Y* implies that Y dies. Such sentences will be incorrectly understood by listeners of an Object-Verb-Subject (OVS) language: they will believe instead that X dies as a result of the killing action performed by the subject Y. It appears that such gross typological differences are rare within groups of closely related languages. Again, to simplify the problem, therefore, I will assume that there are no differences in word order between the language of speaker A and listener B. Or rather, whatever differences in word order may exist between the two languages, they do not compromise intelligibility.

1.3 Approaching the problem

When we listen to someone who speaks in a related language that we have not heard before in our life, speech understanding is compromised to a greater or lesser extent. Situations in which speech input is non-optimal abound in everyday life. The speaker may be handicapped by some language or speech pathology (e.g. stuttering, cleft palate speech, alaryngeal speech, e.g. after surgical removal of the larynx and vocal cords). Special kinds of pathologies are accent, whether foreign or native, and computer speech.[2] Alternatively, the speaker may be perfectly normal but the communication channel may be polluted by noise (ambient noise, competing speech input, harmonic distortion, echoes and reverberation, selective amplification and filtering), which may be continuous or intermittent (perceptual adaptation to intermittent noise is harder).

The amazing fact is that the native listener is generally quite successful in getting the speaker's intentions even if the input speech is highly defective and even if the communication channel is noisy. Human spoken language has evolved such that it is extremely robust and works under the most adverse circumstances. The science of phonetics, more than any other branch of knowledge, studies the process of speech perception. A full-fledged theory of human speech perception should allow us to understand the robustness of speech communication and predict how the listener would reconstruct the speaker's message even if the input speech is defective or when the communication channel is noisy. I refer to relevant chapters in the *Handbook of Speech Perception* (Remez and Pisoni, 2005) for sketches of such theories.

I therefore embrace the null hypothesis that understanding a speaker of a related variety of one's native language does not involve any special mechanisms. Rather, the listener simply marshals up the mechanisms that he routinely brings to bear in the processing of speech input under suboptimal listening conditions. I suggest, in other words, that insights into the normal speech perception mechanism should be sufficient to provide answers to our basic question: how well would a listener B understand speaker A if A and B are related but non-identical languages or language varieties. Note that within the science of phonetics I include, somewhat imperialistically, two specialisations that address the perception of defective input speech. These are (i) the phonetics of foreign language learning and (ii) speech technology, specifically the quality assessment of speech synthesis. There is a large body of research on both (i) and (ii) that we may fruitfully turn to for ideas on speech intelligibility, perceptual assimilation of strange sounds, and word recognition.

2. SPEECH INTELLIGIBILITY

In this section I will argue that the most important and central aspect of speech understanding is the recognition of the words, i.e. of the smallest units of language in which a more or less fixed meaning is coupled with a more or less fixed sequence of sounds. We will then briefly review techniques that have been developed to measure speech intelligibility and express intelligibility scores in terms of the percentage of words correctly recognised.

2.1 Word recognition is key

We will define intelligibility in quite practical terms as the percentage of linguistic units correctly recognised by the listener in the order in which they were spoken. Intelligibility can be tested at several levels of the linguistic hierarchy, be it at the level of meaningless units (sounds or phonemes), or at the level of meaningful units such as morphemes and words.

It has become standard practice in speech intelligibility measurement to test the recognition of linguistic units at several linguistic levels. Typically, intelligibility tests are part of a test battery that addresses sounds, words and sentences separately (see van Bezooijen and van Heuven, 1997 and references given there). When we want to apply speech intelligibility tests to the problem of establishing the success of communication between speaker and hearer of related language varieties, we are not so much interested in the success with which the listener identifies individual sounds. Rather, we are interested in the percentage of words that the listener gets right. Therefore, measuring the success of phoneme identification is only useful in so far as this measure helps us to predict the success of word recognition. The underlying assumption here is that word recognition is the key to speech understanding. As long as the listener correctly recognises words, he will be able to piece the speaker's message together.

2.2 *Functional testing versus opinion testing*

In the literature on quality assessment of speech synthesis a division is often made between functional intelligibility testing and opinion testing (e.g. van Bezooijen and van Heuven, 1997). Functional intelligibility tests measure the real thing. They measure to what extent a listener actually recognises linguistic units (words) in spoken stimuli. A traditional functional test is dictation; here listeners simply write down what (they believe) the speaker said. Dictation draws heavily on the listeners' memory. In intelligibility testing it is not realistic to repeat the spoken utterance, since speakers in a real-life situation normally say things only once. In order to reduce memory load, sentences can be exploded, i.e. read in short phrase-like chunks with pauses in between to write down the response, or parts of the message may be printed on the listener's answer sheet such that he has to recognise selected (blanked-out) words only. Typically, the score of a functional intelligibility test is a percentage that expresses what proportion of the linguistic units present in the stimulus materials were correctly recognized by the listener.

When listeners have recognised a word, that word will remain active in the listeners' memory for a long time (up to several hours or even a whole day, see e.g. Morton, 1969). The next time the listeners hear the same word, they will recognise it with very little effort. This so-called priming phenomenon results in ceiling effects. This is a problem if the same word has to be recognised by the same listener in different versions, for instance when spoken in the listener's native language B and in a related language A. In order to avoid priming effects, word recognition experiments block the different versions of stimulus words over different listeners so that each listener hears only one version of each stimulus word. Blocking of versions over listeners is not a problem when the number of versions is limited. In some studies on intelligibility of related language varieties, however, the number of versions is as much as fifteen (e.g. Gooskens and Heeringa, 2004 for Norwegian dialects, or Tang and van Heuven 2007, 2009 for Chinese dialects). In such more complicated experiments, blocking is done through Latin square designs in which each listener hears one-fifteenth part of the stimulus material in each of 15 different varieties, and yet hears materials in each of the 15 varieties in equal proportions, and never hears the same word twice (not even in a different variety). The blocking of versions of groups of listeners makes functional intelligibility testing a laborious undertaking. For this reason functional intelligibility testing is shunned when the number of language varieties under study is large.

It was discovered (or at least claimed) in work on quality assessment of talking machines that so-called opinion testing is an adequate shortcut to functional intelligibility testing. In opinion testing, listeners are asked how well *they think* they would understand a speech sample presented to them. The same sample can be presented to the same listener in several different versions, for instance synthesised by several competing brands of reading machines and by a human control speaker (Pisoni, Greene and Nusbaum, 1985; van Bezooijen and van Heuven, 1997). The listener is familiarised with the contents of the speech sample before it is presented so that recognition does not play a role in the process. All the listener has to do is to imagine that he has not heard the sample before and to estimate how much of its contents he thinks he would grasp. The response is an intelligibility judgment, between 0 'I think I would not get a single word of what this speaker says' and 10 for 'I would understand this speaker perfectly, I would not miss a single word.' It has been shown that the mean score averaged over a group of listeners/judges (so-called Mean Opinion Score or MOS) very strongly differentiates between speech of differing quality (high concurrent validity with functional intelligibility scores).

Tang and van Heuven (2009) computed the correlation between functional and opinion tests of intelligibility among 15 Chinese dialects. They found correlation coefficients around $r = .8$. This is a high degree of correlation but it also shows that opinion test do not account for all the variability in the functional test scores: some 35 per cent of the variance in the functional test scores goes unaccounted for. On the basis of this finding it seems advisable to attempt functional testing if at all possible; only if the number of language pairs targeted is very large, is opinion testing an option as a non-ideal but manageable alternative. And even in such large-scale comparisons it would always be advisable to cross-validate the opinion test results with functional counterparts for a subset of language pairs sampled from the larger ensemble.

2.3 Avoiding ceiling effects

When the language varieties of the speakers only differ in very subtle ways from that of the listener, it may be difficult to differentiate between close and not so very close varieties. In order to avoid such ceiling effects it may be useful to make the listener's task more difficult. What is generally done in such situations is that information in the stimulus is reduced by some form of signal degradation. There are many ways to degrade the input speech. It can be achieved by filtering (removing amplitude from the signal in specific frequency bands), by signal compression, by adding various kinds of noise to the signal or by replacing selected fragments of the signal by silence (or noise).

Filtering the speech signal is done when we listen to someone over an ordinary telephone. Here frequencies below 300 Hz and above 3300 Hz are removed from the signal. Normally, communication between native speakers and native listeners remains perfectly feasible with this impoverished kind of signal. When either the speaker or the listener is non-native, communication tends to become problematic.

Signal compression such as Linear Predictive Coding (LPC) is the basis of GMS telephony. It reduces input speech to a relatively small set of numbers that describe successive speech samples of, say, 10 ms. At the receiver end the speech is regenerated but with considerable loss of quality. The severity of the data reduction can be varied in small steps, which makes this a very useful research tool in intelligibility studies.

Adding noise to the communication channel is an effective method of making perfectly intelligible speech difficult to understand. Many types of noise have been tested for their effectiveness as a masker of speech. White noise affects all frequencies from low to high indiscriminately. This makes it a relatively in-effective masker, since speech has its energy concentrated at low frequencies. A more effective masker would be pink noise (which emphasises low frequencies) but the most effective way to mask speech is by adding more speech to it, i.e. competing voices. Lately, so-called speech noise or babble noise has become a very popular masker. This is basically speech recorded from many speakers added together. The masking noise can have a fixed intensity, for instance equal to the mean peak intensity of the vowels in the utterance. Alternatively, the noise may be intensity modulated such that when the intensity of the speech signal goes up by a particular number of decibels, so does the intensity of the masking noise. Communication between native speakers and native listeners withstands a lot of masking noise. The masking noise may be up to 12 dB stronger than the speech signal and the listener may still get the gist of the message. When either the speaker or the listener is non-native, however, communication fails at less extreme signal-to-noise ratios (van Wijngaarden, 2001).

In the preceding paragraphs we have considered the measurement of the dependent variable in intelligibility research, i.e. the quality of word recognition in sentential context. In the following sections we will address the question how the quality of word recognition can be predicted from a comparison of closely related languages at the level of smaller units, such as phonemes and allophones.

3. PERCEPTUAL ASSIMILATION OF STRANGE SOUNDS

3.1 Ask the listener

The way we perceive sounds is shaped by our linguistic experience. Native listeners of English sort incoming speech sounds into categories that are specific to English; Chinese listeners have learnt from childhood onwards to sort sounds in terms of the categories that are most appropriate for Chinese. At the centres of these native language categories prototypes are set up, which act like magnets. Tokens of speech sounds that differ from the prototype are perceptually drawn closer to it (the nearer they physically are to the prototype, the stronger the magnet effect), so that the listener is never aware of the (small) mismatch between the token and the prototype (Kuhl and Iverson, 1995). At the boundary between adjacent categories in perceptual space, however, even small differences can be adequately heard, so that sound discrimination at category boundaries is sharper than within categories.

When we hear sounds spoken in a language variety that differs from our native language, the incoming sounds will deviate to a lesser or greater extent from the prototypes we are used to. Nevertheless we categorise the large majority of the incoming sounds to the prototypes that we have learnt. Only when the discrepancy between an incoming sound and any existing prototype is very large, will the listener refuse to categorise the incoming sound. Best, McRoberts and Goodell (2001) have set up a typology of what they call assimilation patterns that may be observed when a listener is first confronted with sounds that deviate from the prototypes in the native language. Basically a non-native phone may be assimilated to a native category in one of three ways:

(i) *C (categorised)*: it may be categorized as an exemplar of a native phone. It may vary from a very good (prototypical) exemplar to a poor one (on a 1–7 goodness scale).

(ii) *U (uncategorised)*: the token may be at the boundary between two (or more) native categories such that the listener cannot decide which category to assimilate the token to. The sound falls within the native phonological space but in between existing categories.

(iii) *N (non-assimilable)*: the token is not assimilated into the native phonological space at all. It is heard as a non-speech sound instead. This may happen, for instance, when an English listener is first confronted with African click sounds. Here the listener often thinks the speaker clapped hands while speaking.

When studying the perception of sounds in a related language variety, category N will be extremely rare. It seems impossible, by today's standards, to predict whether a non-native sound will be categorised, and if so how, just by comparing sound recordings or physiological measurements of such tokens. Phonetic theory has just not come far enough. As a practical way out, the assimilation behaviour should be tested through experimentation, as in the example below.

In the field of second-language learning, the learner's native language is called the source language, and the language to be learnt is called the target language.

In a sound assimilation experiment, the learner is asked to categorise foreign (target) sounds in terms of his native (source) language with forced choice, and to rate each token for goodness (or 'typicality'), for instance on a scale from 0 (very poor token) to 10 (excellent token). Table 1 presents the results of such an assimilation experiment (Sun and van Heuven, 2007) in which Mandarin listeners were asked to identify the 19 vowels of British English in terms of 14 Mandarin (surface) vowel categories.

The results show, for instance, that any (half) open English monophthong is assimilated to Mandarin /ɑ/, although some are considered a very poor token (e.g. English /ɛ/ is rated as a token of Mandarin /ɑ/ at 2.8 on the 10-point goodness scale)

If we are to predict how well listener B will understand speaker A in a related language, we would first have to know how the sounds in speaker A's variety map onto the inventory of listener B, and how easy it would be for listener B to assimilate a particular sound to the category of his choice. Experiments such as the one exemplified here, would be a necessary first step. Such experiments have not been done in the context of predicting intelligibility of closely related languages.

3.2 Prediction of sound categorisation through learning algorithms

An interesting and promising development, and also an alternative to asking native listeners directly how they perceive strange sounds, is offered by learning algorithms. Suppose we have collected a large number of tokens, by many speakers, of all the sounds in the inventory of a language, for instance, all the monophthongs of English as spoken by American adults. One may then measure relevant acoustic properties of these vowel tokens, such as the first and second formant frequencies F1 and F2 – which would adequately represent vowel height and backness, respectively. The distances between the vowel tokens in the acoustic space can be scaled so as to be perceptually more realistic through Bark transformation (e.g. Traunmüller, 1990). Next, differences between speakers (and between sexes) can be substantially reduced through some simple normalisation procedure (most successful one is the Lobanov transformation, which is simply a z-normalisation within speakers, Lobanov, 1971). We may then submit these transformed and normalised data to an automatic classification procedure such as Linear Discriminant Analysis (LDA; for details on the above procedures, and references, see Wang and van Heuven, 2006). By comparing category membership and the (transformed) acoustic properties of the vowel tokens, the LDA will automatically set up category boundaries in the vowel space such that vowel tokens are optimally sorted (i.e. with the least number of classification errors) into the native categories.

Table 1. Mean percent identification and goodness rating (in parentheses) of English vowel stimuli in terms of Mandarin vowel categories. Boldfaced values indicate the modal identification response. Only identification scores > 10 per cent are included.

English Vowel Stimuli	Chinese Vowel Responses (percent identification and rating 1–10)													
	ɨ	i	ɿ	y	ei	æ	ə	u	ɤ	ou	ɔ	ɑ	au	ɚ
iː	23				**66 (5.9)**									
ɪ					**73 (6.4)**		11							
eɪ					**91 (7.4)**									
ɛ						11			13			**33 (2.8)**		16
æ												**66 (5.4)**		16
e									**86 (6.9)**					
uː								**91 (6.9)**						
ʊ										**63 (7.3)**			13	
oʊ										**86 (7.5)**				
ɔː											**53 (6.6)**	**88 (7.7)**	11	
ɔ												**89 (7.1)**		
ʌ												**70 (7.1)**		
ɑː												**64 (6.1)**	25	
aʊ												**52 (3.4)**	20	
ɔɪ											**61 (7.4)**	11	**81 (7.1)**	
eʊ								28						
eɜ		11			**61 (5.5)**			31						14
eɪ					**48 (4.8)**	13								17

48

Once the LDA is trained on a given set of native speech sounds, we may apply the same set of decision rules to a new dataset, which may be another set of vowel tokens produced by native speakers of the same language as the training data (in which case performance will be very good to excellent). We may also use the decision rules to categorise a dataset with vowel tokens that deviate from the training data. This may be a set of vowel tokens produced by foreign-language learners but it may also be a set of vowels of a different (in this case related) language. The LDA will then tell us how a native listener of the target language would classify each input vowel token. In this way, the LDA is a model of the native listener of the target language. Such a model can be used to predict how listeners of source language B would assimilate the vowels of target language A to their native language categories (Strange et al. 1998, 2004). The same methodology should also work for the assimilation of consonant sounds, provided, of course, that the targeted acoustic dimensions are appropriate for consonant classification.

I have not yet seen this methodology applied to the problem of predicting the perception of a closely related language. Note, however, that although the method described here would probably yield the desired result, it is not driven by theoretical insight; it merely uses the mediating device of a empirically derived computational model. The method does not allow us to directly compare linguistic-phonetic descriptions of the vowel systems of the languages concerned and predict how listeners of one language would categorise the vowels of the other language.

Let us suppose that we now know how the sounds of language A are mapped onto the inventory of a closely related language B, so that we know which vowels and consonants in listener B's language are activated to what extent by the successive incoming sounds produced by the speaker of language A. How would listener B be able to recognise words in the defective input? This is what we will consider in the next section.

4. FROM SOUNDS TO WORD RECOGNITION

4.1 Model of human word recognition

We know from psychophysics that short-term memory keeps a faithful representation of the auditory input no longer than 250 ms (e.g. Crowder and Morton, 1969; Massaro, 1972). After a quarter of a second, the details of the auditory input have evaporated from memory. In a language such as English most words last longer than 250 ms. Therefore, a major problem in spoken word recognition is how the human listener is able to recognise a word even though the acoustic information that defines it is never available for inspection in its entirety. In this respect spoken word recognition presents a challenge that is absent in visual word recognition, where the reader may always refocus on earlier text input.

In order to account for spoken word recognition a range of models have been proposed. Here I will be eclectic and describe in quite general terms what a reasonable model of human word recognition might look like.

It is widely accepted that the human brain is a massive parallel processor. For every word we know, there is a specialised group of brain cells, also called 'word recognition unit' or 'logogen' (Morton, 1969) that has learnt to respond only to information that is characteristic of that particular word. If we know, say, 50,000 different words, then we have 50,000 logogens. When we listen to speech, the auditory information is fed to all 50,000 logogens in parallel. When the incoming sound matches the internal specification of the logogen, its activation is increased; when there is no match (or an outright clash between what is actually heard and what should have been heard), the logogen's activation remains stationary (or is reduced). The better the incoming sound matches the internal specification of the logogen, the greater its contribution to the overall activation of the logogen.[3]

However, incoming speech sounds do not activate words directly. At a lower level in the system there are recognition units for sound categories (phonemes or similar). The phone units are bi-directionally connected with the logogens. When the input acoustics activate the phoneme /k/, all words with a /k/ in their specification will increase their activity. When, for instance, the word *cat* is being said, any word with a /k/ in it is activated. As the logogen for *cat* is activated, so are (through back-propagation) all the phonemes that are internally specified in the logogen for *cat*, such as the /æ/ and the /t/. When the subsequent sound input indeed contains /æ/ and /t/, these phonemes will be active on two counts: by bottom-up activation through sensory input and by top-down activation through back-propagation. Phonemes in words that are not being activated by sensory input receive negative signals ('inhibition') from more successful candidates, so that very soon after the onset of a word only one feasible candidate remains, which is then recognised (winner takes all). Moreover, activation of a word leads to activation of all other words that are semantically (and syntactically) related to it. When a word is deactivated the activation of all related words is also reduced. When a word is actually recognised, it remains active for a long time, and so are all words that are neurally connected to it. This is how semantic and syntactic dependencies are accounted for. This view of human word recognition draws heavily on ideas behind the TRACE model (McClelland and Elman, 1986, see also additional references in note 3).

There are several more effects that have been found to affect word recognition. These effects will also play a role when listeners do not get input in their native language but when the input speech is distorted due to the fact that the speaker has a foreign accent or speaks a closely related language.

50

4.2 Frequency effects

Words that we have heard often before tend to be recognised sooner (from less sensory input) than infrequent words. This frequency effect is accounted for by the fact that the activation of a word that was actually recognised, remains high for a long time, and never fully returns to its previous resting level. Highly frequent words, therefore, have acquired a permanent headstart in the recognition process. As a result, when the input speech in the related language is ambiguous or otherwise unclear, thereby activating multiple recognition candidates in the mind of the listener, high-frequency recognition candidates will be favoured.

These, and other, models of auditory word recognition neatly account for the phenomenon that a listener may recognise a long word without having to keep the entire sound shape of the word in auditory memory. Incoming sound is short-lived. All it does is activate phonemes to a greater or lesser degree, and then it dies. Acoustic information is thereby recoded into a more abstract neural representation with a longer life cycle.

4.3 Superiority of the word beginning?

Older models of word recognition (whether auditory or visual) attached special importance to the beginning of words. For instance, the Cohort model (Marslen-Wilson and Welsh, 1978; Nooteboom, 1981) claimed that a word could never be recognised if the sounds in the word onset (defined as the first 200 ms of the word) could not be heard. In later experiments, however, it was shown that the word onset is not indispensable, and that, in fact, auditory information in any part of the word contributes equally in principle to the recognition process (Nooteboom and van der Vlugt, 1988) – as is implied by the neural network view presented in Section 4.1.

Earlier sounds in a word enter the auditory system before the later sounds. It is advantageous for the word recognition system to reduce the number of competing candidates as rigorously as possible. Keeping many alternatives open requires extra processing capacity, which is a commodity. There are clear indications that the languages in the world tend to concentrate contrastive information in the beginning of words. For instance, in any language I know, the number of different sounds that may occur at the beginning of a word is larger than the inventory of sounds that may occur at the end of a word. The advantage of this organisational principle is that words can be recognised sooner (i.e. from a shorter onset portion) than in the case of a more even distribution of contrastive elements over the length of the words.

Ideally, words are recognised before their acoustic end is reached. This is typically the case in longer, polysyllabic words. In the word *elephant*, for instance, after the fourth phoneme (i.e. when the sounds [ɛləf] have been heard) no other words remain in the lexicon than *elephant* (and its derivations). In the Cohort model, the lexical uniqueness point (UP, the point from the word onset where it is uniquely distinguished from all competitors in the lexicon) plays an important role. It is at the UP that the listener gets access to the lexical entry, and retrieves all information on the word that is stored in the lexicon (including its meaning, syntactic properties and sound shape). From the UP onwards, the word form is predictable. The listener will check whether indeed the next sounds are as expected, and as a bonus, the listener will know where the next word begins.

4.4 Neighbourhood density

A more sophisticated account of lexical competition during word recognition is offered by the Neighbourhood Activation Model (NAM, Luce and Pisoni, 1998). A practical way of defining a word's neighbourhood is by listing all words that deviate from the target by just one sound. Thus the (British) English word *cat* has a total of 30 neighbours:[4]

bat, pat, mat, fat, vat, that, gnat, sat, chat, rat, hat	(11)
kit, Kate, coat, caught, cot, cart, court, curt, coot, cut, kite	(11)
cap, cab, cam, can, cash, Cass, Cal, catch	(8)

Generally, short words live in densely populated neighbourhoods. Long words live in sparsely populated neighbourhoods. An everyday word such as *computer* has no neighbours at all. Generally, words with many neighbours will be more difficult to recognise than words in small neighbourhoods. This is a matter of lexical redundancy.

Especially when the input sounds are non-prototypical, the human listener cannot definitely rule out competitors. On account of this, short words with many competitors in a dense neighbourhood will be more difficult to recognise. These predictions were born out by the results reported by Luce and Pisoni (1998) in a study in which they carefully controlled token frequencies, neighbourhood density and word length.

4.5 Vowels versus consonants

To conclude this section, let us consider the potentially different contributions of vowels versus consonants to the word recognition process. On the one hand, vowels are louder than consonants; they have more carrying power and can therefore be better heard in adverse circumstances. From a structural, linguistic view, vowels are the heads of syllables.

In spite of the structural and acoustic dominance of vowels, it seems that the contribution of vowels to word recognition is less important than that of consonants. Van Ooijen (1994:110–117; 1996) asked listeners to correct non-words to words in a so-called word reconstruction task. Here the non-words differed from the nearest word in one vowel and one consonant. Replacing either the vowel or the consonant was enough to change the non-word back to a word, as shown in the examples below (three out of a total of 60):

Non-word	Words after V-change	Words after C-change
irmy	army	early
nottice	notice	novice
tisk	task tusk	risk disk

Subjects who were instructed to change vowels only, failed to reconstruct the word in 28 percent of the responses and restored the non-word to the nearest word by inadvertently changing a consonant in another 7 percent of the cases. Subjects who were told only to change consonants failed to reconstruct the word in 42 percent or changed a vowel instead in 15 percent of the cases. When, in a third condition, subjects were left free to choose whether they wished to change either a vowel or a consonant, they opted for each solution in equal proportion. Crucially, however, when they opted for a vowel substitution, reaction time was much faster (1595 ms) than when they resorted to consonant substitution (1922 ms).

It is not entirely clear why vowels contribute less to the identity of words than consonants. It is true that languages typically have more consonant than vowel phonemes. So, from an information-theoretic point of view it should be easier to restore the vowels than to restore the consonants simply because the number of alternatives to choose from is smaller in the case of vowels. Next, in most languages there are more consonants in the shape of words than vowels. Even though CV is the optimally simple and universally preferred syllable type, most languages have more complex syllable types as well. The number of vowels per syllable will always be one, no more, no less. The number of consonants will be at least one, but often more. This skew would also lend more importance to consonants in word recognition. It may also be the case that all vowels resemble each other more than consonants resemble other consonants. Vowels typically only differ in their formants coding height (F1) and backness/rounding (F2). Variation in duration and nasality is secondary (and the same two features are also available for consonants). Consonants differ in many more dimensions, and the acoustic differences along the various dimensions seem to be more contrastive.

Given the evidence presented above, then, it would be reasonable to expect deviations in vowels to be less damaging when listening to speech in a related language variety than deviations in the consonants. Gooskens, Heeringa and Beijering (this volume) are the first to examine the relative weight of vowels versus consonants in the context of intelligibility of related languages. In their correlational study they found that the intelligibility of 17 Scandinavian (Danish, Norwegian, Swedish) dialects for Standard Danish listeners, as determined by a functional translation test, could be predicted better from deviations in the consonants ($r = -.74$) than in the vowels ($r = -.29$). It would make sense, therefore, to incorporate the different contribution of vowels versus consonants in future models of intelligibility of related languages.

5. ROLE OF PROSODY

5.1 Defining (word) prosody

Prosody is the ensemble of all properties of the speech signal that cannot be accounted for by the properties of the constituent phonemes in their early-to-late order (van Heuven and Sluijter, 1996 and references therein). An example of prosody at the word level is stress. Stress is defined here as the abstract linguistic property of a word that tells us which syllable in the word is stronger than any other. In a language with stress, every (content) word has a stress position.[5] The sounds in a stressed syllable are pronounced with greater effort, which results in (i) longer duration, (ii) more extreme articulatory positions (spectral expansion of vowels), (iii) greater loudness (higher intensity and flatter spectral tilt) and (iv) more resistance to coarticulation. When a word is communicatively important in the discourse (depending on the intentions of the speaker) the stressed syllable in the word is additionally marked by a conspicuous change in vocal pitch (a rise, fall, or both).

Some languages have so-called fixed stress; the position of the stress is fixed for the entire vocabulary by a single rule. In Finnish (and related languages) the stress is always on the first syllable. In Polish, the stress is always on the prefinal syllable. In languages with fixed stress, hearing a stress tells the listener where one word ends and where the next word begins. This demarcative function may be important in the perception of continuous speech, as a way to reduce the problem of finding the word boundaries. I am not familiar with any research on perceptual problems caused by incorrect stress in languages with fixed, demarcative stress.

Other languages may have variable, or contrastive, stress. Here the position of the stress differs from one word to the next. Either the stress position can be derived by a set of rules (weight-sensitive stress systems) or has to be learnt by heart for each word in the vocabulary as a lexical property. In such languages identical segment strings may yet be distinct words solely because they differ in the position of the stress. An example would be the English minimal stress pair *trusty* ('trustworthy', initial stress) versus *trustee* (board member of a foundation, final stress). The number of minimal stress pairs in Germanic languages is very limited. Therefore, it seems unlikely that the primary function of stress in such languages is to differentiate between words (Cutler, 1986). Rather, it would appear that differences in stress position allow the listener to subdivide the vocabulary into a small number of rhythmic types, within which words can be recognised more efficiently because of the reduced lexical search space.

As far as we know, the majority of the languages in world have stress. Other languages have lexical tone.[6] In a prototypical tone language any syllable in a word may be pronounced with a different melody, for instance at a high tone (H) or at a low tone (L). In such a tone language there would be four types of word melody on two-syllable words: HH, HL, LH and HH. It is not the case that prominence (or greater perceived strength) is associated with either the H or the L tone; this is the crucial formal difference between stress and tone. The primary function of tone would be to help differentiate between words in the lexicon. Tone languages such as Mandarin, a language with four lexical tones, contain many minimal word pairs, triplets and even quartets, that only differ in the tone pattern. An often cited example is the Mandarin syllable /ma/, which means 'mother' with high level tone (HH), 'hemp' with mid-rising tone (MH), 'horse' with low dipping tone (MLH) and 'scold' with high falling tone (HL). One would expect word recognition, even in connected speech, to depend considerably on tonal information; the role of tonal information should increase and be more or less indispensable when speech is heard in severe noise. There is very little research on the role of lexical tone in speech recognition, and virtually none at all when it comes to understanding speech in a closely related language. I will present some (preliminary) data below. In the next two sections I will first review some work on the role of stress in word recognition and then of tone.

5.2 *Stress and word recognition*

It has often been remarked that the contribution of stress to the process of word recognition should be a modest one. Orthographies reflect effects of stress only in exceptional cases. In the writing systems of European languages, the position of the stress is not indicated in the spelling (with the exception of Spanish, which writes accent marks on syllables with stress in irregular position). Word tones are not written in the orthographies of Norwegian, Swedish, Serbo-Croatian and Welsh. The basic idea is that the words in languages can be recognised from their segmental make up, and that word prosody is largely redundant (especially in sentence contexts).

Table 2. Percent correctly named words (left) and naming latency of correct responses (ms). Words with a melodic accent synthesised on the lexically stressed syllable are listed along the main diagonal of the matrix (boldface).

Lexical stress on syll. #	Stress synthesised on syll #			Stress synthesized on syll #		
	1	2	3	1	2	3
1	**66**	44	56	**1500**	1800	1650
2	34	**81**	31	1630	**1510**	1640
3	34	25	**63**	1700	1690	**1390**

My take on the role of stress (and of prosody in general) is that it is extremely robust against noise and distortion. Because it is a slowly varying property of the speech code, it will normally not be needed in the recognition of words when listening to speech in one's native language. However, when communication suffers from noise, prosody fulfils the role of a safety catch. Listening to speech in a closely related language is basically listening to speech in noise. So, in these circumstances I would predict that stress is important to word recognition; especially incorrect stress, i.e. stressed realised in unexpected positions, will be highly detrimental to word recognition. Such effects should be even stronger when the language does not have stress but word tone (see below).

If it is true that stress becomes more important as the quality of the input speech degrades, we predict that word recognition will suffer if stress is on the wrong syllable in low quality speech. This was clearly shown in van Heuven (1985). Correct recognition of words synthesised from low-quality diphones was severely reduced (and delayed by 120 to as much as 310 ms) if medial or final stress was shifted to an incorrect position in Dutch words. However, shifting an initial stress to a later position was less detrimental in terms of percent correct naming but still yielded severe delays (see Table 2).

On the basis of such results I would predict that unexpected stress positions play an important negative role in understanding speech in a closely related variety. Given that the sounds in the related language do not match the prototypes of the listener's system, word prosody will assume a more prominent role. Now, if the stress were marked in the wrong position, chances of the listener accessing the right portion of his lexicon are very small, and failure of the word recognition process will be the result.[7]

5.3 Lexical tone and word recognition

Gooskens and Heeringa (2004) studied judged distance between 15 Norwegian dialects. In Norwegian, stressed syllables may have one of two different tones (unstressed syllables have no tone), which makes it a restricted tone system.

Similarly, Tang and van Heuven (2007) investigated judged distance and judged intelligibility between 15 (Mandarin and non-Mandarin) Chinese dialects – with four to nine lexical tones, depending on the particular dialect. To get some grip on the contribution of tonal information to distance and intelligibility, speech materials in both studies were presented both with full tonal information and in monotonised versions (using PSOLA analysis and resynthesis, a technique that allows the researcher to change the melody of a speech utterance but leaves the segmental quality unaffected).[8] The results of both studies showed that removing tonal information from the speech utterances did not clearly influence the judgments by the listeners – except that they were somewhat less outspoken.

Yang and Castro (this volume) computed tonal distance between dialects of tone languages (Bai and Zhuang) spoken in the South of China, close to the Vietnamese border. They then regressed tonal distance (computed in several different ways) against functional intelligibility measurements and found that segmental and tonal distance correlated roughly equally strongly with intelligibility (both around $r = .7$). irrespective of the method used. Curiously enough, Tang (2009), who correlated similar tonal distance measures with both functional and judged intelligibility measures for all pairs of 15 Mandarin and non-Mandarin Chinese dialects obtained no r-values better than .4.

In order to get some idea of the relative importance of tonal information for word recognition in tone languages, an experimental set-up is required in which segmental and tonal information is manipulated independently. Such experiments are difficult to find in the literature. Zhang, Qi, Song and Liu (1981) report recognition scores for several versions of Mandarin materials. Recognition of tones was close to ceiling no matter what kind of filtering had been applied to the signals (whether low pass or high pass) while correct identification of segments (vowels, consonants) was severely affected. This shows that tone, like other prosodic features, is an extremely robust property in speech communication. When melodic properties were removed from the stimuli (using resynthesis with noise excitation or excited by a monotonised sawtooth wave), word recognition scores dropped to 24 and 16 percent, respectively; while sentence intelligibility was at 24 and 33 percent, respectively. When the sawtooth excitation was given its original melody, word and sentence scores rose to 50 and 73 percent correct; adding noise excitation (during obstruents) to the frequency-modulated sawtooth source yielded word and sentence scores of 60 and 90 percent correct.

A more direct study on the relative importance of segmental versus tonal information for the intelligibility of a tone language is reported by Zhu (2009). He established the intelligibility of the 25 Mandarin SPIN test sentences (male voice) used by Tang and van Heuven (2009).[9] Sentences were presented with high-quality segments, with moderate loss of quality (low-pass filtered at 1 kHz) and with practically all spectral information removed (low-pass filtered at

Table 3. Intelligibility (per cent correct recognition of sentence-final word) broken down by melodic version (presence versus absence of pitch information) and by segmental information (excellent, reduced, none). Data from Zhu (2009).

Melodic	Segmental quality			
version	High	Moderate	Poor	Mean
Original	97	83	23	69
Monotonised	98	47	10	52
Mean	98	68	17	61

300 Hz). Each of these three versions were presented with full melodic information as well as monotonised (in a fully blocked design). Intelligibility scores were as shown in Table 3.

These results show that information on tones is fully redundant when segmental quality is high. However, when segmental quality is compromised, tone information makes a large contribution to word recognition and sentence intelligibility. The effect is especially important when segmental quality is moderate. Here the presence of tone information keeps intelligibility at a high level; when the pitch information is eliminated, scores drop below the intelligibility threshold (commonly set at 50 percent word error rate).

Note that in the studies reviewed here, there is always some residual information in the signal that carries information on the identity of the word tones. We know that the tones of Mandarin are also cued by differences in duration and by differences in intensity contour. Follow-up experiments are needed here in which these secondary acoustic properties are also controlled in the stimulus materials.

I should also point out that the results reported above on the importance of word tone and of word stress cannot be compared directly. In the stress experiment, stress was either on the correct or in some wrong position, it was never absent.[10] In the tone experiment, the tones were (nearly) absent but never wrong or misleading. Additional research will be needed in order to come to a more balanced view of the relative importance of stress and tone (as two typologically competing manifestations of word prosody) for speech intelligibility.

6. CONCLUSION

The upshot of the review presented in the sections above is that we are still a long way off from being able to predict success in speech understanding (or word recognition in continuous speech, as a more modest intermediate goal) from a comparison of the two languages engaged in semi-communication. At the same time, however, I have tried to show that the problem is not insoluble. Given some realistic simplifications and a substantial research effort to apply known techniques that have proven their value in other contexts, accurate predictions of mutual intelligibility should be feasible.

As a short-term research agenda, I would recommend in-depth, detailed studies of the effects at the lower levels of the linguistic hierarchy on the recognition of words (isolated and in short sentences). We need to establish how the vowels, consonants and word-prosodic categories (stress, tone) are perceived by the listener of a related language. Once we know what perceptual confusions arise due to the deviant phonetic properties of the related input language, can we attempt to predict the effects at the higher linguistic levels (understanding of sentences and paragraphs). And only if we know the precise effects of the deviant input at the phonetic level, will it be possible to predict intelligibility of a related language by comparing source and target languages at the symbolic levels (i.e. by comparing segmental and tonal transcriptions of words and sentences).

REFERENCES

R. van Bezooijen and V. J. van Heuven (1997), 'Assessment of speech synthesis', in D. Gibbon, R. Moore and R. Winksi, eds., *Handbook of standards and resources for spoken language systems* (Berlin/New York), 481–653.

C. T. Best, G. W. McRoberts and E. Goodell (2001), 'Discrimination of non-native consonant contrasts varying in perceptual assimilation to the listener's native phonological system', *Journal of the Acoustical Society of America*, 109, 775–794.

P. Boersma (2001), 'Praat, a system for doing phonetics by computer', *Glot International*, 5, 341–345.

P. Boersma and D. Weenink (1996), *Praat, a system for doing phonetics by computer*. Report nr. 136, Institute of Phonetic Sciences, University of Amsterdam (Amsterdam).

Y. Chen, M. Robb, H. Gilbert and J. Lerman (2003), 'Vowel production by Mandarin speakers of English', *Clinical Linguistics & Phonetics*, 15, 427–440.

B. Comrie, M. S. Dryer, M. Haspelmath and D. Gil, eds., (2005), *World Atlas of Language Structures*. Oxford: Oxford University Press.

R. G. Crowder and J. Morton (1969), 'Precategorical acoustic storage (PAS)', *Perception & Psychophysics*, 5, 365–373.

A. Cutler (1986), 'Forbear is a homophone: Lexical stress does not constrain lexical access', *Language and Speech*, 29, 201–220.

C. Gooskens, W. Heeringa and K. Beijering (this volume), 'Phonetic and lexical predictors of intelligibility'.

C. Gooskens and W. Heeringa (2004), 'Perceptive evaluation of Levenshtein dialect distance measurements using Norwegian dialect data', *Language Variation and Change*, 16, 189–207.

W. Heeringa (2004), 'Measuring dialect pronunciation differences using Levenshtein distance' (Ph-D thesis, University of Groningen).

V. J. van Heuven (1984), 'Segmentele versus prosodische invloeden van klemtoon op de herkenning van gesproken woorden' [Segmental versus prosodic influences of stress on the recognition of spoken words], *Verslagen van de Nederlandse Vereniging voor Fonetische Wetenschappen*, 159/162, 22–38.

V. J. van Heuven (1985), 'Perception of stress pattern and word recognition: recognition of Dutch words with incorrect stress position', *Journal of the Acoustical Society of America*, 78, S21.

V. J. van Heuven and A. M. C. Sluijter (1996), 'Notes on the phonetics of word prosody', in R. Goedemans, H. van der Hulst and E. Visch, eds., *Stress patterns of the world, Part 1: Background*, HIL Publications (volume 2), Holland Institute of Generative Linguistics (The Hague), 233–269.

R. van Hout and H. Münsterman (1981), 'Linguïstische afstand, dialect en attitude' [Linguistic distance, dialect and attitude], *Gramma*, 5, 101–123.

D. N. Kalikow, K. N. Stevens and L. L. Elliott (1977), 'Development of a test of speech intelligibility in noise using sentence materials with controlled word predictability', *Journal of the Acoustical Society of America*, 61, 1337–1351.

P. K. Kuhl and P. Iverson (1995), 'Linguistic experience and the "perceptual magnet effect"', in W. Strange, ed., *Speech perception and linguistic experience: Issues in cross-language research* (Timonium, MD), 121–154.

B. M. Lobanov (1971), 'Classification of Russian vowels spoken by different speakers', *Journal of the Acoustical Society of America*, 49, 606–608.

P. A. Luce and D. B. Pisoni (1998), 'Recognizing spoken words: The neighborhood activation model', *Ear and Hearing*, 19, 1–36.

W. D. Marslen-Wilson and A. Welsh (1978), 'Processing interactions and lexical access during word recognition in continuous speech', *Cognitive Psychology*, 10, 29–63.

D. W. Massaro (1972), 'Preperceptual images, processing time and perceptual units in auditory perception', *Psychological Review*, 79, 124–145.

J. L. McClelland and J. L. Elman (1986), 'The TRACE model of speech perception', *Cognitive Psychology*, 18, 1–86.

J. Morton (1969), 'Interaction of information in word recognition', *Psychological Review*, 76, 165–178.

E. Moulines and E. Verhelst (1995), 'Time-domain and frequency-domain techniques for prosodic modification of speech', in W. B. Kleijn and K. K. Paliwal, eds., *Speech coding and synthesis* (Amsterdam), 519–555.

S. G. Nooteboom (1981), 'Lexical retrieval from fragments of spoken words: beginnings versus endings', *Journal of Phonetics*, 9, 407–424.

S. G. Nooteboom and M. J. van der Vlugt (1988), 'A search for a word-beginning superiority effect', *Journal of the Acoustical Society of America*, 84, 2018–2032.

D. Norris (1994), 'Shortlist: A connectionist model of continuous speech recognition', *Cognition*, 52, 189–234.

D. Norris, J. M. McQueen and A. Cutler (2000), 'Merging information in speech recognition: Feedback is never necessary', *Behavioral and Brain Sciences*, 23, 299–370.

B. A. van Ooijen (1994), 'The processing of vowels and consonants' (doctoral dissertation, Leiden University).

B. van. Ooijen (1996), 'Vowel mutability and lexical selection in English: Evidence from a word reconstruction task', *Memory & Cognition*, 24, 573–583.

S. Peperkamp and E. Dupoux (2002), 'A typological study of stress deafness', in C. Gussenhoven and N. Warner, eds., *Papers from the Seventh Laboratory Phonology Conference* (Berlin), 203–240.

D. Pisoni, B. Greene and H. Nusbaum (1985), 'Perception of synthetic speech generated by rule', *Proceedings of the IEEE*, 73, 1665–1676.

B. Remijsen and V. J. van Heuven (2005), 'Stress, tone and discourse prominence in the Curaçao dialect of Papiamentu', *Phonology*, 22, 205–235.

B. Remijsen and V. J. van Heuven (2006), 'Introduction: between stress and tone', *Phonology*, 23, 121–123.

W. Strange, R. Akahane-Yamada, R. Kubo, S. A. Trent, K. Nishi and J. J. Jenkins (1998), 'Perceptual assimilation of American English vowels by Japanese listeners', *Journal of Phonetics*, 26, 311–344.

W. Strange, S.-O. Bohn, S. A. Trent and K. Nishi (2004), 'Acoustic and perceptual similarity of North German and American English vowels', *Journal of the Acoustical Society of America*, 115, 1791–1807.

L. Sun and V. J. van Heuven (2007), 'Perceptual assimilation of English vowels by Chinese listeners. Can native-language interference be predicted?', in B. Los and M. van Koppen, eds., *Linguistics in the Netherlands 2007* (Amsterdam), 150–161.

C. Tang and V. J. van Heuven (2007), 'Mutual intelligibility and similarity of Chinese dialects. Predicting judgments from objective measures', in B. Los and M. van Koppen, eds., *Linguistics in the Netherlands 2007* (Amsterdam), 223–234.

C. Tang and V. J. van Heuven (2009), 'Mutual intelligibility of Chinese dialects experimentally tested', *Lingua*, 119, 709–732.

H. Traunmüller (1990), 'Analytical expressions for the tonotopic sensory scale', *Journal of the Acoustical Society of America*, 88, 97–100.

H. Wang and V. J. van Heuven (2006), 'Acoustical analysis of English vowels produced by Chinese, Dutch and American speakers', in J. M. Van de Weijer and B. Los, eds., *Linguistics in the Netherlands 2006* (Amsterdam/Philadelphia), 237–248.

S. J. van Wijngaarden (2001), 'Intelligibility of native and non-native Dutch speech', *Speech Communication*, 35, 103–113.

C. Yang and A. Castro (this volume), 'Representing tone in Levenshtein distance'.

E. van Zanten and R. W. N. Goedemans (2007), 'A functional typology of Austronesian and Papuan stress systems', in V. J. van Heuven and E. van Zanten, eds., *Prosody in Indonesian languages* LOT Occasional Series 9 (Utrecht), 63–88.

L. Zhu (2009), 'The relative contribution of segmental and tonal information to the intelligibility of Standard Mandarin' (MA thesis, Dept. English, Shenzhen University).

END NOTES

[1] In some studies a one-dimensional distance value was obtained by having listeners judge the overall distance or strangeness of some language (variety) relative to their own (van Hout and Münsterman, 1981; Gooskens and Heeringa, 2004; Tang and van Heuven, 2007). This measure correlates almost perfectly with judged intelligibility (Tang and van Heuven, 2007), so that it seems that intuitions about linguistic distance are primarily based on intelligibility. However, in the studies mentioned, the varieties were always related to the language of the judges. It would be crucial to check whether listeners also have clear and reliable intuitions on linguistic distance if they do not understand the stimulus languages at all. As far as I have been able to ascertain, such research has not been done.

[2] That foreign accent is a speech pathology is implied by Chen et al. (2003), who published a study of Chinese accent in English in the journal *Clinical Linguistics & Phonetics*.

[3] The logogen model can be seen as an early model that involves the concept of neural networks. In more recent developments of such theories of word recognition, such as Trace (McClelland and Elman, 1986) and Shortlist A (Norris 1994), and computational implementations of the latter in Merge (Norris, McQueen and Cutler, 2000) the term logogen is no longer used but the concept of a word (or stem morpheme) as a configuration of specialised neurons still plays a central role.

[4] Here we will ignore neighbors that could be generated by deletion or addition of a sound, although established practice requires that we include these in the neighborhood.

[5] Monosyllabic function words may have unstressable vowels (lexical schwa).

[6] The World Atlas of Linguistic Structures (WALS, Comrie, Dryer, Haspelmath and Gil, 2005) lists 220 tone languages versus 307 no-tone languages (chapter 13); at the same time it lists 502 stress languages, divided in chapter 14 between 282 with fixed stress (281 in chapter 15) versus 220 with no-fixed stress (219 in chapter 15). Van Zanten and Goedemans (2007:64) estimate that languages with stress-based word prosody, tone-based systems and languages without word prosody occur in 80, 16 and 4 per cent of the world's languages, respectively. Clearly, languages without word prosody are rare; moreover, languages that independently exploit both stress and tone seem to be anomalous and may develop only as a result of contact between a stress language and a non-related tone language (Remijsen and van Heuven, 2005, 2006). It would seem, therefore, that word prosody of the world's languages is either stress-based or tone-based.

[7] These predictions could be made for all other languages with variable (distinctive) stress systems. I do not know what to predict in the case of incorrect stress in languages with a fixed stress system. It has been shown that French listeners, for example, are 'stress deaf' (Peperkamp and Dupoux, 2002), since French with its fixed final stress never uses stress to distinguish one word from another. However, French listeners could use stress as a word separator. Whether they do, and what happens when French words are incorrectly stressed, has not been researched in any detail.

[8] PSOLA: Pitch-Synchronous Overlap and Add is an analysis-resynthesis technique in the time domain. For a description see e.g. Moulines and Verhelst, 1995). The technique is widely available through Praat speech processing software (Boersma 2001, Boersma and Weenink, 1996).

[9] SPIN test stands for Speech in Noise test. This functional intelligibility test was developed for use in audiology (establishing the extent of patients' deafness) by Kalikow, Stevens and Elliot (1977).

[10] In van Heuven (1984) I included Dutch materials with no acoustic marking of word stress at all – by synthesizing words from diphones exclusively excerpted from strongly accented source syllables and omitting all temporal, dynamic and melodic stress marking from the synthesis. Word intelligibility appeared unaffected by this manipulation. It would seem therefore that only stress in incorrect position should be penalized. I similar vein, I would predict that simply removing tone information from Mandarin stimuli (as in the experiments reviewed) is not nearly as detrimental to intelligibility as is pronouncing the words with (phonetically correct) tones of the wrong type.

PHONETIC AND LEXICAL PREDICTORS
OF INTELLIGIBILITY

CHARLOTTE GOOSKENS, WILBERT HEERINGA
AND KARIN BEIJERING

Abstract   *In the present investigation, the intelligibility of 17 Scandinavian language varieties and standard Danish was assessed among young Danes from Copenhagen. In addition, distances between standard Danish and each of the 17 varieties were measured at the lexical level and at different phonetic levels. In order to determine how well these linguistic levels can predict intelligibility, we correlated the intelligibility scores with the linguistic distances and we carried out a number of regression analyses. The results show that for this particular set of closely related language varieties phonetic distance is a better predictor of intelligibility than lexical distance. Consonant substitutions, vowel insertions and vowel shortenings contribute significantly to the prediction of intelligibility.*

I. INTRODUCTION

Gooskens (2007) correlated lexical and phonetic distances with mutual intelligibility scores for the Mainland Scandinavian standard languages, Danish, Norwegian and Swedish. Subjects from different places in Denmark, Norway and Sweden listened to the two standard languages spoken in the neighbouring countries and linguistic distances were measured between the language varieties of the listeners and the test languages. In total there were 18 mean intelligibility scores and 18 corresponding linguistic distances. The distances were measured at the two linguistic levels that are generally taken to be most important for mutual intelligibility in Scandinavia, namely the lexical and the phonetic level (Delsing and Lundin Åkesson, 2005; Torp, 1998). The results showed a high

International Journal of Humanities and Arts Computing 2 (1–2) 2008, 63–81
DOI: 10.3366/E1753854809000317
© Edinburgh University Press and the Association for History and Computing 2009

correlation between intelligibility scores and phonetic distances ($r = -.80$, $p < .01$). The correlation with lexical distances was low and not significant ($r = -.42$, $p = 0.11$), probably due to the fact that the lexical differences between the Scandinavian language varieties are small.

The purpose of the present paper is similar to the goal of the study we mentioned above: investigating the relationship between the intelligibility of closely-related language varieties and linguistic distances among these varieties. In our study a larger set of languages varieties is tested including *dialect* varieties, while Gooskens (2007) focused on standard languages. The intelligibility of 17 Scandinavian language and dialect varieties was tested among speakers of standard Danish. Like in the previous study, we correlated intelligibility scores with lexical and phonetic distances. However, in the present study the phonetic distances were also split up into consonant and vowel distances and subclassified by type (substitutions, insertions, deletions, lengthening and shortening of consonants and vowels).

Since only aggregate phonetic distances were included in the investigation by Gooskens (2007), no conclusions could be drawn about the nature of the phonetic differences that contribute most to intelligibility. It is generally assumed that consonants are more important than vowels for the identification of a word and that vowels carry less information than consonants. Consonants function as reference points in words while vowels tend to be more variable and change over time more rapidly than consonants do (Ashby and Maidment, 2005). Therefore, the occurrence of deviant segments in the consonantal structure of a word is presumably more disturbing for the intelligibility than changes in the vowels of a word. Ashby and Maidment illustrate this observation by an example. They assume that if all vowels in the sentence *Mary has a little lamb* are replaced by for example [ɛ], most people will probably still understand the sentence. However, when replacing all consonants with [d] and keeping the correct vowel qualities, the sentence will be unintelligible. The relative contribution of consonants and vowels to intelligibility may be different across languages since the size of consonant and vowel inventories can vary considerably and so can the number of vowels and consonants used in running speech. In the present investigation we measured consonant and vowel distances separately in order to test the hypothesis that consonants are more important for intelligibility than vowels in a Scandinavian setting.

We also took a closer look at the role of vowel and consonant distances subclassified by formal operation. We made a distinction between the following operations: substitutions, insertions, deletions, lengthening and shortening of vowels and consonants. The effect of these operations on intelligibility may vary. For example, substitutions change the basic framework of a word. In case of insertion or deletion of a segment, there is either a sound segment too many or too few in comparison with the native variety of the listeners and this may change the structure of the words. Also the lengthening and shortening of segments may make words more difficult to understand.[1]

The research questions posed in the study are as follows:

1. What is the relative contribution of lexical and phonetic distances to the intelligibility of Scandinavian language varieties to standard Danish listeners?
2. What is the relative contribution of aggregate consonant and vowel distances to the intelligibility of Scandinavian language varieties to standard Danish listeners?
3. What is the relative contribution of subclassified consonant and vowel distances (insertions, deletions, substitutions, lengthening, shortening) to the intelligibility of Scandinavian language varieties to standard Danish listeners?

2. MATERIAL

We included recordings and transcriptions of the fable *The North Wind and the Sun*[2] in 18 different language varieties in our investigation (see Figure 1). One of the varieties, standard Danish, was only included in order to be able to check that the test was feasible. From a selection of recordings in more than 50 different Norwegian dialects, we chose eight dialects that form a good representation of the dialectological and geographical diversity of Norway.[3] In addition, we made extra recordings of Faroese (Torshavn), standard Swedish (as spoken in Stockholm), four Swedish dialects representing the four major dialect groups (including Finland Swedish), standard Danish (as spoken in Lyngby, close to Copenhagen) and three Danish dialects spoken on the peninsula of Jutland. The standard varieties of Danish, Norwegian[4] and Swedish all belong to the Mainland Scandinavian branch of the North Germanic language family and are known to be mutually intelligible. Speakers of these varieties can communicate with each other in their own language, though sometimes with some effort, see e.g. Delsing and Lundin Åkesson (2005). So far, the intelligibility of non-standard language varieties in a Scandinavian context has not been investigated. Faroese belongs to the Insular Nordic branch of the North Germanic language family and without prior instruction it is almost unintelligible to speakers of Mainland Scandinavian (Torp 1998: 34).

The Norwegian version of *The North Wind and the Sun* was first translated into Danish, Swedish and Faroese. The texts were then presented to speakers of the 18 varieties in the standard language of their country. The 18 text versions comprised between 91 and 111 words, with a mean of 98 words. The 18 recordings were used for the intelligibility experiment (see Section 3). In addition, phonetic transcriptions were made of all recordings.[5] These transcriptions were used to calculate the Levenshtein distances (see Section 4).

Figure 1. Map of Scandinavia with the locations of the 18 Scandinavian language varieties.

3. INTELLIGIBILITY

Design

The fable *The North Wind and the Sun* consists of six sentences. Each listener heard these six sentences, each sentence being presented in another Scandinavian language variety. In total 18 Scandinavian language varieties (including standard Danish) had to be tested. In order to be able to test all varieties we divided them into three groups. Every group contained a standard variety of one of the Mainland Scandinavian languages (Danish, Norwegian or Swedish). Furthermore, the three groups contained an equal number of Danish, Norwegian and Swedish dialects. We distributed the varieties among the groups in such a way that all groups contained both varieties that were likely to be difficult to understand, as well as varieties that were expected to be easy to understand. Faroese is the most deviant language variety in the test and the dialects of Oppdal and Storliden also differ considerably from standard Danish. Hence, each test contained one Danish, Norwegian or Swedish standard variety, one 'deviant'

66

variety, and an equal number of other Danish, Norwegian and Swedish dialects. In (1) an overview of the three groups is given. The abbreviations behind the dialects represent the language areas, i.e. NO stands for Norwegian, SW for Swedish, DA for Danish, FA for Faroese, and 's' preceding an abbreviation stands for the standard variety.

(1) | **group 1** | **group 2** | **group 3** |
| --- | --- | --- |
| Oslo (sNO) | Stockholm (sSW) | Lyngby (sDA) |
| Torshavn (sFA) | Oppdal (NO) | Storliden (SW) |
| Høgsted (DA) | Hjordkær (DA) | Katrad (DA) |
| Tromsø (NO) | Bjugn (NO) | Rana (NO) |
| Fyresdal (NO) | Gaular (NO) | Trysil (NO) |
| Lidköping (SW) | Gryttinge (SW) | Finland Swedish (SW) |

In order to test all sentences in all varieties, 18 different versions of the listening experiment were needed (6 versions per group). For example, test 1A contained sentence 1 in the Tromsø dialect, test 1B contained sentence 2 in the Tromsø dialect and so on (crossed design). The order of the sentences was randomised for each version, except that the first sentence, which contains the title of the fable and therefore reveals the content of the story, always occurred as the last sentence in the test. Furthermore, we also made sure that the sentences did not follow each other in the original order (for example sentence 3 preceding sentence 4). In this way, the listeners could not derive the content of a sentence from the context.[6]

Listeners

The subjects were 351 native speakers of standard Danish between 15 and 20 years of age (average 17.6) from 18 high-school classes in Copenhagen. Since the listeners lived in Copenhagen, we assumed that they all spoke standard Danish or at least were familiar with this language variety. Some of the listeners may have been familiar with some of the language varieties presented in the test. However, people living in Copenhagen do not generally have much contact with the Danish dialects of Jutland or the other Scandinavian dialects.

Procedure

While listening to the six sentences from the fable *The North Wind and the Sun*, the subjects had to translate each word they heard into standard Danish. Each sentence was presented twice. First the whole sentence was presented and next it was presented once more in smaller pieces of four to eight words, depending on the position of prosodic breaks. In this way we made sure that saturation of the listeners' short-term memory would not influence the results and that the listeners had enough time to write down their translations.[7] Between the sentences there was a pause of 3 seconds and every sentence was preceded by a beep. The listening experiment started with an example sentence in Swedish (not from *The North Wind and the Sun*) so that the listeners could get used to the task.

Intelligibility scores

The percentage of correctly translated words constituted the intelligibility score of a given language variety. A correctly translated word was awarded one point and partly correctly translated words half a point. For example, if only the last part of the word *nordenvinden* 'The North Wind' was correctly translated, half a point was given.[8] We excluded Lyngby, representing standard Danish, from the analysis. This recording was only included to check that the test was feasible. Since 99 per cent of the Lyngby words were translated correctly, we conclude that this was indeed the case. So the remaining analyses were based upon 17 varieties.

4. LINGUISTIC DISTANCES

4.1 Phonetic distances

Phonetic distances between standard Danish (Lyngby) and each of the other 17 Scandinavian language varieties were calculated by means of the Levenshtein algorithm (see detailed explanations in Heeringa 2004). The distance between two phonetic transcriptions of two cognate pronunciations is calculated as the number of operations needed to transform one transcription into the other. There are three types of operations: insertions, deletions and substitutions of phonetic segments. The power of the Levenshtein distance is that it chooses the least costly set of operations that transform one pronunciation into another.

We will illustrate the algorithm with an example. The form *enige* (meaning 'in agreement') is pronounced as [ʔeːni] in Lyngby (standard Danish) and as [eːnɪɡɑ] in Stockholm (standard Swedish). Ignoring suprasegmentals and diacritics (including length marks), the Levensthein algorithm will find the alignment as shown in (2).[9]

(2)

	1	2	3	4	5	6
Lyngby	ʔ	e	n	i		
Stockholm		e	n	ɪ	ɡ	ɑ
	del			sub	ins	ins

The pronunciation of Lyngby is changed into the pronunciation of Stockholm by one deletion, one substitution and two insertions, four operations in total. Since we are using Levenshtein distance to model intelligibility, we want to calculate the extent to which a speaker of the Lyngby variety understands the pronunciation of Stockholm as a percentage. In our example we get six alignment slots, therefore the phonetic distance is $4/6 = 0.67$ or 67 per cent. This is the distance for one word. The distance for the whole text is the summed distances for all words divided by the number of words.

In order to obtain distances which are based on linguistically motivated alignments that respect the syllable structure of a word or the structure within a syllable, the algorithm was adapted so that a vowel may only correspond to a vowel and a consonant only to a consonant. The semi-vowels [j] and [w] may also correspond to a vowel or the other way around, their vowel counterparts [i] and [u] may correspond to a consonant or the reverse. The central vowel schwa [ə] may correspond to any sonorant. In this way, unlikely matches like [o] and [t] or [s] and [e] are prevented.

In the example above, all operations have the same cost. In the present study, we used graded operation weights calculated on the basis of sound samples from *The Sounds of the International Phonetic Alphabet* (1995). On the basis of the spectrograms, distances were measured between the IPA vowels and pulmonic consonants (see Heeringa 2004, pp. 97–107). We used a Barkfilter representation, which we consider a perceptually-oriented spectrogram since it has a more or less logarithmic frequency scale, a logarithmic power spectral density and the 24 first critical bands are modeled (see Heeringa 2004, pp. 87–88 for more details). The Barkfilter distances are used as operation weights. In this way the fact that for example [i] and [e] are phonetically closer to each other than [i] and [a] is taken into account. On average the Bark filter distances among vowels are smaller than among consonants. The vowel space is about one third of the consonant space (Heeringa 2004, p. 94). Gradual weights for insertions and deletions are obtained by measuring distances between the IPA sounds and silence. Using the Barkfilter representation, the glottal stop is closest to silence, and the [a] is most distant.

In validation work Heeringa (2004) found the tendency that Levenshtein distances based on logarithmic gradual segment distances approach perception better than Levenshtein distances based on linear gradual segment distances (see pp. 185–186). Although the Barkfilter represention already is logarithmic in itself since it has a logarithmic power spectral density, the use of logarithmic Barkfilter segment distances still gave some further improvement.

The length of different segment types is represented by changing the phonetic transcriptions as in (4).

(4) extra short sounds are retained as they are [ă] = a
    normal sounds are doubled [a] = aa
    half long sounds are trebled [aˑ] = aaa
    long sounds are quadrupled [aː] = aaaa

Differences in length are formalised as insertions or deletions (indels), for example [a] versus [aː] is represented as *aa* versus *aaaa*, which results in two indels. Lengthening of a segment compared to standard Danish is processed as the insertion of a segment whereas shortening of a segment compared to standard Danish is processed as the deletion of a segment. Indels of this type are not regarded as 'real' indels, but as 'indels because of length difference' so that we are able to distinguish between insertions/deletions and lengthening/shortening. Diphthongs are processed as sequences of two monophthongs, or as sequences of a monophthong and a glide ([j] or [w]).

First Levenshtein distances on the basis of all segments (full phonetic distance) were calculated between each Scandinavian language variety and standard Danish. Together with the lexical distances (see Section 4.2) these distances were used to answer the first research question formulated in Section 1. Next, in order to be able to answer the second research question, the full phonetic distance was subdivided for consonants on the one hand and vowels on the other hand. When we calculated distances on the basis of consonants only, the full phonetic strings of the corresponding pronunciations were initially compared to each other using the Levenshtein algorithm. Once the optimal alignment was found, the distances were based on the alignment slots in which only consonants are involved, i.e. slots with either consonant insertion, deletion or substitution.[10] This distance was divided by the length of the full alignment. Vowel distance is calculated in a similar way, including only operations where vowels are involved.

We may illustrate this with example (2). The length of the alignment on the basis of all segments is 6. The slots 2, 4 and 6 concern vowels, involving a substitution and an insertion. Therefore the vowel distance is $2/6 = 0.33$. We find one vowel substitution, therefore the vowel substitution distance is $1/6 = 0.17$. Likewise the vowel insertion distance is $1/6 = 0.17$. We do not find vowel deletions, therefore the vowel deletion distance is $0/6 = 0$. For the consonant (sub)levels the distances may *mutatis mutandis* be calculated in the same way.

Above we mentioned that an [i] may match with a [j], and a [u] with a [w]. These matches are counted both as vowel (substitution) distances and consonant (substitution) distances.

4.2 Lexical distances

The lexical distance between standard Danish and the 17 other language varieties is measured in the simplest way like Séguy (1973) did. The lexical distance is expressed as the percentage of non-cognates (words that are not historically related to the corresponding words in standard Danish) in the 17 language varieties. For each word in the 17 varieties the corresponding cognate was aligned if existent. If no cognate exists the corresponding non-cognate was aligned. Some words may appear several times in the text. For example, *Nordenvinden* 'The North Wind' appears four times. In such cases four word pairs are considered.

Non-cognates are, in principle, unintelligible to listeners with no prior knowledge of the test variety. A large number of non-cognates should necessarily decrease the extent to which another language variety is intelligible. An example is *krangla* in the dialect of Fyresdal and *skændes* in standard Danish. Lexical differences hardly concern internationalisms in our material and therefore loan words are not excluded in the analyses.

The lexical and the phonetic measurements and the intelligibility scores are given in Appendix A, Tables A.1 and A.2.

5. THE RELATION BETWEEN LINGUISTIC DISTANCES AND INTELLIGIBILITY

We correlated the intelligibility scores of 17 Scandinavian language varieties (see Section 3) with lexical distance measures and different phonetic distance measures. In addition, we also correlated the major linguistic distances (lexical, phonetic, consonants and vowels) with all the linguistic distance measures. This provides information about colinearity. The results are shown in Table 1. In addition, we carried out regression analyses in order to investigate the relative contribution of the various linguistic levels to intelligibility. In Sections 5.1 to 5.3, the results of the correlations and the regression analyses that are relevant to the three research questions will be discussed.

5.1 Lexical and phonetic distances

We correlated the intelligibility scores of the 17 Scandinavian language varieties with the lexical and the phonetic distances, see Table 1. Both correlations are significant at the .01 level, and the correlation with phonetic distances is higher than with lexical distances, but not significantly higher ($r = -.86$ versus $r = -.64$, $p = .08$).[11] The corresponding scatterplots are presented in Figures 2 and 3. Most lexical distances are rather small (below five percent) and the

71

Table 1. Correlations between linguistic distances, intelligibility scores and major linguistic distances.

Linguistic levels	Intelligibility	Lexical	Phonetic	Consonants	Vowels
lexical	−.64**		.49*	.46	.50*
phonetic	−.86**	.49**		.88**	.36
consonants	−.74**	.46	.88**		.21
substitutions	−.57*	−.08	.66**	.56*	−.10
insertions	−.11	.47	.17	.43	.03
deletions	−.22	.13	.26	.25	.56
lengthening	.07	−.25	−.15	−.22	−.79**
shortening	−.22	.40	.42	.39	.11
vowels	−.29	.50*	.36	.21	
substitutions	.11	.16	−.18	−.34	.77*
insertions	−.39	.67**	.47	.53	.41
deletions	−.44	−.02	.53*	.35	.07
lengthening	−.42	.06	.51*	.37	−.45
shortening	−.49*	.21	.29	.07	.05
schwa vs. sonorant	.33	−.10	−.47	−.37	−.38

* $p \leq .05$; ** $p \leq .01$.

corresponding intelligibility scores vary greatly. As expected from the fact that Faroese belongs to another branch of the North Germanic language family, the Faroese variety from Torshavn is most deviant from standard Danish, both lexically and phonetically, and it was also most difficult to understand for the Danish listeners. Storliden is lexically and Oppdal phonetically almost as deviant as Faroese and both varieties are also hard to understand. The standard languages of Sweden and Norway (Oslo and Stockholm, plotted on top of each other in Figure 2) are most similar to standard Danish and also most easily understood, even more so than the Danish dialects of Hjordkær, Katrad and Høgsted.

The strong correlations between the linguistic distances and the intelligibility scores show that the intelligibility of closely related languages and language varieties can be predicted well from the linguistic distances between the target language and the language of the listener (the larger the distances, the more difficult it is to understand the varieties). The correlation between the lexical and phonetic distances is rather low ($r = .49$, $p = .05$), which shows that the two levels are to a large degree independent. Still, a stepwise regression analysis excludes lexical distances from the model. A regression analysis including both lexical and phonetic distances results in a non-significantly higher prediction of intelligibility ($r = .90$, $p < .0001$) than phonetic distances only ($r = .86$, $p < .0001$), see Table 2.

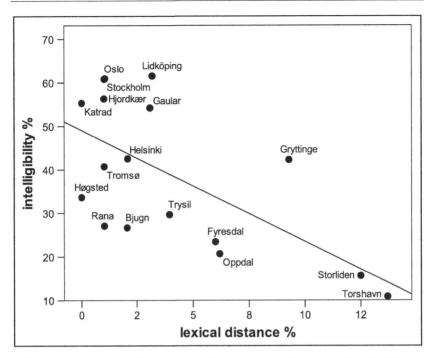

Figure 2. Scatterplot of the correlation between lexical distances and intelligibility scores ($r = -.64$, $p < .05$).

5.2 *Consonants and vowels*

We calculated the phonetic distances for vowels and consonants separately (see Section 4.1) and correlated these two distance measurements with the intelligibility scores. We expected consonants to play a more important role in intelligibility than vowels (see Section 1). The correlations for the consonants were indeed significantly stronger than for the vowels ($r = -.74$ versus $r = -.29$, $p = 0.04$), see Table 1. The correlations are lower than in the case of the full phonetic distances ($r = -.86$) but the consonant distances are still significant at the one percent level while the vowel distances are not. In Figure 4 a scatterplot is presented with the correlation of intelligibility with both the vowels and the consonants. Only consonant distances correlate significantly with the full phonetic distances ($r = .88$). The correlation between consonant distances and vowel distances is low and not significant ($r = -.21$, $p = .41$), which shows that the two levels are independent of each other. A regression analysis with vowels and consonants as independent variables and intelligibility as the dependent variable results in a correlation of .76. In a stepwise regression analysis, only consonants are included in the first step ($r = .74$).

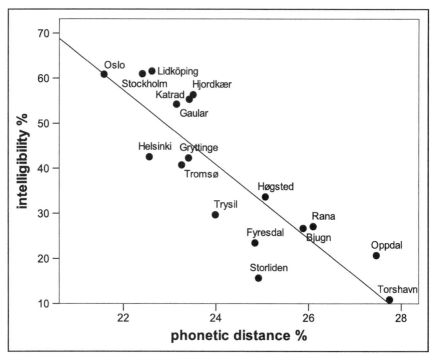

Figure 3. Scatterplot of the correlation between phonetic distances and intelligibility scores ($r = -.86$, $p < .01$).

Table 2. Regression analyses where intelligibility scores are the dependent variable and phonetic and lexical distances are the independent variables.

Method	Entered variables	Model	Result
Enter	Full phonetic distance, lexical distance	Full phonetic distance, lexical distance	$R = .90$ $R^2 = .81$ $p < .001$
Stepwise	Full phonetic distance, lexical distance	Full phonetic distance	$R = .86$ $R^2 = .74$ $p < .001$

5.3 Phonetic sublevels

Finally, we made separate analyses of the consonants and vowels for the different kinds of consonant and vowel operations (insertions, deletions, substitutions, lengthenings and shortenings). Only consonant substitutions ($r = -.57$, $p < .05$) and vowel shortenings ($r = -.49$, $p < .05$) correlate significantly with the intelligibility scores. A regression analysis with all phonetic sublevels gives

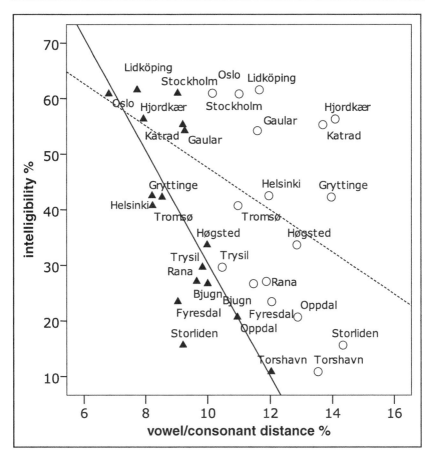

Figure 4. Scatterplot of the correlation between intelligibility and vowel distances (circles, $r = -.29$, $p = .25$) and between intelligibility and consonant distances (triangles, $r = -.74$, $p = .001$).

Table 3. Regression analyses where intelligibility scores are the dependent variable and consonant and vowel distances are the independent variables.

Method	Entered variables	Model	Result
Enter	Consonants, vowels	Consonants, vowels	$R = .76$ $p < .001$
Stepwise 1ˢᵗ step	Consonants, vowels	Consonants	$r = .74$ $p < .001$

Table 4. Regression analyses where intelligibility scores are the dependent variable and different phonetic sublevels are the independent variables.

Method	Entered variables	Model	Result
Enter	All phonetic sublevels	All phonetic sublevels	$R = .93$ $p < .001$
Stepwise 1st step	All phonetic sublevels	Consonant substitutions	$R = .57$ $p = .017$
Stepwise 2nd step	All phonetic sublevels	Consonant substitutions, vowel insertions	$R = .78$ $p < .001$
Stepwise 3rd step	All phonetic sublevels	Consonant substitutions, vowel insertions, vowel shortenings	$R = .87$ $p < .001$

a multiple correlation of $R = .93$ ($p = .05$). A stepwise regression analysis results in three models. As could be expected from the correlations, consonant substitutions are the most important factor. Even though vowel insertion does not correlate significantly with intelligibility ($r = -.39$, $p > .05$) it is included as the second factor and this results in a correlation of .78 ($p = .001$). Vowel shortening is included in the third model and results in a correlation of .87 ($p < .0001$).

6. DISCUSSION AND CONCLUSIONS

We investigated the role of different linguistic levels in the intelligibility of 17 Scandinavian language varieties among young Danes from Copenhagen. First, we wanted to investigate the relative contribution of lexical and phonetic distances (research question 1 in Section 1). We found significant correlations with both lexical and phonetic distances, but a multiple regression analysis included only phonetic distances, which suggests that phonetic distance is a significant predictor. We found the tendency that lexical distances correlate less strongly with intelligibility scores than phonetic distances, but the difference was not significant. The lower correlation with lexical distances is probably due to the fact that it is difficult to predict the effect of individual lexical differences. One single non-cognate word in a sentence or even a larger part of a text can lower intelligibility considerably if the non-cognate word is a central concept. On the other hand, if the non-cognate words in a text have little semantic content, it has less influence on intelligibility. Furthermore, it is possible that the listeners understand some non-cognate words because they are familiar with the words from previous experience with the test language. Finally, the lexical differences between the varieties in our investigation are rather small (see Appendix A).

Next, we investigated the relative contribution of consonant and vowel distances to intelligibility (research question 2). We found that there is a significantly stronger correlation between consonant distances and intelligibility than between vowel distances and intelligibility ($r = -.74$ versus $r = -.29$, $p = 0.04$). This suggests that consonants play a more important role in intelligibility than vowels and it confirms the assumption by Ashby and Maidment (2005) that vowels carry less information than consonant, see introduction. We measured the distances between the individual sound on the basis of spectograms. As mentioned in Section 3 distances between vowels are generally smaller than between consonants. However, our results show larger mean distances between vowels than between consonants (see Figure 3 and Appendices A and B), which means that there is much more vowel variation than consonant variation. The fact that consonants still show a higher correlation with intelligibility confirms the important role that consonants play for the intelligibility. Since our investigation is based on the overall intelligibility of a whole speech sample we are not able to make conclusions about the importance of the quantity and quality of the vowel and consonant differences. In future work, more controlled experiments would have to be set up in order to investigate the relative importance of these two factors in the intelligibility of different languages.

Finally, we took a closer look at the role of the different consonant and vowel operations (research question 3). A stepwise regression analysis showed that consonant substitutions, vowel insertions and vowel shortenings contribute significantly to the prediction of intelligibility. As far as the consonants are concerned, substitution is the only operation that correlates significantly with intelligibility. The first model in a stepwise regression analysis includes this level and excludes all other levels. It does not come as a surprise that consonant substitutions play an important role in intelligibility. When consonants in a word are substituted the framework of the word is changed (see Section 1). Insertions and deletions of consonants are likely to alter the framework of a word as well because the number of reference points change. However both operations play an insignificant role in our investigation. This can probably be explained by the fact that many insertions are found at the end of words which may be less important for the identity of a word than the beginning. Furthermore, Danish has many reduced spoken word forms and as a consequence consonant insertions often result in a word form that is known to Danish listeners from the written or underlying form of the Danish equivalent. Lengthening and shortening of consonants will not disturb the Danish listeners since in Danish consonant length is not phonemically distinct.

In contrast with consonant substitutions, vowel substitutions play a negligible role in intelligibility. Considering the large amount of vowel variation in Danish this may not come as a surprise. Van Ooijen (1994:108) suggested that 'listeners are both aware of and equipped to meet [vowel] variability, especially in the case of a vowel-rich language.' The correlation between vowel insertions and intelligibility scores is low, but vowel insertions are still added to consonant substitutions in the second model resulting from the stepwise regression analysis. Vowel insertions may result in additional syllables or diphthongs in comparison to the corresponding words in Danish. This may conceal the identity of the words for Danish listeners. In the third model resulting from the multiple regression analysis, vowel shortening is added. This is also the only vowel operation that correlates significantly (at the 5 per cent level) with intelligibility. Vowel length is phonemically distinct in Danish and deviant vowel lengths may therefore be rather disturbing.

Our analysis is based on a limited number of words (a mean of 98 words). This sample may be too limited for a lexical analysis, while a small number of words has been proven to be sufficient for reliable measurements of phonetic distance by means of the Levenshtein distance (Heeringa 2004). Furthermore, the results found in this study may not generalise to other situations. If the number of non-cognates varies around the critical breakdown threshold, as it may well be when varieties of other languages (or languages families) are compared, lexical distance will be more important than phonological/phonetic distance within the cognates. Similarly, if a language has more (or fewer) consonants relative to vowels in its phoneme inventory, the importance of vowel and consonant distance will be different. Typically, the relationship between number and magnitude of deviations for the stored representation and intelligibility of a linguistic unit is non-linear. Identification of a sound or recognition of a word remains very good for small discrepancies from the norm, and then abruptly breaks down. Future work with different language varieties and more controlled representations of the various linguistic units can hopefully give more insight into the relative contribution of linguistic phenomena to intelligibility and show when the limits of intelligibility are reached.

APPENDIX A

Table A.1. Distances between standard Danish and 17 Scandinavian language varieties. The table shows lexical and phonetic distances, and (sublevel) consonant distances. Distances are expressed as percentages, see Sections 4.1 and 4.2. The range, mean and standard deviation are given in the last three rows.

Dialect	Lexical	Phonetic	Phon. Cons. Subst.	Phon. Cons. Ins.	Phon. Cons. Del.	Phon. Cons. Leng.	Phon. Cons. Short.
Høgsted	.00	25.07	9.98	5.97	1.46	2.56	.02	1.17
Lidköping	3.19	22.61	7.74	3.90	2.33	1.51	.72	.21
Oslo	1.03	21.58	6.81	4.41	1.39	1.01	1.65	.33
Torshavn	13.68	27.75	12.03	5.00	4.76	1.76	.32	.41
Fyresdal	6.00	24.84	9.05	4.14	2.83	2.07	1.28	.19
Tromsø	1.03	23.16	8.23	5.29	.83	2.01	1.19	.60
Oppdal	6.19	27.46	10.95	6.30	2.06	2.26	.79	.79
Gaular	3.09	23.15	9.27	4.99	2.31	1.80	1.12	.12
Stockholm	1.06	22.41	9.04	3.90	3.89	1.08	1.03	.13
Hjordkær	1.02	23.51	7.94	4.24	1.87	1.83	.11	.38
Gryttinge	9.28	23.41	8.54	3.82	2.46	1.75	.36	.07
Bjugn	2.06	25.88	10.00	7.13	1.74	.97	1.37	.76
Helsinki	2.08	22.56	8.21	3.91	2.71	1.60	.57	.20
Katrad	.00	23.42	9.21	4.57	2.29	2.18	.06	1.12
Rana	1.04	26.09	9.65	6.98	1.22	1.19	1.21	.85
Storliden	12.50	24.92	9.21	5.25	1.68	1.81	.29	.20
Trysil	3.96	23.99	9.83	5.81	2.46	1.30	1.04	.57
Range	13.68	6.17	5.22	3.31	3.93	1.59	1.63	1.10
Mean	3.95	24.22	9.16	5.04	2.25	1.69	.78	.48
Std. dev.	4.24	1.78	1.24	1.08	.96	.46	.51	.35

79

Charlotte Gooskens et al.

Table A.2. Distances between standard Danish and 17 Scandinavian language varieties. The table shows (sublevel) vowel distances, expressed as percentages (see Section 4.1) and intelligibility scores representing the percentage of correctly translated words (see Section 3). The range, mean and standard deviation are given in the last three rows.

Dialect	Phon. Vow.	Phon. Vow. Subst.	Phon. Vow. Ins.	Phon. Vow. Del.	Phon. Vow. Leng.	Phon. Vow. Short.	Schwa versus Sonor.	Intelligibility
Høgsted	12.86	10.51	.79	.96	1.10	.31	.21	33.68
Lidköping	11.66	10.21	1.30	.14	1.47	.36	.46	61.57
Oslo	11.01	9.21	.89	.84	1.28	.40	.18	60.85
Torshavn	13.54	9.05	4.16	.27	1.60	.35	.06	10.86
Fyresdal	12.05	9.51	2.11	.43	1.39	.36	.53	23.46
Tromsø	10.97	9.48	.70	.80	1.27	.65	.33	40.74
Oppdal	12.89	9.15	1.49	2.25	1.64	.62	.12	20.70
Gaular	11.59	9.36	1.52	.71	.71	.32	.17	54.24
Stockholm	10.16	8.42	1.21	.52	1.08	.32	.81	60.97
Hjordkær	14.09	11.46	1.37	1.00	.50	.47	.29	56.34
Gryttinge	13.96	10.57	1.85	.61	.82	.44	.66	42.30
Bjugn	11.47	8.86	1.07	1.54	1.59	.57	.28	26.68
Helsinki	11.96	10.24	1.57	.15	.64	.50	.48	42.54
Katrad	13.70	10.34	1.54	.68	.26	.31	.06	55.32
Rana	11.88	8.84	1.18	1.86	1.98	.57	.20	27.10
Storliden	14.34	11.59	1.20	1.48	.54	.71	.15	15.63
Trysil	10.46	8.30	.84	1.33	1.41	.56	.37	29.68
Range	4.18	3.29	3.46	2.10	1.72	.40	.75	50.71
Mean	12.27	9.71	1.46	.92	1.13	.46	.32	38.98
Std. dev.	1.31	.98	.79	.60	.48	.13	.21	16.99

REFERENCES

M. Ashby and J. Maidment (2005), *Introducing phonetic science* (Cambridge).
K. Beijering, C. Gooskens, and W. Heeringa (2008), 'Predicting intelligibility and perceived linguistic distance by means of the Levenshtein algorithm' in M. van Koppen and B. Botma, eds, *Linguistics in the Netherlands 2008* (Amsterdam), 13–24.
L. O. Delsing and K. Lundin Åkesson (2005), *Håller språket ihop Norden?: en forskningsrapport om ungdomars förståelse av danska, svenska og norska* (Copenhagen).
C. Gooskens (2007), 'The contribution of linguistic factors to the intelligibility of closely related languages', *Journal of Multilingual and multicultural development*, 28(6), 445–467.
C. Gooskens and W. Heeringa (2004), 'The position of Frisian in the Germanic language area'. In D. Gilberts, M. Schreuder, and N. Knevel, eds, *On the Boundaries of Phonology and Phonetics* (Groningen), 61–87.
C. Gooskens and W. Heeringa (2006), 'The relative contribution of pronunciation, lexical and prosodic differences to the perceived distances between Norwegian dialects', *Literary and Linguistic Computing, special issue on Progress in Dialectometry: Toward Explanation* 21 (4), 477–492.

N. Grønnum (2003), 'Why are the Danes so hard to understand?' In H. Galberg Jacobsen et al., eds, *Take Danish – for instance: linguistic studies in honour of Hans Basbøll presented on the occasion of his 60th birthday, 12 July 2003* (Odense), 119–130.

W. Heeringa (2004), 'Measuring dialect pronunciation differences using Levenshtein distance' (Ph.D. thesis, University of Groningen).

B. van Ooijen (1994), 'The processing of vowels and consonants' (Ph.D. thesis, University of Leiden).

J. Séguy (1973), 'La dialectométrie dans l'atlas linguistique de la Gascogne', *Revue de linguistique romane*, 37, 1–24.

P. J. Scharpff and V. J. van Heuven (1988), 'Effects of pause insertion on the intelligibility of low quality speech', in W. A. Ainsworth and J. N. Holmes, eds, *Proceedings of the 7th FASE/Speech-88 Symposium, The Institute of Acoustics* (Edinburgh), 261–268.

C. Tang and V. J. van Heuven (2007), 'Mutual intelligibility and similarity of Chinese dialects. Predicting judgments from objective measures' in B. Los and M. van Koppen, eds, *Linguistics in the Netherlands 2007* (Amsterdam), 223–234.

A. Torp (1998), *Nordiske språk i nordisk og germansk perspektiv* (Oslo).

END NOTES

[1] At first glance it may look strange to consider lengthenings and shortenings as separate classes rather than particular kinds of substitutions. In Section 4.1 we explain the way in which lengthenings and shortenings are treated and come back to this.

[2] *The North Wind and the Sun* is a well-known text in phonetic research. In *The principles of the International Phonetic Association* (1949) the text is transcribed in 51 different languages.

[3] The recordings were made by Jørn Almberg and Kristian Skarbø. They are available via http://www.ling.ntnu.no. We are grateful for their permission to use the material.

[4] In Norway there is no spoken standard language. The Oslo variety represented the standard variety in this investigation. This variety functions as a spoken standard to some extent, even though it does not have a very strong position compared with spoken standards in many other European countries.

[5] The phonetic transcriptions of the Norwegian varieties were made by Jørn Almberg. The rest of the transcriptions were made by Andreas Vikran and corrected by Jørn Almberg to ensure consistency.

[6] The listeners were asked if they were familiar with the fable. Listeners who reported that they knew the story were excluded from the investigation.

[7] It also makes the task easier, but still not so easy that a ceiling effect is reached as becomes clear from the results in Section 5.1.

[8] Alternatively, we could have adopted the stem morpheme as scoring unit, so that getting the compound right would have counted as two units (cf. Scharpff & Van Heuven 1988).

[9] [ʔ] is the symbol used for the Danish phoneme called *stød* in Danish.

[10] Lengthenings and shortenings are excluded since they do not affect the structure of words, but in future work we want to include them as well.

[11] Significance of correlations and significance of differences between correlations are calculated with the Mantel test.

LINGUISTIC DETERMINANTS OF THE INTELLIGIBILITY
OF SWEDISH WORDS AMONG DANES

SEBASTIAN KÜRSCHNER, CHARLOTTE GOOSKENS
AND RENÉE VAN BEZOOIJEN

Abstract   In the present investigation we aim to determine to which degree various linguistic factors contribute to the intelligibility of Swedish words among Danes. We correlated the results of an experiment on word intelligibility with eleven linguistic factors and carried out logistic regression analyses. In the experiment, the intelligibility of 384 frequent Swedish words was tested among Danish listeners via the Internet. The choice of eleven linguistic factors was motivated by their contribution to intelligibility in earlier studies. The highest correlation was found in the negative correlation between word intelligibility and phonetic distances. Also word length, different syllable numbers, foreign sounds, neighbourhood density, word frequency, orthography, and the absence of the prosodic phenomenon of 'stød' in Swedish contribute significantly to intelligibility. Although the results thus show that linguistic factors contribute to the intelligibility of single words, the amount of explained variance was not very large (R^2 (Cox and Snell) = .16, R^2 (Nagelkerke) = .21) when compared with earlier studies which were based on aggregate intelligibility. Partly, the lower scores result from the logistic regression model used. It was necessary to use logistic regression in our study because the intelligibility scores were coded in a binary variable. Additionally, we attribute the lower correlation to the higher number of idiosyncrasies of single words compared with the aggregate intelligibility and linguistic distance used in earlier studies. Based on observations in the actual data from the intelligibility experiment, we suggest further steps to be taken to improve the predictability of word intelligibility.

International Journal of Humanities and Arts Computing 2 (1–2) 2008, 83–100
DOI: 10.3366/E1753854809000329
© Edinburgh University Press and the Association for History and Computing 2009

I. INTRODUCTION

Danish and Swedish are closely related languages within the North Germanic language branch. The two languages are mutually intelligible to such a high degree that in Danish-Swedish communication speakers mostly use their own mother tongues, a mode of communication termed semi-communication by Haugen (1966). In previous research it was shown that intelligibility scores correlate highly with global phonetic distances between the languages involved (cf. e.g. Beijering, Gooskens and Heeringa, 2008; Gooskens, 2007). Hence, linguistic factors play a major role in determining mutual intelligibility. Additionally, it is often assumed that attitudes and prior exposure to the variety in question are important factors (e.g. Delsing and Lundin Åkesson, 2005). However, correlations between intelligibility scores and the latter two factors are low, and the direct relationship is difficult to prove (Van Bezooijen and Gooskens, 2007).

Earlier research has mostly involved testing text understanding. Intelligibility scores were based on the text as a whole. This means that the influence of different linguistic dimensions such as textual and sentence context, morphology, and phonology could not be distinguished. In our study, we wanted to determine the role of linguistic factors in more detail. Therefore, we chose to focus on single words instead of sentences or texts. We conducted an Internet experiment assessing the intelligibility of isolated Swedish words among Danish subjects, excluding the influence of sentence and textual context.[1] The underlying assumption here is that word recognition is the key to speech understanding. If the listener correctly recognizes a minimal proportion of words, he or she will be able to piece the speaker's message together. In particular, we tested the impact of linguistic factors such as segmental and prosodic phonetic distance, Swedish sounds lacking in the Danish sound system, word frequency, and orthography on word intelligibility. In this way we hoped to obtain more detailed information on the precise role of various linguistic factors in the intelligibility of Swedish words among Danes.

The way in which we tested intelligibility on the Internet may be relevant for research in other experimental disciplines within the humanities such as psycholinguistics, neurolinguistics, and psychology. Furthermore, the algorithms we used to measure linguistic distances might be of interest to any discipline in need of tools for automatic comparison of numbers or strings, for example in history and literary studies. The computationally based methods for intelligibility and distance measurement are also highly relevant for inter-disciplinary studies combining political and linguistic sciences concerned with the multilingual Europe.

2. EXPERIMENT

To test word intelligibility, an Internet-based experiment was conducted.[2] In this experiment, Danish subjects were confronted with 384 isolated Swedish nouns. These nouns were randomly selected from a list of 2575 highly frequent words.[3] In a pre-test, we assured that all these nouns were known to subjects from the test group, i.e. pupils aged 16–19.

The 384 words were read aloud by a male Swedish native speaker from the city of Uppsala and recorded in a professional sound studio. Each subject heard one quarter, i.e. 96 of the 384 Swedish words and was requested to write the Danish translation into a text field within ten seconds. Prizes were promised to the participants, and especially to the best-scoring participants, to stimulate the subjects to make an effort to do well. The choice of the words and the order of presentation were randomized in order to reduce tiredness effects. Since the word blocks were automatically assigned to the subjects in random order, some word blocks were presented to more subjects than others. The lowest number of subjects who heard a word block was seven, the highest number 19, with an average of 10.5 subjects per word block.

52 secondary school pupils, all mother tongue speakers of Danish aged 16–19 who grew up with no additional mother tongue, participated in the experiment. Since we are interested in intelligibility at a first confrontation, we needed subjects who had had little contact with the test language. We therefore excluded 10 subjects living in regions close to the Swedish border. As an extra precaution, we also had the subjects translate a number of Swedish non-cognates. Such words should be unintelligible to subjects with no prior experience with the language. Indeed, hardly any of the non-cognates were translated correctly. An exception is formed by the word *flicka* 'girl' (Danish *pige*), which was translated correctly by 68 per cent of the subjects. This word is probably known to most Danes as a stereotypical Swedish word. For example, it was used in the popular Danish pop song *sköna flicka* ('beautiful girl') by Kim Larsen. On the basis of these results we decided not to exclude any of the 42 remaining subjects.

The results were automatically categorized as right or wrong through a pattern match with expected answers. Those answers which were categorized as wrong were subsequently checked manually by a Danish mother tongue speaker. Responses which deviated from the expected responses due to a mere spelling error were counted as correct identifications. Spelling errors were objectively defined as instances where only one letter had been spelt wrongly without resulting in another existing word. So, for example the mistake in *ærende* (correct *ærinde*) 'errand' is considered a spelling mistake and therefore counted as correct (only one wrong letter without resulting in another existing word), while *aske* (correct *æske* 'box') was not counted as correct because the mistake results in an existing word meaning 'ash'. Some Swedish words have more than one possible translation. For example the Swedish word *brist* 'lack' can be translated into Danish *brist* or *mangel*, both meaning 'lack'. Both translations were counted as correct. In the case of homonyms, both possible translations were accepted as correct. For example, Swedish *här* can be translated correctly into Danish *hær* 'army' or *her* 'here'.

After this procedure, we had obtained a score of zero (word not identified) or one (word identified) per word for each subject. The obtained scores were subsequently used as the dependent variable in a regression model with several linguistic factors as covariates (see Section 3) to identify the degree to which these determine intelligibility.

We only investigated the intelligibility of cognates since non-cognate forms should, almost by definition, be unrecognizable. Cognates are historically related word pairs that still bear the same meaning in both languages. We use a broad definition of cognates, including not only shared inherited words from Proto-Nordic, but also shared loans such as Swedish/Danish *perspektiv* 'perspective', which is borrowed from the same Latin source in both languages. We also excluded words that have a cognate root but a derivational morpheme that is different between the corresponding cognates in Swedish and Danish. So, for example, the word pair Swedish *undersökning* – Danish *undersøgelse* 'examination' was excluded from the analyses. Of the 384 Swedish nouns, 347 proved to be cognate with Danish nouns.

3. FACTORS CONSIDERED FOR EXPLANATION

In this section we will explain eleven factors that we considered to be possible determinants of the variance in the intelligibility scores. Most of the factors are known to play a role in word intelligibility from psycho-phonetic literature (cf., e.g., Van Heuven, this volume). Other factors are assumed to play a role in the special case of Swedish-Danish communication by Scandinavian scholars. We aimed to include as many factors as possible. However, we were limited by the fact that they had to be quantifiable, since we wanted to test their contribution to intelligibility statistically.

3.1 Levenshtein distance

As mentioned in the introduction, aggregate phonetic distances between languages are good predictors of intelligibility of whole texts (cf. e.g. Beijering et al., 2008, Gooskens, 2007). Also at the word level small phonetic distances can be assumed to correlate with high intelligibility scores, while large distances can be expected to correlate with low intelligibility scores. We measured the phonetic distances by means of the Levenshtein algorithm.

Alignment	1	2	3	4
Swedish	g	ɵ	l	d
Danish	g	u	l	

	subst.		insert.		
0	1	0	1	=	2

Figure 1. Calculation of Levenshtein distance.

Levenshtein distance is a measure of string edit distance based on the smallest number of operations necessary to map a given string on another string. Applied in linguistics, a string of sounds from one variety can thus be mapped on the corresponding string in another variety (cf. Heeringa, 2004). Insertions, deletions, and substitutions are possible operations. The example in Figure 1 shows the calculation of string edit distance between Danish and Swedish *guld* 'gold', pronounced as [gul] in Danish and as [gɵld] in Swedish.

First, the two strings are aligned, with identical sounds being matched with each other (cf. [g] and [l]). Subsequently, the number of operations necessary to transform one string into another is calculated. In our example two sounds are identical and therefore they do not add any costs. In contrast, operations are necessary for the vowel which has to be substituted, and for the final sound which has to be inserted in order to change the Swedish pronunciation into the Danish. Since operations have to be conducted at two slots, the Levenshtein distance is 2. To relate the distance to word length, we divide by the number of alignments, i.e. 4 in the example. The normalised distance is $2/4 = 0.5$, i.e. 50 per cent for our example.

In order to obtain distances which are based on linguistically motivated alignments that respect the syllable structure of a word or the structure within a syllable, the algorithm was adapted so that in the alignment a vowel may only correspond to a vowel and a consonant to a consonant. The semi-vowels [j] and [w] may also correspond to a vowel or the other way around. The central vowel schwa [ə] may correspond to any sonorant. In this way, unlikely matches – like [o] and [t] or [s] and [e] – are prevented.

The Swedish test words were transcribed by a phonetician who is a mother tongue speaker of Swedish, and the corresponding Danish words were represented by their pronunciation in Standard Danish. Levenshtein distance was calculated automatically for all 347 pairs of cognates. The distance was only calculated for segments, i.e. we did not include any prosodic features other than segment length in our calculations. Instead, prosodic features are integrated in Sections 3.4, 3.6, and 3.7. The mean segmental distance across all words was 52.1 per cent. Eight word pairs had a distance of zero, for example Swedish *team* – Danish *team* 'team' that are both pronounced as [tiːm]. Six word pairs had the maximum distance of 100 per cent, for example Swedish *ljud* [jʉːd] Danish *lyd* [lyːˀð̞] 'sound'. For each word, Levenshtein distance was coded as a fraction representing a percentage. The distribution of the distances across the data proved to be normal.

3.2 Foreign sounds

When a listener being confronted with a language (variety) for the first time hears unusual or unknown sounds, he may be distracted and this may influence intelligibility negatively (cf. Van Heuven, this volume). To explore the effect of this factor we listed for each Swedish word the number of sounds which do not exist in the Danish sound system. The following sounds are described as foreign in the literature (from Karker, 1997; Nordentoft, 1981):

- Retroflex consonants produced according to the phonological rule that [r] and a following alveolar consonant merge, cf. Swedish, *art* [ɑːʈ] 'sort', *bord* [buːɖ] 'table', *alternativ* [altəɳatiːv] 'alternative', *orsak* [uːʂɑːk] 'cause', *parlament* [paɭamɛnt]
- The postalveolar-velar fricative [ɧ], cf. Swedish *aktion* [akɧuːn].

We only considered single sounds, i.e. in our list of foreign sounds we did not include any combinations of sounds which exist in Danish but are phonotactically uncommon, cf. [lj] or [ŋn]. Neither did we include sounds which are possible in the Danish system, but in contrast to Swedish do not establish a phonemic opposition, such as long plosives, some voiced consonants, and the vowels [ʉ] and [ɵ].

For each word, the number of foreign sounds was coded. 46 of the words contained a retroflex consonant or a postalveolar-velar fricative. Three words contained two foreign sounds: *koordination* [kuɔɖɪnaɧuːn] 'coordination', *ordning* [oːɖɳɪŋ] 'order', and *stjärna* [ɧæːɳa] 'star'.

3.3 Word length

Previous research has shown that word length plays a role in word recognition (Wiener and Miller, 1946, Scharpff and Van Heuven, 1988). According to these studies longer words are better recognized than shorter words. This, in turn, is explained in terms of the relationship between word length and the number of 'neighbours', i.e. competing word forms that are very similar to the stimulus word (see Section 3.7). Longer words have fewer neighbours than shorter words

(Vitevitch and Rodriguez, 2005). Furthermore, redundancy increases with word length, which is assumed to enhance intelligibility as well (see Section 3.7). Swedish words were annotated for word length in terms of the number of phonetic segments. The mean word length across all words was 5.57 segments. The four longest words consisted of 12 segments, for example *uppmärksamhet* [ɐp:mærksamhe:t] 'attention', while the shortest word had only one segment, *ö* [øː] 'island'.

3.4 Word stress differences

Van Heuven (this volume) found that correct recognition of words was severely reduced and delayed if stress was shifted to the initial syllable in Dutch words with medial or final stress. Extrapolating this result he hypothesized that unexpected stress positions play a (negative) role not only in understanding the mother tongue but also a closely related variety (Van Heuven, this volume). For each Swedish word, we annotated whether the place of the word stress was different from that in the corresponding Danish cognate, assuming that such a difference makes the word more difficult to identify. The coding was categorical, either 1 when word stress was different, or 0 when this was not the case. Danish *kontekst* ['kɔntᵉgsd] vs. Swedish *kontext* [kɔn'tɛkst] 'context' may serve as an example of word stress differences, which were found in ten of the word pairs.

3.5 Differences in number of syllables

Cognates between Danish and Swedish can differ in the number of syllables, cf. Danish *mængde* [mɛŋ'də] vs. Swedish *mängd* [mɛŋd] 'quantity'. Since a missing or extra syllable could cause confusion in word identification, we annotated instances with different syllable numbers by coding the number of additional or lacking syllables. Ten of the Swedish words contained one syllable extra compared to the corresponding Danish word, while 22 words had one syllable less. Two Swedish words were even two syllables shorter than the Danish cognate, namely *choklad* [ɸjɔklɑːd] (Danish *chokolade* [ɕogolæːðə]) 'chocolate' and *tjänst* [ɕɛnst] (Danish *tjeneste* [tjeˌneˑsdə]) 'service'.

3.6 Lexical tones

According to Van Heuven (this volume), in ideal circumstances the contribution of word prosody to the process of word recognition is a modest one. Because word prosody is a slowly varying property of the speech code, it will normally not be needed in the recognition of words. However, when communication suffers from noise, prosody fulfils the role of a safety catch. Listening to speech in a closely related language bears similarities to listening to speech in noise (cf. Van Heuven, this volume). Therefore differences in presence and realization of lexical tones are predicted to be detrimental to word recognition.

In Danish, no lexical tones are used, while Swedish has two word tones, an acute accent (or accent I) and a grave accent (accent II). Minimal pairs occur, e.g. *ánden* (acc. I), definite singular form of *and* 'duck' vs. *ànden* (acc. II), definite singular form of *ande* 'spirit'. Accent I is most similar to the Danish stress accent, while there is no 'musical accent' comparable to the Swedish accent II in Danish. We therefore hypothesize that words with accent II may distract the Danish subjects when hearing such Swedish words. We coded the word accent for each test word, using a binary categorical variable. 253 words had accent I and 94 had accent II.

3.7 Stød

Danish has a special prosodic feature at the word level which does not occur in Swedish. The so-called 'stød' is a kind of creaky voice. It occurs in long vowels and in voiced (sonorant) consonants. Presence versus absence of 'stød' creates an abundance of minimal contrasts, for example [hɛnˀɐ] 'hands' versus [hɛnɐ] 'happen'. We assumed that the absence of this phenomenon in corresponding Swedish words may cause confusion on the part of the Danish listeners. However, since 'stød' is also missing in several Danish dialects to the south of the 'stød isogloss' without any reported influence on intelligibility, the influence on intelligibility may be limited. We used a binary categorical variable to code for each word if it included a 'stød' or not. 164 words had a 'stød', and 161 words had no 'stød'.

3.8 Neighbourhood density

Neighbours are linguistically defined as word forms that are very similar to the stimulus word and may therefore serve as competing responses. For an extensive description of the neighbourhood activation model, see Luce and Pisoni (1998). Since a high neighbourhood density enlarges the number of possible candidates for translation, we assume that the higher the density is, the lower the number of correct identifications will be. Short words in general have a denser neighbourhood. From this we would predict that the possible advantage of short words being more frequent than long words (see Section 3.11) is neutralised by the neighbourhood density problem.

Here we define neighbourhood density as the number of Danish words which deviate from the Swedish stimulus in only one sound, disregarding the correct counterpart. For example, the Swedish word *säng* 'bed' with the correct Danish translation *seng* has four Danish neighbours: *syng* 'sing', *senge* 'beds', *hæng* 'hang', and *stæng* 'close', while the Swedish word *adress* 'address' has no neighbours. For each Swedish word we counted the number of neighbours in Danish and coded it into the database. The mean number of neighbours was 0.93, which means that on average each correct answer has one competing incorrect answer. 244 words had no neighbours and the largest number of neighbours was 16 for the Swedish word *ö* 'island'.

3.9 Etymology

Work in progress by Gooskens, van Bezooijen and Kürschner showed that loan words that have been introduced into both Swedish and Danish are easier to understand by Danish subjects listening to Swedish than native cognate words. Presumably this is due to the fact that the loan words were affected by fewer sound changes differentiating Swedish from the other Nordic languages than native words. Additionally, on average loan words are longer than native words.[4]

The Swedish words in our database were categorized according to their etymology. We distinguished between native words and loan words. All words originating in Proto-Germanic which, as far as we could tell from etymological dictionaries such as Hellquist (1980) and Wessén (1960), have been present in Swedish at all times are defined as native words. There were 196 native words. All words which were newly introduced as loans from other languages are defined as loan words, i.e. even words of Proto-Germanic origin which have been lost in Swedish and were re-introduced through language contact. For this reason, also the quite high number of Low-German words, which have been introduced due to the strong language contact with the Hanseatic league in the Middle Ages, is part of the loan word group. 151 of the words were loan words. We used a binary categorical variable to code the etymology for each word.

3.10 Orthography

There is evidence that knowledge of orthography influences spoken word recognition (e.g. Ziegler and Ferrand, 1998; Chéreau, Gaskell and Dumay, 2007). The evidence comes from experiments with words that differ in degree of sound-to-spelling consistency and from recent neuroimaging research (Blau et al., 2008). Doetjes and Gooskens (accepted) correlated the percentages of correct translations of 96 words with simple Levenshtein distances between the Swedish and Danish pronunciations and got a correlation of $r = .54$. Next, they measured the Levenshtein distances again but this time corrected the distances in such a way that they took into account that Danes may be able to use the Danish orthography when decoding certain Swedish spoken words. The corrected distances showed a higher correlation with the intelligibility scores ($r = .63$), which provides evidence that Danes have support from their own orthography when hearing Swedish words.

Danish is generally described as the Scandinavian language which has gone through the most drastic sound changes (Brink and Lund, 1975; Grønnum, 1998). As the spelling remained conservative, the number of sound-to-letter correspondences has therefore decreased heavily. In contrast, the sound changes in Swedish have not differentiated spoken and written language to such a high extent. In some cases, spoken and written language has even converged because people tend to pronounce the words as they are spelt (Wessén, 1965: 152; Birch-Jensen, 2007). Because of the Danish conservative orthography, it is plausible that Danes may use their orthographical knowledge in the identification of Swedish words. To measure the help Danes might get through their orthography, for each word we counted the number of Swedish sounds which (1) did not match with a corresponding sound in Danish, but (2) were equivalent with the corresponding letter in Danish. For example, consider the different pronunciations of the words for 'hand': Danish *hånd* [hɔnˀ] vs. Swedish *hand* [hand]. The final consonant is not pronounced in Danish but it can be assumed that Danish subjects identifying the Swedish word make use of their knowledge of Danish orthography, which includes the consonant. For this reason the insertion of the *d* was given one point in this example. The number of such helpful letters was coded into the database for each word. The mean number of sounds per word that could be identified by means of the Danish orthography was 1.27, with a minimum of 0 (118 of the words) and a maximum of 6 in one case.

3.11 Danish word frequency

We assume that the token frequency of words may influence correct identification, since frequent words are more likely to come to the subjects' minds immediately than infrequent words. The activation of a word that was recognized before remains high for a long time, and never fully returns to its previous resting level. Highly frequent words therefore have a permanent advantage in the recognition process (Luce and Pisoni 1998).

Since we make assumptions about the performance of the Danish subjects, the frequency in their mother tongue must be decisive. We therefore annotated all words for token frequency in Danish. The numbers were based on the frequency list of a large written language corpus, the Korpus 90.[5] The most frequent word was *dag* 'day', which occurred 222,159 times in the corpus. There were seven stimulus words which did not occur in the corpus and thus had a frequency of 0. The smallest positive frequency was found for *overføring* 'transmission', which occurred 11 times. Since the raw frequency data was heavily positively skewed, we changed the coding of this variable by recalculating it as log frequency. Based on log frequency, the data was normally distributed.

Table 1. Point-biserial correlation of the intelligibility scores with continuous linguistic factors.

Factor	Correlation (r)	Significance (p)
Levenshtein distance	$-.27$	$< .001$
Foreign sounds	$-.11$	$< .001$
Word length of Swedish words	$.21$	$< .001$
Difference in syllable number	$-.17$	$< .001$
Neighbourhood density	$-.13$	$< .001$
Orthography	$.13$	$< .001$
Log frequency	$.01$	not sign.

4. RESULTS

The intelligibility test resulted in an overall percentage of 61 per cent correct identifications of the Swedish cognates among the Danish subjects. To identify the independent contribution of each of the linguistic factors, we correlated the intelligibility scores with each factor separately. Since the intelligibility scores were coded in a binary variable, we had to calculate correlation coefficients considering this coding scheme. To correlate binary variables with continuous variables, point-biserial correlation coefficients using Pearson correlations are commonly used. We used this calculation for correlating the intelligibility scores with the continuous variables coding linguistic factors. The results are listed in Table 1.

The results show that apart from log frequency, all linguistic factors coded in continuous variables correlate significantly with the intelligibility scores. Table 1 reveals the highest correlation between the intelligibility scores and Levenshtein distance, which confirms results from previous research that phonetic distance is an important predictor of intelligibility (see Section 1). Nevertheless, the correlation is much lower than in previous research which dealt with aggregate distance and intelligibility scores ($r = -.27$ compared to, e.g., $r = .86$ in Beijering, Gooskens and Heeringa, 2008). The correlations with word length ($r = .21$) and difference in syllable numbers ($r = -.17$) are comparatively high as well. Additionally, neighbourhood density ($r = -.13$), orthography ($r = .13$), and foreign sounds ($r = .11$) correlate significantly with the intelligibility scores.

In order to identify the independent contribution of the variables which were coded categorically, we conducted logistic regression analyses with only one covariate each. The results of these analyses are found in Table 2.

Table 2 shows that lexical tones and 'stød' do not explain the variance to a significant extent. By contrast, word stress difference and etymology are found to explain parts of the variance. Nevertheless, the amount of explained variance is low for both factors.

93

Table 2. Results from logistic regression analyses in enter method with the intelligibility scores as dependent variable and a single categorical linguistic factor as covariate.

	Step	Model χ^2	Significance	-2LL	Cox and Snell R^2	Nagelkerke R^2
	0			4921.00		
Word stress difference	1	6.432	$p < .05$	4914.57	.00	.00
Lexical tones	1	3.442	not sign.	4917.56	.00	.00
Stød	1	1.806	not sign.	4919.19	.00	.00
Etymology	1	23.787	$p < .001$	4897.21	.01	.01

We were not only interested in the contribution of each single factor, but we also wanted to find out which combination of factors served best to explain intelligibility. To identify which factor combination reveals the best prediction for the intelligibility scores, we conducted regression analyses with multiple factors. The intelligibility scores were defined as the dependent variable, and the eleven linguistic factors were chosen as covariates. Since the dependent variable was binary and thus did not meet the requirements of linear regression models, we used a generalized linear model in binary logistic regression. Table 3 summarizes the results of the regression analyses, conducted first with the enter method to identify the effect of all factors in combination and then with the forward method to identify the best stepwise combination of factors.

Table 3 summarizes the results of two linear regression analyses. The improvement of the model for each step and the significance of the improvement are calculated based on the χ^2 score. The -2 Log likelihood (-2LL) indicates how poorly the model fits the data: The more the value of -2LL is reduced in comparison to the beginning state or the previous step, the better the model fits, i.e. the higher is the contribution of the added factor. We report two 'pseudo' R^2 scores (Cox and Snell as well as Nagelkerke R-square) which – comparable with linear regression – serve to indicate the model's effect size. These R^2 scores are calculated cautiously and therefore seem rather low in comparison with R^2 scores from linear regression models. The analyses show that the linguistic factors can explain the variance partly, but not to a very high extent. Including all factors, we arrive at a χ^2 of 624.99 with R^2 (Cox and Snell) = .16, and R^2 (Nagelkerke) = .22.

The stepwise analysis, done in the forward method, reveals eight models. Levenshtein distance is revealed as the most important factor ($\chi^2 = 286.14$, R^2 (Cox and Snell) = .08, R^2 (Nagelkerke) = .10). The second model explains the variance to a higher extent by including word length ($\chi^2 = 461.05$, R^2 (Cox and Snell) = .12, R^2 (Nagelkerke) = .16). Steps 3 to 7 include different syllable number, foreign sounds, neighbourhood density, log frequency, and orthography.

Table 3. Results of binary logistic regression analyses with the intelligibility scores as dependent variable and all linguistic factors as independent variables.

Method	Model	Model χ^2	Significance	-2LL	Cox and Snell R^2	Nagel-kerke R^2
Enter						
Step 0				4810.03		
Step 1	all linguistic factors	624.99	$p < .001$	4185.04	.16	.22
Forward						
Step 0				4810.03		
1st step	Levenshtein distance	286.14	$p < .001$	4523.89	.08	.10
2nd step	previous factor +word length	461.05	$p < .001$	4348.98	.12	.16
3rd step	previous factors +different syllable no.	508.73	$p < .001$	4301.30	.13	.18
4th step	previous factors +foreign sounds	544.35	$p < .001$	4265.67	.14	.19
5th step	previous factors +neighbourhood density	567.85	$p < .001$	4242.18	.15	.20
6th step	previous factors +log frequency	593.03	$p < .001$	4217.00	.15	.21
7th step	previous factors +orthography	610.45	$p < .001$	4199.58	.16	.21
8th step	previous factors +'stød'	618.31	$p < .001$	4191.72	.16	.21

Finally, in step 8 'stød' is added, resulting in $\chi^2 = 618.31$, R^2 (Cox and Snell) = .16, and R^2 (Nagelkerke) = .21. Although log frequency as a separate variable has a low correlation with the intelligibility results, it is nonetheless identified as a relevant factor in the prediction of word intelligibility in a combined model. The same goes for 'stød', which did not explain the variance to a significant extent when used as the only covariate in a logistic regression model. The remaining factors (word stress difference, lexical tones, etymology) do not add significantly to the model, although both word stress difference and etymology were identified to explain parts of the variance significantly when used as the only covariate in logistic regression. Presumably, this might partly be attributed to the binary categorical coding scheme of both lexical tones and etymology.

Section 3 showed that the variables were not totally independent from each other but interact in certain dimensions. For example, word length presumably correlates negatively with frequency and the number of neighbours. This interaction might weaken the regression models. We therefore conducted a multicollinearity analysis. We calculated the variance inflation factors (VIF) of each of the predicting variables to see if the variables had a strong linear relationship with any of the other predictors. Since the mean VIF of 1.43 is higher than 1, we need to assume that our regression model is slightly biased by multicollinearity. The highest VIF is 2.46 (for word length). Since none of the variables thus reveals a VIF higher than 10, collinearity is not a serious problem for the model.

Collinearity diagnostics reveal that the strongest collinearity exists between word length, Levenshtein distance, and lexical tones. The reason for the collinearity between word length and Levenshtein distance is probably that Levenshtein distance increases with longer words. We tried to reduce this effect by normalizing by the length of the alignment, but the results of the diagnostics reveal that collinearity remains. Word length and lexical tones interact because accent II is impossible in monosyllabic words and thus only found in long words.

The existence of collinearity means that we cannot always precisely decide which of the interdependent factors makes the main contribution to explain the variance. A possible solution to this problem would be to reduce the number of factors, integrating covarying variables into one and the same variable. For example, lexical tones could be somehow integrated into the calculation of Levenshtein distance. Nevertheless, such a solution would cause new problems: When combining segmental and suprasegmental differences into a single measure, how would we know how to weigh the contribution of segmental and prosodic differences, respectively? Since we were mostly interested in tracing the contribution of each of the single linguistic factors and their combination in explaining the intelligibility of isolated words, and since the multicollinearity analysis showed that collinearity does not cause serious problems in our models, we conclude that the current analyses are thus well-suited to reveal models to answer our research questions.[6]

5. DISCUSSION

Compared to earlier studies on linguistic predictors of intelligibility, the degree to which the intelligibility covaries with phonetic distances is low. Earlier studies showed high correlations between intelligibility scores and Levenshtein distance. Gooskens (2007), e.g., obtained a correlation of $r = -.80$, $r^2 = .64$ ($p < .001$) for intelligibility scores with Levenshtein distance between varieties of the Scandinavian languages Danish, Norwegian, and Swedish. Beijering, Gooskens and Heeringa (2008) even found an overall correlation of $r = -.86$,

$r^2 = .74$ ($p < .01$) between intelligibility scores and Levenshtein distances of Copenhagen Danish and a range of other Scandinavian varieties. In our study, the correlation with Levenshtein distance reveals lower scores, namely $r = -.27$, $r^2 = .07$ in point biserial correlations, and R^2 (Cox and Snell) $= .08$, R^2 (Nagelkerke) $= .10$ in logistic regression models. The eight factors combined in model 8 are revealed as most important for the intelligibility of Swedish words by Danes. In comparison with earlier studies, this model also reveals a rather low score of R^2 (Cox and Snell) $= .16$, R^2 (Nagelkerke) $= .21$. It remains to be discussed why the factors considered cannot explain more of the variance and which other factors are likely to play an additional role in intelligibility. In what follows, we will consider some possible explanations.

Partly, the low scores must be ascribed to the rather cautious calculation of R^2 scores in logistic regression modelling. In addition, the reason for the low correlation in the current study is probably that we focus on the intelligibility of single words rather than aggregate intelligibility. Aggregating is a mode of calculation which is known to inflate correlation coefficients because it reduces noise. Whereas the aggregate intelligibility score – which is obtained as the mean of all single word scores in a whole corpus – may be consistent, the intelligibility of single words may be influenced by rather unpredictable factors such as prosodic differences (cf. voice quality, speech rate, etc.) and idiosyncratic characteristics of the single words.

In order to get an impression of such idiosyncratic characteristics we had a closer look at the mistakes that the listeners made. A number of different categories of mistakes can be distinguished. First, we found that many subjects confused the stimulus with (or searched for help in) another foreign language they had learned. Swedish *art* 'sort', e.g. was often translated into Danish *kunst* 'art', presumably through confusion with English. Checking the corpus for words which are potentially confusable with English and German words could reveal an additional factor for intelligibility. Nevertheless, finding potential candidates for this kind of confusion is a hard task since the confusability is not always obvious.

Second, the mistakes give reason to believe that the way in which we operationalised the neighbourhood factor may not be optimal. It looks as if the number of neighbours is not as decisive as the proximity of the neighbours to the test words. For example, the Swedish word *fel* [feːl] 'mistake' was translated with Danish *fæl* [fæ'l] 'foul' by a majority of the listeners, probably due to the fact that *fæl* is phonetically closer to *fel* than the correct *fejl* [faj'l]. Examples like this suggest that qualitative characteristics of neighbours are more decisive in word identification than the total number of neighbours. Nevertheless, it is challenging to operationalise such a qualitative neighbourhood model, because the question of how to measure similarity between sounds is difficult, particularly when addressed in two specific languages (cf. the following point).

Third, a number of sounds cause problems for the listeners because they are confused with non-corresponding phonemes in Danish. For example, Swedish /ɑ/ mostly corresponds with [ɛ] in Danish. Only in combination with /r/, it is pronounced as /ɑ/ in Danish, too. Therefore Swedish *stat* [stɑːt] 'state' is translated as Danish *start* [sdɑːˀd] 'start' instead of *stat* [sdɛːˀd] by many listeners. Swedish /ø/ is often confused with /ø/ or with /y/ which results in the translation of Swedish *luft* 'air' with Danish *løft* 'lift' instead of the correct *luft*, cf. also Swedish *frukt* 'fruit' translated as Danish *frygt* 'fear' instead of the correct *frugt*. On the other hand, Doetjes and Gooskens (accepted) showed that Danes in general have no problems in understanding words with an /u/ that is pronounced as [u] in Swedish and as [o] in Danish (cf., e.g., Swedish *fot* [fuːt] – Danish *fod* [foð]). This can probably be explained by the fact that the two sounds are so similar that the Danes think they hear an /o/, when a Swede pronounces an /u/. Disner (1983: 59) showed that there is large phonetic overlap between Danish /o/ and Swedish /u/.

Also some consonants are confused. Danish, e.g., has no voicing distinction but an aspiration-based distinction in plosives. Therefore, the Swedish difference between voiced and voiceless plosives corresponds to a difference between aspirated and unaspirated sounds at word onset in Danish. This is probably the reason why Swedish *klass* 'class' is translated as *glas* 'glass' instead of the correct *klasse* by the Danish listeners. These examples all suggest that the effect of rather fine phonetic differences on the intelligibility is significant and probably language dependent. In order to model intelligibility more successfully, communicatively relevant sound distances therefore need to be incorporated into the Levenshtein algorithm.

The three kinds of mistakes discussed here give some indications of how we may proceed to improve the predictability of word intelligibility. However, it may turn out that there is a limit to the extent to which the model can be improved. Clearly some factors pertain to only a limited number of words and also the combination of factors plays a role. The listener may use different strategies for each word to match it with a word in his own language. Furthermore, such a model may have to be language dependent since each language combination provides different challenges to the listener.

REFERENCES

K. Beijering, C. Gooskens and W. Heeringa (2008), 'Modeling intelligibility and perceived linguistic distances by means of the Levenshtein algorithm', in M. Koppen and B. Botma, eds, *Linguistics in the Netherlands* (Amsterdam), 13–24.

R. van Bezooijen and C. Gooskens (2007), 'Interlingual text comprehension: linguistic and extralinguistic determinants', in J. D. ten Thije and L. Zeevaert, eds, *Receptive Multilingualism* and intercultural communication: Linguistic analyses, language policies and didactic concepts (Amsterdam) 249–264.

J. Birch-Jensen (2007), *Från rista till chatta. Svenska språkets historia* (Gothenburg).

V. Blau, N. van Atteveldt, E. Formisano, R. Goebel, and L. Blomert (2008), 'Task-irrelevant visual letters interact with the processing of speech sounds in heteromodal and unimodal cortex', *European Journal of Neuroscience*, 28 (3): 500–509.

L. Brink and J. Lund (1975), *Dansk rigsmål: lydudviklingen siden 1840 med særligt henblik på sociolekterne i København* (Copenhagen).

C. Chéreau, M. G. Gaskell and N. Dumay (2007), 'Reading spoken words: Orthographic effects in auditory priming', *Cognition*, 102, 341–360.

L.-O. Delsing and K. Lundin Åkesson (2005), *Håller språket ihop Norden? En forskningsrapport om ungdomars förståelse av danska, svenska och norska* (Copenhagen).

S. F. Disner (1983), *Vowel quality: The relation between Universal and language specific factors* (Los Angeles).

G. Doetjes and C. Gooskens (accepted), 'Skriftsprogets rolle i den dansk-svenske talesprogsforståelse', *Språk och Stil*.

C. Gooskens (2007), 'The contribution of linguistic factors to the intelligibility of closely related languages', *Journal of Multilingual and multicultural development*, 28 (6), 445–467.

N. Grønnum (1998), *Fonetik og fonologi. Almen og dansk* (Copenhagen).

E. Haugen (1966), 'Semicommunication: The language gap in Scandinavia', *Sociological inquiry*, 36, 2, 280–297.

W. Heeringa (2004), *Measuring dialect pronunciation differences using Levenshtein distances* (Groningen).

E. Hellquist (1980 [1922]), *Svensk etymologisk ordbok*. Tredje upplagan. (Malmö). Also available at: http://runeberg.org/svetym/.

V. J. van Heuven (1985), 'Perception of stress pattern and word recognition: recognition of Dutch words with incorrect stress position', *Journal of the Acoustical Society of America*, 78, S21.

V. J. van Heuven (this volume), 'Making sense of strange sounds: (mutual) intelligibility of related language varieties. A review', *International journal of humanities and arts computing*.

A. Karker (1997), 'Det danske sprog', in A. Karker, B. Lindgren and S. Løland, eds, *Nordens språk* (Oslo).

P. A. Luce and D. B. Pisoni (1998), 'Recognizing spoken words: The Neighborhood Activation Model', *Ear and hearing*, 19, 1–36.

A. M. Nordentoft (1981), *Nordiske nabosprog: dansk-norsk-svensk sproglære for lærerstuderende* (Copenhagen).

P. J. Scharpff and V. J. van Heuven (1988), 'Effects of pause insertion on the intelligibility of low quality speech', in W. A. Ainsworth, J. N. Holmes, eds, *Proceedings of the 7th FASE/Speech-88 Symposium* (Edinburgh), 261–268.

M. S. Vitevitch and E. Rodriguez (2005), 'Neighborhood density effects in spoken word recognition in Spanish', *Journal of Multilingual Communication Disorders*, 3, 64–73.

E. Wessén (1960), *Våra ord. Deras uttal och ursprung. Kortfattad etymologisk ordbok* (Stockholm).

E. Wessén (1965), *Svensk språkhistoria. Ljudlära och ordböjningslära* (Stockholm).

F. M. Wiener and G. A. Miller (1946), 'Some characteristics of human speech', in *Transmission and reception of sounds under combat conditions. Summary Technical Report of Division 17, National Defense Research Committee* (Washington, DC), 58–68.

J. C. Ziegler and L. Ferrand (1998), 'Orthography shapes the perception of speech: The consistency effect in auditory word recognition', *Psychonomic Bulletin and Review*, 5, 683–689.

END NOTES

[1] The intelligibility of words without any possible influence from the semantic context can also be tested by presenting words in nonsense contexts, which might resemble usual language decoding more than identifying isolated words. However, since Swedish is characterised by a high number of sandhi phenomena, the correct segmentation of the test words would be an additional task when presented in syntactic context. By using words without any syntactic context we thus made sure that the subjects' task was only to identify words, without the additional need to segment them correctly.

[2] The experiment may be found on the Internet at http://www.let.rug.nl/lrs. It is possible to participate in the test with a guest account (login: germanic, password: guest). We thank Johan van der Geest for programming the experimental interface and databases.

[3] The list was prepared for investigating several Germanic languages. It was based on the most frequent words occurring in large corpora of both formal language (Europarl, cf. http://www.statmt.org/europarl/) and informal language (Corpus of Spoken Dutch, cf. http://lands.let.kun.nl/cgn/home.htm).

[4] The mean word length of native Swedish words in our dataset was 4.8 sounds, while the mean length of loan words was 5.9 sounds. This difference was significant (df $= 345$, $p < .001$).

[5] The corpus provides texts from different written language genres (journals, magazines, fiction) from 1988–1992 and consists of 28 million words. The frequency lists are freely accessible at http://korpus.dsl.dk. To our knowledge, there is no corpus of comparable size available for spoken Danish.

[6] Still, there is a chance that the models are influenced by the fact that some of the variables are not well-balanced. For example, with lexical tones 253 words have accent I, and only 94 have accent two. Only 46 of the 347 words reveal foreign sounds, etc. A possible solution to this problem would be a Latin square design, but this is rather complicated and might even be impossible to build with eleven factors. We therefore chose to include all words into the analysis.

100

MUTUAL INTELLIGIBILITY OF STANDARD AND REGIONAL DUTCH LANGUAGE VARIETIES

LEEN IMPE, DIRK GEERAERTS AND DIRK SPEELMAN

Abstract   *In this experimental study, we aim to arrive at a global picture of the mutual intelligibility of various Dutch language varieties by carrying out a computer-controlled lexical decision task in which ten target varieties are evaluated – the Belgian and Netherlandic Dutch standard language as well as four regional varieties of both countries. We auditorily presented real as well as pseudo-words in various varieties of Dutch to Netherlandic and Belgian test subjects, who were asked to decide as quickly as possible whether the items were existing Dutch words or not. The experiment's working assumption is that the faster the subjects react, the better the intelligibility of (the language variety of) the word concerned.*

I. INTRODUCTION

1.1 Research framework

When speakers of different languages or language varieties communicate with each other, one group (generally the economically and culturally weaker one) often switches to the language or language variety of the other, or both groups of speakers adopt a third, common *lingua franca*. However, if the languages or language varieties are so much alike that the degree of mutual comprehension is sufficiently high, both groups of speakers might opt for communicating in their own language variety.

This type of interaction between closely related language varieties, which Haugen (1966) coins *semicommunication* and Braunmüller and Zeevaert (2001) refer to as *receptive multilingualism*, has been investigated between speakers

International Journal of Humanities and Arts Computing 2 (1–2) 2008, 101–117
DOI: 10.3366/E1753854809000330

of native Indian languages in the United States (Pierce 1952), between Spaniards and Portuguese (Jensen, 1989), between speakers of Scandinavian languages (Zeevaert, 2004; Gooskens, 2006; Lars-Olof Delsing, 2007) and between Slovaks and Czechs (Budovičová, 1987). Though primarily referring to interlingual intelligibility situations as exemplified above, this concept may also be employed in the description of the intralingual Dutch intelligibility situation. Both diachronically and synchronically, Belgian Dutch and Netherlandic Dutch are closely related varieties that are often held to be mutually intelligible so that speakers do not need to switch to another language variety to be understood.

However, even though the various Dutch language varieties share a great deal of similarity, there also exist clear differences amongst them at the morphological, lexical, syntactic, semantic and especially the phonetic level. Although a considerable amount of descriptive and theoretical work has been done on the linguistic variation in Dutch (Geeraerts, Grondelaers and Speelman, 1999; van Hout and Van de Velde, 2001), few data are available on the implication of this variation for comprehensibility. As illustrated by the fact that more and more television programmes from both countries are being intralingually subtitled when broadcast in the other, this variation often seems to cause comprehensibility difficulties between Dutch speakers. Moreover, such difficulties may exist within each of the two national varieties of Dutch, especially amongst the Flemish regiolects (van Bezooijen and van den Berg, 1999a). Also within both countries, certain groups of non-standard speakers are frequently intralingually subtitled (Vandekerckhove, 2006). According to Hendrickx (2003) this implies that 'Nederlandstaligen elkaar steeds minder goed blijken te verstaan en te begrijpen, als je bedenkt hoe vaak ze zichzelf ondertitelen. Nederlanders ondertitelen Vlamingen, Vlamingen ondertitelen Nederlanders én andere Vlamingen' (Dutch speakers seem to understand each other increasingly worse, if you consider how often they subtitle themselves. Netherlandic Dutch speakers subtitle Flemish speakers, Flemish speakers subtitle Netherlandic Dutch speakers *and* other Flemish speakers). The few studies that have tackled this topic for the Dutch situation have exclusively relied upon subjective introspection by informants (Boets and De Schutter, 1977); no research exists that carries out statistically supported measurements in an extensive experimental design.

1.2 Definition of the problem

Considering the Dutch language situation as outlined above, several research questions arise. Do the various Dutch language varieties hold enough similarities so that Dutch speakers do not experience real comprehension problems in mutual communication? Or, on the contrary, is there so much mutual variation that serious comprehension difficulties amongst Dutch speakers actually arise? And if so, are the intelligibility problems symmetric or asymmetric, or in other words, is comprehension more likely in one direction than in the other? Specifically, do Netherlandic and Belgian Dutch speakers understand one another with equal ease? The same holds for the regional level: is the West-Flemish regiolect, to pick a random example, more easily understood by Limburgish subjects than the Limburgish regiolect is by West-Flemings? Moreover, are there also significant differences in the intelligibility of standard compared to regional varieties?

To answer these questions, we presented an array of existing and non-existing words, recorded in ten different standard and regional Dutch language varieties (2.1), to a group of Belgian and Netherlandic Dutch test subjects (2.2). Via a computer-controlled intelligibility test (2.3), which consists of a lexical decision task and an identification task, we registered the response time and accuracy of the test subjects' responses.

We will discuss some first results of this study at two distinct levels. First, we treat the mutual intelligibility in the Dutch language area at the national level (3.1), focussing on the comprehension difficulties between speakers of Belgian and Netherlandic Dutch in general. Second, we zoom in on the regional level (3.2) and consider the mutual intelligibility relations within each of the Dutch-speaking countries. Finally, we briefly discuss which factors most probably determine this experiment's intelligibility scores and account for the variation found (3.3). As several studies on the mutual intelligibility of closely related varieties have shown or suggested (cf. van Bezooijen and Gooskens 2007), factors such as linguistic distance as well as factors such as familiarity or language attitude can play an important role in predicting intelligibility scores. These two groups of determinants correspond to the distinction between 'the objective division of dialectal features' and 'the subjective awareness of cohesion between dialects' (Weijnen 1946) as made in the perceptual dialectological tradition (Preston 1999). This field of study has been the driving force for several dialectological, sociolinguistic and variationist studies in the Low Countries, such as van Bezooijen's research (2002) on the influence of (especially) subjective factors on aesthetic evaluations of Dutch language varieties.

2. INTELLIGIBILITY

2.1 Target varieties

2.1.1 Selection

The word list we used in the intelligibility test contains 200 existing and as many non-existing words recorded in ten different varieties of Dutch, viz. a Netherlandic and Belgian Dutch realisation of the standard language as well as four regional varieties from both countries. Nowadays, most Dutch speakers are

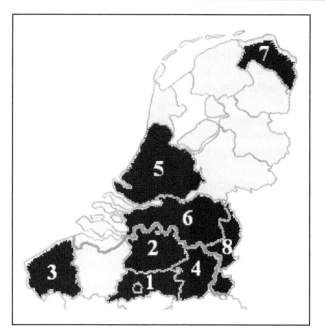

Figure 1. Map of Flanders and the Netherlands.

able to use a non-dialectal, regional or standard variety. In supraregional – and especially in supranational – communication, we expect them to actually do so as that facilitates comprehension for a speaker of a different dialectal or regional variety to a large extent. Since we wanted to model the interregional intelligibility relations in the Dutch language area as realistically as possible, we only selected standard and regional target varieties without including any local dialects.

Both in Flanders and in the Netherlands, we selected regiolects from the most central area, from an intermediary region and from the peripheral regions – based upon socio-geographical as well as dialectological criteria (Musterd and De Pater 1994). In Flanders, Brabant (indicated on Figure 1 as *1*) constitutes the central area, the economical, cultural and linguistic centre of Flanders (Geerts, 1983). In the Netherlands, the Randstad (*5*) holds that central position. Further, we selected somewhat less central regiolects from the Flemish intermediary region Antwerp (*2*) and its Dutch equivalent Northern Brabant (*6*). The most peripheral varieties for this study were selected in the Flemish areas West-Flanders (*3*) and Limburg (*4*) and in the Netherlandic regions Groningen (*7*) and Netherlandic Limburg (*8*). In comparison with the more central regions, dialectal language use seems to have preserved quite a strong position here and most Dutch-speaking language users perceive the linguistic distance between dialect and standard language in these peripheral regions as the greatest.

2.1.2 Recordings

In a sound-proof radio studio with high-standard audio equipment, the stimulus words were recorded by eight male radio commentators (four from each country) between 27 and 34 years of age, each born and bred in one of the eight regions described above. For each regional variety we selected, a set of 40 (20 existing and 20 non-existing) regional words was recorded by one of the eight speakers, whereas the two (Belgian and Netherlandic Dutch) sets of 40 standard words were composed by recordings of four different speakers (i.e. each speaker pronounced ten words in the standard variety of his country). The speakers were asked to make no lexical changes to the stimulus words. The words are therefore not lexically, but only phonetically regionally marked. We levelled out word length differences between the stimuli by composing the word sets in such a way that there were no statistical differences in the mean stimulus duration of (each condition within) each word set.

The fact that each regional variety is recorded by only one speaker has serious disadvantages as compared to studies in which several speakers per variety are included, since it prohibits a watertight check on the effect of speaker individual characteristics. We tried to tackle this problem as well as possible by a strict speaker selection. Given the speakers' professional background, all voices had a priori been screened for quality and clarity. In our opinion, all speakers *we* selected had an excellent quality speaking voice. None of them had a nasal articulation, nor a whispery, creaky or harsh voice. During the recordings, we also instructed the speakers, if necessary, to slow down or speed up their speech tempo. According to our evaluation, the final recordings have a highly comparable speech rate. In order to objectively check this factor's effect, we will correlate the average speech rate per speaker with the intelligibility scores obtained for that speaker by test subjects of the same variety (as in Tang and van Heuven, 2009). Further, via Adobe Audition, we normalised the recordings (amplitude peak scale 0.98), removed clicks and checked the average pitch for each speaker that ranged between 112 and 118 Hz.

Moreover, it should be noted that the request to talk with a regional accent does not presuppose that regiolects exist as clearly distinguishable linguistic systems that are equidistant from the standard language (Auer, 2005). What speakers recognise as 'regional varieties' may be more or less remote from the standard variety. In order to obtain a comparable degree of regionality between the words recorded across the eight regional varieties, we *identically* instructed speakers with a *highly comparable profile*, used to employ both regional and standard language for their professional ends. As Auer argues, speakers adapt the degree of regionality of their speech depending on situational changes. Therefore, we did not direct the speakers which specific regional markers they had to use, but rather referred to similar communicative situations by defining regiolect on the basis of its functional use, i.e. *informal regionally accented speech* comprehensible in the speaker's entire region, differentiated from the *formal* standard and from *local* dialect with a smaller geographical reach and a more restricted intelligibility. Moreover, since the word sets for the two standard varieties included words recorded by four different speakers, also the standard recordings inevitably contain some regional colourings. In spite of the speakers' profession that assumes the mastery of neutral standard language, spoken standard is usually not totally free of regional variation. All the same, this (slight) intrastandard variation ties in with our attempt to model the Dutch linguistic situation as realistically as possible. Importantly, phonetic distance calculations between all regional and standard recordings, which we will carry out in future research (3.3), will enable us to take into account all existing *intraregiolect* and *intrastandard* variation in eventual analyses.

2.2 Test subjects

The test subjects are 16- to 20-year-old secondary school pupils (46 per cent boys and 54 per cent girls) that follow pre-university education. We selected 641 pupils in Flanders and 404 subjects in the Netherlands, originating from the same eight regions as indicated in Figure 1. To obtain a more generalisable picture of the intelligibility within each area, we selected three geographically scattered measurement points per region, none of which represent a border town with another selected region. The number of selected subjects ranges from 75 to 206 pupils per region.

At the onset of the intelligibility test, we asked all test subjects to complete an extensive list of personal questions. The results of non-native speakers of Dutch and of pupils who reside in another region than the school's region (and consequently probably speak a (slightly) other regional variety) were excluded from analysis.

2.3 Experiment

We developed a computer-controlled intelligibility test by means of the software package *E-Prime* (Schneider, Eschman and Zuccolotto, 2002), that allows us to register reaction times with great accuracy. The test consists of three main components, namely a lexical decision task (2.3.1), a multiple choice task (2.3.2) and a questionnaire (2.3.3).

2.3.1 Lexical decision task

Design

After a short practice trial, all test subjects took part in a lexical decision task in which we auditorily presented them with the full, randomised list of 400 existing and non-existing isolated words. To prevent a learning effect, no item was presented twice. After each word, the test subjects were asked to decide as quickly as possible whether the word exists in Dutch or not. The experiment's working assumption is that the faster the subjects react, the better the intelligibility of the word, and by extension, of the language variety in which the word was recorded.

Stimulus material

Both the existing and non-existing items are subdivided according to structural and linguistic criteria. The existing words are subdivided according to nationality-based typicality, frequency and word class. As Table 1 shows, each set of words contains ten binational words and ten national words typical of the country in which the standard or regional variety in which the word set is recorded, is spoken. This selection results from a Stable Lexical Marker analysis (Speelman, Grondelaers and Geeraerts, 2008) on three large corpora, viz. an internet blog corpus, an online football forum corpus and the CGN (Corpus of Spoken Dutch), all containing Belgian and Netherlandic Dutch language material. The first two corpora predominantly contain informal language, while the CGN also contains more formal material. A Stable Lexical Marker analysis, which is based on a log likelihood test, highlights the typical lexical items (i.e. the stable lexical markers) of a (sub)corpus, enabling us to extract, for example, typically Flemish words. Binational words are words that are as typical in Flanders as in the Netherlands, such as the word *aandacht (attention)*, while national words are typically Belgian Dutch, such as *kotmadam (a students' landlady)*, or typically Netherlandic Dutch, such as *gozer (fellow)*. We did not extract any typically regional words (such as typically West-Flemish words). In other words, whereas the stimuli are *phonetically* regionally marked (since each word set is recorded in a standard or regional variety), they are *lexically* only nationally marked (since we only selected nationally typical, but no regionally typical words). Each set of binational and national words also contains an equal number of high- and low-frequent items.

On top of the corpus-based selected 200 existing words, we created 200 non-existing words. Each set of non-words, recorded in one of the ten target varieties, is based upon a (for each set of non-words identical) set of 20 existing words that are not used elsewhere in the experiment and that are as typical in Flanders as in the Netherlands. Each non-word was checked for its distance from the word upon

Table 1. Numerical data and examples on the main subdivisions of the existing words. (h) represents 'high-frequent', (l) represents 'low-frequent'.

WORDS (200)

4 BELGIAN DUTCH SPEAKERS

	regiolect Brabant (20)	regiolect Antwerp (20)	regiolect W-Flanders (20)	regiolect Limburg (20)	standard Belgian Dutch (20)
binational (10)	(h) eerlijk 'honest'	(h) winkel 'shop'	(h) schrijven 'write'	(h) aandacht 'attention'	(h) keuken 'kitchen'
	(l) wrijven 'rub'	(l) puin 'rubble'	(l) droog 'dry'	(l) leunen 'lean'	(l) stabiel 'stable'
national (10)	(h) schoon 'beautiful'	(h) goesting 'appetite'	(h) spijtig 'regrettable'	(h) plezant 'pleasant'	(h) content 'pleased'
	(l) zeveren 'drivel'	(l) peinzen 'think'	(l) hesp 'ham'	(l) kuisen 'clean'	(l) fameus 'huge'

4 NETHERLANDIC DUTCH SPEAKERS

	Regiolect Randstad (20)	regiolect N-Brabant (20)	regiolect Groningen (20)	regiolect Limburg (20)	standard Neth. Dutch (20)
binational (10)	(h) vallen 'fall'	(h) gebouw 'building'	(h) water 'water'	(h) kopen 'buy'	(h) zeggen 'say'
	(l) dreiging 'menace'	(l) klinker 'vowel'	(l) goedkoop 'cheap'	(l) brutaal 'brutal'	(l) dieet 'diet'
national (10)	(h) balen 'fed up'	(h) kroeg 'pub'	(h) gaaf 'cool'	(h) snappen 'understand'	(h) aardig 'nice'
	(l) jatten 'steal'	(l) pinnen 'pay by card'	(l) gozer 'fellow'	(l) gezeik 'crap'	(l) gillen 'scream'

which it is based. Since we will not discuss any consequences of the subdivisions at the level of the non-existing words in this paper, we will not elucidate them any further.

2.3.2 Multiple choice task

In order to check whether the results of the lexical decision task reflect the informants' real comprehension of the stimuli, we included a multiple choice task. In this second test, we presented the test subjects with the same 200 existing words that were presented in the lexical decision task, each word having exactly the same accent as it had in the first task. The subjects were asked to decide which out of two possible alternatives reflected the best the meaning of the stimulus words, one of the options being a synonym or semantically strongly related word (such as *triest 'sad'* as synonym for the stimulus word *droevig 'sad'*) and the other alternative being a semantically unrelated word (such as *klein 'small'* as incorrect alternative for *droevig 'sad'*).

2.3.3 Questionnaire on attitude and familiarity

As a third and last task, the test subjects were asked to complete a questionnaire on their language attitudes towards and familiarity with the examined varieties. Both factors, attitude and familiarity, can possibly have influenced the intelligibility scores. To measure the subjects' explicit language attitudes, they were asked to evaluate status-related questions about the language varieties' usefulness and value and solidarity-related questions about the varieties' friendliness and beauty on a seven-point scale. This approach follows an established dichotomy in language attitudinal research (Ryan 1982). In addition, the test subjects specified how often they wrote or spoke each language variety involved in the test (active familiarity) on the one hand, and how often they read or heard each variety (passive familiarity) on the other.

3. RESULTS

We will discuss some first results of the intelligibility test at two distinct levels, the national and the regional level. At the national level (3.1), we consider whether speakers of the two national varieties of Dutch experience word level comprehension problems. At the regional level (3.2), we examine whether there are also intelligibility difficulties within each of the Dutch-speaking countries. We examined the intelligibility relations by means of the test subjects' response time. We only took into account the stimuli that the subjects categorised correctly in the lexical decision task *and* identified correctly in the multiple choice task.

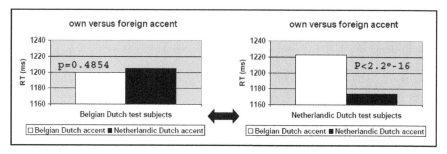

Figure 2. Mutual intelligibility at the national level (accent): mean reaction times (milliseconds) and p-values (t-test, statistical significance < .05).

Furthermore, we will briefly touch upon the mechanisms underlying the intelligibility results and discuss their relevance for this and other studies in the humanities, addressing non-linguistic determinants such as the informants' attitude towards or familiarity with certain language varieties as well as linguistic factors such as phonetic distance (3.3). In future research, we will examine these determinants to gain an insight into their relative contribution in determining the mutual intelligibility of Dutch language varieties.

3.1 Mutual intelligibility at the national level

3.1.1 Results

At the national level, the foremost question is whether speakers of the two national varieties of Dutch are faced with intelligibility problems and additionally, whether or not these difficulties are asymmetric. To this end we compared the extent to which the two groups of speakers understand each other, considering both phonetic and lexical dimensions.

From a phonetic point of view, it is no surprise that both Flemish and Netherlandic Dutch-speaking subjects generally have (slightly) fewer problems with correctly understanding words recorded in their own national accent than in an accent of the other country (see Figure 2). However, comparing the extent to which both groups of speakers understand a foreign accent reveals an asymmetrical intelligibility relation. A two-way ANOVA shows that the interaction between the factor 'test subject's nationality' and the factor 'own versus foreign accent' is significant ($p < 2.2^e\text{-}16$). Comparatively speaking, it appears that the Flemish test subjects have significantly fewer problems understanding words recorded in a Netherlandic Dutch accent than the Netherlandic Dutch subjects have understanding words recorded in a Belgian Dutch accent. These analyses include all existing binational words recorded in

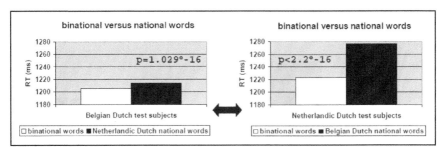

Figure 3. Mutual intelligibility at the national level (lexicon): mean reaction times (milliseconds) and p-values (t-test, statistical significance < .05).

a Belgian versus Netherlandic Dutch standard or regional variety (viz. 50 words per accent per group of test subjects). We excluded the national words in order to be able to clearly distinguish the (phonetic) effect of the national accent in which a word is pronounced from the (lexical) effect of in which Dutch-speaking country a word is most typically used.

Also lexically speaking, we find evidence for this asymmetric intelligibility relation. Predictably, Figure 3 demonstrates that Dutch-speaking subjects generally have a better understanding of the binational words that are equally typically in Flanders and in the Netherlands than of the national words of the other country. More interestingly, a comparison of the extent to which both groups of speakers understand words typically used in the other language community again reflects an asymmetry. A two-way ANOVA demonstrates that the interaction between the factor 'test subject's nationality' and the factor 'binational versus national word' is significant ($p = 2.59^{e}$-13), again with a better understanding on the side of the Flemish subjects. For the Belgian Dutch test subjects, the analyses include binational and typically Netherlandic Dutch national words, all recorded in a Netherlandic Dutch standard or regional variety. For the Netherlandic Dutch subjects, we included binational and typically Belgian Dutch national words, recorded in a Belgian Dutch accent (viz. 50 words per condition per group of test subjects).

3.1.2 Analysis

The asymmetry pictured above fits in with the (historical) language-political situation in the Dutch language area. Since the end of the nineteenth century, Flanders has officially followed the language policy of the Netherlands (Van Hout et al., 1999). Standard pronunciation, as used by the Netherlandic educated classes, patterned the target language of Belgian Dutch speakers. However, as Van de Velde (1996) notes, over the past 70 years, linguistic distances

111

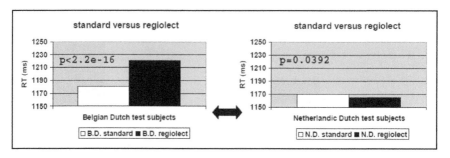

Figure 4. Effect of standardness and regionality within Flanders and the Netherlands: mean reaction times (milliseconds) and p-values (t-test, statistical significance < .05).

between Belgian and Netherlandic Dutch have increased as the Netherlandic Dutch linguistic hegemony decreased. All the same, it has been Flanders that has traditionally been normatively (e.g. via education and state policy) and culturally (e.g. via viewing habits) oriented towards the Netherlands instead of vice versa. Thus, it has also been Flanders that, for many years, has been exposed to and familiarised with the Netherlandic Dutch accent and lexicon, instead of the other way round. In line with this finding, also other studies (cf. Geeraerts, Grondelaers and Speelman, 1999) found indications of Flanders lexically converging towards the Netherlands.

3.2 Mutual intelligibility at the regional level

3.2.1 Results

Shifting our attention to the regional level, we consider the effect of standardness and regionality ('Is standard language effectively better understood than regional language use?'). We will successively discuss the intelligibility of standard versus non-standard speech within Flanders and within the Netherlands. As regards the Flemish situation, Figure 4 depicts that Flemish test subjects (left-hand side of Figure 4) generally need significantly more time to correctly understand non-standard Belgian Dutch varieties than to understand standard Belgian Dutch. Conversely, Netherlandic Dutch test subjects need, unlike Flemish speakers, approximately as much time to correctly understand standard Netherlandic Dutch and Netherlandic Dutch regional varieties (right-hand side of Figure 4). A two-way ANOVA confirms that the interaction between the factor 'test subject's nationality' and the factor 'standard versus non-standard' is significant ($p < 2.2^e\text{-}16$). For both groups of test subjects, all existing words recorded in a variety spoken in their own country are taken into account. Per group of test subjects, the analyses include 20 standard and 80 non-standard words.

3.2.2 Analysis

Summarising the results in Figure 4, the internal intelligibility situations in Flanders and the Netherlands are contrastive. Specifically, the intelligibility difficulties between standard words and (non-dialectal) regional words turn out to be significantly smaller in the Netherlands than in Flanders. In other studies (such as Geeraerts, Grondelaers and Speelman, 1999) indications have been found that the *linguistic distance* between formal standard and informal non-standard Dutch is greater in Flanders than in the Netherlands today, which could hypothetically account for the intelligibility scores discussed above. However, in order to be able to reach firm conclusions and solid interpretations, we must map the linguistic distances between this study's target varieties objectively (which we will do in further research, see 3.3). Moreover, such objective distance calculations will enable us to check whether possibly more intrastandard variation (caused by the fact that the standard words are recorded through four different speakers) among the Netherlandic than among the Belgian Dutch standard recordings have affected the intelligibility scores discussed above.

3.3 Explanatory factors

As discussed above, the intelligibility experiment reveals some highly interesting results. On the basis of the available data, however, we can only speculate on the mechanisms *underlying* these findings. In order to be able to provide solid interpretations, we will examine whether and to what extent the intelligibility scores are determined by several linguistic and non-linguistic factors in future research.

A first explanatory factor we assess is the *phonetic distance* between all language variety pairs concerned, which we will compute by means of the Levenshtein method (Kessler, 1995). This technique has already proven successful for measuring phonetic distances between Dutch dialects in other (socio)phonetic studies in the humanities (Nerbonne et al., 1996; Nerbonne and Heeringa, 1998) and for gaining insight into the linguistic basis of intelligibility (van Bezooijen and Gooskens, 2007).

Importantly, the linguistic knowledge of most Dutch language users probably covers standard-like *and* regional-like varieties. Therefore, Dutch speakers may relate words they perceive to more than one cognitive representation for those words in their minds. The greater the linguistic difference between the perceived words and the mental representation(s), the longer it takes for hearers to recognise the words in question. In order to determine each individual's main mental representation(s) – the standard, the regiolect, or both – we will reckon with familiarity scores that we calculated on the basis of the questionnaire on each subject's active and passive knowledge of all language varieties involved in the intelligibility test (2.3.3). These scores allow us to take into account, for each hearer, the most relevant variety or varieties in calculating phonetic distances, which may determine the hearer's intelligibility scores.

As just mentioned, a second determinant we will address is *familiarity*. Logically, in line with the results of other intelligibility studies (for example Gooskens, 2006), more contact and familiarity imply a better comprehensibility.

Thirdly, several studies (Börestam, 1987; Boets and De Schutter, 1977) have reasoned that *language attitudes* may play a role in determining asymmetrical intelligibility results. It is suggested that positive language attitudes may encourage listeners to try to understand the language variety in question, whereas negative attitudes may hinder intelligibility. However, in an experimental setting in which isolated words are presented, language attitudes have not yet been proven to predict intelligibility. We plan to measure test subject's language attitudes by means of applying the affective priming technique (Fazio et al., 1986), an established and successful tool in socio-psychological research on the implicit measurement of attitudes, and to investigate whether the attitudinal scores correlate with intelligibility scores.

In order to pinpoint the relative contribution of each explanatory factor discussed above, we will carry out a series of multiple regressions with the phonetic distances, the familiarity responses and the attitudinal scores as the independent variables and the intelligibility scores as the dependent variable.

4. DISCUSSION

With this experimental study, we have sought to arrive at a global picture of the mutual intelligibility at the word level of ten different – Belgian and Netherlandic Dutch, standard and regional, central and peripheral – language varieties in Flanders and the Netherlands. The results of a computer-controlled intelligibility test revealed certain word comprehension difficulties and asymmetrical intelligibility relations, arising at two distinct levels, viz. the national and the regional level.

At the national level, in line with the historical language-political situation in the Dutch language area, Flemish test subjects seem to have significantly fewer problems with correctly understanding Netherlandic Dutch stimuli than vice versa, for which we found both phonetic and lexical evidence. At the regional level, we see a clearly positive effect of the degree of standardness on the ease of comprehension. This effect appears to be the most salient within Flanders, where the intelligibility differences between standard and (non-dialectal) regional words are greater than in the Netherlands. Objective linguistic distance measurements, planned in future research, will show whether or not these findings are reflected in a smaller phonetic distance between formal standard and informal non-standard Dutch in the Netherlands than in Flanders.

In future research, we will seek to frame and interpret the intelligibility problems and differences by means of assessing both linguistic and non-linguistic explanatory factors. In order to pinpoint their relative contribution to the mutual intelligibility of Dutch language varieties, we will examine these factors in detail by means of techniques and insights commonly used in other disciplines of the humanities. In this, we will turn to computational linguistics to calculate phonetic distances by means of the Levenshtein method, to sociolinguistics in mapping familiarity and to psycholinguistics and social psychology while carrying out a computer-controlled auditive priming experiment to measure the test subjects' implicit language attitudes.

Finally, we would like to explicitly underline the relevance of the technique employed in this study, viz. computer-controlled intelligibility testing, to other disciplines in the humanities. Experimental computer-controlled research on intelligibility has been a topic of substantial importance in the fields of speech pathology, foreign language testing and speech technology. In research on speech pathology, Maassen (1985) employed intelligibility tests to examine the effect of (supra)segmental corrections on the intelligibility of deaf speech. Also in order to establish the degree of intelligibility of language varieties with a foreign accent (for example Wang 2007 on Chinese, Dutch and American speakers of English), similar tests have been adopted. In the field of speech technology, finally, techniques of the same kind have proven their value in testing the intelligibility of (and detecting problems with) talking computers (van Bezooijen and van Heuven, 1997).

REFERENCES

P. Auer (2005), 'Europe's sociolinguistic unity, or: A typology of European dialect/standard constellations', in N. Delbecque, J. van der Auwera and D. Geeraerts, eds, *Perspectives on variation. Sociolinguistic, historical, comparative* (Berlin/New York), 7–42.

H. Boets and G. De Schutter (1977), 'Verstaanbaarheid en appreciatie. Nederlandse dialekten uit België zoals inwoners van Duffel die ervaren', *Taal en Tongval*, 29, 156–177.

U. Börestam (1987), *Dansk-svensk språkgemenskap påundantag*, FUMS rapport 137 (Uppsala).

K. Braunmüller and L. Zeevaert (2001), *Semikommunikation, rezeptive Mehrsprachigkeit und verwandte Phänomene. Arbeiten zur Mehrsprachigkeit* (Hamburg).

V. Budovičová (1987), 'Literary languages in contact', in J. Chloupek et al., eds, *Reader in Czech sociolinguistics* (Amsterdam/Philadelphia), 156–175.

L. O. Delsing (2007), 'Scandinavian intercomprehension today', in J. D. ten Thije and L. Zeevaert, eds, *Receptive multilingualism* (Amsterdam), 231–248.

R. H. Fazio, D. M. Sanbonmatsu, M. C. Powell and F. R. Kardes (1986), 'On the automatic activation of attitudes', *Journal of Personality and Social Psychology*, 50(2), 229–238.

D. Geeraerts, S. Grondelaers and D. Speelman (1999), *Convergentie en divergentie in de Nederlandse woordenschat. Een onderzoek naar kleding- en voetbaltermen* (Amsterdam).

G. Geerts (1983), 'Brabant als centrum van standaardtaalontwikkeling in Vlaanderen', *Forum der Letteren*, 24(1), 55–63.

C. Gooskens (2006), 'Linguistic and extra-linguistic predictors of inter-Scandinavian intelligibility', *Linguistics in the Netherlands*, 23(1), 101–113.

C. Gooskens (2007), 'Contact, attitude and phonetic distance as predictors of inter-Scandinavian communication', in J. M. Eloy and T. Óhlfearnáin, eds, *Near languages – collateral languages* (Limerick), 99–109.

E. Haugen (1966), 'Semicommunication: the language gap in Scandinavia', *Sociological Inquiry*, 36, 280–297.

R. Hendrickx (2003), 'Wat zegt ie?', in J. Stroop, ed., *Waar gaat het Nederlands naartoe? Panorama van een taal* (Amsterdam), 74–81.

J. Jensen (1989), 'On the mutual intelligibility of Spanish and Portuguese', *Hispania*, 72, 849–852.

B. Kessler (1995), 'Computational dialectology in Irish Gaelic', *Proceedings of the European ACL* (Dublin), 60–67.

B. Maassen and D. J. Povel (1985), 'The effect of segmental and suprasegmental corrections on the intelligibility of deaf speech', *Journal of the Acoustical Society of America*, 78(3), 877–886.

S. Musterd and B. de Pater (1994), *Randstad Holland. Internationaal, regionaal, lokaal* (Assen).

J. Nerbonne, W. Heeringa, E. van den Hout, P. van de Kooi, S. Otten and W. van de Vis (1996), 'Phonetic distance between Dutch dialects', in G. Durieux, W. Daelemans and S. Gillis, eds, *Proceedings of Computational Linguistics in the Netherlands '95* (Antwerpen), 185–202.

J. Nerbonne and W. Heeringa (1998), 'Computationele vergelijking en classificatie van dialecten', *Taal en Tongval*, 50(2), 164–193.

J. E. Pierce (1952), 'Dialect distance testing in Algonquian', *International Journal of American Linguistics*, 18, 203–210.

D. Preston (1999), *Handbook of perceptual dialectology*, 1st ed. (Amsterdam).

E. B. Ryan and H. Giles (1982), *Attitudes towards language variation – social and applied contexts* (UK).

W. Schneider, A. Eschman and A. Zuccolotto (2002), *E-Prime user's guide* (Pittsburgh).

D. Speelman, S. Grondelaers and D. Geeraerts (2008), 'Variation in the choice of adjectives in the two main national varieties of Dutch', in G. Kristiansen and R. Dirven, eds, *Cognitive sociolinguistics: language variation, cultural models, social systems* (Berlin/New York).

C. Tang and V. J. Van Heuven (2009), 'Mutual intelligibility of Chinese dialects experimentally tested', *Lingua* 119(5), 709–732.

R. van Bezooijen and V. J. Van Heuven (1997), 'Assessment of speech synthesis', in D. Gibbon, R. Moore and R. Winski, eds, *Handbook of Standards and Resources for Spoken Language Systems* (Berlin/New York), 481–653.

R. van Bezooijen and R. van den Berg (1999a), 'Taalvariëteiten in Nederland en Vlaanderen: hoe staat het met hun verstaanbaarheid?', *Taal en Tongval*, 51(1), 15–33.

R. van Bezooijen and R. van den Berg (1999b), 'Word intelligibility of language varieties in the Netherlands and Flanders under minimal conditions', in R. van Bezooijen and R. Kager, eds, *Linguistics in the Netherlands* (Amsterdam/Philadelphia), 1–12.

R. van Bezooijen (2002), 'Aesthetic evaluations of Dutch. Comparison of dialects, accents and languages', in D. Long and D. R. Preston, eds., *Handbook of perceptual dialectology*, 2nd ed. (Amsterdam/Philadelphia), 13–30.

R. van Bezooijen and C. Gooskens (2007), 'Interlingual text comprehension: linguistic and extralinguistic determinants', in J. D. ten Thije and L. Zeevaert, eds, *Receptive multilingualism and intercultural communication. Hamburger studies in multilingualism* (Amsterdam), 249–264.

H. Van de Velde (1996), 'Variatie en verandering in het gesproken Standaard-Nederlands (1935–1993)' (Ph.D. thesis, University of Nijmegen).

H. Van de Velde and R. van Hout (2001), *R-atics. Sociolinguistic, Phonetic and Phonological Characteristics of /r/.* Special Issue of Etudes & Travaux 4 (Brussel).

R. van Hout et al. (1999), 'De uitspraak van het Standaard-Nederlands: variatie en varianten in Vlaanderen en Nederland', in E. Huls and B. Weltens, eds, *Artikelen van de derde sociolinguïstische conferentie* (Delft), 183–196.

R. Vandekerckhove et al. (2006), 'Intralinguale ondertiteling van Nederlandstalige televisieprogramma's in Vlaanderen: linguïstische en extra-linguïstische determinanten', in T. Koole, J. Nortier and B. Tahitu, eds, *Artikelen van de vijfde sociolinguïstische conferentie* (Delft), 503–513.

H. Wang (2007), *English as a lingua franca: Mutual Intelligibility of Chinese, Dutch and American speakers of English* (LOT Dissertation Series 147, Utrecht).

A. A. Weijnen (1946), 'De grenzen tussen de Oost-Noordbrabantse dialecten onderling', in A. A. Weijnen, J. M. Renders and J. Van Ginneken, eds, *Oost-Noordbrabantse dialectproblemen. Bijdragen en Mededelingen der Dialectencommissie van de Koninklijke Nederlandse Akademie van Wetenschappen 8* (Amsterdam), 1–15.

L. Zeevaert (2004), *Interskandinavische Kommunikation. Strategien zur Etablierung von Verständigung zwischen Skandinaviern im Diskurs* (Hamburg).

THE DUTCH–GERMAN BORDER: RELATING LINGUISTIC, GEOGRAPHIC AND SOCIAL DISTANCES

FOLKERT DE VRIEND, CHARLOTTE GIESBERS, ROELAND VAN HOUT AND LOUIS TEN BOSCH

Abstract *In this paper we relate linguistic, geographic and social distances to each other in order to get a better understanding of the impact the Dutch-German state border has had on the linguistic characteristics of a sub-area of the Kleverlandish dialect area. This area used to be a perfect dialect continuum. We test three models for explaining today's pattern of linguistic variation in the area. In each model another variable is used as the determinant of linguistic variation: geographic distance (continuum model), the state border (gap model) and social distance (social model). For the social model we use perceptual data for friends, relatives and shopping locations. Testing the three models reveals that nowadays the dialect variation in the research area is closely related to the existence of the state border and to the social structure of the area. The geographic spatial configuration hardly plays a role anymore.*

I. INTRODUCTION

The Dutch-German state border south of the river Rhine was established in 1830. Before that time, the administrative borders in this region frequently changed. The Kleverlandish dialect area, which extends from Duisburg in Germany to Nijmegen in The Netherlands, crosses the state border south of the Rhine. The area is demarcated by the Uerdingen line in the south, the diphthongisation line of the West Germanic 'i' in the West, and the border with the Low Saxon dialects of the *Achterhoek* area in the North-East. The geographic details of the area can be found in Figure 1 (the state border is depicted with a dashed-dotted line).

International Journal of Humanities and Arts Computing 2 (1–2) 2008, 119–134
DOI: 10.3366/E1753854809000342

Figure 1. Geographic details of the Kleverlandish dialect area (Cornelissen 2003).

Hinskens, Kallen and Taeldeman (2000) pointed out that European state borders that cut across old dialect continua had a strong impact on dialect change. Boberg (2000) investigated the dialects on both sides of the border between Canada and the US and criticised Trudgill's gravity model (Trudgill, 1974). The gravity model says that language varieties may be subject to a 'gravity-like law'. In the model, population size plays the role of mass, so that settlements with large populations are particularly likely to adopt each other's changes. However, the effects of state borders are not taken into account in the model.

The Kleverlandish area, in its original form, is a prototypical example of a dialect continuum. There were no natural borders or sharp dialect borders. Kremer (1984; 1990) and Niebaum (1990) discussed the increased significance of the Dutch-German state border as a dialect border. Later, both Heeringa, Nerbonne, Niebaum, Nieuweboer and Kleiweg (2000) and Giesbers (2008) quantatively examined the effect of the Dutch-German state border. The area Heeringa et al. (2000) were interested in is situated north of the Rhine, around

Figure 2. Position of the research area of Giesbers (2008), relative to The Netherlands. The map also includes provincial borders.

the German town of Bentheim. Giesbers (2008) investigated a sub-area of the Kleverlandish dialect area that is situated south of the Rhine between the Dutch towns of Nijmegen (in the north) and Venray (in the south), as depicted in Figure 2. Both studies showed that the political border had a significant impact on the dialect continuum and separated the Dutch from the German dialects.

In this paper we test three models to explain the linguistic characteristics of the area depicted in Figure 2. The three models are the continuum model, the gap model and the social model.

When closely related language varieties in an area form a continuum, their distribution is marked by a direct, monotonic relationship between geographic and linguistic distance. Chambers and Trudgill (1985) formulate this as:

'If we travel from village to village, in a particular direction, we notice linguistic differences which distinguish one village from another. Sometimes the differences will be larger, and sometimes smaller, but they will be cumulative. The further we get from our starting point, the larger the differences will become.'

A cumulative model implies that the linguistic distance can be estimated fairly precisely on the basis of geographic distance: the larger the geographic distance, the larger the linguistic distance. The default model for a perfect dialect continuum can be defined as follows:

continuum model
linguistic distance = f(geographic distance)

f is a monotonic increasing function in this model, and, in a particularly simple case, a linear function. An error term could be added to the model since there may be some variability across the area. Hard (1972) simulated a continuum model for the Rhenish Fan (cf. Bloomfield, 1933), a famous example of a cumulative dialect continuum consisting of a stepwise isoglossic structure, with a random variability component.

The Kleverlandish dialects in The Netherlands and Germany came under the hegemony and influence of the two respective standard languages after the establishment of the state border in 1830. In addition, political, administrative and cultural developments became different in the area that was divided then over two countries. What was the impact of the state border on the dialects? The central research hypothesis in Giesbers (2008) is that the Dutch-German state border has given rise to a linguistic gap in the Kleverlandish dialect continuum. If this is true, the continuum model could be extended by adding a constant value to *f* representing the state border gap. In its most outspoken form we may assume that the gap became the main determinant of the linguistic distance, overshadowing remaining differences and patterns of dialect variation. Such an outspoken model can be defined as:

gap model
linguistic distance = f(gap)

The gap can only have two values in this model. It is zero when two locations are not separated by the state border. It has a specific, fixed value when two locations are separated by the state border. Again, an error term could be added to account for variability across the area.

The usefulness of the continuum model and the gap model is supported by historical marriage data collected in the research area by Giesbers (2008). In the period 1850–1870 30 per cent of the marriages were mixed, indicating a continuous socio-geographic network structure, with no notable effect of the state border. Nowadays the number of mixed marriages has dropped to less than 5 per cent, indicating that the state border has formed a gap in marital exchange. Intensive contact between speakers is an essential condition for dialects to continue to cohere. Could the linguistic distances in our research area be more directly related to social distances than to geographic distances? Assuming that marriage data reflect the intensity of cross-border contact, the question arises which other properties correlate with the social contact structure of the area. These properties could contribute to our understanding of the new linguistic structure in the Kleverlandish area. No objective data, however, are available on the social structure of the research area. Alternatively, one can ask people living in the area about how they perceive the geographic distribution of relevant social phenomena. We will look at perceptual social contact data for friends, relatives and shopping places. An explanatory model based on these social data can be defined as follows:

social model
linguistic distance = f(social distance)

The social model is similar to the continuum model but takes social distance as the determinant of linguistic distance instead of geographic distance. *f* is again a monotonic increasing function in this model and an error term could be added here too.

We want to test the explanatory power of the three models. In section 2 we first describe the data that will be used to test the models. These data were collected along the state border in the Kleverlandish area. In section 3 we derive distances from the data and test the three models. We first compare the continuum and gap models and then check to see if the social model has more explanatory power. In section 4 we discuss the results followed by a conclusion.

2. DATA COLLECTION

We collected data for 10 locations in the northern part of the Kleverlandish dialect area. Five locations on each side of the border were selected, as is shown in Figure 3. The area does not contain any natural borders and the 10 locations lie close to the state border. In the selection process, locations on the Dutch side of the border were paired with similar locations on the German side of the border based on information about population size, infrastructure and distance to the border. This resulted in five cross-border pairs of locations. The town centres of both Huelm (Germany) and Siebengewald (The Netherlands) for instance are 3.7 kilometres from the border. Two locations with a larger distance to the border are Gennep and Goch: 17 kilometres. The population size of the locations varies between 721 (Huelm) and 19,961 (Goch) in Germany, and 777 (Ven-Zelderheide) and 11,403 (Groesbeek) in The Netherlands. For these 10 locations we collected linguistic and social data.

Figure 3. The 10 locations on both sides of the Dutch-German state border; cross-border paired locations are connected by lines. The rightmost line is the state border.

2.1 Linguistic data

The linguistic data were collected by recording 20 respondents in the research area. In each of the 10 locations two dialect speakers (one younger and one older speaker) that spoke their dialect on a daily basis were asked to give their dialect words (nouns) for a list of a hundred concepts related to everyday life. We only used the data from the 10 older speakers (> 60 years) since these data are expected to be closer to typical dialect speech and less likely to have been influenced by the standard languages of the two areas (Dutch and German) (cf. Giesbers, 2008). The list of concepts we used was developed by Van Bezooijen to measure lexical and phonetic-phonological variation between closely related (Germanic) language varieties (cf. Heeringa, Nerbonne, Van Bezooijen and Spruit, 2007).

The recordings were transcribed on a detailed phonetic level. Table 1 shows an example of the phonetic transcriptions. It shows the pronunciation for the concept *aardappel* ('potato') as realised by the older respondent of the location

124

Table 1. Example of the phonetic transcriptions used.

Location	Concept	Phonetic transcription
Gennep (> 60 yrs)	Aardappel	ERdAp@l

Gennep. The transcription system used was a combination of German and Dutch X-SAMPA.

Many subtle differences were transcribed, such as the voicing of fricatives, differences in place and manner in [r] pronunciations and the height, rounding and length of vowels. The frequency of each phoneme and phoneme cluster in the dataset was representative for the range of sounds in the dialect speech (cf. Giesbers, 2008).

2.2 Social data

The social data were collected using a questionnaire that was filled in by 268 respondents from the 10 locations in the research area. The respondents belonged to two age groups (i.e., 30–40 years, 60 years and over) and they were balanced for age and gender. The respondents were recruited through a regional Dutch and a regional German newspaper. Both newspapers published an article about the research project together with the questionnaire. Of the 340 informants that returned the questionnaire, 268 also met the selection criteria: they grew up in the location where they were living today and they spoke the local dialect.

Respondents were asked to indicate and rank in which locations they had friends and family and where they went shopping. These three types of data give information on the degree of social contact between the locations in the area. Respondents were asked to name and rank order 10 locations for friends and family, and five for shopping locations.

3. METHODOLOGY AND RESULTS

We first obtained geographic distances and distances for the linguistic and social data to test the three models. Next, we performed Multi-Dimensional Scaling on the distances and plotted the two-dimensional result. We also plotted the distances after transforming them to a similar scale. By visually comparing the plots to each other we can interpret the explanatory power of the three models. To compare the different distance topologies (Pearson product-moment) correlations were also used. Finally, the three models were tested statistically using regression analysis.

3.1 The continuum model versus the gap model

We used a Dutch route planner website by the *Dutch* Automobile Association ('ANWB') to obtain geographic distances. The geographic distances obtained

Table 2. Range and mean for the geographic distances.

	Dutch	German	Dutch–German
Range	4.90–22.00	3.70–26.10	3.40–20.00
Mean	12.14	12.98	10.25

were not distances 'as the crow flies' but the shortest travel distance when following the normal road infrastructure. Travel distances are not equal to distances 'as the crow flies' and Gooskens (2005) for instance notes that in Norway they can be quite different because of the mountainous characteristics of the country. In our research area, however, there are no natural borders and the travel distances we obtained are quite comparable to distances 'as the crow flies'. The longest geographic distance in our data set is the distance between Groesbeek and Huelm; 26.1 kilometres. The smallest geographic distance is between Goch and Huelm; 3.4 kilometres.

The locations were selected in such a way that they were geographically balanced, but the border may have had an effect on the actual connectedness between locations. To validate our sample we looked at the Dutch, the German and the Dutch-German distances separately. Table 2 shows the range and mean for the three types of geographic distances. The distances are evenly distributed over the three groups of locations and no significant differences were found (F $(2.42) = 0.787$, p $= 0.462$).

We used the Levenshtein method (Kruskal, 1983) to obtain linguistic distances. The Levenshtein method computes linguistic distances between locations based on all pairs of phonetic transcriptions (strings). The distance between the two phonetic transcriptions involved is calculated on the basis of the minimum number of operations needed for string A to be transformed into string B. The three types of operations permitted are insertion, deletion or substitution of characters.

We calculated Cronbach's Alpha (Cronbach, 1951) with the dialectometric software RuG/L04 to make sure that the number of words used is a sufficient basis for the Levenshtein analysis. With Cronbach's Alpha we can measure the minimum reliability of our Levenshtein distance measurements when applied to our dataset. In the social sciences values higher than 0.70 are considered sufficient (Nunnally, 1978). Cronbach's Alpha was 0.93 for our dataset of a hundred concepts.

Next, we used RuG/L04 to compute the linguistic distances with the Levenshtein method. We used the simplest version of the method in which phonetic overlap is binary: non-identical phones contribute to phonetic distance, identical ones do not. No feature-based segment distance table was used and no weights were assigned to the different types of operations. The RuG/L04

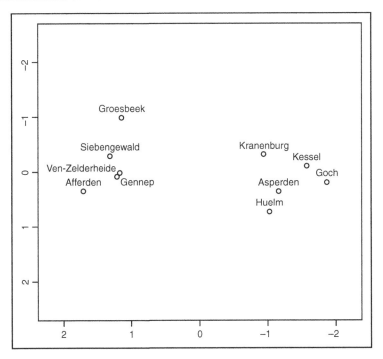

Figure 4. Two-dimensional MDS plot of the linguistic distances.

software was used to obtain a 10 by 10 dissimilarity matrix for the locations. The diagonal of this matrix is always zero and only half of the matrix is used since the lower half is the mirror image of the upper half.

To test the continuum model we first performed Multi-Dimensional Scaling (MDS) on the distances. Point sets are projected and visualised in two-dimensional space with MDS (see for instance Nerbonne, Heeringa and Kleiweg, 1999; Spruit, 2008). The MDS analysis on the linguistic distances (Alscal) gave a nearly perfect two-dimensional solution (Stress = 0.050, RSQ = 0.990). Both the x-axis and the y-axis are mirrored in this plot, depicted in Figure 4, to make it easier to visually compare the result of the analysis to the topology of the distances 'as the crow flies' depicted in Figure 3. The topology of the linguistic distances is clearly different from the geographic distances 'as the crow flies'.

The most remarkable outcome is that distances between locations within the *same* country are always (much) smaller than distances between locations that are in *different* countries. The continuum model does not apply to the linguistic distances. It is the gap model that seems to give the required topology.

Table 3. Correlation values for linguistic distance and the three types of location pairs; one-tailed p values.

	Geographic distance *Dutch (N = 10)*	Geographic distance *German (N = 10)*	Geographic distance *Dutch-German (N = 25)*
Linguistic distance	0.495 (p = 0.073)	0.577 (p = 0.041)	0.098 (p = 0.321)

To investigate the topological structures and their relations in more detail we also calculated the correlations between the geographic and the linguistic distances for all 45 pairs of locations. The continuum model predicts a high correlation, the gap model no correlation at all. The correlation is 0.291, with a one-tailed p value of 0.038. We opted for a one-tailed test, since the values must be positive if there is a correlation. Since the distances are not independent measurements, the probability values of the correlation coefficients were calculated using the Mantel test (Mantel, 1967). The conclusion is that the correlation is significant but low. Geographic distances hardly play a role in explaining the linguistic distances. Does this mean we have to reject the continuum model completely?

We divided the 45 location pairs into three groups to test the continuum model in more detail: 10 Dutch pairs, 10 German pairs and 25 Dutch-German pairs. The gap model predicts that the linguistic distances within Dutch-German pairs should be relatively large and constant. The linguistic distances in the Dutch pairs and in the German pairs may be arbitrary, but under the assumption of the remains of a continuum model, a relationship between geography and linguistic distance may still hold. The correlations for the three groups of pairs are given in Table 3. The correlation coefficients were calculated using a classical statistical test instead of the Mantel test because of the asymmetric nature of the three distance matrices.

The correlation for the Dutch-German location pairs is not significant. The correlations for the Dutch and German location pairs are clearly higher, although the correlation for the Dutch pairs fails to reach significance. Given the low number of location pairs, the statistical test of the correlations does not have much power to detect lower correlations.

Next, we visualised the relationship between the geographic and linguistic distances after having transformed the linguistic distances to a similar scale as the geographic distances (we used the same maximum). Standardising the scaling helps in interpreting the relationship and does not change the intrinsic structural characteristics of the distances. We now expect to find the location pairs adhering to the continuum model, in which the linguistic distance equals the geographic distance, on the diagonal. The scatter plot is given in Figure 5. The three groups of location pairs were given different symbols.

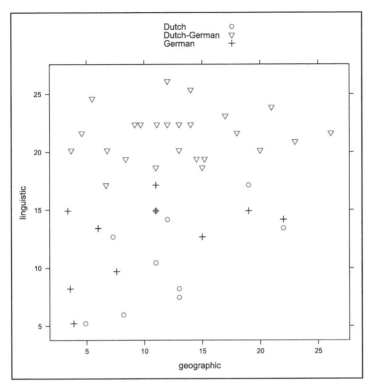

Figure 5. Linguistic distance by geographic distance for the three groups of location pairs on the same scale of magnitude.

The Dutch-German pairs (the triangles) show a distinct pattern. Their geographic distance varies between 3 and 26 kilometres, but their (scaled) linguistic distance ranges from 17 to 26 kilometres. There is no further explanation for the variation within the range found. The smallest distance in the Dutch-German pairs (17) is equal to the largest distance found for the Dutch and German pairs. The gap model clearly applies to the Dutch-German pairs. The distances for the Dutch and German pairs are smaller, and they are roughly on the diagonal. For both the Dutch pairs and the German pairs the linguistic distance on average increases as the geographic distance increases. This relationship was also reflected in the higher correlation values in Table 3. The continuum model no longer applies to the whole research area, but only (moderately) to the within-country linguistic distances. Location pairs across the Dutch-German border are nowadays separated by a clear linguistic gap.

Our interpretation of the plot in Figure 5 is further corroborated by the high correlation between linguistic distance and the gap as a nominal variable

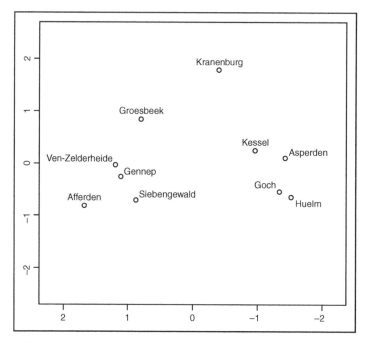

Figure 6. Two-dimensional MDS plot of the social variable friends.

(two locations are separated by the border, yes or no): 0.850 (N = 45, p = 0.000). Looking at the strong division between the Dutch-German location pairs and the Dutch or German location pairs in Figure 5, this high correlation was to be expected. When entering both the gap and geographic distance in a (linear) regression analysis, the effect of geographic distance turns out to be not significant, even when we use a one-tailed test. Our conclusion is that we need to reject the continuum model and accept the gap model.

3.2 *The gap model versus the social model*

Can other types of data tell us more about the linguistic structure in the Kleverlandish area? In this section we test the social model to see if it has more explanatory power than the gap model. We used the social data Giesbers (2008) collected about friends, family, and shopping for this. In these data no effect was found for the respondent variables *gender* and *age*. The weighted data were computed per location and three separate 10 by 10 dissimilarity matrices were obtained for each of the social variables. MDS returned excellent results for a two-dimensional representation for all three variables. The two-dimensional

Table 4. Correlation values for linguistic distance and the distance for shopping, family or friends; one-tailed p values.

	Shopping distance (N = 45)	Family distance (N = 45)	Friends distance (N = 45)
Linguistic distance	0.623 (p = 0.001)	0.737 (p = 0.001)	0.818 (p = 0.000)

MDS results for *friends* (Stress = 0.070, RSQ = 0.972) are given in Figure 6. Again we mirrored the x-axis.

The plot in Figure 6 shows that the general topology for *friends* resembles the MDS plot for the linguistic distances depicted in Figure 4. Next, we checked the correlations for linguistic distance and each of the three social variables. The correlations can be found in Table 4. Again we used the Mantel test to determine their statistical significance.

The social variable *friends* shows the strongest correlation, but the correlation for the other two variables is also clearly present. Linguistic distance is not a property on its own, but is embedded in the social structure of the research area.

To get a more detailed picture of the relationship between the variable *friends* and linguistic distance, we used the same visualisation method as applied in Figure 5. This time, we scaled up both the *friends* distances and the linguistic distances to the same maximum value of the geographic distances. Next, we plotted the relation between the *friends* distances and the linguistic distances in Figure 7, for the three groups of pairs: Dutch, German and Dutch-German.

Figure 7 shows that all location pairs are on the diagonal this time, although the relationship is not perfect, but scattered. The diagonal pattern applies to all three groups of pairs. This means that the two variables really share a similar configuration or topology. Figure 7 supports our finding that the linguistic distances appear to belong to an overarching socio-geographic pattern that has developed in the research area over the last two centuries.

A regression analysis was also performed to see if a combination of social variables gives an even better result. However, no better model could be found. The simple model in which *friends* is the only explanatory variable still gave the best result. We also entered both *friends* and geographic distances in a (linear) regression analysis. The effect of geographic distance here turned out not to be significant.

The explanatory power of the gap model (explained variance: 0.723) is higher than that of the social model (explained variance: 0.668). However, the difference between the two models is not big enough to make a final choice for one of them. Combining the two variables in a regression analysis returned a better model with a higher amount of explained variance (0.781). Both variables are significant, although the strongest predictor is the gap variable. This is

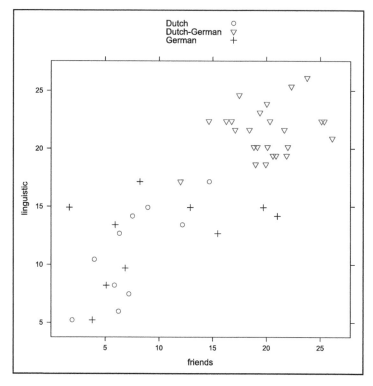

Figure 7. Linguistic distance by friends distance for the three groups of location pairs on the same scale of magnitude.

not surprising since the correlation value for the gap was higher. Explaining linguistic distance in the Kleverlandish area clearly requires combining the assumption of a gap and data about the social structure of the area.

4. DISCUSSION AND CONCLUSIONS

In this paper we tested three models to explain the pattern of linguistic variation in a sub-area of today's Kleverlandish dialect area: the continuum model, the gap model and the social model. We first compared the continuum model to the gap model and concluded that the continuum model nowadays no longer applies to the whole research area. It applies only moderately to the within-country locations. The gap model explains the linguistic distances between the cross-border pairs of locations very precisely. There, the state border has become the main determinant of the linguistic distances, overshadowing remaining differences and patterns of dialect variation. Next, we checked to see if the social model had more explanatory power. We therefore looked at contact data about friends, relatives and shopping places and found that linguistic distance nowadays is embedded in the socio-geographic structure of the research area. Especially the friends data very much resembled the linguistic data. Combining the gap model and the social model turned out to be the most successful way to explain the linguistic distances. Clearly, the dialect variation in our research area is closely related to the existence of the state border and to the social structure of the area. The geographic spatial configuration hardly plays a role anymore.

We have shown that political and social contact variables nowadays are more important than geography in explaining the topological structure for linguistic variation in our research area. The pattern of linguistic variation that existed about 200 years ago in the Kleverlandish area was the result of human contact. Without natural or political borders or dominant population centres, the Kleverlandish dialect area developed into a dialect continuum in which linguistic distance was closely related to geography. The cohesive social system between locations across the state border diverged after the establishment of the state border in the area in 1830, and as a result, so did the dialect variation. Others have also pointed at the importance of such political and social variables (cf. Bailey, Wikle, Tillery and Sand, 1993; Boberg, 2000; Horvath and Horvath, 2001). What other variables might help to come to a better understanding of the topological structure of linguistic variation? Giesbers (2008) shows that the divergence of dialect variation in the Kleverlandish area was further stimulated by the influence the two standard language varieties, Dutch and German, had on the dialects. Gooskens (2005) points at the influence mass media and demographic factors like migration and immigration might have on the spreading of linguistic variables. Also, social contact data about mobility and telecommunication possibilities could be helpful.

ACKNOWLEDGEMENTS

The authors would like to thank Janienke Sturm, Joanne van Emmerik and three anonymous reviewers for their valuable comments on previous versions of this paper.

REFERENCES

G. Bailey, T. Wikle, J. Tillery and L. Sand (1993), 'Some patterns of linguistic diffusion', *Language Variation and Change*, 3(3), 241–264.

L. Bloomfield (1933), *Language* (New York).

C. Boberg (2000), 'Geolinguistic diffusion and the U.S.-Canada border', *Language Variation and Change*, 12(1), 1–24.

J. K. Chambers and P. Trudgill (1998), *Dialectology* (Cambridge).

G. Cornelissen (2003), *Kleine Niederrheinische Sprachgeschichte (1300–1900): eine regionale Sprachgeschichte für das deutsch-niederländische Grenzgebiet zwischen Arnheim und Krefeld* (Geldern – Venray).

133

L. J. Cronbach (1951), 'Coefficient alpha and the internal structure of tests', *Psychometrika*, 16, 297–334.

F. De Vriend, J. P. Kunst, L. Ten Bosch, C. Giesbers and R. Van Hout (2008), 'Evaluating the relationship between linguistic and geographic distances using a 3D visualization', *Proceedings of the sixth international conference on language resources and evaluation* (Marrakech), 2212–2215.

C. Giesbers, R. Van Hout and R. Van Bezooijen (2006), 'De geografische en perceptieve afstand tussen dialecten: de rol van de staatsgrens in het Kleverlandse dialectcontinuüm', *Artikelen van de vijfde sociolinguïstische conferentie* (Delft), 175–186.

C. Giesbers (2008), 'Dialecten op de grens van twee talen. Een dialectologisch en sociolinguïstisch onderzoek in het Kleverlands dialectcontinuüm' (Ph.D. thesis, Radboud University Nijmegen).

C. Gooskens, Charlotte (2005). 'Traveling time as a predictor of linguistic distance', *Dialectologia et Geolinguistica*, 13, 38–62.

G. Hard (1972), 'Ein geographisches Simulationsmodell für die rheinische Sprachgeschichte', in E. Essen and G. Wiegelmann, eds, *Festschrift Matthias Zender, Studien zur Volkskultur, Sprache und Landesgeschichte* (Bonn), 5–29.

W. Heeringa, J. Nerbonne, H. Niebaum, R. Nieuweboer and P. Kleiweg (2000), 'Dutch-German contact in and around Bentheim. Languages in Contact', *Studies in Slavic and General Linguistics*, 28, 145–156.

W. Heeringa (2004), 'Measuring dialect pronunciation differences using Levenshtein distance' (Ph.D. thesis, Rijksuniversiteit Groningen).

W. Heeringa, J. Nerbonne, R. Van Bezooijen and M. Spruit (2007), 'Geografie en inwoneraantallen als verklarende factoren voor variatie in het Nederlandse dialectgebied', *Nederlandse Taal- en Letterenkunde*, 123(1), 70–82.

F. Hinskens, J. L. Kallen and J. Taeldeman (2000), 'Dialect convergence and divergence across European borders', *International Journal of the Sociology of Language*, 145.

B. M. Horvath and R. J. Horvath (2001), 'A multilocality study of a sound change in progress: The case of /l/ vocalization in New Zealand and Australian English', *Language Variation and Change*, 13(1), 37–57.

L. Kremer (1984), 'Die niederländisch-deutsche Staatsgrenze als subjektive Dialektgrenze', *Driemaandelijkse Bladen*, 36, 76–83.

L. Kremer (1990), 'Kontinuum oder Bruchstelle? Zur Entwicklung der Grenzdialekte zwischen Niederrhein und Vechtegebiet', in L. Kremer and H. Niebaum, eds, *Grenzdialekte. Studien zur Entwicklung kontinentalwestgermanischer Dialektkontinua* (Hildesheim, Zürich and New York), 85–123.

J. B. Kruskal (1983), 'An overview of sequence comparison: time warps, string edits, and macromolecules', *SIAM Rev.*, 25, 201–237.

N. Mantel (1967), 'The detection of disease clustering and a generalized regression approach', *Cancer Research*, 27, 209–220.

J. Nerbonne, W. Heeringa and P. Kleiweg (1999), 'Edit Distance and Dialect Proximity', in D. Sankoff and J. B. Kruskal, eds, *Time Warps, String Edits and Macromolecules: The Theory and Practice of Sequence Comparison* (Stanford), 5–15.

H. Niebaum (1990), 'Staatsgrenze als Bruchstelle? Die Grenzdialekte zwischen Dollart und Vechtegebiet', in L. Kremer and H. Niebaum, eds, *Grenzdialekte. Studien zur Entwicklung kontinentalwestgermanischer Dialektkontinua* (Hildesheim, Zürich and New York), 49–83.

J. Nunnally (1978), *Psychometric theory* (New York).

RuG/L04, Software for dialectometrics and cartography. http://www.let.rug.nl/ kleiweg/L04/.

M. Spruit (2008), 'Quantitative perspectives on syntactic variation in Dutch dialects' (Ph.D. thesis, University of Amsterdam).

P. Trudgill (1974), 'Linguistic change and diffusion: Description and explanation in sociolinguistic dialect geography', *Language in Society*, 2, 215–246.

THE SPACE OF TUSCAN DIALECTAL VARIATION:
A CORRELATION STUDY

SIMONETTA MONTEMAGNI

Abstract   *The paper illustrates the results of a correlation study focusing on linguistic variation in an Italian region, Tuscany. By exploiting a multi-level representation scheme of dialectal data, the study analyses attested patterns of phonetic and morpho-lexical variation with the aim of testing the degree of correlation between a) phonetic and morpho-lexical variation, and b) linguistic variation and geographic distance. The correlation analysis was performed by combining two complementary approaches proposed in dialectometric literature, namely by computing both global and place-specific correlation measures and by inspecting their spatial distribution. Achieved results demonstrate that phonetic and morpho-lexical variations in Tuscany seem to follow a different pattern than encountered in previous studies.*

I. INTRODUCTION

It is a well-known fact that different types of features contribute to the linguistic distance between any two locations, which can differ for instance with respect to the word used to denote the same object or the phonetic realisation of a particular word. Yet, the correlation between different feature types in defining patterns of dialectal variation represents an area of research still unexplored. In traditional dialectology, there is no obvious way to approach this matter beyond fairly superficial and impressionistic observations. The situation changes if the same research question is addressed in the framework of dialectometric studies, where it is possible to measure dialectal distances with respect to distinct linguistic levels and to compute whether and to what extent observed distances correlate. Another related question concerns the influence of geography on

International Journal of Humanities and Arts Computing 2 (1–2) 2008, 135–152
DOI: 10.3366/E1753854809000354
© Edinburgh University Press and the Association for History and Computing 2009

linguistic variation. Answering this question can help to shed light on whether observed correlations among linguistic levels should instead be interpreted as a separate effect of the underlying geography. Over the last years, both Groningen and Salzurg schools of dialectometry have been engaged in providing answers to these questions from different perspectives and working with different data from various languages. Concerning the former, it is worth mentioning the contributions by Nerbonne (2003), Gooskens and Heeringa (2006) and Spruit *et al.* (in press); the latter is represented by the 'correlative dialectometry' studies of Goebl (2005; 2008). In both cases, this appears to be a promising line of research.

The main goal of this study is to gain insight into the nature of linguistic variation by investigating the degree to which a) patterns of dialectal variation computed with respect to different linguistic levels correlate in the language varieties spoken in Tuscany (a region which has a special status in the complex puzzle of linguistic variation in Italy),[1] and b) linguistic patterns of variation correlate with geographic distance. The study was performed on the corpus of dialectal data *Atlante Lessicale Toscano* ('Lexical Atlas of Tuscany', henceforth ALT), by combining complementary approaches proposed in the dialectometric literature: two dialectometric software packages have been used, namely RUG/L04 developed by P. Kleiweg and VDM by E. Haimerl.[2] The starting point is represented by the results of a dialectometric study focusing on phonetic and lexical variation in Tuscany (Montemagni, 2007). By exploiting a multi-level representation scheme of dialectal data, the linguistic distances among the investigated locations were measured with respect to different linguistic levels. Correlational analyses were then performed on the resulting distance matrices in order to estimate the degree of association between the different levels and to evaluate the role played by geography in explaining observed correlations.

2. THE DATA SOURCE

2.1 The Atlante Lessicale Toscano

ALT is a regional linguistic atlas focusing on dialectal variation throughout Tuscany, a region where both Tuscan and non-Tuscan dialects are spoken; the latter is the case of dialects in the north, namely Lunigiana and small areas of the Apennines (so-called Romagna Toscana), which rather belong to the group of Gallo-Italian dialects. ALT interviews were carried out in 224 localities of Tuscany, with 2,193 informants selected with respect to a number of parameters ranging from age and socio-economic status to education and culture. The interviews were conducted by a group of trained fieldworkers who employed a questionnaire of 745 target items, designed to elicit variation mainly in vocabulary, semantics and phonetics. A dialectal corpus with these features lends itself to investigations concerning geographic or horizontal (diatopic) variation as well as social or vertical (diastratic) variation: in this study we will focus on the diatopic dimension of linguistic variation. ALT, originally published in the year 2000 (Giacomelli *et al.*, 2000) as a CD-Rom, is now available as an on-line resource, ALT-Web[3].

2.2 *ALT-Web representation of dialectal data*

In ALT, all dialectal items were phonetically transcribed.[4] In order to ensure a proper treatment of these data, an articulated encoding schema was devised in ALT-Web in which all dialectal items are assigned different levels of representation: a first level rendering the original phonetic transcription as recorded by fieldworkers; other levels containing representations encoded in standard Italian orthography. In this multi-level representation scheme, dialectal data are encoded in layers of progressively decreasing detail going from phonetic transcription to different levels of orthographic representations eventually abstracting away from details of the speakers' phonetic realisation.[5]

For the specific concerns of this study, we will focus on the following representation levels: phonetic transcription (henceforth, PT) and normalised representation (henceforth, NR) where the latter is the representation level meant to abstract away from within-Tuscany vital phonetic variation. At the NR level a wide range of phonetic variants is assigned the same normalised form: e.g. words such as [skjaˈttʃata], [skjaˈttʃaθa], [skjaˈttʃada], [skjaˈttʃaða], [stjaˈttʃata], [stjaˈttʃaθa], [stjaˈttʃada], [stjaˈttʃaða], [stʃaˈssɛda] etc. (denoting a traditional type of bread, flat and crispy, seasoned on top with salt and oil) are all assigned the same normalised form, SCHIACCIATA. Note that at this level neutralisation is only concerned with phonetic variants resulting from productive phonetic processes: this is the case, for instance, of variants involving spirantisation or voicing of plosives like /t/, as in [skjaˈttʃaθa] and [skjaˈttʃada]. On the contrary, there are word forms like [ˈkaʎʎo] and [ˈgaʎʎo] (meaning 'rennet') which are assigned distinct NRs, CAGLIO and GAGLIO respectively: this follows from the fact that the [k] vs [g] alternation in word-initial context represents a no longer productive phonetic process in Tuscany. It should also be noted that the NR level does not deal with morphological variation (neither inflectional nor derivational). This entails that words such as [skjaˈttʃata] (singular) and [skjaˈttʃate] (plural) as well as [skjattʃaˈtina] (diminutive) are all assigned different NFs. Currently, NR is the most abstract representation level in ALT-Web.

3. INDUCTION OF PATTERNS OF PHONETIC AND LEXICAL VARIATION

3.1 *Building the experimental data sets*

The representation scheme illustrated in section 2.2 proved to be particularly suitable for dialectometric analyses of dialectal data at various linguistic description levels.

First, patterns of phonetic and lexical variation could be studied with respect to different representation levels, providing orthogonal perspectives on the same set of dialectal data. In particular, the study of phonetic variation was based on PTs, whereas NRs were used as a basis for the investigation on lexical variation.

Second, the alignment of the representation levels was used to automatically extract all attested phonetic variants of the same normalised word form (henceforth, NF). In practice, the various phonetic realisations of the same lexical unit were identified by selecting all phonetically transcribed dialectal items sharing the same NF. Since the ALT-Web NR level does not abstract away from either morphological variation or no longer productive phonetic processes, we can be quite sure that phonetic distances calculated against phonetic variants of the same NF testify vital phonetic processes only, without influence from any other linguistic description level (e.g. morphology).

The experimental data used for the study of phonetic variation was thus formed by the normalised forms attested in the ALT corpus, each associated with the set of its phonetically transcribed variants; this is exemplified in the first two columns of Table 1 for the normalised form SCHIACCIATA. For the study of lexical variation we instead used ALT onomasiological questions (i.e. those looking for the attested lexicalisations of the same concept) with their associated normalised answers; this is exemplified in the last two columns of Table 1 in which the NFs collected as answers to the question n. 290 'schiacciata' are reported.

3.2 Measuring linguistic distances in Tuscany

3.2.1 Methodology

The linguistic distances across the locations of the ALT geographic network were calculated with the Levenshtein Distance measure (henceforth, LD), a string-distance measure originally used by Kessler (1995) as a means of calculating the distance between the phonetic realisations of corresponding words in different dialects. Kessler showed that with LD it is possible to 'reliably group a language into its dialect areas, starting from nothing more than phonetic transcriptions as commonly found in linguistic surveys' (Kessler, 1995:66). The LD between two strings is given by the minimum number of operations needed to transform one string into the other; the transformation is performed through basic operations (namely the deletion or the insertion of a string character, or the substitution of one character for another), each of which is associated a cost.

With LD, comparing two dialectal varieties results in the mean distance of all performed word-pair comparisons. The use of LD in calculating the linguistic distance between language varieties was further extended and improved by Nerbonne *et al.* (1999) and Heeringa (2004) who worked on different languages and with different representation types (i.e. phone-based, feature-based and acoustic representations). In these dialectal studies based on LD, the standard

Table 1. Excerpts from the experimental data sets used for the study of phonetic and lexical variation.

	NF = SCHIACCIATA		question = n. 290 'schiacciata' (traditional type of bread, flat and crispy, seasoned on top with salt and oil)	
Location	Phonetic realisation		Location	Normalised answer(s)
15 Vergemoli	[scaˈttʃata]		15 Vergemoli	FOCACCIA, FOCACCINA, **SCHIACCIATA**
16 Pieve Fosciana	[scaˈttʃada]		16 Pieve Fosciana	FOCACCIA, **SCHIACCIATA**
18 San Pellegrino in Alpe	[scaˈttʃata], [stʲaˈttʃata]		17 Barga	FOCACCIA
19 Brandeglio	[scaˈttʃaθa], [stʲaˈttʃaθa]		18 San Pellegrino in Alpe	FOCACCIA, PATTONA, **SCHIACCIATA**
22 Prunetta	[stʲaˈttʃaθa]		19 Brandeglio	FOCACCIA, SCHIACCIA, **SCHIACCIATA**
23 Orsigna	[skjaˈttʃaθa], [scaˈttʃaθa], [stjaˈttʃata]		20 Rivoreta	FOCACCIA
24 Spedaletto	[stjaˈttʃaθa]		21 Popiglio	SCHIACCIA
25 Castello di Sambuca	[scaˈttʃada]		22 Prunetta	**SCHIACCIATA**
28 Barberino di Mugello	[skjaˈttʃata], [stjaˈttʃata]		23 Orsigna	COFACCIA, SCHIACCIA, **SCHIACCIATA**
...			...	

measure was also refined to cope with dialectology-specific issues, dealing with: a) the normalisation of the distance measure with respect to the length of compared words (Nerbonne *et al.*, 1999); b) the treatment of multiple responses (Nerbonne and Kleiweg, 2003).

In the present study, we use LD to calculate linguistic distances between the ALT locations:[6] the distance between each location pair is obtained by averaging the LDs calculated for individual word pairs, be they phonetic realisations of the same NF or lexicalisations of a given concept (see section 3.1). Missing dialectal items are ignored due to their uncertain origin.[7] In what follows, we will focus on issues specific to the measure of linguistic distances with the ALT data.

3.2.2 Measuring phonetic distances

Using LD, the phonetic distance between two linguistic varieties A and B is computed by comparing the phonetic variants of NFs in A with the phonetic variants of the same NF set in B. The phonetic realisation of a given word can be represented in different ways giving rise to different approaches to the measure of phonetic distance, respectively denominated by Kessler (1995) 'phone string comparison' and 'feature string comparison'. In the former, LD operates on sequences of phonetic symbols, whereas in the latter comparison is carried out with respect to feature-based representations. Both approaches were experimented with in the study of phonetic variation in Tuscany;[8] due to the almost equivalent results achieved in the two experiments,[9] in what follows we will focus on the distance matrix calculated on the basis of phone-based representations.

The experimental data set included only NFs having at least two phonetic variants attested in at least two locations. A collection of 9,082 NFs was thus selected, with associated 32,468 phonetic variants types: within this NF set, geographical coverage ranges between 2 and 224 and phonetic variability between 2 and 34. The resulting phonetic distance matrix was built on the basis of the 206,594 phonetic variants attested as instantiations of the selected NFs. In order to assess the reliability of the data set, we calculated the coefficient Cronbach α (Heeringa, 2004:170–173) which was 0.99. This means that this data set provides a reliable basis for an analysis of phonetic differences based on LD.

The distance between the phonetic variants of the same NF in different locations was calculated on the basis of the raw LD, without any type of normalisation by the length of compared transcriptions: in this way, all sound differences add the same weight to the overall distance and are not inversely proportional to the word length as in the case of normalised distances. This choice is in line with the Heeringa *et al.* (2006) findings which notice that raw LD represents a better approximation of phonetic differences among dialects as perceived by dialect speakers than results based on normalised LD.

3.2.3 Measuring lexical distances

Whereas a study of phonetic variation based on phonetically transcribed data could only be conducted with LD, this choice is not to be taken for granted in the case of lexical distances. In fact, in the pioneering research by Seguy (1971) and Goebl (1984) the comparison between any two sites is performed starting from the proportion of shared answers to a given questionnaire item and of those which differ. Yet, it is often the case that answers elicited from informants are different forms of the same lexical item: typically, they are inflectional or derivational variants of the same lemma. Moreover, they can also include diacronically (e.g. etymologically) related words. By adopting a binary notion of lexical distance, related but different lexical items are treated as completely unrelated answers. To overcome this problem, in their study of lexical variation in LAMSAS Nerbonne and Kleiweg (2003) applied LD to measure also the lexical distance of the answers on the basis of the encouraging results previously obtained in the study of phonetic variation. With LD, related lexical items are no longer treated as irrelated answers and their partial similarity is taken into account.[10]

We felt that the use of LD for measuring lexical distances was also appropriate in the ALT case. This choice appears even more crucial if we consider the type of representation of dialectal data we are dealing with. Although we are using previously normalised dialectal forms, we have seen that this representation level does not abstract away from morphological variation or from no longer productive phonetic processes. To keep with the SCHIACCIATA example, the questionnaire item meant to gather lexicalisations of the concept of this traditional type of bread includes answers both in the singular and in the plural forms (e.g. *schiacciatina* vs *schiacciatine*), gender variants (e.g. *schiaccino*-masculine vs *schiaccina*-feminine), as well as derivationally related variants such as *schiaccia*, *schiaccina* and *schiacciata* or multi-word expressions like *schiacciata unta* (lit. SCHIACCIATA with oil) or *schiacciata al sale* (lit. salted SCHIACCIATA). At the NR level, all these forms still represent distinct answers. By resorting to LD, their relatedness can be accounted for in the measure of lexical distance.[11]

The present study of lexical variation in Tuscany is based on the entire set of ALT onomasiological questions (see section 3.1), namely 460 questionnaire items which gathered a total of 39,761 normalised answer types geographically distributed into 227,555 tokens. In this case, the coefficient Cronbach α was 0.97, showing that this was a sufficient basis for a reliable analysis.

Lexical distances were measured using LD operating on NFs. Given the features peculiar to the NR level, the resulting measure of lexical distance has to be seen as reflecting patterns of morphological variation as well, especially for what concerns derivation. For this reason, from now on we will refer to the distances computed against NFs as 'morpho-lexical distances'. Differently from the phonetic distance computation, here it makes sense to normalise LD so that it is independent from the length of compared words (as suggested in Nerbonne *et al.*, 1999). This choice follows from the fact that in the study of lexical variation words are to be considered as the linguistic units with respect to which the distance computation is performed.

4. LINGUISTIC AND GEOGRAPHIC DISTANCES: WITHIN AND BETWEEN CORRELATIONS

4.1 Methodology

Following Heeringa and Nerbonne (2001), the phonetic and morpho-lexical distance matrices were explored with complementary techniques, namely agglomerative hierarchical clustering and multidimensional scaling: the results of this study are reported in Montemagni (2007). Here it suffices to say that the iconic profiles of phonetic and morpho-lexical variation are visually quite different. Besides the borders identifying non-Tuscan dialects from Lunigiana and Romagna Toscana, proposed phonetic and morpho-lexical dialectal subdivisions do not overlap. This fact needs further investigation aimed at exploring the reasons underlying this state of affairs. In particular, two research questions need to be addressed:

a) whether and to what extent observed patterns of phonetic and morpho-lexical variation are associated with one another;

b) whether and to what extent phonetic and morpho-lexical distances correlate with geographic distance. In particular, if this turns out to be the case, we need to investigate whether they correlate with geography in the same way.

Following Nerbonne (2003), Goebl (2005), Gooskens (2005), Gooskens and Heeringa (2006) and Spruit *et al.* (in press), the correlation between the distances observed at different linguistic levels on the one hand and between linguistic and geographic distances on the other hand is calculated in terms of the Pearson's correlation coefficient. Two approaches can be recognised in the dialectometric correlation literature:

1. the correlation is measured with respect to the whole place x place matrix, thus providing a global measure of whether and to what extent the distance matrices are correlated: this is the approach followed in the Groningen school of dialectometry;

2. the correlation is calculated separately for each of the investigated locations giving rise to place-specific measures which can then be visualised on a map highlighting the areas characterised by similar correlation patterns; this corresponds to the 'correlative dialectometry' by Goebl (2005).

Interestingly enough, the two approaches complement each other nicely, providing at the same time global and place-specific correlation measures; in this study of Tuscan dialectal variation, both approaches are experimented with.

For the specific concerns of this study, we will focus on Tuscan dialects only, i.e. on the 213 out of the 224 ALT locations where Tuscan dialects are spoken.

4.2 Correlation between phonetic and morpho-lexical distances

By focussing on Tuscan dialects only, the global correlation between phonetic and morpho-lexical distances turns out to be 0.4125, with only 17 per cent of explained variance. This situation is not reflected in the analyses of Tuscan dialects by the main scholar of Tuscan dialectology – Giannelli (2000) – whose proposed subdivision seems to result from the combination of phonetic, phonemic, morpho-syntactic and lexical features.

This global correlation value suggests that within Tuscan-speaking localities it can often be the case that two dialects differ at the level of phonetic features but still have a common vocabulary, or the other way around. In order to check whether and most importantly where this is the case, following the correlative dialectometry approach by Goebl (2005) phonetic/morpho-lexical correlation scores have been calculated separately for each of the investigated locations and then projected on a map: the result is shown in Figure 1.

Following Goebl (2005), the distance values (*dist*) obtained with LD were converted into proximity values (*prox*) with the formula $dist + prox = 100$. For each site, obtained phonetic and morpho-lexical proximity values were correlated showing a variability range from 0.17 to 0.74: in the map, the correlation values are organised into 6 intervals according to the MINMWMAX visualisation algorithm (Goebl, 2006), where intervals 1–3 and 4–6 gather correlation values respectively below and above the arithmetic mean. The resulting spatial distribution is quite interesting: the darker zones of the map (intervals 5 and 6) indicate those areas in which phonetic variation is in lock-step with morpo-lexical variation. This happens to be the case in the area around Florence (identified in the map by the white polygon), expanding in all directions, in particular west and south. This 'harmony' between phonetic and morpho-lexical variation progressively fades in the areas corresponding to intervals from 4 to 1. It is interesting to note that these results are in line with the dialectometric study of the Italian AIS atlas by Goebl (2008:55) who records relatively low phonetics-vocabulary correlation values in the peripheral areas of Tuscany.

4.3 Correlation between linguistic and geographical distances

Before drawing any conclusion, we need to take into account a third factor, geography. How much of the observed linguistic variation can be accounted

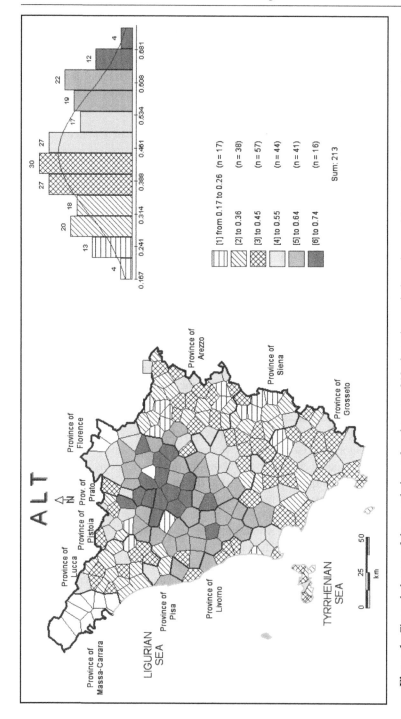

Figure 1. Choropleth map of the correlation values between 213 phonetic proximity values and 213 morpho-lexical proximity values. Proximity = 100-distance. Algorithm of visualisation: MINMWMAX (6-tuple). Software: VDM.

Table 2. Global correlation between geographic and linguistic distances.

	Correlation (r)	Explained variance (r² * 100)
Geographic vs phonetic distances	0.1358	1.8%
Geographic vs morpho-lexical distances	0.6441	41.0%

for by the underlying geography? In previous dialectometric correlation studies, geography has been shown to correlate strongly with variation at different linguistic levels within the same language (Heeringa and Nerbonne, 2001, Spruit *et al.*, in press). This appears to hold true, with some significant differences due to the underlying geography (see below), also for other languages such as Norwegian (Gooskens, 2005). Let us consider whether this is the case for Tuscany as well.

Table 2 reports observed correlations for the 213 Tuscan-speaking localities between geographical distances[12] on the one hand and phonetic and morpho-lexical distances on the other hand; note that all computed correlation coefficients are significant with $p = 0.0001$. The results show that the differences observed at the morpho-lexical level are more strongly associated with geographic distances ($r = 0.6441$) than variation at the phonetic level ($r = 0.1358$). The percentages in the rightmost column indicate the amount of variation at the specified linguistic level which can be explained with geographical distance. Interestingly enough, it turned out that only 1.8 per cent of phonetic variation can be explained with geographical distance.

Tuscany presents quite a peculiar situation concerning the correlation of linguistic variation with geography, which differs in two different respects from what has been observed in the dialectometric literature so far. Consider first the association between phonetic and geographic variation: different correlations were observed in the literature, going from $r = 0.67$ in the case of Dutch (Nerbonne *et al.*, 1996) to a significantly lower value, i.e. $r = 0.22$, in the case of Norwegian (Gooskens, 2005). Gooskens (2005) explains such a different correlation as the impact of geography on dialect variation in Norway, where the central mountain range prevented direct travel until recently: she found out that in Norway travel time is correlated more strongly with linguistic distance than linear geographic distance.

Consider now the second peculiar aspect of Tuscan dialectal variation with respect to geography. Spruit *et al.* (in press) report the correlation observed for Dutch between distances at different linguistic levels and geography: such a correlation appears to be quite high and constant across all levels taken into account, namely pronunciation ($r = 0.68$), syntax ($r = 0.66$) and lexicon ($r = 0.57$). The authors take these results to confirm the fundamental postulate in dialectology that language varieties are structured geographically (Nerbonne and Kleiweg, 2007). This does not appear to be the case in Tuscany where significantly different correlations are recorded across distinct levels of linguistic description; because of this, the low phonetics/geography correlation observed in Tuscany cannot be explained in terms of the underlying geography.

Following the correlative dialectometry approach of Goebl, the correlation between linguistic proximity values and geographic proximity values was computed for each site. The results are summarised in Figure 2, with the left map focussing on the spatial distribution of phonetic vs geographic proximity correlation and the right one on morpho-lexical vs geographic proximity correlation. By comparing the variability range in the two maps, it can be observed that the situation differs significantly. Whereas in the case of the phonetics/geography correlation it goes from -0.35 to 0.59, in the case of morpho-lexical variation the correlation values are higher and characterised by a narrower variation span (oscillating from 0.32 to 0.83). Interestingly, the phonetics-geography variation range of intervals 5–6 (0.33–0.59) covers approximately the variation span of intervals 1–3 (0.32–0.64) in the case of the morpho-lexical/geography correlation. The spatial distribution of phonetics/geography correlation values (Figure 2, left map) follows a pattern similar to what has been observed in Figure 1. Again, the darker zones of the map (intervals 5 and 6), marking those areas in which phonetic and geographic proximity are 'in tune', are located in the area around Florence, expanding south-west down to the coast; the surrounding areas, corresponding to intervals from 4 to 1, are characterised by progressively lower correlation scores. Again, these results are in line with Goebl (2008:54–55), whose linguistics vs geography correlation maps (namely maps 23, 24 and 25) characterise Tuscany as having low correlation scores, especially in the northern part.

4.4 Discussion

The Tuscan situation can be summarised as follows. Phonetic and morpho-lexical variation patterns do not correlate strongly ($r = 0.4125$); the correlation between phonetic and geographic distances is much lower ($r = 0.1358$), differing significantly from the correlation between morpho-lexical distances and geography which appears to be considerably higher ($r = 0.6441$). Due to this combined evidence, we cannot explain the low correlation between phonetic and geographical distances in terms of the underlying geography of Tuscany as hypothesised in the case of Norway. Rather, the different correlation with respect to geography seems to suggest that phonetic and morpho-lexical variation in Tuscany is regulated by distinct patterns of linguistic diffusion.

Morpho-lexical variation in Tuscany appears to conform to the dialectological postulate that 'geographically proximate varieties tend to be more similar

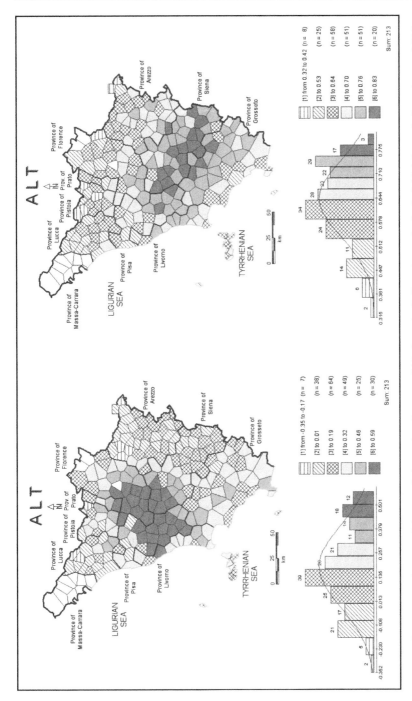

Figure 2. Choropleth maps of the correlation values between 213 phonetic (left) and morpho-lexical (right) proximity values and 213 geographic proximity values. Algorithm of visualisation: MINMWMAX (6-tuple). Software: VDM.

than distant ones' (Nerbonne and Kleiweg, 2007). On the contrary: Tuscan phonetic variation presents itself as an exception to the above mentioned dialectological postulate, since phonetic distances are not fully cumulative and there are geographically remote areas which appear to be linguistically similar (Montemagni, 2007). Tuscan phonetic variation can thus be seen as resulting from a different pattern of linguistic diffusion: we hypothesise that it is the result of 'the displacement of a formerly widespread linguistic feature by an innovation' (Chambers and Trudgill, 1998:94).

In order to test this hypothesis, a closer look at phonetic variation is necessary, especially for what concerns the linguistic properties playing a major role in determining identified patterns of phonetic variation. Current research in this direction shows that among the linguistic features playing a major role in determining identified phonetic variation patterns there appears to be spirantisation phenomena (so-called 'Tuscan gorgia').[13] Tuscan gorgia is accepted as being a local and innovative (presumably dating back to the Middle Ages) natural phonetic phenomenon (consonantal weakening) spreading from the culturally influential center of Florence in all directions, especially southward and westward. Interestingly enough, the spatial distribution of Tuscan gorgia is very close to distribution of the darker zones in Figures 1 and 2, i.e. the areas where phonetic variation appears to correlate more strongly with morpho-lexical variation (Figure 1) and geographic proximity (Figure 2, left map). The converse is also true: surrounding areas, corresponding to the zones not affected by Tuscan gorgia, show in both cases low correlation values; this means that in these areas phonetic variation is no longer aligned with neither morpho-lexical variation nor geography.

5. CONCLUSIONS

The paper reports the results of a correlation study focusing on phonetic and morpho-lexical variation in Tuscany. The study was performed on the data extracted from the entire ALT corpus. Phonetic and morpho-lexical distances among Tuscan language varieties were calculated using LD against different representation types (PT and NR respectively). The resulting distance matrices were analysed in order to test the degree of correlation between observed patterns of phonetic and morpho-lexical variation on the one hand, and between linguistic variation and geographic distances on the other hand. The correlation analysis, restricted to the Tuscan dialects area, was performed by combining the two different but complementary approaches proposed in the dialectometric literature, namely by computing both global and place-specific correlation measures and by inspecting their spatial distribution. Differently from the results of previous correlation studies, phonetic and morpho-lexical variation in Tuscany does not appear to conform to the same pattern: whereas the latter can be taken to confirm the postulate that language varieties are structured geographically, the former rather suggests that a different pattern of linguistic variation is at work, characterised by the spread of phonetic features from a core locality to neighbouring ones and by the existence of linguistically related but geographically remote areas.

The contribution of this study is twofold. From the point of view of Tuscan dialectology, it helps gain insight into the nature of diatopic variation at different linguistic description levels, a topic which to our knowledge has never been investigated so far. From a more general dialectometric perspective, one of the innovative contributions of this study consists of identifying radically different patterns of linguistic variation for different description levels with respect to the same area. Obviously, these results need further investigation in different directions. Firstly, it would be interesting to widen the range of linguistic levels taken into account to assess whether there are levels which are more closely associated than others. First experiments in this direction suggest that morphological and lexical variation are more strongly associated than phonetic variation appears to be with them. Secondly, one could extend this correlation study by considering socio-economical factors playing a role in the linguistic variation process as well. Through this, identified variation patterns could result from the complex interaction of geographic and social factors. Note that ALT could be conveniently exploited for this purpose due to the simultaneous diatopic and diastratic characterisation of its data. Last but not least, it would be interesting to apply the adopted correlation methodology to study the relationship between patterns of linguistic variation and genetic or demographic variation, hopefully leading to a deeper understanding of the role of population movements in determining dialect diversity.

ACKNOWLEDGEMENTS

I would like to thank the anonymous reviewers for their valuable comments and suggestions to improve this paper. I would like to thank John Nerbonne for his precious suggestions on previous versions of this work, and Peter Kleiweg for his support in the use of the RUG/L04 software. I would also like to thank Hans Goebl for the stimulating comments on the results of the correlational analyses illustrated in this paper, and Slavomir Sobota with Edgar Haimerl for their support with the VDM software. Finally, thanks are also due to Eva Maria Vecchi who reviewed the manuscript.

REFERENCES

J. K. Chambers and P. Trudgill (1998), *Dialectology*, 2nd Edition (Cambridge).

S. Cucurullo, S. Montemagni, M. Paoli, E. Picchi and E. Sassolini (2006), 'Dialectal resources on-line: the ALT-Web experience', *Proceedings of LREC-2006* (May 2006, Genoa, Italy), 1846–1951.

G. Giacomelli, L. Agostiniani, P. Bellucci, L. Giannelli, S. Montemagni, A. Nesi, M. Paoli, E. Picchi and T. Poggi Salani (2000), eds, *Atlante Lessicale Toscano* (Roma).

L. Giannelli (2000), *Toscana*, 2nd Edition (Pisa) (1976, 1st edition).

H. Goebl (1984), *Dialektometrische Studien: Anhand italoromanischer, rätoromanischer und galloromanischer Sprachmaterialien aus AIS und ALF* (Tübingen).

H. Goebl (2005), 'La dialectométrie corrélative. Un nouvel outil pour l'étude de l'aménagement dialectal de l'espace par l'homme', *Revue de linguistique romane*, 69, 321–367.

H. Goebl (2006), 'Recent Advances in Salzburg Dialectometry', *Literary and Linguistic Computing*, 21(4), 411–435.

H. Goebl (2008), 'La dialettometrizzazione integrale dell'AIS. Presentazione di primi risultati', *Revue de linguistique romane*, 72, 25–113.

C. Gooskens (2005), 'Traveling time as a predictor of linguistic distance', *Dialectologia et Geolinguistica*, 13, 38–62.

C. Gooskens and W. Heeringa (2006), 'The Relative Contribution of Pronunciation, Lexical and Prosodic Differences to the Perceived Distances between Norwegian dialects', *Literary and Linguistic Computing*, 21(4), 477–492.

C. Grassi, A. Sobrero and T. Telmon (1997), *Fondamenti di Dialettologia Italiana* (Roma-Bari).

B. Kessler (1995), 'Computational Dialectology in Irish Gaelic', *Proceedings of the 7th Conference of the European Chapter of the Association for Computational Linguistics (EACL)* (Dublin), 60–67.

G. Kondrak (2002), 'Algorithms for Language Reconstruction' (unpublished Ph.D. Thesis, University of Toronto).

W. Heeringa and J. Nerbonne (2001), 'Dialect Areas and Dialect Continua', *Language Variation and Change*, 13, 375–400.

W. Heeringa (2004), 'Computational Comparison and Classification of Dialects' (Ph.D. thesis, University of Groningen), available at http://www.let.rug.nl/~heeringa/dialectology/thesis/.

W. Heeringa, P. Kleiweg, C. Gooskens and J. Nerbonne (2006), 'Evaluation of string distance algorithms for dialectology', in J. Nerbonne and E. Hinrichs, eds, *Linguistic Distances* (Shroudsburg, PA), 51–62.

S. Montemagni (2007), 'Patterns of phonetic variation in Tuscany: using dialectometric techniques on multi-level representations of dialectal data', in P. Osenova, E. Hinrichs and J. Nerbonne, eds, *Proceedings of the Workshop on Computational Phonology at RANLP-2007, 26 September 2007* (Borovetz, Bulgaria), 49–60.

J. Nerbonne, W. Heeringa, E. van den Hout, P. van de Kooi, S. Otten and W. van de Vis (1996), 'Phonetic Distance between Dutch Dialects', in G. Durieux, W. Daelemans and S. Gillis, eds, *Proceedings of the Sixth CLIN Meeting* (Antwerp, Centre for Dutch Language and Speech, UIA), 185–202.

J. Nerbonne, W. Heeringa and P. Kleiweg (1999), 'Edit Distance and Dialect Proximity', in D. Sankoff and J. Kruskal, eds, *Time Warps, String Edits and Macromolecules: The Theory and Practice of Sequence Comparison* (Stanford), v–xv.

J. Nerbonne (2003), 'Linguistic Variation and Computation', *Proceedings of the 10th Meeting of the European Chapter of the Association for Computational Linguistics, 15–17 April 2003* (Budapest), 3–10.

J. Nerbonne and P. Kleiweg (2003), 'Lexical Distance in LAMSAS', in J. Nerbonne and W. Kretzschmar, eds, *Computers and the Humanities (Special Issue on Computational Methods in Dialectometry)*, 37(3), 339–357.

J. Nerbonne and P. Kleiweg (2007), 'Toward a Dialectological Yardstick', *Journal of Quantitative Linguistics*, 14(2), 148–167.

J. Prokić (2007), 'Identifying Linguistic Structure in a Quantitative Analysis of Dialect Pronunciation', *Proceedings of the ACL 2007 Student Research Workshop, June 2007* (Prague), 61–66.

J. Séguy (1971), 'La relation entre la distance spatiale et la distance lexicale', *Revue de Linguistique Romane*, 35, 335–357.

M. R. Spruit, W. Heeringa and J. Nerbonne (in press), 'Associations among Linguistic Levels', *Lingua (Special Issue on Syntactic Databases)*, available at http://marco.info/pro/pub/shn2007dh.pdf.

END NOTES

[1] According to the main scholar of Tuscan dialectology (Giannelli, 2000), Tuscan dialects are neither northern nor southern dialects: this follows from their status as the source of Italian as well as from their representing a compromise between northern and central-southern dialects. Their linguistic characterisation is not so easy, since there appear to be very few features – if any at all – which are common to all and only Tuscan dialects. If elements of unity are hard to find, those of differentiation are present at the different levels of linguistic description.

[2] The RUG/L04 package can be downloaded from http://www.let.rug.nl/kleiweg/L04/; the Visual DialectoMetry (VDM) is a freely available software package documented at http://ald.sbg.ac.at/dm/Engl/default.htm.

[3] http://serverdbt.ilc.cnr.it/altweb/

[4] The ALT transcription system is a geographically specialised version of the *Carta dei Dialetti Italiani* (CDI) (Grassi *et al.*, 1997). In what follows, for the reader's convenience phonetically transcribed data are reported in IPA notation.

[5] For more details on the representation scheme adopted in ALT-Web, see Cucurullo *et al.* (2006).

[6] Used software: RUG/L04.

[7] In principle, they could be due to the fact that interviewers did not ask the corresponding question or did not get a useful reply from informants.

[8] Two experiments were conducted, operating respectively on atomic and feature-based representations. Feature-based representations of phonetic variants were automatically generated with a software module in the RUG/L04 package on the basis of a system of 18 features, identified starting from the ALT phonetic transcription system. The adopted feature-based representation distinguishes vowel-specific features (i.e. height, advancement, length and roundedness) as well as consonantal features covering place of articulation (e.g. bilabial, dental, alveolar, velar, etc.), manner of articulation (e.g. stop, lateral, fricative, lateral, etc.) and presence/absence of voice; other features are concerned with prosodic properties such as stress and the vowel/consonant distinction. For more details, see Montemagni (2007).

[9] The distances resulting from the two experiments were compared with the Pearson's correlation coefficient which turned out to be $r = 0.99$. This shows that when working with large data sets feature- and phone-based representations do not lead to significantly different results: if on the one hand feature-based representations do not lead to much improved analyses, on the other hand the rough measure working on phone-based representation appears to be reliable.

[10] A potential problem of this approach is to treat as lexically related accidentally close variants. However, the occurrence of cases like this one within the set of answers to the same questionnaire item is extremely rare.

[11] In principle, a viable alternative could have been resorting to lemmatisation: as Nerbonne and Kleiweg (2003) point out, the application of LD for measuring lexical distance provides 'only a rough estimate of what more correctly lemmatizing ought to to'. In practice, we believe that in the case of ALT data lemmatisation is not an easy solution at all, especially for what concerns derivationally related words: the question is if and when word forms such as *schiaccina* or *schiaccetta* should be lemmatised as instances of the base lemma *schiaccia* or if they represent lemmata in their own right. Lemmatisation criteria for dialectal data of this type are not easy to find and involve careful examination of the geographic distribution of words as well as of paradigmatic relations holding within the lexicon of a given locality. Therefore, recourse to LD in the ALT case should not be seen as a second best but rather as a way to overcome inherent lemmatisation problems which are not easily solvable.

[12] The geographical distances have been calculated using the 'll2dst' programme included in the RuG/L04 software package.

[13] Following Kondrak (2002) and Prokic (2007), extraction of regular sound correspondences from aligned word pairs was carried out. We focused on the aligned phonetic variants of 519 normalised forms selected on the basis of extra-linguistic criteria, namely geographical coverage and variation range. The experimental data set includes 5,218 phonetic variants types corresponding to 89,715 tokens. Attested phonetic variants were aligned using RUG/L04: alignments were induced by enforcing the syllabicity constraint. In the case of multiple alignments, only the first one was considered. From all aligned word pairs both matching and non-matching phonetic segments were extracted for a total of 25,132,756 segment pairs. A coarse-grained classification of non-matching phonetic segments (4,877,928) shows that consonants play a major role in Tuscan phonetic variation, covering the 70 per cent of non-matching phonetic segments. A finer-grained classification of non-matching phonetic segments involving consonants demonstrates that a significant part of them (i.e. 42 per cent) corresponds to spirantization phenomena, partitioned as follows: 35 per cent spirantization of plosives (/k t p/ > [h ɸ θ]) and 7 per cent weakening of palatal affricates (e.g. /ʃt/ > [ʃ]). These percentages grow further if we focus on Tuscan dialects only. We also measured the correlation between overall phonetic distances and phonetic distances focussing on non-matching phonetic segments involving spirantization of plosives which turned out to be rather high, with $r = 0.61$.

RECOGNISING GROUPS AMONG DIALECTS

JELENA PROKIĆ AND JOHN NERBONNE

Abstract   In this paper we apply various clustering algorithms to the dialect pronunciation data. At the same time we propose several evaluation techniques that should be used in order to deal with the instability of the clustering techniques. The results have shown that three hierarchical clustering algorithms are not suitable for the data we are working with. The rest of the tested algorithms have successfully detected two-way split of the data into the Eastern and Western dialects. At the aggregate level that we used in this research, no further division of sites can be asserted with high confidence.

I. INTRODUCTION

Dialectometry is a multidisciplinary field that uses various quantitative methods in the analysis of dialect data. Very often those techniques include classification algorithms such as hierarchical clustering algorithms used to detect groups within certain dialect area. Although known for their instability (Jain and Dubes, 1988), clustering algorithms are often applied without evaluation (Goebl, 2007; Nerbonne and Siedle, 2005) or with only partial evaluation (Moisl and Jones, 2005). Very small differences in the input data can produce substantially different grouping of dialects (Nerbonne et al., 2008). Without proper evaluation, it is very hard to determine if the results of the applied clustering technique are an artifact of the algorithm or the detection of real groups in the data.

The aim of this paper is to evaluate algorithms used to detect groups among language dialect varieties measured at the aggregate level. The data used in this research is dialect pronunciation data that consists of various pronunciations of 156 words collected all over Bulgaria. The distances between words are calculated using Levenshtein algorithm, which also resulted in the calculation of

International Journal of Humanities and Arts Computing 2 (1–2) 2008, 153–172
DOI: 10.3366/E1753854809000366

the distances between each two sites in the data set. We apply seven hierarchical clustering algorithms, as well as the k-means and neighbor-joining algorithm to the calculated distances and examine these using various evaluation methods. We evaluate using several external and internal methods, since there is no direct way to evaluate the performance of the clustering algorithms.

The structure of this paper is as follows. Different classification algorithms are presented in the next section. In Section 3 we discuss our data set and how the data was processed. Various evaluation techniques are described in Section 4. The results are given in Section 5. In Section 6 we present discussion and conclusions.

2. CLASSIFICATION ALGORITHMS

In this section we briefly introduce seven hierarchical clustering algorithms, k-means and neighbor-joining algorithm, originally used for reconstructing phylogenetic trees.

2.1 Hierarchical clustering

Cluster analysis is the process of partitioning a set of objects into groups or clusters (Manning and Schütze, 1999). The goal of clustering is to find structure in the data by finding objects that are similar enough to be put in the same group and by identifying distinctions between the groups. Hierarchical clustering algorithms produce a set of nested partitions of the data by finding successive clusters using previously established clusters. This kind of hierarchy is represented with a dendrogram – a tree in which more similar elements are grouped together. In this study seven hierarchical clustering algorithms will be investigated with regard to their performance on dialect pronunciation data. All these agglomerative clustering algorithms proceed from a distance matrix, repeatedly choosing the two closest elements and fusing them. They differ in the way in which distances are recalculated from the newly fused elements to the others. We now review the various calculations.

Single link method, also known as nearest neighbor, is one of the oldest methods in cluster analysis. The similarity between two clusters is computed as the distance between the two most similar objects in the two clusters.

$$d_{k[ij]} = minimum(d_{ki}, d_{kj})$$

In this formula, as well as in other formulae in this subsection, i and j are the two closest points that have just been fused into one cluster $[i, j]$, and k represents all the remaining points (clusters). As noted in Jain and Dubes (1988), single link clusters easily chain together, producing the so-called *chaining effect*,

154

and produce elongated clusters. The presence of only one intermediate object between two compact clusters is enough to turn them into a single cluster.

Complete link, also called furthest neighbor, uses the most distant pair of objects while fusing two clusters. It repeatedly merges clusters whose most distant elements are closest.

$$d_{k[ij]} = maximum(d_{ki}, d_{kj})$$

Unweighted Pair Group Method using Arithmetic Averages (UPGMA) belongs to a group of average clustering methods, together with three methods that will be described below. In UPGMA, the distance between any two clusters is the average of distances between the members of the two clusters being compared. The average is weighted naturally, according to size.

$$d_{k[ij]} = (n_i/(n_i + n_j)) \times d_{ki} + (n_j/(n_i + n_j)) \times d_{kj}$$

As a consequence, smaller clusters will be weighted less and larger ones more.

Weighted Pair Group Method using Arithmetic Averages (WPGMA), just as UPGMA, calculates the distance between the two clusters as the average of distances between all members of two clusters. But in WPGMA, the clusters that fuse receive equal weight regardless of the number of members in each cluster.

$$d_{k[ij]} = \left(\frac{1}{2} \times d_{ki}\right) + \left(\frac{1}{2} \times d_{kj}\right)$$

Because all clusters receive equal weights, objects in smaller clusters are more heavily weighted than those in the big clusters.

Unweighted Pair Group Method using Centroids (UPGMC) In this method, the members of a cluster are represented by their middle point, the so-called centroid. This centroid represents the cluster while calculating the distance between the clusters to be fused.

$$d_{k[ij]} = (n_i/(n_i + n_j)) \times d_{ki} + (n_j/(n_i + n_j)) \times d_{kj}$$
$$-((n_i \times n_j)/(n_i + n_j)^2) \times d_{ij}$$

In the unweighted version of the centroid clustering the clusters are weighted based on the number of elements that belong to that cluster. This means that bigger clusters receive more weight, so that centroids can be biased towards bigger clusters. Centroid clustering methods can also occasionally produce reversals – partitions where the distance between two clusters being joined is smaller than the distance between some of their subclusters (Legendre and Legendre, 1998).

Weighted Pair Group Method using Centroids (WPGMC) Just as in WPGMA, in WPGMC all clusters are assigned the same weight regardless of the number of objects in each cluster. In that way the centroids are not biased

155

towards larger clusters.

$$d_{k[ij]} = \left(\frac{1}{2} \times d_{ki}\right) + \left(\frac{1}{2} \times d_{kj}\right) - \left(\frac{1}{4} \times d_{ij}\right)$$

Ward's method This method is also known as the minimal variance method. At each stage in the analysis clusters that merge are those that result in the smallest increase in the sum of the squared distances of each individual from the mean of its cluster.

$$d_{k[ij]} = ((n_k + n_i)/(n_k + n_i + n_j)) \times d_{ki} + ((n_k + n_j)/(n_k + n_i + n_j))$$
$$\times d_{kj} - ((n_k/(n_k + n_i + n_j)) \times d_{ij}$$

This method uses an analysis of variance approach to calculate the distances between clusters. It tends to create clusters of the same size (Legendre and Legendre, 1998).

2.2 K-means

The k-means algorithm belongs to the non-hierarchical algorithms which are often referred to as *partitional* clustering methods (Jain and Dubes, 1988). Unlike hierarchical clustering algorithms, partitional clustering methods generate a single partition of the data. A partition implies a division of the data in such a way that each instance can belong only to one cluster. The number of groups in which the data should be partitioned is usually determined by the user.

The k-means is the most commonly used partitional algorithm, that despite its simplicity, works sufficiently well in many applications (Manning and Schütze, 1999). The main idea of k-clustering is to find the partition of *n* objects into *K* clusters such that the total error sum of squares is minimized. In the most simple version, the algorithm consists of the following steps:

1. pick at random initial cluster centers
2. assign objects to the cluster whose mean is closest
3. recompute the means of clusters
4. reassign every object to the cluster whose mean is closest
5. repeat steps 3 and 4 until there are no changes in the cluster membership of any object

Two main drawbacks of the k-means algorithm are the following:

- the user has to define the number of clusters in advance
- the final partitioning depends on the initial position of the centroids

Possible solutions to these problems, as well as the detailed descriptions of the k-means algorithm can be found in some of the classical references to k-means: Hartigan (1975), Everitt (1980) and Jain and Dubes (1988).

2.3 Neighbor-joining

Apart from the seven hierarchical clustering algorithms and k-means, we also investigate the performance of the neighbor-joining algorithm. We introduce this technique at more length as it is less familiar to linguists. Neighbor-joining is a method for reconstructing phylogenetic trees that was first introduced by Saitou and Nei (1987). The main principle of this method is to find pairs of taxonomic units that minimize the total branch length at each stage of clustering. The distances between each pair of instances (in our case data collection sites) are calculated and put into the $n \times n$ matrix, where n represents the number of instances. The matrices are symmetrical since distances are symmetrical, i.e. distance (a,b) is always the same as distance (b,a). Based on the input distances, the algorithm finds a tree that fits the observed distances as closely as possible. While choosing the two nodes to fuse, the algorithm always takes into account the distance from every node to all other nodes in order to find the smallest tree that would explain the data. Once found, two optimal nodes are fused and replaced by a new node. The distance between the new node and all other nodes is recalculated, and the whole process is repeated until there are no more nodes left to be paired. The algorithm was modified by Studier and Kepler (1988), and the complexity was reduced to $O(n^3)$. The steps of the algorithm are as follows (taken from Felsenstein (2004)):

- For each node compute u_i which is the sum of the distances from node i to all other nodes

$$u_i = \sum_{j: j \neq i}^{n} \frac{D_{ij}}{(n-2)}$$

- Choose i and j for which $D_{ij} - u_i - u_j$ is smallest
- Join i and j. Compute the length from i and j to the newly formed node v using the equations below. Note that the distances from the new node to its children (leaves) need not be identical. This possibility does not exist in hierarchical clustering.

$$v_i = \frac{1}{2} D_{ij} + \frac{1}{2}(u_i - u_j)$$

$$v_j = \frac{1}{2} D_{ij} + \frac{1}{2}(u_j - u_i)$$

157

- Compute the distance between the new node and all of the remaining nodes

$$D_{(ij),k} = \frac{(D_{ik} + D_{jk} - D_{ij})}{2}$$

- Delete nodes i and j and replace them by the new node

This algorithm produces a unique unrooted tree under the principal of minimal evolution (Saitou and Nei, 1987). In biology, the neighbor-joining algorithm has become very popular and widely used method for reconstructing trees from distance data. It is fast and can be easily applied to a large amount of data. Unlike most hierarchical clustering algorithms, it will recover the true tree even if there is not a constant rate of change among the taxa (Felsenstein, 2004).

3. DATA PREPROCESSING

The data set used in this research consists of transcriptions of the pronunciations of 156 words collected from 197 sites equally distributed all over Bulgaria. All measurements were done based on the phonetic distances between the various pronunciations of these 156 words. No morphological, lexical or syntactic variation between the dialects were taken into account.

Word transcriptions were preprocessed in the following way:

- First, all diacritics and suprasegmentals were removed from word transcriptions. In order to process diacritics and suprasegmentals, they should be assigned weights appropriate for the specific language that is being analyzed. Since no study of this kind was available for Bulgarian, diacritics and suprasegmentals were removed, which resulted in the simplification of data representation. For example, [u], [uː], ['u], and ['uː] counted as the same phone. Also, all words were represented as series of phones which are not further defined. The result of comparing two phones can be 1 or 0; they either match or they do not. For example, pair [e, ɛ] counts as different to the same degree as pair [e, i]. Although it is linguistically counterintuitive to use less sensitive measures, Heeringa (2004:p. 186) has shown that in the aggregate analysis of dialect differences more detailed feature representation of segments does not improve the results obtained by using simple phone representation.
- All transcriptions were aligned based on the following principles: a) a vowel can match only with a vowel b) a consonant can match only with a consonant; and c) high vowels, semivowels ([j], [w]) and sonorant consonants can also match. The alignments were carried out using the Levenshtein algorithm, which also results in the calculation of a distance between each pair of words. A detailed explanation of the Levenshtein algorithm can be found in Heeringa (2004). The distance is the smallest

number of insertions, deletions, and substitutions needed to transform one string to the other. In this work all three operations were assigned the same value: 1. An example of an aligned pair of transcriptions can be seen here:

$$- \quad e \quad d \quad e \quad m$$
$$j \quad \mathrm{\alpha} \quad d \quad \mathrm{\alpha} \quad -$$

The distance between two sites is the mean of all word distances calculated for those two sites. The final result is a distance matrix which contains the mean distances between each two sites in the data set. This distance matrix was further analyzed using seven hierarchical algorithms, k-means and the neighbor-joining algorithm described in the previous section.

4. EVALUATION

We analyzed the results obtained by the above mentioned methods further using a variety of measures. Multidimensional scaling was performed in order to see if there were any separate groups in the data and to determine the optimal number of clusters in the data set. External validation of the clustering results included the modified Rand index, purity and entropy. External validation involves comparison of the structure obtained by different algorithms to a *gold standard*. In our study we used the manual classification of all the sites produced by traditional dialectologist as a *gold standard*. Internal validation included examining the cophenetic correlation coefficient, noisy clustering and a consensus tree, which do not require comparison to any *a priori* structure, but rather try to determine if the structure obtained by algorithms is intrinsically appropriate for the data.

Multidimensional scaling is a dimension-reducing method used in exploratory data analysis and a data visualization method, often used to look for separation of the clusters (Legendre and Legendre, 1998). The goal of the analysis is to detect meaningful underlying dimensions that allow the researcher to explain observed similarities or dissimilarities between the investigated objects. In general then, MDS attempts to arrange 'objects' in a space with a certain small number of dimensions, which, however, accord with the observed distances. As a result, we can 'explain' the distances in terms of underlying dimensions. It has been frequently used in linguistics and dialectology since Black (1973) .

4.1 External validation

The **modified Rand index** (Hubert and Arabie, 1985) is used for comparing two different partitions of a finite set of objects. It is a modified form of the Rand index (Rand, 1971), one of the most popular measures for comparing partitions. Given a set of n elements $S = o_1, \ldots o_n$ and two partitions of S, $U = u_1, \ldots u_R$ and $V = v_1, \ldots v_C$ we define

a the number of pairs of elements in S that are in the same set in U and in the same set in V

b the number of pairs of elements in S that are in different sets in U and in different sets in V

c the number of pairs of elements in S that are in the same set in U and in different sets in V

d the number of pairs of elements in S that are in different sets in U and in the same set in V

The Rand index R is

$$R = \frac{a+b}{a+b+c+d}$$

In this formula a and b are the number of pairs of elements in which two classifications agree, while c and d are the number of pairs of elements in which they disagree. The value of the Rand index is between 0 and 1, with 0 indicating that the two data clusters do not agree on any pair of points and 1 indicating that the data clusters are exactly the same. In dialectometry, this index was used by Heeringa et al. (2002) to validate dialect comparison methods. A problem with the Rand index is that it does not return a constant value (zero) if two partitions are picked at random. Hubert and Arabie (1985) suggested a modification of Rand index that corrects this property. It can be expressed in the general form as:

$$\frac{Rand\,Index - Expected\,Index}{Maximum\,Index - Expected\,Index}$$

The value of the modified Rand index is between -1 and 1.

Entropy and **purity** are two measures used to evaluate the quality of clustering by looking at the reference class labels of the elements assigned to each cluster (Zhao and Karypis, 2001). Entropy measures how different classes of elements are distributed within each cluster. The entropy of a single cluster is calculated using the following formula:

$$E(S_r) = -\frac{1}{\log q} \sum_{i=1}^{q} \frac{n_r^i}{n_r} \log \frac{n_r^i}{n_r}$$

where S_r is a particular cluster of size n_r, q is the number of classes in the reference data set, and n_r^i is the number of the elements of the ith class that were assigned to the rth cluster. The overall entropy is the weighted sum of all cluster entropies weighted by the size of the cluster:

$$E = \sum_{r=1}^{k} \frac{n_r}{n} E(S_r)$$

The **purity** measure is used to determine to which extent a cluster contains objects from primarily one class. The purity of a cluster is calculated as:

$$P(S_r) = \frac{1}{n_r} max(n_r^i)$$

while the overall purity is the weighted sum of the individual cluster purities:

$$P = \sum_{r=1}^{k} \frac{n_r}{n} P(S_r)$$

4.2 Internal validation

The **cophenetic correlation coefficient** (Sokal and Rohlf, 1962) is Pearson's correlation coefficient computed between the cophenetic distances produced by clustering and those in the original distance matrix. The cophenetic distance between two objects is the similarity level at which those two objects become members of the same cluster during the course of clustering (Jain and Dubes, 1988) and is represented as branch length in dendrogram. It measures the extent to which the clustering results correspond to the original distances. When the clustering functions perfectly, the value of the cophenetic correlation coefficient is 1. In order to check the significance of this statistics we performed the simple Mantel test as implemented in **zt** software (Bonet and de Peer, 2002). A simple Mantel test is used to compare two matrices by testing the correlation between them using the standard Pearson correlation coefficient and testing its statistical significance (Mantel, 1967).

Noisy clustering, also called composite clustering, is a procedure in which small amounts of random noise are added to matrices during repeated clustering. The main purpose of this procedure is to reduce the influence of outliers on the regular clusters and to identify stable clusters. As shown in Nerbonne et al. (2008) it gives results that nearly perfectly correlate with the results obtained by bootstrapping – a statistical method for measuring the support of a given edge in a tree (Felsenstein, 2004). The advantage of the noisy clustering, compared to bootstrapping, is that it can be applied on a single distance matrix – the same one used as input for the classification algorithms.

A **consensus dendrogram**, or consensus tree, is a tree that summarizes the agreement between a set of trees (Felsenstein, 2004). A consensus tree that contains a large number of internal nodes shows high agreement between the input trees. On the other hand, if a consensus tree contains few internal nodes, it

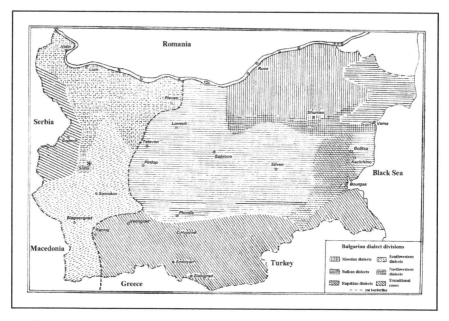

Figure 1. Traditional map of Bulgarian dialects.

is a sign that input trees classify the data in conflicting ways. The majority rule consensus tree, used in this study, is a tree that consists of the groups, i.e. clusters, which are present in the majority of the trees under study. In this research a consensus dendrogram was created from four dendrograms produced by four different hierarchical clustering methods. Clusters that appear in the consensus tree are those supported by the majority of algorithms and can be taken with greater confidence to be true clusters.

5. RESULTS

Before describing the results of applying various algorithms to our data set, we give a short description of the traditional division of the Bulgarian dialect area that we used for external validation in our research.

5.1 Traditional scholarship

Traditional scholarship (Stojkov, 2002) divides the Bulgarian language into two main groups: Western and Eastern. The border between these two areas is so-called 'yat' border that reflects different pronunciations of the old Slavic vowel 'yat'. It goes from Nikopol in the North, near Pleven and Teteven down to Petrich in the South (bold dashed line in Figure 1).

Stojkov divides each of these two areas further into three smaller dialect zones, which can also be seen on the map in Figure 1. This 6-fold division is based on the variation of different phonetic features. No morphological or syntactic differences were taken into account. In order to evaluate the performance of different clustering algorithms, all sites present in our data set were manually assigned by an expert to one of the two, and later six, main dialect areas according to Stojkov's classification. This was done by Professor Vladimir Zhobov, phonetician and dialectologist from the Faculty of Slavic Philologies 'St. Kliment Ohridski', University of Sofia.

Due to various historical events, mostly migrations, some villages are dialectological islands surrounded by language varieties from groups different from the one they belong to. This lack of geographical coherence can be seen, for example, in the north-central part on the map in Figure 2.

5.2 MDS

Multidimensional scaling was performed in order to check if there are any separate clusters in the data. The results can be seen in the Figure 3, where the first two extracted dimensions are plotted against the x and y axes. In addition, all three extracted dimensions are represented by different shades of red, blue and green colors. This represents the third MDS dimension.

The first three dimensions represented in Figure 3 explain 98 per cent of the variation in the data set – the first dimension extracted explains 80 per cent of the variation, and the second dimension 16 per cent. In Figure 3 we can see two distinct clusters along the x-axis, which, if put on the map, correspond to the Eastern and Western group of dialects (Figure 4).

Variation along the y-axis corresponds to the separation of the dialects in the South from the rest of the country. Using MDS to screen the data, we observe that there are two distinct clusters in the data set – even though MDS is fully capable of representing continuous data. This finding fully agrees with the expert opinion (Stojkov, 2002) according to which the Bulgarian dialect area can be divided into Eastern and Western dialect areas along the 'yat' border. A third area that can be seen in Figure 4 is the area in the South of the country – the area of the Rodopi mountains. In the classification of dialects done by Stojkov (2002), this area is identified as one of the six main dialect areas based on the phonetic features.

5.3 External validation

The results of the multidimensional scaling and dialect divisions done by expert can be used as a first step in the evaluation of the clustering algorithms. Visual inspection shows that three algorithms fail to identify any structure in the data, including East-West division of the dialects: single link and two centroid

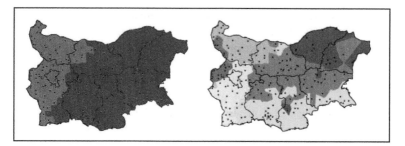

Figure 2. The two-way and six-way classification of sites done by expert.

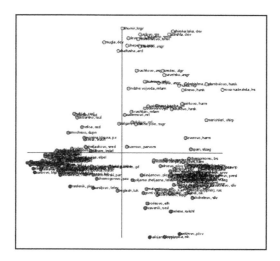

Figure 3. MDS plot.

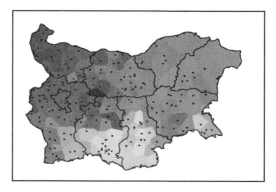

Figure 4. MDS map.

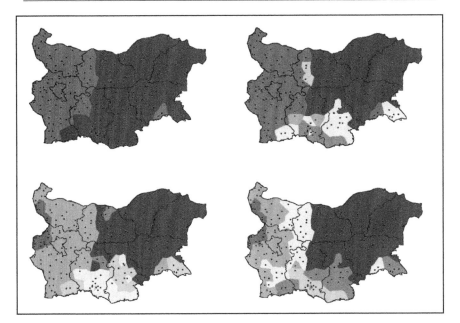

Figure 5. Top left map: 2-way division produced by UPGMA, WPGMA and Ward's method. Top right map: 6-way division produced by UPGMA. Bottom maps: 6-way divisions produced by WPGMA and Ward's method respectively.

algorithms, UPGMC and WPGMC. Dendrograms drawn using UPGMC and WPGMC reveal a large number of reversals, while closer inspection of the single link dendrogram clearly shows the presence of the *chain effect*. The remaining algorithms reveal the East-West division of the country clearly (Figure 5). For that reason, in the rest of the paper the main focus will be on those four clustering algorithms, as well as on the k-means and neighbor-joining.

In order to compare divisions done by clustering algorithms with the division of sites done by expert we calculated the modified Rand index, entropy and purity for the 2-fold, 3-fold, and 6-fold divisions done by algorithms on the one hand, and those divisions according to the expert on the other. The results can be seen in Table 1.

The neighbor-joining algorithm produced an unrooted tree (Figure 6), where only 2-fold and 3-fold divisions of the sites can be identified. Hence, all the indices were calculated only for the 2-fold and 3-fold divisions in neighbor-joining.

In Table 1 we can see that the values of the modified Rand index for single link and two centroid methods are very close to 0, which is the value we would get if the partitions were picked at random. UPGMA, WPGMA, Ward's method

Table 1. Results of external validation: the modified Rand index (MRI), entropy (E) and purity (P). Results for the 2, 3 and 6-fold divisions are reported.

Algorithm	MRI(2)	MRI(3)	MRI(6)	E(2)	E(3)	E(6)	P(2)	P(3)	P(6)
single link	−0.004	0.007	−0.001	0.958	0.967	0.881	0.614	0.396	0.360
complete link	0.495	0.520	0.350	0.510	0.542	0.467	0.848	0.766	0.645
UPGMA	**0.700**	**0.627**	0.273	0.368	**0.445**	0.583	0.914	**0.853**	0.568
WPGMA	**0.700**	0.626	0.381	0.368	0.445	0.448	0.914	**0.853**	0.665
UPGMC	−0.004	0.007	−0.006	0.959	0.967	0.926	0.614	0.396	0.310
WPGMC	−0.004	0.007	−0.005	0.958	0.967	0.925	0.614	0.396	0.305
Ward's method	**0.700**	**0.627**	0.398	0.368	**0.445**	0.441	0.914	**0.853**	0.675
k-means	**0.700**	0.625	**0.471**	**0.354**	0.451	**0.355**	**0.919**	0.756	**0.772**
NJ	0.567	0.461	-	0.442	0.550	-	0.873	0.777	-

and k-means, which gave nearly the same 2-fold division of the sites, show the highest correspondences with the divisions done by expert. For 3-fold and 6-fold divisions the values for the modified Rand index went down for all algorithms, which was expected since the number of groups increased. The two algorithms with the highest values of the index are Ward's method and UPGMA for 3-fold, and k-means for the 6-fold division. Just as in the case of the 2-fold division, the single-link, UPGMC, and WPGMC algorithms have values of the modified Rand index close to 0. Neighbor-joining produced a relatively low correspondence with expert opinion for the 3-fold division – 0.461. Similar results for all algorithms and all divisions were obtained using entropy and purity measures. External validation of the clustering algorithms has revealed that single link, UPGMC and WPGMC algorithms are not suitable for the analysis of the data we are working with, since they fail to recognize any structure in the data.

5.4 Internal validation

In the next step internal validation methods were used to check the performance of the algorithms: the cophenetic correlation coefficient, noisy clustering and consensus trees. Since k-means does not produce a dendrogram, it was not possible to calculate the cophenetic correlation coefficient. The values of the cophenetic correlation coefficient for the remaining eight algorithms can be seen in Table 2. We can see that clustering results of the UPGMA have the highest correspondence to the original distances of all algorithms – 90.26 per cent. They are followed by the results obtained by using complete link and neighbor-joining algorithm. All correlations are highly significant with $p < 0.0001$. Given the poor performance of the centroid and single-link methods in detecting the dialect divisions scholars agree on, we note that cophenetic correlation coefficients are not successful in distinguishing the better techniques from the weaker ones. We

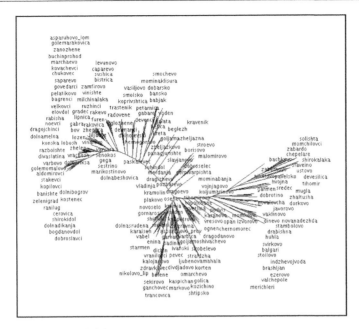

Figure 6. Neighbor-joining tree.

Table 2. Cophenetic correlation coefficient.

Algorithm	CCC	p
single link	0.7804	0.0001
complete link	0.8661	0.0001
UPGMA	**0.9026**	0.0001
WPGMA	0.8563	0.0001
UPGMC	0.8034	0.0001
WPGMC	0.6306	0.0001
Ward's method	0.7811	0.0001
Neighbor-joining	0.8587	0.0001

conjecture that the reason for this lies in the fact that the cophenetic correlation coefficient so dependent is on the lengths of the branches in the dendrogram, while our primary purpose is the classification.

Noisy clustering, that was applied with the seven hierarchical algorithms, has confirmed that there are two relatively stable groups in the data: Eastern and Western. Dendrograms obtained by applying noisy clustering to the whole data set show low confidence for the two-way split of the data, between 52 and 60 per cent. After removing the Southern villages from the data set, we obtained dendrograms that confirm two-way split of the data along the 'yat' border with

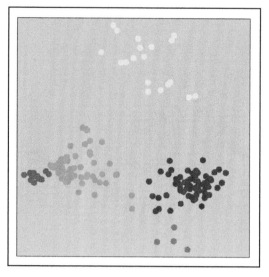

Figure 7. MDS plot of 6 clusters produced by WPGMA. Note that the good separation of the clusters is often spoiled by unclear margins.

much higher confidence ranging around 70 per cent. These values are not very high. In order to check the reason of the influence of the Southern varieties on the noisy clustering we examine an MDS plot in two dimensions with cluster groups marked by colours. In Figure 7 we can see MDS plot of 6 groups produced by WPGMA algorithm. MDS plot reveals two homogeneous groups and a third, more diffuse, group that lies at a remove from them. The third group of the sites represents the Southern group of varieties, colored light blue and yellow, and is much more heterogeneous than the rest of the data. Closer inspection of the MDS plot in Figure 3 also shows that this group of dialects has a particularly unclear border to the Eastern dialects, which could explain the results of the noisy clustering applied to the whole data set.

Since different algorithms gave different divisions of sites, we used a consensus dendrogram in order to detect the clusters on which most algorithms agree. Since single link, UPGMC and WPGMC have turned to be inappropriate for the analysis of our data, they were not included in the consensus dendrogram. The consensus dendrogram drawn using complete link, UPGMA, WPGMA and Ward's method can be seen in Figure 8. The names of the sites are colored based on the expert's opinion, i.e. the same as in Figure 2. The dendrogram shows strong support for the East-West division of sites, but no agreement on the division of sites within the Eastern and Western areas. At this level of hierarchy, i.e. 2-way division, there are several sites classified differently by algorithms and by expert. These sites go along the 'yat' border and represent the marginal

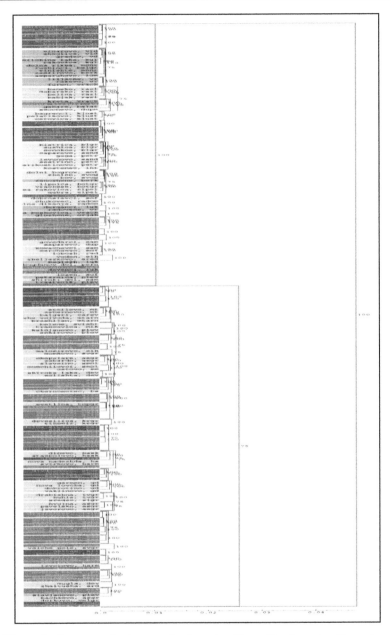

Figure 8. Consensus dendrogram for four algorithms. The four algorithms show agreement only on the 2-way division. It is not possible to extract any hierachical structure that would be present in the majority of four analyses. (For the explanation of colors see Figure 2.)

cases. The only two exceptions are villages in the South-East, namely Voden and Zheljazkovo. However, according to many traditional dialectologists these villages should be classified as Western dialects due to many features that they share with the dialects in the West (personal communication with prof. Vladimir Zhobov). The four algorithms show agreement only on the very low level where several sites are grouped together and on the highest level. It is not possible to extract any hierarchical structure that would be present in the majority of four analyses.

6. DISCUSSION AND CONCLUSIONS

Different clustering validation methods have shown that three algorithms are not suitable at all for the data we are working with, namely single link, UPGMC and WPGMC. The remaining four hierarchical clustering algorithms gave different results depending on the level of hierarchy, but all four algorithms had high agreement on the detection of two main dialect areas within the dialect space. At the lower level of hierarchy, i.e. where there are more clusters, the performance of the algorithms is poorer, both with respect to the expert opinion and with respect to the mutual agreement as well. As shown by noisy clustering, the 2-fold division of the Bulgarian language area is the only partition of sites that can be asserted with high confidence.

The results of the neighbor-joining algorithm were a bit less satisfactory. The reason for this could be in the fact that our data is not tree-like, but rather contains a lot of borrowings due to contact between different dialects. A recent study (Hamed and Wang, 2006) of Chinese dialects has shown that their development is not tree-like and that in such cases usage of tree-reconstruction methods can be misleading.

The division of sites done by the k-means algorithm corresponded well with the expert divisions. Two and three-way divisions also correspond well with the divisions of four hierarchical clustering algorithms. What we find more important is the fact that in the divisions obtained by the k-means algorithm into 2, 3, 4, 5 and 6 groups the two-way division into the Eastern and Western groups is the only stable division that appears in all partitions.

This research shows that clustering algorithms should be applied with caution as classifiers of language dialect varieties. Where possible, several internal and external validation methods should be used together with the clustering algorithms in order to validate their results and make sure that the classifications obtained are not mere artifacts of algorithms but natural groups present in the data set. Since performance of clustering algorithms depends on the sort of data used, evaluation of algorithms is a necessary step in order to obtain results that can be asserted with high confidence.

The fact that there are only two distinct groups in our data set that can be asserted with high confidence, as opposed to six found in the traditional atlases, could possible be due to the simplified representation of the data (see Section 3). It is also possible that some of the features responsible for the traditional 6-way division are not present in our data set. At the moment, we are investigating these two issues. Regardless of the quality of the input data set, we have shown that clustering algorithms will partition data into the desired number of groups even if there is no natural separation of the data. For this reason it is essential to use different evaluation techniques along with the clustering algorithms.

Classification algorithms are nowadays applied in different subfields of humanities (Woods et al., 1986; Boonstra et al., 1990). It is a general technique that can be applied to any sort of data that needs to be put into different groups in order to discover various patterns. Document and text classification, authorship detection and language typology are just some of the areas where classification algorithms are nowdays successfully applied. The problem of choosing the right classification algorithm and obtaining stable results goes beyond dialectometry and is present whenever applied. For this reason the present paper is valuable not only for the research done in dialectometry, but also for other branches of humanities that are using clustering techniques. It shows how unstable the results of clustering algorithms can be, but also how to approach this problem and overcome it.

REFERENCES

P. Black (1973), 'Multidimensional scaling applied to linguistic relationships', in *Cahiers de l'Institut de Linguistique Louvain*, Volume 3 (Montreal). Expanded version of a paper presented at the Conference on Lexicostatistics. University of Montreal.

E. Bonet and Y. V. de Peer (2002), 'zt: a software tool for simple and partial mantel tests', *Journal of Statistical software*, 7(10), 1–12.

O. Boonstra, P. Doorn and F. Hendrickx (1990), *Voortgezette Statistiek voor Historici* (Muiderberg).

B. S. Everitt (1980), *Cluster Analysis* (New York).

J. Felsenstein (2004), *Inferring Phylogenies* (Massachusetts).

H. Goebl (2007), 'On the geolinguistic change in Northern France between 1300 and 1900: a dialectometrical inquiry', in J. Nerbonne, T. M. Ellison, and G. Kondrak, eds, *Computing and Historical Phonology. Proceedings of the Ninth Meeting of the ACL Special Interest Group in Computationa Morphology and Phonology* (Prague), 75–83.

M. B. Hamed and F. Wang (2006), 'Stuck in the forest: Trees, networks and Chinese dialects', *Diachronica*, 23(1), 29–60.

J. A. Hartigan (1975), *Cluster algorithms* (New York).

W. Heeringa (2004), *Measuring Dialect Pronunciation Differences using Levensthein Distance* (PhD Thesis, University of Groningen).

W. Heeringa, J. Nerbonne and P. Kleiweg (2002), 'Validating dialect comparison methods', in W. Gaul and G. Ritter, eds, *Classification, Automation, and New Media. Proceedings of the 24th Annual Conference of the Gesellschaft für Klassifikation, University of Passau, March 15–17, 2000* (Heidelberg), 445–452.

L. Hubert and P. Arabie (1985), 'Comparing partitions', *Journal of Classification*, 2, 193–218.

A. K. Jain and R. C. Dubes (1988), *Algorithms for Clustering Data* (New Jersey).

P. Legendre and L. Legendre (1998), *Numerical Ecology*, second ed. (Amsterdam).

C. Manning and H. Schütze (1999), *Foundations of Statistical Natural Language Processing* (Cambridge, MA).

N. Mantel (1967), 'The detection of disease clustering and a generalized regression approach', *Cancer Research*, 27, 209–220.

H. Moisl and V. Jones (2005), 'Cluster analysis of the Newcastle Electronic Corpus of Tyneside English: a comparison of methods', *Literary and Linguistic Computing*, 20, 125–146.

J. Nerbonne, P. Kleiweg, W. Heeringa and F. Manni (2008), 'Projecting Dialect Differences to Geography: Bootstrap Clustering vs. Noisy Clustering', in H. B. Christine Preisach, Lars Schmidt-Thieme and R. Decker, eds, *Data Analysis, Machine Learning, and Applications. Proc. of the 31st Annual Meeting of the German Classification Society* (Berlin), 647–654.

J. Nerbonne and C. Siedle (2005), 'Dialektklassifikation auf der Grundlage Aggregierter Ausspracheunterschiede', *Zeitschrift für Dialektologie und Linguistik*, 72(2), 129–147.

W. M. Rand (1971), 'Objective criteria for the evaluation of clustering methods', *Journal of American Statistical Association*, 66(336), 846–850.

N. Saitou and M. Nei (1987), 'The neighbor-joining method: A new method for reconstructing phylogenetic trees', *Molecular Biology and Evolution*, 4, 406–425.

R. R. Sokal and F. J. Rohlf (1962), 'The comparison of dendrograms by objective methods', *Taxon*, 11, 33–40.

S. Stojkov (2002), *Bulgarska dialektologiya* (Sofia).

J. A. Studier and K. J. Kepler (1988), 'A note on the neighbor-joining algorithm of Saitou and Nei', *Molecular Biology and Evolution*, 5, 729–731.

A. Woods, P. Fletcher and A. Hughes (1986), *Statistics in Language Studies* (Cambridge).

Y. Zhao and G. Karypis (2001), 'Criterion functions for document clustering: Experiments and analysis', Technical report 01-40, Department of Computer Science, University of Minnesota, Minneapolis, MN.

COMPARISON OF COMPONENT MODELS IN ANALYSING THE DISTRIBUTION OF DIALECTAL FEATURES

ANTTI LEINO AND SAARA HYVÖNEN

Abstract   *Component models such as factor analysis can be used to analyse spatial distributions of a large number of different features – for instance the isogloss data in a dialect atlas, or the distributions of ethnological or archaeological phenomena – with the goal of finding dialects or similar cultural aggregates. However, there are several such methods, and it is not obvious how their differences affect their usability for computational dialectology. We attempt to tackle this question by comparing five such methods using two different dialectological data sets. There are some fundamental differences between these methods, and some of these have implications that affect the dialectological interpretation of the results.*

I. INTRODUCTION

Languages are traditionally subdivided into geographically distinct dialects, although any such division is just a coarse approximation of a more fine-grained variation. This underlying variation is usually visualised in the form of maps, where the distribution of various features is shown as isoglosses. It is possible to view dialectal regions, in this paper also called simply dialects, as combinations of the distribution areas of these features, where the features have been weighted in such a way that the differences between the resulting dialects are as sharp as possible. Ideally, dialect borders are drawn where several isoglosses overlap.

As more and more dialectological data is available in electronic form, it is becoming increasingly attractive to apply computational methods to this problem. One way to do this is to use clustering methods (e.g. Kaufman and Rousseeuw, 1990), especially as such methods have been used in dialectometric

International Journal of Humanities and Arts Computing 2 (1–2) 2008, 173–187
DOI: 10.3366/E1753854809000378

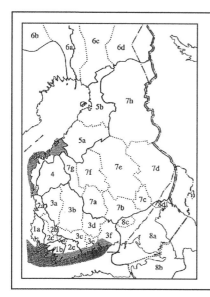

- Western dialects

  1 Southwestern dialects

  2 Mid-southwestern dialects

  3 Tavastian dialects

  4 Southern Ostrobothnian dialect

  5 Central and northern Ostrobothnian dialects

  6 Northernmost dialects

- Eastern dialects

  7 Savonian dialects

  8 Southeastern dialects

Figure 1. Traditional division of Finnish dialects (Savijärvi and Yli-Luukko, 1994).

studies (e.g. Heeringa and Nerbonne, 2002; Moisl and Jones, 2005). However, in our initial studies (Leino et al., 2006; Hyvönen et al., 2007) clustering did not seem to be the best tool for finding dialects from a large corpus of spatial distributions. Instead, it would appear that it is easier to analyse dialectal variation with methods that do not impose sharp boundaries but rather present each 'dialect' as a diffusion pattern.

There are several methods that can be applied to a large corpus of feature to find 'dialects', or more precisely regularities that can be interpreted as dialectal variation. However, choosing the right method for such a task is not easy, as there is little information available about their relative merits. Our goal here is to compare several such methods with two data sets describing Finnish dialectal variation.

Our first test corpus comprises the 213 isogloss maps of the Dialect Atlas of Kettunen (1940a), later edited into a computer corpus (Embleton and Wheeler, 1997). Its emphasis is on phonological features, with morphology also relatively well represented; Kettunen (1940b:V) regrets that he could not expand it to include lexical variation. The traditional view of Finnish dialects, seen in Figure 1, is by and large based on these features, so it is also possible to compare the computational results to the division that dialectologists have agreed on.

We also use a second test corpus, a set of some 9,000 lexical distribution maps that were drawn as a part of the editing process for the Dictionary of Finnish

Dialects (Tuomi, 1989). We have already performed some initial analyses of this same corpus (Hyvönen et al., 2007), and using it here makes it possible to build on the prior work. The main advantage, however, is that it is very different from the Dialect Atlas corpus. The Atlas corpus is much smaller but for the most part comprehensive, while the Dictionary corpus is significantly larger but contains a massive amount of noise, as different regions have been surveyed to widely varying degrees.

At this point we would also like to note that the methods we compare here are in no way specific to dialectological data but are instead general-purpose computational methods suitable for a wide range of multivariate analyses. We chose Finnish dialects as our test subject mainly because the corpora were readily available to us, and secondarily because of our prior knowledge of the field. Nevertheless, geographically distributed presence–absence data is common also in other disciplines, and the methods would be equally useful for analysing such variation.

2. METHODS

According to the traditional view Finland is divided into separate dialect regions. The borders of these regions are commonly drawn along the borders of Finnish municipalities, since these were the basic geographical units used for collecting most of the original data. It is very natural to consider the data as a binary presence–absence matrix, with zeros indicating the absence and ones the presence of a feature in a municipality. It would therefore be attractive to apply clustering methods to our data sets and divide the municipalities of Finland into separate clusters, each corresponding to a particular dialect region. However, in reality dialect regions do not have sharp borders, and assigning each municipality to a particular cluster is not necessarily a good approach (Hyvönen et al., 2007).

An alternative is to use component methods to analyse the data. While we shall see later on that different methods do indeed perform differently, what all of the methods used in this study have in common is that they produce a small number of components that capture the most significant aspects of the overall variation. Because of this, the methods can also be thought of as latent variable methods: the components, or latent variables, capture the hidden structure of the data. For historical reasons different methods use different names to refer to these components, so that they are also called aspects or factors. In this paper, when we talk of latent variables or components or aspects or factors we are talking about the same thing, although strictly speaking we could make a distinction between the actual phenomena underlying the data and the components which are used to model them.

Ideally the components found are interpretable in terms of the dialect regions. We consider features as observations and municipalities as variables, and each element of a component corresponds to a municipality. Each component can be visualised as a choropleth map, with a colour slide between the extremes.

In mathematical terms we can express the data as follows:

$$D = FX \tag{1}$$

where D is the data matrix, F contains our factors and X is the mixing matrix. If the factors in F correspond to dialect regions, the elements of X tell how these factors are combined to get the data matrix. One dialect word or feature is represented by one column in D, and the corresponding column of X tells how the k factors, stored in columns of F, combine to explain that dialect word.

2.1 Factor analysis

Factor analysis (FA) aims to find a small set of factors which explain the data. For example, if solar radiation and temperature correlate strongly only one factor ('sun') can be used to explain them both. In our case, all Tavastian dialect features correlate strongly, so only one factor ('Tavastian') can be used to explain them. In other words, we would expect some correspondence between factors and dialects.

As Factor Analysis is a well-established method, there are several implementations that are readily available. In this study we have used a matlab implementation by Trujillo-Ortiz et al. (2006). For more information on factor analysis see for example Rencher (2002).

2.2 Non-negative matrix factorisation

Non-negative matrix factorisation (NMF) (Paatero, 1997; Lee and Seung, 1999) differs from factor analysis in that it aims to find *non-negative* factors which explain the data in a non-negative way. For example, a municipality in Kainuu could be explained using Savonian and Ostrobothnian components with weights 1 and 2 ('this municipality is one part Savonian and 2 parts Ostrobothnian'). Similarly, a certain dialect word or feature could be half Tavastian and half southwestern.

In many applications non-negativity is intuitively appealing. For example, one of the classic tasks in exploratory data analysis is so-called market basket analysis, or finding regularities in the combinations of different items that customers buy during a single trip to a market. In this case, it is obvious that the original data is non-negative: one cannot easily have -2 cartons of milk. Dialectological data is also non-negative – a feature may not appear in a local dialect but its frequency cannot be negative. The same applies to factors extracted from dialect data, as it is very difficult to understand what it would mean to characterise a municipality as '-0.5 Tavastian'.

NMF forces all elements of both matrices on the right side in equation 1 to be non-negative. This means that in the 'Tavastian' factor the elements corresponding to Tavastian municipalities are positive, while elements corresponding distinctively non-Tavastian municipalities are zero. Similarly, if a dialect word is used in Savonia and Ostrobothnia, which are represented by two factors, then the elements of X in equation 1 corresponding to that word will be positive for the Savonian and Ostrobothnian factors and zero otherwise. It is thus possible to interpret these factors as approximating the relative weight of the different dialectal influences.

While the components are always non-negative there is no similar guarantee regarding the high end of the range. This is important if one wishes to compare the relative weights of the components; in such a case one must add a separate post-processing step to normalise the components.

2.3 Aspect Bernoulli

The aspect Bernoulli (AB) method (Kaban et al., 2004) differs from the methods introduced previously in that it is designed for binary data. Moreover, interpretation can in this case be given in terms of probabilities, so that for instance a municipality (or dialect word or feature) is 83% Savonian. This makes the method attractive for our use.

The AB method is also designed to distinguish between false and true presence and absence in data, which means it is suitable for dealing with noisy data. This should be good news for dealing with the Dialect Dictionary data set, which has a very large number of false absences, as all municipalities have not been thoroughly sampled. However, it seems that too much is too much: the missing values in the data set, far from being randomly distributed, are a consequence of systematic differences in sampling frequencies, and AB did not deal well with this kind of missing data.

2.4 Independent component analysis

Independent component analysis (ICA) (Hyvärinen et al., 2001) is typically used to separate signals with several measurements and a few measuring points. A classical problem would be the so-called cocktail party problem: we have five microphones in a room with five people talking, and we wish to separate these speech signals. Here we consider dialect words or features as the signal, and by 'monitoring' this signal in each municipality we use ICA to discover the the source of those signals, i.e. the dialects themselves.

ICA aims to find factors, or in this context components, that are statistically independent. ICA uses PCA as a standard preprocessing step, so that the number of principal components used depends on the number of factors sought. In our study we only use a small number of the principal components, as otherwise the resulting components tend to be too localised.

2.5 *Principal components analysis*

Principal components analysis (PCA) (Hotelling, 1933) is the oldest and probably also the best known method used in this study. PCA finds the direction in the data which explains most of the variation in the data. This is the first principal component. After this each consecutive component explains the variation left in the data after the variation explained by previous components has been removed. Note that each component must be interpreted bearing the previous components in mind. The principal components, especially the first ones, give a global view of dialects, but in general the components do not directly correspond to individual dialect regions.

In all of the previous methods described the number of factors chosen is crucial: different choices give different components. If the number of components k is large, the components are more localised, whereas for small k we tend to get components which correspond to a rough partitioning of dialects. In contrast, no matter how many components are computed by PCA the first k components are always the same. The first principal component will always present the main direction of variation. Principal components will therefore in general not represent the different dialect regions per se, but instead they give a global view of the variation. For example in Figure 2 we see that in the Dialect Dictionary data, after east-west variation is accounted for the next most important factor is the north-south variation.

In explaining the data PCA certainly does as well as the other methods, but unlike these it does not directly summarise the contributions of different dialects as the components. This is often done using rotation as a post-processing step, but the rotation of the first few principal components does result in something that should not strictly speaking be called principal components any more.

3. COMPARISON OF THE METHODS

In order to compare the five different methods we have used each to divide both data sets into ten components, or in the case of PCA looked at the first ten components. In comparing the results we have used two criteria: spatial autocorrelation and the degree to which the components conform to the existing dialectological view.

It should be kept in mind that the traditional view of Finnish dialects is largely based on the material presented in the Dialect Atlas. Even though this has been supplemented by later research, the relationship is strong enough that the traditional view can be considered the primary criterion for comparing the

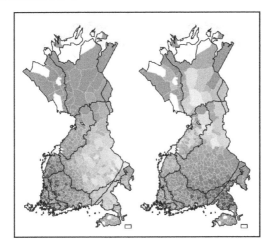

Figure 2. Dialect Dictionary, principal components 2 and 3. The first principal component (not shown) captures the sampling rate (Hyvönen et al., 2007). The second component captures east–west variation, with the western influence shown as the blue and the eastern influence the yellow end of the colour scale. Similarly, the third component shows the north–south variation as the most significant direction after the east–west variation has been removed.

methods, especially for the Dialect Atlas data. The correspondence is not perfect, as is easily seen from comparing the traditional division in Figure 1 to a nine-way aspect Bernoulli analysis in Figure 3, and with the Dialect Dictionary data this relationship is somewhat weaker still. Nevertheless, the traditional view is a useful yardstick for comparing the methods.

Measuring spatial autocorrelation shows essentially how cohesive each of the components is. When dealing with dialectal phenomena, it is reasonable to assume that the underlying phenomena do not have spatial discontinuities: in general, linguistic innovations spread across space in such a way that there are no major gaps within the resulting region. However, noise in data may result in noisy components. Using spatial autocorrelation as a quality measure favours methods which are more robust with respect to noise.

We use two different measures for autocorrelation. On the one hand, we use Moran's I statistic (Bailey and Gatrell, 1995:269–71):

$$I = \frac{n \sum_{i=1}^{n} \sum_{j=1}^{n} w_{ij}(y_i - \bar{y})(y_j - \bar{y})}{\left(\sum_{i=1}^{n}(y_i - \bar{y})^2\right)\left(\sum\sum_{i \neq j} w_{ij}\right)} \tag{2}$$

Here n is the number of municipalities, w_{ij} is 1 where municipalities i and j are neighbours and 0 otherwise, y_i is the value of the component in municipality i and $\bar{y}$ the average value of the component.

179

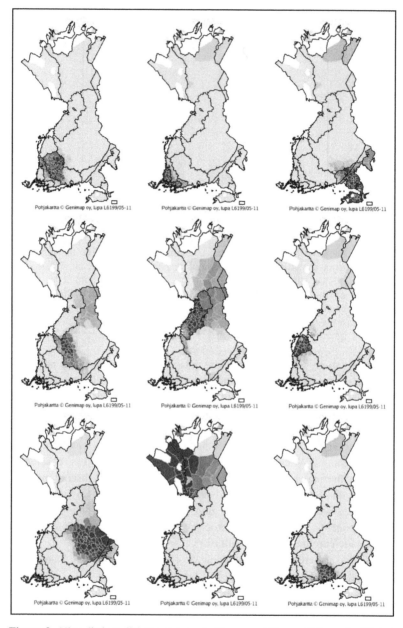

Figure 3. Nine distinct dialects as extracted by aspect Bernoulli from the Dialect Atlas data.

Table 1. Comparison of different analyses. For spatial autocorrelation, the column I should be > 0 and $C < 1$; for correlation between the analysis results and the traditional view of dialects, the column Dialect should be > 0.

	Atlas			Dictionary		
	I	C	Dialect	I	C	Dialect
FA	0.88	0.12	0.75	0.74	0.30	0.59
NMF	0.90	0.13	0.81	0.66	0.48	0.58
AB	0.89	0.14	0.83	0.53	0.52	0.47
ICA	0.93	0.07	0.60	0.71	0.41	0.50
PCA	0.87	0.12	0.55	0.67	0.46	0.41

Values of $I > 0$ indicate that the value of the measured phenomenon tends to be similar in nearby locations, while $I < 0$ when the values at nearby locations tend to differ.

On the other hand, we also use Geary's C statistic (Bailey and Gatrell, 1995:270):

$$C = \frac{(n-1)\sum_{i=1}^{n}\sum_{j=1}^{n} w_{ij}(y_i - y_j)^2}{2\left(\sum_{i=1}^{n}(y_i - \bar{y})^2\right)\left(\sum\sum_{i\neq j} w_{ij}\right)}$$

The C statistic shows the variance of the difference of neighbouring values, and thus tends to favour smaller-scale autocorrelation effects than the more globally oriented I statistic. The C statistic varies between 0 and 2, and values < 1 indicate positive autocorrelation.

To augment these two autocorrelation measures we use the correlation between a component and the closest traditional dialect region, as this gives some indication of how well these methods agree with more conventional dialectology. Correlations in the usual sense were calculated for a component and all the traditional regions over the municipalities, and the greatest of these correlations was chosen. Values between -1 and 0 indicate negative and those between 0 and 1 positive correlation.

Table 1 shows the summary of our results. It shows for each of the methods and data sets the average of the I and C statistics of the ten components; similarly, it shows the average of the correlation between each component and the closest-matching traditional dialect region. It is not possible to give absolute guidelines on which values are significant, as this depends very much on the properties of the original data, but in short the I statistic and the correlation should be as large and the C statistic as small as possible. To illustrate the differences between the methods, Figure 4 shows the component that corresponds most closely with the northern and central Tavastian dialects in the two corpora.

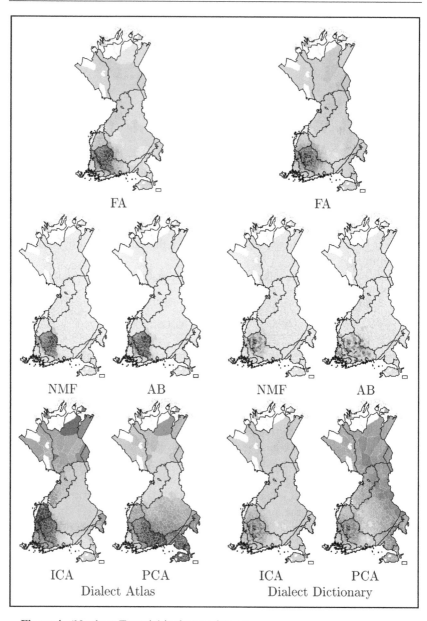

Figure 4. 'Northern Tavastia' in the two data sets.

The maps derived from the Dialect Atlas in Figure 4 show how non-negative matrix factorisation and aspect Bernoulli give much more clearly defined dialects than the other methods. This is also reflected in Table 1: in the columns for the Dialect Atlas, both I and C show strong autocorrelation, and the components correlate highly with traditional dialect regions. However, the columns for the Dialect Dictionary in Figure 4 and Table 1 show that both methods are sensitive to noise in the data, so that in this case the components are spotty, with the least degree of autocorrelation among the five methods.

Independent component analysis has the strongest autocorrelation with the Dialect Atlas data and performs quite well also with the much more noisy Dialect Dictionary data. On the other hand, the components it discovers do not bear as much resemblance to the traditional dialectological understanding. This is especially apparent in the Dialect Atlas data, as evidenced by Figure 4; it is much less visible in the Dialect Dictionary data, where the other methods do not perform much better. In estimating the reliability of the components one should remember that the Dialect Atlas data set is relatively small, whereas ICA in general works better when the sample size is large.

Factor analysis performs reasonably well with the Dialect Atlas data: while it is not the best it still gives results that are both reasonably well autocorrelated and easily interpretable in dialectological terms. With the Dialect Dictionary data, however, it is the clear winner.

Finally, principal components analysis gives components that are spatially cohesive, with autocorrelation measures that are on par with the other methods. However, it is not very good in discovering dialects themselves – but that is because it does not attempt to do so. Instead, it finds directions of variation that are in a sense one step further, underlying the dialects themselves. This means that the first few components may give new insight, but very soon the further components become hard to interpret.

4. COMPARISON OF THE CORPORA

It is also interesting to take the opportunity to look briefly at how the different corpora – one dealing largely with morphological and phonological, the other entirely with lexical variation – show a slightly different division of the Finnish dialects. The subdivision of the southwestern and southeastern dialects is particularly interesting.

As seen in Figure 5, factor analysis of the Dialect Atlas data finds both the traditional southwestern and mid-southwestern dialects as expected. The latter is usually considered a group of transitional dialects between the southwestern and Tavastian dialects, and its existence is explained by settlement history and trade routes in the middle ages. A similar analysis of the Dialect Dictionary data, however, divides the dialect into a northern and eastern group along the coastline,

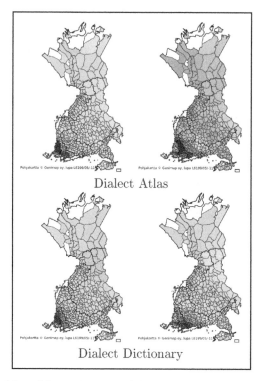

Dialect Atlas

Dialect Dictionary

Figure 5. Division of the southwestern dialects given by factor analysis.

with the dividing line following the medieval highway from the coast inland. The contacts within each of these regions are still strong, and it is possible to view the difference between the two corpora as reflecting, in one case, Viking-age settlement and medieval contacts and, in the other, more modern cultural unity.

Figure 6 shows a similar division of the southeastern dialects. The Dialect Atlas gives the Carelian isthmus and the Finnish-speaking areas in Ingria as one group and the northwestern coasts of Lake Ladoga as the other. This is historically understandable, as Ingria was settled from Finland in the 17th century, after Sweden took the area from Russia; on the other hand, the northern coast of Lake Ladoga was historically bilingual between Finnish and the closely related Carelian. The Dialect Dictionary, however, divides the dialect along the pre-World War II border between Finland and Russia.

In both cases the differences seem to stem from the differences in how grammatical and lexical features spread. Words are easily borrowed from neighbours, so lexical data divides these two regions along the lines where people had most contact – in the case of southwestern dialects from the late

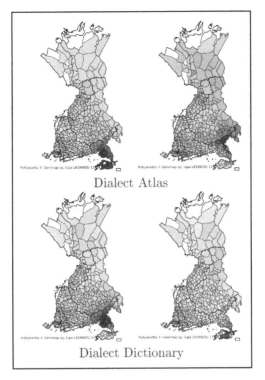

Dialect Atlas

Dialect Dictionary

Figure 6. Division of the southeastern dialects given by factor analysis.

medieval or early modern period onwards, in the case of southeastern dialects since the pre-WWII borders were established in the early 19th century. The morphological and phonological features, however, reflect a significantly older contact, and in this case it is even plausible to consider that the differing features did not spread by borrowing from neighbours but instead by the people themselves moving.

5. CONCLUSIONS

There are several component analysis methods that can be used to analyse corpora of isogloss or other presence–absence data. Such data exists in a wide range of disciplines, from archaeology to zoology; from a methodological point of view it is rather arbitrary and even irrelevant that we have chosen dialectal variation as our subject. The methods are all useful, but each has its own limitations, and these limitations should be kept in mind when selecting the method for a particular dialectological task. Similarly, the properties of the chosen method are relevant when interpreting the results.

The oldest of the methods in this study, principal components analysis, can be useful for trying to get one step beyond the dialect division itself: the components it finds should not be viewed as separate dialects but rather as a layered view of the variation. In interpreting each of the components one should always keep in mind that the bulk of the variation has already been explained away by the earlier components. This makes interpretation hard.

Although almost as old as PCA, factor analysis is still one of the most useful methods here. In fact, a large part of this study can be summarised as a general guideline: 'if in doubt, start with factor analysis'. This method may not be the best, but in analysing the two quite different corpora it gave solid and easily interpretable results in both cases.

Turning to the more recent methods, Independent component analysis may be useful for giving a fresh look into the variation, especially if there is a large amount of data. In the present case, its results have less resemblance with traditional dialectological notions, and in some cases such new insight can be useful. For a more mainstream view of the dialect variation, however, the other methods would likely be more useful.

With the last two methods, Non-negative matrix factorisation and aspect Bernoulli, one of the key questions is the amount of noise in the data. These two seem to be the most sensitive to the effects of uneven gathering of the raw data. On the other hand, when the data results from a survey that has treated the whole study area with equal thoroughness, these methods give very good results.

Finally, the two corpora we used were different in that one consists mostly of grammatical and the other of lexical features. This difference is reflected in the results, so that while analysis of both corpora shows mostly quite similar dialects there are also differences. These differences can be explained by the different ways that lexical and grammatical innovations spread: in short – and getting dangerously close to oversimplifying – lexical elements are transferred via cultural contacts, while morphological and phonological features seem to spread most easily when the speakers of a dialect themselves move to a new area. In the future it would be interesting to do a more thorough study of these differences, and also to compare dialects to the distributions of place names (e.g. Leino, 2007) or ethnological features (e.g. Vuorela, 1976).

REFERENCES

T. C. Bailey and A. C. Gatrell (1995), *Interactive Spatial Data Analysis* (Harlow).

S. Embleton and E. S. Wheeler (1997), 'Finnish dialect atlas for quantitative studies', *Journal of Quantitative Linguistics*, 4(1–3), 99–102.

W. Heeringa and J. Nerbonne (2002), 'Dialect areas and dialect continua', *Language Variation and Change*, 13, 375–398.

H. Hotelling (1933), 'Analysis of a complex of statistical variables into principal components', *Journal of Educational Psychology*, 24, 417–441, 498–520.

A. Hyvärinen, J. Karhunen, and E. Oja (2001), *Independent Component Analysis*.

S. Hyvönen, A. Leino and M. Salmenkivi (2007), 'Multivariate analysis of finnish dialect data – an overview of lexical variation', *Literary and Linguistic Computing*, 22(3), 271–290.

A. Kaban, E. Bingham and T. Hirsimäki (2004), 'Learning to read between the lines: The aspect bernoulli model', in *Proceedings of the 4th SIAM International Conference on Data Mining*, 462–466.

L. Kaufman and P. J. Rousseeuw (1990), *Finding Groups in Data: An Introduction to Cluster Analysis*.

L. Kettunen (1940a), *Suomen murteet III A. Murrekartasto*.

L. Kettunen (1940b), *Suomen murteet III B. Selityksiä murrekartastoon*.

D. Lee and H. Seung (1999), 'Learning the parts of objects by non-negative matrix factorization', *Nature*, 401, 788–791.

A. Leino (2007), 'Regional variation in Finnish lake and hill names', in B. Eggert, B. Holmberg, and B. Jørgensen, eds, *Nordiske navnes centralitet og regionalitet. Rapport fra NORNAs 35. symposium på Bornholm 4.–7. maj 2006, Volume 82 of NORNA-rapporter*, 123–144.

A. Leino, S. Hyvönen and M. Salmenkivi (2006), 'Mitä murteita suomessa onkaan? murresanaston levikin kvantitatiivista analyysiä', *Virittäjä*, 110, 26–45.

H. Moisl and V. Jones (2005), 'Cluster analysis of the newcastle electronic corpus of tyneside english: A comparison of methods', *Literary and Linguistic Computing*, 20, 125–146.

P. Paatero (1997), 'Least squares formulation of robust non-negative factor analysis', *Chemometrics and Intelligent Laboratory Systems*, 37, 23–35.

A. C. Rencher (2002), *Methods of Multivariate Analysis*, Wiley Series in probability and statistics.

I. Savijärvi and E. Yli-Luukko (1994), *Jämsän äijän murrekirja*, Suomalaisen Kirjallisuuden Seuran toimituksia.

A. Trujillo-Ortiz, R. Hernandez-Walls, A. Castro-Perez, M. Rodriguez-Ceja, A. Melendez-Sanchez, E. del Angel-Bustos, M. Melo-Rosales, B. Vega-Rodriguez, C. Moreno-Medina, A. Ramirez-Valdez, J. D'Olivo-Cordero, L. Espinosa-Chaurand, and G. Beltran-Flores (2006), 'Anfactpc: Factor analysis by the principal components method', A MATLAB file. http://www.mathworks.com/matlabcentral/fileexchange/loadFile.do?objectId=10601.

T. Tuomi, ed. (1989), *Suomen murteiden sanakirja. Johdanto (Dictionary of Finnish Dialects. Introduction)*, Kotimaisten kielten tutkimuskeskuksen julkaisuja.

T. Vuorela, ed. (1976), *Atlas of Finnish folk culture*.

FACTOR ANALYSIS OF VOWEL PRONUNCIATION IN SWEDISH DIALECTS

THERESE LEINONEN

Abstract   *In this study 91 local Swedish dialects were analysed based on vowel pronunciation. Acoustic measurements of vowel quality were made for 18 vowels of 1,014 speakers by means of principal component analysis of vowel spectra. Two principal components were extracted explaining more than $\frac{3}{4}$ of the total variance in the vowel spectra. Plotting vowels in the PC1-PC2 plane showed a solution with strong resemblance to vowels in a formant plane. Per location averages of all speakers were calculated and factor analysis was run with the 91 locations as data cases and the two acoustic component of the 18 words as variables. Nine factors were extracted corresponding to distinct geographic distribution patterns. The factor scores of the analysis revealed co-occurrence of a number of linguistic features.*

I. INTRODUCTION

The traditional method of identifying dialect areas has been the so-called isogloss method, where researchers choose some linguistic features that they find representative for the dialect areas and draw lines on maps based on different realisations of these features. One problem with the isogloss method is that isoglosses rarely coincide, and a second is that the choice of linguistic features is subjective and depends on what the researcher chooses to emphasise. Dialectometric research has been trying to avoid these problems by aggregating over large data sets and using more objective data-driven methods when determining dialect areas (Séguy, 1973; Goebl, 1982; Heeringa, 2004; Nerbonne, 2009).

International Journal of Humanities and Arts Computing 2 (1–2) 2008, 189–204
DOI: 10.3366/E175385480900038X
© Edinburgh University Press and the Association for History and Computing 2009

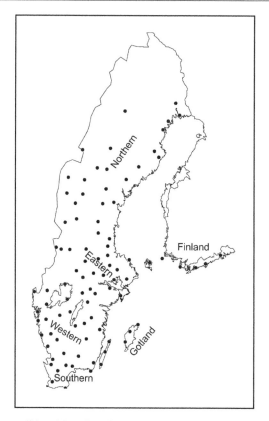

Figure 1. The traditional Swedish dialect areas according to Wessén (1969) and the 91 data sites for the current study.

In the Swedish language area the traditional dialect divisions have been based on particularly phonetic, phonological and morphological features, usually seen from a historical perspective. Wessén (1969:13) notes that the borders of two or more linguistic traits seldom coincide and that every single dialect division therefore will be a construct depending on what the researcher considers to be important. Nonetheless, a sketch of a dialect division will help to give an overview of the varying linguistic phenomena. For the Swedish dialect area no sharp dialect borders have been suggested. In the dialect continuum, however, some main dialect groups have been identified. Figure 1 shows the six traditional Swedish dialect areas according to Wessén (1969). The English labels on the map are according to Rendahl (2001), who also suggested that the Eastern dialect area would actually reach much further to the south than in Wessén's division and thus would divide the mainland Swedish dialects more strongly in the east-west direction.

Recently studies have been carried out where the Swedish dialects have been categorised according to some specific linguistic features. Bruce (2004) classified Swedish dialects according to intonational variation and found seven distinct dialect regions. Schaeffler (2005) categorised the Swedish dialects based on phonological quantity and found a clear division into three areas: Southern Swedish, Northern Swedish and Finland-Swedish.

Lundberg (2005) used clustering methods for analysing differences in the pronunciation of the vowel in the word *lat* in 95 Swedish dialects. The study included samples from an average of three speakers per location analysed with Mel-frequency cepstral coefficients. A comparison of Swedish dialects based on acoustic measurements of the whole vowel system is nonetheless lacking. In other language areas, however, large scale studies of regiolects and sociolects based on acoustic measures of vowel pronunciation have been carried out. Labov et al. (2005) described regional varieties of North American English by measuring the first two formants of on average 300 vowel tokens of 439 speakers. Adank et al. (2007) investigated regional differences in vowel pronunciation in Standard Dutch based on measurements of duration and formant frequencies of 15 vowels of 160 Dutch and Flemish speakers.

In dialectometric research statistical methods like cluster analysis and multidimensional scaling have successfully been used to determine dialect areas and to explore dialect continua (Heeringa, 2004). These methods are based on aggregate pair-wise distances between dialects, which makes it difficult to trace the underlying linguistic features determining the dialect division. In order to identify linguistic structure in aggregate analysis, Nerbonne (2006) applied factor analysis to transcribed vowel data from the Southern states of the U.S. The analysis revealed which vowels could explain most of the variation and also which vowels show similar variation patterns. However, the statistic analysis only revealed which vowels were the most important ones for the analysis, but manual investigation of the data was needed in order to identify the exact qualitative differences between dialects for the vowels concerned.

Factor analysis was also used by Clopper and Paolillo (2006) to analyse formant frequencies and duration of 14 American English vowels as produced by 48 speakers from six dialect regions. The analysis showed regional patterns and co-occurrence of some vowel features, but the analysis was complicated by interactions with gender.

The purpose of the current study is to describe the Swedish dialect landscape based on acoustic measurements of vowel pronunciation. The aim is to find dialect regions, and additionally to characterise the dialect areas linguistically. The latter has attracted too little attention in dialectometric research. Moreover, a goal was to investigate whether there are vowel features that seem to bundle together, on the one hand, and, on the other hand, whether there are vowel features with clearly different geographic distributions. The study is based on acoustic measurements of the vowels of more than 1,000 speakers, which is more speakers than in any acoustic study mentioned above. Hence, it was crucial to use an acoustic method that could be automated to a higher degree than formant measurements, which is the most common method for assessing vowel quality from spectra but which requires manual correction. An other aim was to reduce the effect of sex on the acoustic measurements.

Developing exact dialect-geographical techniques is of importance for describing diffusion of linguistic phenomena, the results, however, also play a role in a larger context of cultural history.

2. DATA

The data were recorded within the project Swedia, a collaboration between the universities of Lund, Stockholm and Umeå (Bruce et al., 1999). The data were gathered during the period 1998–2001 at 107 locations in Sweden and the Swedish-speaking parts of Finland. At each location recordings were made of twelve speakers: three elderly women, three elderly men, three younger women and three younger men.

Vowel segments were elicited with existing mono- or bi-syllabic words. To keep the phonetic context of the vowels as stable as possible, the target vowels were always surrounded by coronal consonants. For the current study the vowels from the stressed syllables in the following 18 words were used (Standard Swedish pronunciation in square brackets): *dis* [diːs], *disk* [dɪsk], *dör* [dœːr], *dörr* [dœr], *flytta* [flʏta], *lass* [las], *lat* [lɑːt], *leta* [leːta], *lett* [let], *lott* [lɔt], *lus* [lʉːs], *lär* [læːr], *lös* [løːs], *nät* [nɛːt], *sot* [suːt], *särk* [særk], *söt* [søːt], *typ* [tyːp]. Each speaker repeated these words 3–5 times. The words were chosen so that they would cover the whole vowel space of Standard Swedish and also reflect some language historical developments. For example, nowadays the words *lös* and *söt* have the same vowel phoneme in Standard Swedish. However, historically the former originates from a diphthong /au/, which has been monophthongised in most varieties of Swedish, while the latter one is an original monophthong. Some of the Swedish dialects have preserved these vowels as two different phonemes. The deviant phoneme systems of Swedish dialects were also the reason that real words were used instead of a fixed consonant context, which is often the case in vowel research.

The recordings in the data base were annotated and segmented within the Swedia project. However, some of the 107 sites in the data base were only partly segmented. Moreover, it was not the case that all words mentioned above were elicited at all sites and by all speakers. Consequently, a subset of the Swedia data is used in the current study: 1,014 speakers from 91 sites. For some of these 91 sites data are missing for some speakers. This means that the number of speakers is not constant across locations,and that the number of women and men or older and younger speakers is not always equal. Figure 1 shows a map with dots for the 91 data sites in the current study and the approximate areas of the traditional Swedish dialect division according to Wessén (1969).

3. METHODS

3.1 Principal components and factor analysis

In the current study methods for data reduction were used twice. Section 3.2 explains how principal component analysis (PCA) was used on band filtered vowel spectra in order to obtain a representation of vowel quality. Subsequently, the results of this acoustic analysis were used as variables in a factor analysis (FA) which aimed at discovering the patterns of dialectal variation, as explained in Sections 3.3.

PCA and FA are closely related statistical methods. Thorough comparisons of the differences between the two methods can be found in handbooks, for example Tabachnik and Fidell (2007). A short description of the differences is offered by Leino and Hyvönen (this volume). In the following a short overview of the usage of these methods is given.

Both PCA and FA aim at reducing a bigger number of variables into a smaller set of components or factors. They enable the researcher to identify which variables in a data set show similar patterns of variation and whether the variables can be divided into relatively independent subsets. Variables that correlate with each other are combined into components, which means that the total amount of data can be reduced.

The starting point for a PCA or FA is a variance-covariance matrix or a standardised correlation matrix of the observed variables. The result is a set of *factor loadings* and a set of *factor scores*. Factor loadings are correlations that show to what degree each of the original variables correlates with the extracted components. Factor scores, on the other hand, are values assigned to cases. They estimate the value of a factor (regarded as an implicit variable) for each case. Loadings and scores can be interpreted as describing the data. Alternatively, the scores can be used as input to further analyses replacing the larger number of original variables for each case, and thus reducing the data set.

3.2 Acoustic measure of vowel quality

The traditional way of assessing vowel quality acoustically involves formant measurements. A problem with measuring formants, however, is that algorithms for automatically determining formants in a spectrum always give a large number of false measurements. If two formants are very close to each other they sometimes cannot be separated by the algorithms; on the other hand, if two successive formants are separated by a big distance, the algorithms sometimes find false formants in the gap between the real formants. For example in a study by Adank et al. (2004), where formants were first measured automatically and subsequently verified manually, 20–5 per cent of the measurements had to be hand corrected.

Since the current study involved 1,014 speakers pronouncing 18 different vowels 3–5 times, measuring formants and hand-correcting the data was not a feasible option. Instead we chose PCA on band filtered spectra, which is a method introduced by Pols et al. (1973). This method can be fully automated, and Jacobi et al. (2005) have shown that there is a high correlation between principal components of Bark filtered vowel spectra and the two first formants.

Because of the anatomic differences between women and men, women in general have both a higher fundamental frequency and higher formant frequencies than men. This is why the acoustic analysis was carried out separately on the female and male data. The spectra of all vowel pronunciations were Bark filtered in the frequency area covering the two first formants (3–15 Bark for women and 2–14 Bark for men). The analysis was made in the centre of each vowel segment with a window length of 13 ms. Intensities were equalised at 80 dB. The measurements were done automatically in Praat (Boersma and Weenink, 2009). After the Bark filtering each vowel pronunciation was described by 13 different values, that is, the decibel levels in each of the filters. Since every speaker repeated the words 3–5 times, averages were calculated per word per speaker. PCA on a variance-covariance matrix with Varimax rotation (see Tabachnik and Fidell (2007) for rotation techniques) was performed separately on the female and male subset of the data. Following Jacobi et al. (2005) the loadings were calculated using only corner vowels (vowels with the most extreme values for F1 and F2; for the Swedish data the vowels transcribed as [i], [æ], [ɑ] and [u] in the data base were chosen). This is done in order to weigh all articulatory dimensions equally in the PCA. Some dialects, however, show such strong deviation from Standard Swedish that not all corner vowels could be found in the set of 18 words. Therefore corner vowels were not available for all of the speakers and subsets of 230 women and 230 men were used for calculating the loadings. The average of all occurrences per vowel per speaker were used, resulting in inputs of 920 rows, each containing 13 values. Subsequently, factor scores were calculated for the full data set of 18 vowels per speaker (due to some missing data: 9,398 rows in the analysis of the female data and 8,802 rows in the analysis of the male data). Two factors were extracted explaining 77.8 per cent of the variance for the female data and 76.6 per cent for the male data.

Figure 2 shows the loadings of the analyses of the female and male data. The curves of the two components look very similar for women and men. They only

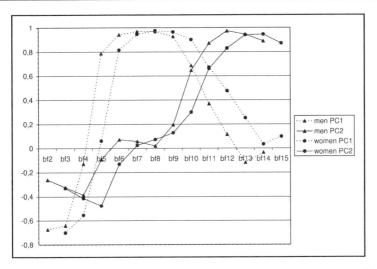

Figure 2. Loadings on the Bark filters (bf) of the two extracted components of the female analysis (3–15 Bark) and the male analysis (2–14 Bark).

seem to be placed differently on the frequency scale. In Figure 3 the scale has been shifted so that instead of the real frequency bands (reaching from 2 to 14 Bark in the male analysis and from 3 to 15 Bark in the female analysis) the x-axis shows the 13 subsequent variables for both sexes. This figure shows that the curves are indeed almost identical for women and men, which indicates that the same information is extracted in both analyses. Because of the anatomical differences between women and men this information can be found on average 1 Bark higher in the female data.

The advantage of running separate PCA's for women and men can be seen in Figures 4 and 5. Figure 4 shows the scores of the corner vowels after running the two separate PCA's for women and men. Just as in a formant plot, the scores are plotted with the first component on the y-axis and the second component on the x-axis with both scales reversed. The ellipses covering one standard deviation of the corner vowels of women and men respectively fit each other almost perfectly. Figure 5 shows the vowel scores of a PCA where women and men were included in the same analysis (2–15 Bark analysed for all speakers) instead of two separate analyses. Because the sexes were analysed together the anatomical differences between women and men led to higher scores for the vowels produced by women. Separate analyses for women and men compensate for the anatomical differences.

The next section (Section 3.3) describes that means per site were calculated for the further analysis, since the aim of this paper was to analyse dialect-geographic variation. If there had been as many women as men pronouncing all the vowels

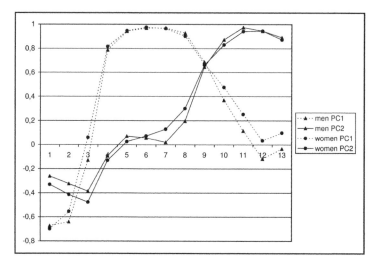

Figure 3. Loadings of the two extracted components of the female analysis (3–15 Bark) and the male analysis (2–14 Bark). In contrast to Figure 2 the loadings in this graph are not plotted against the frequency scale, but so that the curves for women and men start and end at the same point. Variable 1 in the figure thus represents Bark filter 3 for women and Bark filter 2 for men etc.

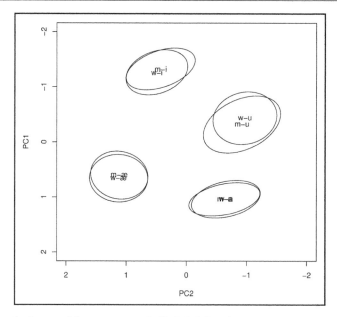

Figure 4. Scores of the corner vowels [i], [æ], [ɑ] and [u] based on separate PCA's for women (w) and men (m). Ellipses cover one standard deviation of the speakers.

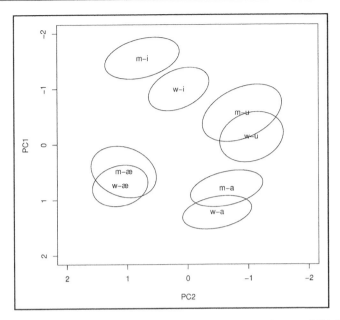

Figure 5. Scores of the corner vowels [i], [æ], [ɑ] and [u] based on one PCA for the speakers of both sexes. Ellipses cover one standard deviation of the female speakers (w) and the male speakers (m) respectively. In contrast to Fig. 4 this analysis fails to normalize vowel quality with respect to sex.

at each location, averaging over the speakers would eliminate any variation caused by anatomical differences between the sexes. However, as mentioned in Section 2, for some sites there are speakers missing. In a factor analytic study (Clopper and Paolillo, 2006) of formant frequencies of the vowels of 48 North American speakers (24 of each sex) from six dialect regions, the two first factors had a stronger connection to sex than to region of origin. By analysing the acoustic data of women and men separately we were able to eliminate variation caused by anatomical differences in the measure of vowel quality. Hence, the mean values per site were not heavily affected by varying amount of data from women and men at each site.

The plot of the vowels in the PC1-PC2 plane (Figure 4) can be compared to formant plots of vowels. As previously mentioned Jacobi et al. (2005) found high correlations between principal components of Bark filtered vowel spectra and the two first formants. However, one should bear in mind that using this method means that rather broadly defined frequency regions determine the representation of vowel quality. Some finer differences in formant levels between dialects, possible to find by manual analysis and correction, may be lost. Because of the similarities between a vowel quadrilateral and the vowels plotted in the

PC1-PC2 plane we can still roughly interpret the first principal component as having a connection to vowel height, while the second is connected to vowel backness.

3.3 Dialectal variation

The results from the PCA of the acoustic data (Section 3.2) were used as input for analysing dialectal variation. The variables for this analysis were the two acoustic components of each of the 18 vowels; in total 36 variables. In articulatory terms these variables roughly correspond to vowel height and backness. Since the aim was to study dialect-geographic variation, for each site in the data set the means of all speakers were calculated. The data, therefore, comprises 91 rows (one for each site) with 36 values.

By comparing different component methods for finding dialect regions Leino and Hyvönen (this volume) concluded that FA is the most stable one providing easily interpretable results. Following their recommendation FA was performed in order to analyse the geographic variation in the present data set. Since the data rows in the analysis were geographic locations each factor clustered acoustic variables with similar geographic distributions. The factor loadings showed the correlations between the acoustic variables and each factor. The results of the FA are presented in Section 4 and the scores for the locations on the factors are visualised on maps. On the maps every site is represented by a dot surrounded by a coloured area scaled between yellow and blue. Yellow means that the score is low, while blue indicates a high score. Hence, sites with similar scores have similar colours, which indicates similar pronunciations.

Factors with an eigenvalue greater than 1 were extracted using Varimax rotation, which led to a solution with nine factors. These factors together explain 71.4 per cent of the variance. Thus, using only nine factors instead of the original 36 variables a large part of the dialectal variation could be explained.

4. RESULTS

In the dialect-geographic analysis nine factors were extracted. In this section, the factor loadings and scores of each factor are presented. Table 1 shows the variables with high loadings on the nine factors. Following Tabachnik and Fidell (2007) loadings above 0.71 are considered *excellent*, above 0.63 *very good* and above 0.55 *good*. Loadings below this are not analysed here.

On the *first factor* a number of front vowels show high positive correlations. For all of these, the correlation concerns the second component of the acoustic analysis, that is the one connected to the front-back dimension. Vowels with excellent correlations are the close vowels [iː], [ɪ], [yː], [ʏ], [eː], [e]. Some more open front vowels show less strong correlations with this factor. Figure 6a

Table 1. Variables with high loadings on the nine extracted factors.

Factor 1			Factor 2			Factor 3		
disk [ɪ]	(pc2)	0.812	dör [œ:]	(pc1)	0.816	typ [y:]	(pc1)	0.867
typ [y:]	(pc2)	0.807	lär [æ:]	(pc1)	0.774	dis [i:]	(pc1)	0.829
leta [e:]	(pc2)	0.799	dör [œ:]	(pc2)	−0.755	sot [u:]	(pc1)	0.683
flytta [ʏ]	(pc2)	0.760	leta [e:]	(pc1)	0.694			
lett [e]	(pc2)	0.758						
dis [i:]	(pc2)	0.750						
lär [æ:]	(pc2)	0.681						
nät [ɛ:]	(pc2)	0.668						
särk [æ]	(pc2)	0.640						
dörr [œ]	(pc2)	0.584						
söt [ø:]	(pc2)	0.559						

Factor 4			Factor 5			Factor 6		
lös [ø:]	(pc1)	0.881	lott [ɔ]	(pc1)	0.702	lus [ʉ:]	(pc2)	0.697
söt [ø:]	(Pc1)	0.809	lat [ɑ:]	(pc1)	0.615	lös [ø:]	(pc2)	0.572
			lass [a]	(pc1)	0.568			

Factor 7			Factor 8			Factor 9		
disk [ɪ]	(pc1)	0.838	dörr [œ]	(pc1)	0.743	nät [ɛ:]	(pc1)	0.653

shows the scores of the dialects on this factor. The more blue the colouring on the map the higher the score. The dialects in the Eastern dialect area, in the parts around Stockholm and Uppsala called *uppsvenska* 'Core Eastern' in the dialect literature, have low scores on this factor, while most of the dialects in the rest of the language area have higher scores.

The *second factor* has a high positive correlation with the first acoustic component of the vowels [œ:] and [æ:] in the words *dör* and *lär* and a high negative correlation with the second acoustic component of [œ:]. There is also a somewhat lower correlation with [e:] in *leta*. A high score on this factor implies a high value on the first acoustic component for the vowels concerned, which indicates a more open pronunciation (compare Figure 4). Since both [æ:] and [œ:] have high correlations on this factor, the conclusion can be drawn that if a dialect has an open pronunciation of one of these vowels, this will also be true for the other one. The quality of the /ö/- and /ä/-sounds is considered an important marker for characterising dialectal identity in Swedish (Elert, 1978). In front of an /r/ these vowels are pronounced more openly than in other positions in Standard Swedish. Dialects with high scores on this factor are the Southern Swedish dialects, Core Eastern dialects, the dialects on Gotland and in Finland, and some of the most Northern dialects (Figure 6b). The high scores in these areas indicate open pronunciations of the vowels (and for [œ:] also a less fronted

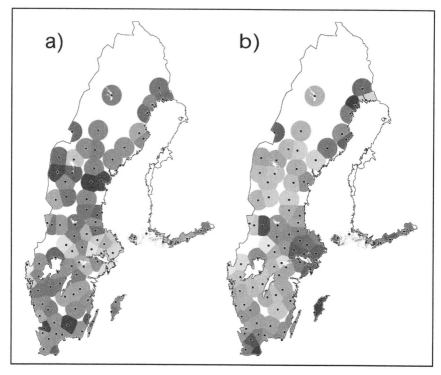

Figure 6. Factor scores of the first (a) and the second (b) factor. Vowels with high loadings on the first factor: [ɪ], [yː], [eː], [ʏ], [e] [iː], [æː], [ɛː], [æ], [œ], [øː]. Vowels with high loadings on the second factor: [œː], [æː], [eː]. Yellow = low score, blue = high score.

pronunciation). The rest of the dialects have a more closed pronunciation of these vowels.

The *third factor* correlates with the first acoustic component of the long high vowels [yː], [iː] and [uː]. The map in Figure 7a shows a north-south division. The dialects in the south of the language area have the highest scores. In articulatory terms this suggests that the vowels are pronounced more openly in the southern parts of the language area.

The first acoustic component of the vowel in *lös* and *söt*, both pronounced [øː] in Standard Swedish, shows excellent correlation with the *fourth factor*. Two areas with quite high scores on this factor can be identified in Figure 7b. One is the area between the Western and the Eastern dialects, also called *mellansvenska* 'Central Swedish' in Swedish dialectology. The other one is in the more south part of the Northern dialect area.

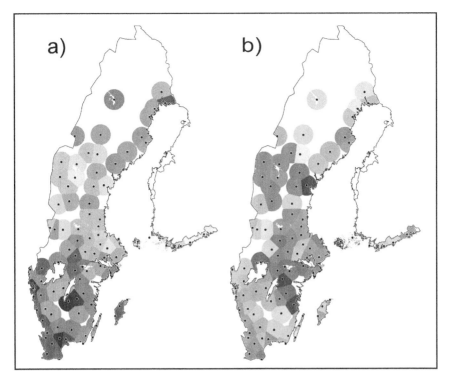

Figure 7. Factor scores of the third (a) and the fourth (b) factor. Vowels with high loadings on the third factor: [y:], [i:], [u:]. Vowels with high loadings on the fourth factor: [ø:]. Yellow = low score, blue = high score.

The *fifth factor* correlates with [ɔ] and somewhat less with the Swedish long and short /a/ ([ɑ:], [a]). There is one outlier in the south of Sweden on this factor (Figure 8a). Also the other Southern Swedish dialects have rather low scores, as have many of the Northern.

The *sixth factor* (Figure 8b) divides the Swedish mainland roughly into a western and an eastern part. Dialects in the west have low scores, while dialects in the east have high scores. The dialects of the Gotland island and in Finland have low scores. The second acoustic component of [ʉ:] and [ø:] are the main variables responsible for this division.

As can be seen in Table 1 factors seven, eight and nine each have only one variable with a high loading. These factors do not have an aggregating effect, since they do not clearly cluster variables. On the other hand they show that there are acoustic variables in the data that show geographical distributions that are not shared by any other variables. The *seventh factor* does not show much geographical coherence, but factors eight and nine identify two rather small

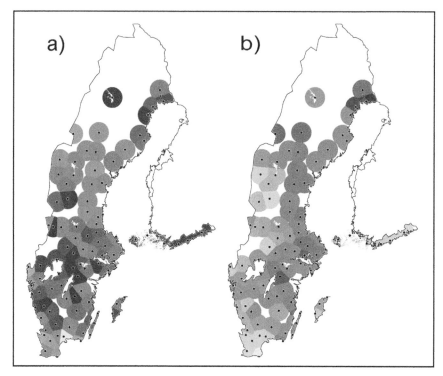

Figure 8. Factor scores of the fifth (a) and the sixth (b) factor. Vowels with high loadings on the fifth factor: [ɔ], [ɑː], [a]. Vowels with high loadings on the sixth factor: [ʉː], [øː]. Yellow = low score, blue = high score.

dialect areas. On the *eighth factor*, described by [œː] in *dörr*, the Northern Swedish dialects closest to the Norwegian border (the province of *Jämtland*) obtain low scores while the rest of the dialects are assigned higher scores. On the *ninth factor* the dialects of the island Gotland are distinguished from the rest by obtaining very low scores.

5. DISCUSSION AND CONCLUSIONS

In this study data reduction methods were used for acoustic analysis of vowel spectra, and for analysing relationships between acoustic-phonetic variables as well as their geographic distribution.

Vowel spectra were Bark filtered and analysed by means of principal component analysis. Vowel pronunciations by women and men were analysed separately, which showed a systematic difference of one Bark in the factor loadings between the sexes. By extracting the acoustic components separately for women and men variation due to anatomical differences between the sexes could be eliminated.

For the analysis of dialectal variation factor analysis was used. Nine factors were extracted showing different geographical distribution patterns in the data, rather than defining distinct dialect areas. For example the third factor showed a north-south distinction, while the sixth factor showed an east-west division of the Swedish mainland. The Core Eastern dialects of the Swedish mainland seem to be a well-distinguished dialect area, as shown by the two first factors. The loadings of the factor analysis showed co-occurrence of some of the vowel features. For example the first factor clustered the second acoustic component of front vowels. The second factor showed that the Swedish /ä/- and /ö/-vowels in front of an /r/ co-vary, and the third factor showed that the first acoustic component of close vowels has a variation distributed geographically as a north-south continuum.

The traditional Swedish dialect areas could only partly be identified by this study. The data set used was large with regard to the amount of data (1,014 speakers); the number of linguistic features, however, was relatively small consisting of 18 vowels. Using more linguistic features in a factor analysis, might reveal clearer dialect areas. However, the strength of factor analysis lies in being able to identify both different diffusion patterns and co-occurring variables. Aggregating techniques, like cluster analysis and multidimensional scaling, might give more straight forward results if the main aim is to determine groups in data.

The results of the factor analytic approach can be compared to those achieved by the traditional isogloss methods. In both cases the distribution maps can be directly connected to underlying linguistic features. But in contrary to drawing isoglosses factor analysis is completely data-driven with automatic recognition of the features that contribute most to the variation in the data and of co-occurring variables. Factor analysis also enables visualisation of continua and gradual borders in the data as well as non-continuous areas, whereas drawing isoglosses suggests abrupt borders. Subjectivity cannot be completely removed from any analysis since all methods depend on the input given. However, using computational methods allows analysis of larger amounts of data than any manual method, which as such reduces the influence of subjective choices.

The different geographical patterns in the data found by the factor analysis can be interpreted as different diffusion patterns. In addition, the possibility to extract co-occurring linguistic features is valuable for typological considerations. This is not important only for the analysis of language, but also for the analysis of other kinds of human activities as investigated by disciplines like archaeology, ethnology and musicology.

In this study the vowel quality was measured only in the centre of each segment. Adding additional vowel features like diphthongisation and length would be interesting for further analyses of dialectal variation in vowel pronunciation. This study was also restricted to averaging over speakers per location. Analysing variation within a site, for example based on age and/or gender, would give additional valuable information about language variation.

REFERENCES

P. Adank, R. Van Hout and R. Smits (2004), 'An acoustic description of the vowels of Northern and Southern Standard Dutch', *Journal of the Acoustical Society of America*, 116, 1729–1938.
P. Adank, R. Van Hout and H. Van de Velde (2007), 'An acoustic description of the vowels of Northern and Southern Standard Dutch II: Regional varieties', *Journal of the Acoustical Society of America*, 121, 1130–1141.
P. Boersma and D. Weenink (2009), *Praat: doing phonetics by computer*. [phonetic software] [version 5.1] ⟨URL: http://www.praat.org⟩ [18 May 2009].
G. Bruce (2004), 'An intonational typology of swedish', in *Proceedings of Speech Prosody 2004*, (Nara), 175–178.
G. Bruce, C.-C. Elert, O. Engstrand and A. Eriksson (1999), 'Phonetics and phonology of the Swedish dialects: a project presentation and a database demonstrator', in *Proceedings of the 14th International Congress of Phonetic Sciences (ICPhS 99)*, San Francisco, 321–324.
C. G. Clopper and J. C. Paolillo (2006), 'North American English vowels: A factor-analytic perspective', *Literary and Linguistic Computing*, 21(4), 445–462.
C.-C. Elert (1978), 'Diftongeringar och konsonantinslag i svenskans långa vokaler', in I. Jonsson (ed.), *Språken i vårt språk* (Stockholm), 168–181.
H. Goebl (1982), *Dialektometrie; Prinzipien und Methoden des Einsatzes der numerischen Taxonomie im Bereich der Dialektgeographie*, Volume 157 of *Philosophisch-Historische Klasse Denkschriften* (Vienna).
W. Heeringa, (2004), *Measuring Dialect Pronunciation Differences using Levenshtein Distance* (Ph.D. thesis, University of Groningen).
I. Jacobi, L. C. W. Pols and J. Stroop (2005), 'Polder Dutch: Aspects of the /ei/-lowering in Standard Dutch', in *Interspeech'05*, (Lisboa), 2877–2880.
W. Labov, S. Ash and C. Boberg (2005), *The Atlas of North American English* (Berlin).
A. Leino and S. Hyvönen (this volume), 'Comparison of Component Models in Analysing the Distribution of Dialectal Features', *International Journal of Humanities and Arts Computing*
J. Lundberg (2005), 'Classifying dialects using cluster analysis' (Master's thesis, Göteborg University).
J. Nerbonne (2006), 'Identifying linguistic structure in aggregate comparison', *Literary and Linguistic Computing*, 21(4), 463–476.
J. Nerbonne (2009), 'Data-driven dialectology', *Language and Linguistics Compass*, 3(1), 175–198.
L. C. W. Pols, H. R. C. Tromp and R. Plomp (1973), 'Frequency analysis of Dutch vowels from 50 male speakers', *Journal of the Acoustical Society of America*, 53, 1093–1101.
A.-C. Rendahl (2001), 'Swedish dialects around the Baltic See', in Ö. Dahl and M. Koptjevskaja-Tamm, eds, *Circum-Baltic Languages. Vol. I: Past and Present* (Amsterdam), 137–177.
F. Schaeffler (2005), *Phonological Quantity in Swedish Dialects* (Ph.D. thesis, Umeå University).
J. Séguy (1973), 'La dialectométrie dans l'Atlas linguistique de la Gascogne', *Revue de linguistique romane*, 37, 1–24.
B. G. Tabachnik and L. S. Fidell (2007), *Using Mulitvariate Statistics*, 5th ed. (Boston etc.).
E. Wessén, (1969), *Våra folkmål*, 9th ed. (Stockholm).

REPRESENTING TONE IN LEVENSHTEIN DISTANCE

CATHRYN YANG AND ANDY CASTRO

Abstract   Levenshtein distance, also known as string edit distance, has been shown to correlate strongly with both perceived distance and intelligibility in various Indo-European languages (Gooskens and Heeringa, 2004; Gooskens, 2006). We apply Levenshtein distance to dialect data from Bai (Allen, 2004), a Sino-Tibetan language, and Hongshuihe (HSH) Zhuang (Castro and Hansen, accepted), a Tai language. In applying Levenshtein distance to languages with contour tone systems, we ask the following questions: 1) How much variation in intelligibility can tone alone explain? and 2) Which representation of tone results in the Levenshtein distance that shows the strongest correlation with intelligibility test results? This research evaluates six representations of tone: onset, contour and offset; onset and contour only; contour and offset only; target approximation (Xu & Wang, 2001), autosegments of H and L, and Chao's (1930) pitch numbers. For both languages, the more fully explicit onset-contour-offset and onset-contour representations showed significantly stronger inverse correlations with intelligibility. This suggests that, for cross-dialectal listeners, the optimal representation of tone in Levenshtein distance should be at a phonetically explicit level and include information on both onset and contour.

I. INTRODUCTION

The Levenshtein distance algorithm measures the phonetic distance between closely related language varieties by counting the cost of transforming the phonetic segment string of one cognate into another by means of insertions, deletions and substitutions. After Kessler (1995) first applied the algorithm to dialect data in Irish Gaelic, Heeringa (2004) showed that cluster analysis based on Levenshtein distances agreed remarkably with expert consensus on

International Journal of Humanities and Arts Computing 2 (1–2) 2008, 205–219
DOI: 10.3366/E1753854809000391

Dutch dialect groupings. In addition, Gooskens and Heeringa (2004) found a significant correlation between Levenshtein distance and perceived distance among Norwegian listeners (r = .67, r < .001), and Gooskens (2006) found an even stronger correlation with intelligibility among Scandinavian languages (r = −.82, p < .001).

Previously, the application of Levenshtein distance has been limited to Indo-European languages. However, Yang (accepted) showed that hierarchical clustering based on Levenshtein distance paralleled that of historical-comparative analysis in Nisu, a Tibeto-Burman language. Also, Levenshtein distance showed a strong, significant correlation with intelligibility test results (r = −.62, p < .001) in Nisu. This correlation suggests that Levenshtein distance is a good approximation of intelligibility for East Asian tonal languages. We apply Levenshtein distance to word lists from *Bai Dialect Survey* (Allen, 2004) and *Hongshuihe Zhuang Dialect Intelligibility Survey* (Castro and Hansen, accepted) and correlate the results with intelligibility test scores obtained during the respective surveys.

Contour tone is a distinguishing characteristic of many East Asian language families such as Sino-Tibetan and Tai-Kadai. Norwegian also has phonemic tone, but Gooskens and Heeringa (2006) found that prosody in Norwegian as measured by Levenshtein distance showed only a weak correlation with perceived distance (r = .24, p < .01) and could only explain 6 per cent of the variance. However, in their perceptual experiment with Chinese dialects, Tang and van Heuven (2007) compared natural speech recordings with recordings that had the pitch variations synthetically removed. They found that listeners made better subjective judgments about dialect distance with the fully tonal recordings than with the recordings that had the tonal information removed. In this paper, our first question investigates the relationship between tone and intelligibility: how much of the variation in intelligibility test results can be explained by tone alone? We measure tone and segment distance separately, correlate the distances with intelligibility test scores, then use multiple linear regression analysis to see which variable has the greatest relative contribution to intelligibility.

Additionally, we investigate the optimal way of representing tones in the Levenshtein distance algorithm in relation to intelligibility. We evaluate six representations of tone, although there are many more possible ways. We correlate Levenshtein distance using each tone representation with intelligibility to answer the question: Which way of representing tone in the Levenshtein distance algorithm shows the strongest correlation with intelligibility? Phonetically explicit representations, which include information on tonal onset, contour, and offset, are compared with more phonemic representations of tone as autosegments and targets. We also include Chao's pitch numbers, since this is the most widely used method of transcribing tone in East Asian tone languages.

2. MATERIAL

We used material from two dialect surveys on minority languages in China: Allen (2004) on the Bai language of Yunnan Province, and Castro and Hansen (accepted) on Hongshuihe (HSH) Zhuang in Guangxi Zhuang Autonomous Region. Both surveys included 500-item wordlists and intelligibility testing using Recorded Text Testing (RTT) methodology (see Section 3.3).

2.1 Bai

Bai is an ethnic minority language in southwest China with a population of around 1.8 million, with the vast majority located in Dali Bai Autonomous Prefecture (Allen, 2004; Yunnan Provincial Statistics Department, 2004). Although Bai is definitely Sino-Tibetan, linguists disagree as to whether it belongs in the Sinitic or the Tibeto-Burman branch of the family (Wang, 2005; Matisoff, 2003).

Previous research on Bai dialects group varieties into Central, Southern, and Northern (Xu and Zhao, 1984; Allen, 2004). Northern Bai, known to its speakers as Leimei, is considerably different from Central and Southern Bai, though still closely related (Bradley, 2007). Wang (2006) identifies a key tonal innovation that groups Southern varieties together: the development of a mid-rising tone in Proto-Bai *Tone 1a in syllables with *voiceless unaspirated and some *voiced sonorant initials. In other environments, *Tone 1a shows a high tone in Southern Bai dialects. Central and Northern Bai show a high tone in *Tone 1a in all environments. Also, Central and Southern Bai share the devoicing of *voiced stops, while Northern Bai retains a voiced stop series.

Allen (2004) collected 500-item word lists in nine locations, including varieties from each dialect group. Northern Bai was represented by Lushui Luobenzhuo in Nujiang Prefecture to the west of Dali, while Central Bai varieties were represented by Lanping Jinding (also in Nujiang), Jianchuan Diannan, and Heqing Jindun. Southern varieties include Dali Zhoucheng, Dali Qiliqiao, and Xiangyun Hedian. Allen (2004) placed Eryuan Xishan and Yunlong Baishi within the Central Bai group due to their high level of comprehension of other Central Bai varieties. However, Eryuan and Yunlong share the *Tone 1a innovation with other Southern varieties in contrast to Central Bai, so historically they belong to Southern Bai. See Figure 1 for a map of the Bai language area.

Allen also recorded personal narratives in seven of the nine locations (excluding Xiangyun and Qiliqiao) and used them to develop intelligibility tests known as Recorded Text Tests (RTT) (see Section 3.1). We correlate Allen's RTT scores with the Levenshtein distances based on his wordlists.

207

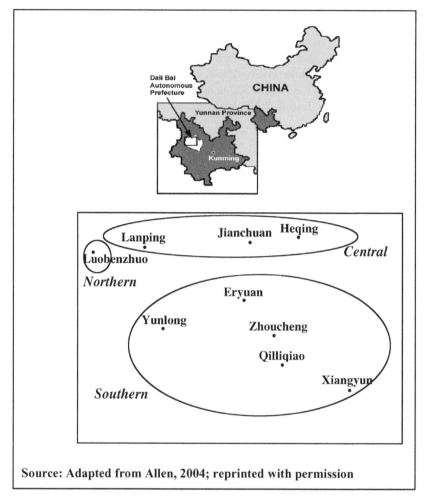

Source: Adapted from Allen, 2004; reprinted with permission

Figure 1. Bai language area.

2.2 Hongshuihe Zhuang

Hongshuihe (HSH) Zhuang, with a population of over 3 million, is spoken in Guangxi Zhuang Autonomous Region in southern China (National Statistics Department, 2003). HSH Zhuang is a Northern Tai language of the Tai-Kadai family. HSH Zhuang is a subgroup of the Zhuang ethnic group, but remains linguistically distinct from other Zhuang languages. See Figure 2 below for the location of Guangxi and HSH Zhuang language area.

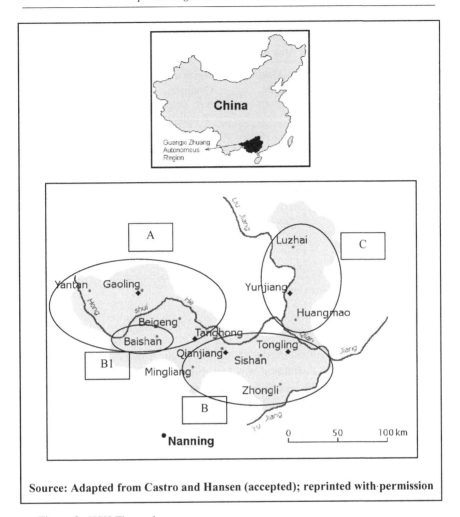

Source: Adapted from Castro and Hansen (accepted); reprinted with·permission

Figure 2. HSH Zhuang language area.

Very little dialect research has been done on HSH Zhuang varieties, but in 2006 Castro and Hansen (accepted) collected 511-item wordlists in 20 locations. Through analysis of the different diachronic developments in the dialect areas' tone systems, they identify three major dialect areas: A, B, and C, seen in Figure 2 below. Using Li's (1977) reconstruction of Proto-Tai tones, Castro and Hansen group the varieties together by tracking their modern reflexes for historic tone categories. Li reconstructs three Proto-Tai tone categories for syllables ending in a vowel or nasal (known as 'unchecked syllables'), which he labels

Table 1. Divergent diachronic developments in HSH Zhuang tone systems.

		Area A	Area B	Area B1	Area C
	Varieties:	Yantan, Gaoling, Beigeng, Tanghong	Mingliang, Qianjiang, Sishan, Zhongli, Tongling	Baishan	Yunjiang, Luzhai, Huangmao
Tone category:					
A1		53	35	35	53, in some places 53ʔ
A2		21, in some places 231	13	31	231
B1		33	55	55	45
B2		31	31	21	31ʔ
C1		453	33	45	53, in some places 453
C2		13, in some places 213	21	13	213

Source: adapted from Castro and Hansen (accepted).

A, B, and C. Voiced initials produced a lower pitch, which became phonemic tone when the voicing distinction was lost, producing six categories: A1, B1, and C1 for syllables with voiceless initials, and A2, B2, and C2 for syllables with originally voiced initials. Table 1 shows the divergent modern reflexes for each tone category in each area, as well as the varieties included in each area. For Areas A and B, the contour shapes are often the converse of each other: Area A's high falling tone in A1 corresponds to Area B's high rising, etc. Area C tones are distinct from the other two groups by the added feature of glottal closure at the end of the contour in tones A1 and B2. Castro and Hansen tentatively group Area B1 with Area B, but the tone correspondences do not match completely.

In each dialect area, Castro and Hansen selected one or two varieties that shared the most lexical items with other locations in their respective areas, for a total of five varieties: Gaoling and Tanghong for A, Qianjiang and Tongling for B, Yunjiang for C. In Figure 2 below, these sites are marked with black diamonds. They then used the personal narratives collected in those five varieties to conduct intelligibility testing (RTT methodology, see Section 3.1) in twelve locations: Yantan, Gaoling, Beigeng, and Baishan in A, Qianjiang, Mingliang, Sishan, Tongling, and Zhongli in B, and Yunjiang, Luzhai and Huangmao in C. See Figure 2 below for their locations. The twelve testing locations were selected in order to provide the widest geographic representation of HSH Zhuang.

Table 2. Cost of operations in Levenshtein distance.

Location	Transcription	Operation	Cost
Eryuan [kʲe³⁵]	kʲe_MRH		
	ke_MRH	delete j	1
	ke_HRH	substitute H for M	1
Jianchuan [ke⁵⁵]	ke_HEH	substitute E for R	1
		total cost	3
		normalised cost	.23

3. METHODOLOGY

To answer our first question about the relation between tone and intelligibility, we calculate the Levenshtein distances for tone separately from that of phonetic segments, correlate the two distances with intelligibility, then use multiple regression analysis to see which variable has the greater contribution to intelligibility. To answer our second question about the optimal representation of tone, we first calculate the Pearson correlation coefficient between intelligibility and the Levenshtein distances using each of the four representations of tone described below in Section 3.1.1. We then use Meng et al's (1992) test for correlated correlation coefficients to see if the highest coefficient is significantly higher than the others.

3.1 Levenshtein distance

Levenshtein distance, also known as edit distance, measures the difference between two strings. The Levenshtein distance between phonetic transcriptions of two cognates is the least number of insertions, deletions and substitutions needed to transform one cognate into another (Heeringa, 2004). One of the strengths of Levenshtein distance is that it always uses the string alignment that incurs the least cost of transformation. We applied Levenshtein distance to the Bai (500-item) and HSH Zhuang (511-item) wordlists using the free RuG-L04 software developed by Kleiweg (2004).

Table 2 calculates the Levenshtein distance between two Bai cognates for the gloss 'chicken,' pronounced [ke⁵⁵] in Jianchuan and [kʲe³⁵] in Eryuan. Tone is represented with tone onset, contour, and offset (see 3.1.1). Insertions, deletions, and substitutions are all weighted the same, with the cost of one. Differences are binary: either the sounds are the same, with no transformation cost, or they are different, with a cost of one. Heeringa et al (2006) found that using binary segment differences was equally valid with that of using gradual measures of distance between segments.

In order to prevent longer words from having undue weight in the calculation of average distance, a normalisation function was used in which the total cost is

Table 3. Sub-lexical variation in HSH Zhuang.

English	Proto-Tai	Liushui	Yantan	Gaoling	Mingliang
chin	khaaŋ A2	haːŋ²³¹	haːŋ²³ kaːu⁴⁴	haːŋ²³pɛ⁴³³	haːŋ³¹ ma³¹

divided by the sum of length of the two strings. In cases where the two strings have no segment in common, the Levenshtein distance is proportional to the sum of the length of the two strings (Kleiweg, 2004).

When measuring phonetic distance, lexical variation is filtered out, and only cognates are accepted as data. However, Bai and HSH Zhuang are isolating languages with many di-syllabic words, in which one syllable may be cognate with other dialects, but the other syllable may not be. Table 3 shows HSH Zhuang words for 'chin', Proto-Tai *khaaŋ A2, in which the first syllable in each variety is the modern reflex of the Proto-Tai, but the second syllables are not cognate with each other. To filter out this 'sub-lexical' variation would place the Levenshtein distance at the morpheme level, not the lexical level, thus removing it even further from the context in which communication occurs. Therefore, we chose not to remove the non-cognate syllables in di-syllabic words. When two words had no overlapping syllables, we treated them as different lexemes.

3.1.1 Representing tone in Levenshtein distance

Phonologists often represent tone as autosegments of H(igh) and L(ow) attached to a tone-bearing unit (Duanmu, 1994; Zsiga and Nitisaroj, 2007). Contour tones like rising or falling are represented as a sequence of autosegments, LH for rising and HL for falling. Xu and Wang (2001), however, propose a Target Approximation (TA) model, in which targets can be static (register tones, e.g. H or L), or dynamic (contour tones, e.g. R for rising). We include both autosegment and target representations of tone in our evaluation.

Autosegments and target representations use salient perceptual cues for native speakers, but the listeners in the intelligibility tests described in section 3.2 are not native speakers of the language they are listening to, but rather speakers of related varieties. Burnham and Francis (1997) suggest that non-native speakers use multiple cues to identify tone, whereas native speakers have already fine-tuned their perception system down to the most salient features. Therefore, a more explicit way of representing tone is introduced, which includes the tonal onset (H for high, M for mid, L for low), contour shape (R for rising, F for falling), and tonal offset.

This moves the representation of tone to a more phonetic level, rather than the more abstract, phonemic level used in autosegmental and target representations. The phonetic representation of onset-contour-offset breaks tone down into three parts, making tone more specified than segments, whose differences are treated

Table 4. Comparison of the impact on Levenshtein distance of different tone representations.

Representation	Southern Bai	Central and Northern Bai	Levenshtein distance
onset-contour-offset	MRH	HEH	2
onset-contour	MR	HE	2
contour-offset	RH	EH	1
target	R	H	1
autosegments	_H	LH	1
Chao's pitch numbers	35	55	1

as binary, as seen in Table 2. Since the specified features of tone may be important perceptual cues to the listeners, the unequal treatment of tone and segment is acceptable for the purposes of this research.

We also include two variations of this more explicit representation: onset-contour and contour-offset. Both the autosegment and TA models agree that it is the offset, or target pitch, of the tone that is most salient to the production and perception of native speakers. However, if the listeners operate more as non-native speakers, they may also use tonal onset as a perceptual cue.

For East Asian tone languages, linguists usually use Chao's (1930) system of transcription. This notation treats tone as a sequence of pitch levels (5 for high, 1 for low), which may not be the optimal representation when modelling intelligibility. The disadvantage of this system is that it treats tone as a series of discrete pitch levels, leaving out explicit information about the contour shape that listeners may use in cross-dialectal comprehension. We include this representation in our evaluation for completeness.

Table 4 shows an example of the impact these various representations of tone have on Levenshtein distance. Southern Bai's mid-rising tone corresponds to Central and Northern Bai's high tone in syllables with Proto-Bai *voiceless unaspirated or *voiced sonorant initials in *Tone 1a. While onset-contour-offset and onset-contour representations count the cost as 2, all other representations count the cost as only 1. This example shows that different representations of tone have a substantial impact on how Levenshtein distance is computed.

3.2 Intelligibility tests

For both the Bai and HSH Zhuang surveys, intelligibility was tested with Recorded Text Tests (RTT), a method developed by Casad (1974) and further refined by Blair (1990). An RTT is a short personal narrative recorded in dialect A and played to a listener from dialect B. The dialect B listener answers content questions about the narrative, and the percentage of correct answers is interpreted as their comprehension level of dialect A.

Allen chose seven sites to record personal narratives in, three sites each from Central and Southern Bai and one from Northern Bai (see Figure 1 for site locations). Castro and Hansen chose five sites, two from dialect area A, two from B, and one from C (see Figure 2 for site locations). Sites were selected to represent speaker population centers, as well as the geographic and linguistic spread of the language. At each site, a native speaker was recorded telling a personal narrative two to five minutes in length, and then the story was translated into the national language (Chinese). The researcher developed 12–20 content questions and asked five to ten local speakers to listen to the narratives and answer the questions. Any question not correctly answered by a local speaker was deemed to be defective, i.e. an irrelevant question that arose from a faulty translation of the text. Defective questions were not included in later testing.

After pilot-testing the narrative recordings, the researcher selected test sites. Allen returned to the same sites as the recording locations, except Luobenzhuo in Northern Bai. Shared vocabulary of less than 60 per cent between Luobenzhuo and all other varieties was deemed a significant enough difference as to make intelligibility unlikely. Allen tested the other six sites on the Luobenzhuo recording with results indicating very low intelligibility. In total, seven tests were conducted in six testing locations (see Figure 1). Castro and Hansen tested five stories at 12 testing sites (see Figure 2); though they did not test every recording at each testing site, they did obtain results for 44 pairs of varieties.

At each testing site, the researcher asked approximately eight to twelve native speakers to listen to the recordings individually using headphones and answer content questions about the text. The listeners were selected to ensure a balance between male and female listeners, between older and younger speakers, and between those with more and less education. Listeners were native speakers who were born and raised in the village, whose parents were both native speakers from the village, and who had minimal contact with speakers from other varieties. Each recording was played twice; the second time, content questions were asked after each section using either the listener's variety or Chinese. If listeners responded with an incorrect answer, the relevant section was played again. Most tests consisted of ten questions, each question being asked immediately after the section that contained the answer. Percentage of correct answers out of the total number of questions constituted the intelligibility test score. Correct answers got one point, while answers that were considered partially correct got half a point.

Tests were individually and orally administered, which substantially increased the time needed for each participant. However, playing the stories for larger groups and asking participants to write down their answers was not viable, since a written test assumes a rate of literacy in Chinese that is unlikely among

Table 5. Pearson's correlation and explained variance of tone and segment levels with respect to intelligibility.

Language	Variable	Correlation (r)	Explained variance ($r^2 \times 100$, %)	Significance
Bai	Tone	−0.75	56	< 0.0001
	Segments	−0.71	51	< 0.0001
HSH Zhuang	Tone	−0.66	43	< 0.0001
	Segments	−0.68	46	< 0.0001

Table 6. Results of multiple linear regression analysis, in which intelligibility is the dependent variable and tone and segments are the independent variables.

Language	Variable	*t*-value	Significance
Bai	Tone	−2.040	0.049
	Segments	−0.604	0.550
HSH Zhuang	Tone	−2.255	0.030
	Segments	−2.934	0.005

ethno-linguistic communities in rural China. Allen had an average sample of ten participants per site, with a total of 419 participants. Castro and Hansen had an average of eight participants, with a total of 372 participants.

4. RESULTS

4.1 Multiple regression analysis for tone and segments

The segmental and suprasegmental distances are each correlated separately with intelligibility test scores for Bai and HSH Zhuang. The correlations are given in Table 5. Tone is represented by onset-contour, since that representation shows a stronger correlation with intelligibility (see Section 4.2 below). For both languages, tone and segments both have a strong, significant correlation with intelligibility.

Multiple regression analysis reveals the relative contribution each level makes to intelligibility, seen in Table 6. For Bai, tone is the main predictor of intelligibility, even more important than the segmental level, which surprisingly appears as an insignificant variable. In contrast, for HSH Zhuang, both tone and segment levels are significant variables in relation to intelligibility. For both languages, tone makes a significant contribution to intelligibility, but in Bai the results suggest that tone is more important than segments. These results suggest

215

Table 7. Comparison of tone representations' correlation with intelligibility for Bai and HSH Zhuang.

Bai	Correlation (r)	Explained variance ($r^2 \times 100$, %)	Significantly higher than others?
onset-contour	−0.75	56	yes, p < .001
onset-contour-offset	−0.75	56	yes, p < .001
contour-offset	−0.75	56	yes, p < .01
target	−0.74	54	no
autosegments	−0.74	54	no
Chao's pitch numbers	−0.72	52	no

HSH Zhuang	Correlation (r)	Explained variance ($r^2 \times 100$, %)	Significantly higher than others?
onset-contour	−0.72	52	yes, p < .001
onset-contour-offset	−0.71	50	yes, p < .05
Chao's pitch numbers	−0.68	46	no
target	−0.65	42	no
autosegments	−0.63	40	no
contour-offset	−0.62	38	no

that the contribution of tone to intelligibility is significant across East Asian tone languages, and for some languages tone may actually be the main predictor of intelligibility.

4.2 Comparison of different representations of tone

Table 7 shows the Pearson correlation coefficients (r) for the various representations of tone described in Section 3.1.1 and intelligibility in Bai and HSH Zhuang, as well as the percentage of variance explained (R^2). All correlation coefficients are highly significant (p < .0001).

For both Bai and Zhuang, the correlations for onset-contour and onset-contour-offset are significantly higher than other representations. In both languages, onset-contour is higher at a significance level of p < .001, while onset-contour-offset is higher at a significance level of p < .001 for Bai and of p < .05 for Zhuang. These results suggest that representing tone with onset-contour and onset-contour-offset better approximates intelligibility than other representations.

In Bai, the correlation for contour-offset was also stronger than others, at a significance level of p < .05. When onset-contour, onset-contour-offset, and contour-offset were compared to each other, without considering target, Chao, or autosegments, none of them was significantly higher. Likewise, for Zhuang, neither onset-contour nor onset-contour-offset was higher than the other.

5. CONCLUSIONS

We applied Levenshtein distance to Bai dialect data from Allen (2004) and HSH Zhuang dialect data from Castro and Hansen (accepted). We correlated Levenshtein distance with intelligibility test scores and found significant inverse correlations in both languages. These findings suggest that Levenshtein distance is a useful tool for dialectologists working with East Asian tone languages, and that Levenshtein distance provides a good model for predicting intelligibility in these languages.

Gooskens and Heeringa (2006) found that the relative contribution of prosody in Norwegian to perceived distance was negligible, but they did not investigate the relative contribution to intelligibility. Tang and van Heuven (2007) assert that in a full-fledged tonal language, like Chinese, the contribution of tone to perceived intelligibility and perceived distance is greater than that found for Norwegian, which only has two tonemes. This research affirms Tang and van Heuven's assertion; we find a strong correlation between tonal information and intelligibility, with tone alone able to explain 43 percent of the variance in HSH Zhuang and 56 percent in Bai. This suggests that, in tonal languages, differences in tone have a significant impact on intelligibility. It would be interesting to compare the relative contributions of consonants, vowels, and tones to intelligibility to see if tone is the single most salient factor in cross-dialectal comprehension in tonal languages.

Finally, we used different representations of tone in Levenshtein distance to see which would show the strongest correlation to intelligibility. For both languages, phonetically explicit representations of tone that included information on tonal onset and contour were superior to others. Representations at a more unspecified, phonemic level such as autosegments and targets showed a weaker correlation with intelligibility. This suggests that cross-dialectal listeners operate as non-native speakers who use a variety of perceptual cues, rather than as native speakers who have narrowed in on a subset of salient features.

For Zhuang, onset and contour were essential ingredients for an optimal approximation of intelligibility, while contour-offset was shown to be less than optimal. But for Bai, contour-offset proved superior to autosegment, target, and Chao's pitch numbers. Thus, at this stage we cannot confirm which is more perceptually salient to cross-dialectal listeners, the onset or the offset. However, given that both Bai and Zhuang show onset-contour as superior, whereas contour-offset is shown only to be optimal in Bai, preference may be given to onset-contour representations.

One explanation for why onset-contour is optimal can be found by reviewing the impact of different tone representations illustrated in Table 4 above (see Section 3.1.1). The distinguishing innovation for Southern Bai is the mid rising (35) tone corresponding to Central and Northern Bai's high level (55) tone. Both onset-contour-offset and onset-contour weighs the distance between 35 and 55 at least twice the amount of the other representations. Even though these two tones end up at the same pitch level, they begin at different levels and have different contour shapes, making them difficult for cross-dialectal listeners to assimilate into their own system. Thus, the greater the weight assigned to this kind of difference, the better the inverse correlation with intelligibility.

This research has relevance for the dialectometry of other East Asian tone languages, many of which have not yet been the object of serious study. Using an optimal representation of tone in Levenshtein distance may result in dialect groupings that are more coherent with the perceptions of listeners, and therefore from a more emic perspective. Our findings also have implications for tone perception research, which has mainly focused on native speakers of major languages such as Thai and Chinese (Gandour et al., 2000; Burnham and Francis, 1997; Zsiga and Nitisaroj, 2007). Since cross-dialectal listeners are somewhat in between native and non-native, perceptual studies of such listeners may reveal that they use a wider range of perceptual cues than native speakers, as suggested by this research.

ACKNOWLEDGEMENTS

We are grateful to David Bradley and Eric Jackson for comments on this work and to the participants at the Methods in Dialectology XIII workshop for their constructive scrutiny. Three anonymous reviewers also gave insightful and helpful comments.

REFERENCES

B. Allen (2004), *Bai dialect survey*, Translated by Zhang Xia. Yunnan Minority Language Commission and SIL International Joint Publication Series (Kunming).
F. Blair (1990), *Survey on a Shoestring*, SIL and UTA Publications in Linguistics 96 (Dallas).
D. Bradley (2007), 'East and South East Asia', in R. E. Asher and C. Moseley, eds, *Atlas of the World's Languages* (London).
D. Burnham and E. Francis (1997), 'Role of linguistic experience in the perception of Thai tones', in A. S. Abramson, ed., *Southeast Asian linguistic studies in honor of Vichin Panupong* (Bangkok).
E. H. Casad (1974), *Dialect intelligibility testing* (Dallas).
A. Castro and B. Hansen (accepted), 'Hongshuihe Zhuang dialect intelligibility survey', *SIL Electronic Survey Reports*.
Y. Chao (1930), 'A system of tone letters', *Le Maitre Phonetique*, 30, 24–27.
S. Duanmu (1994), 'Against contour tone units', *Linguistic Inquiry,* 25.4, 555–608.

J. Gandour, D. Wong, L. Hsieh, B. Wienzapfel, D. Van Lancker, and G. D. Hutchins (2000), 'A crosslinguistic PET study of tone perception', *Journal of Cognitive Neuroscience*, 12, (1), 207–222.

C. Gooskens (2006), 'Linguistic and extra-linguistic predictors of inter-Scandinavian intelligibility', in J. van de Weijer, and B. Los, eds, *Linguistics in the Netherlands 2006* (Amsterdam), 101–113.

C. Gooskens and W. Heeringa (2004), 'Perceptive evaluation of Levenshtein dialect distance measurements using Norwegian dialect data', *Language Variation and Change*, 16, (03), 189–207.

C. Gooskens and W. Heeringa (2006), 'The relative contribution of pronunciational, lexical, and prosodic differences to the perceived distances between Norwegian dialects', *Literary and Linguistic Computing*, 21, (4), 477–492.

W. Heeringa (2004), 'Measuring pronunciation differences with Levenshtein distance' (PhD thesis, University of Groningen).

W. Heeringa, P. Kleiweg, C. Gooskens, and J. Nerbonne (2006), 'Evaluation of string distance algorithms for dialectology', in John Nerbonne and Erhard Hinrichs, eds, *Linguistic Distances Workshop at the joint conference of International Committee on Computational Linguistics and the Association for Computational Linguistics* (Sydney), 51–62.

B. Kessler (1995), 'Computational dialectology in Irish Gaelic', *Proceedings of the European ACL* (Dublin), 60–67.

P. Kleiweg (2004), *RuG/L04, software for dialectometrics and cartography* [computer program]. [2004] < URL: http://www.let.rug.nl/~kleiweg/indexs.html. > [24 May 2008].

F. Li (1977), *A Handbook of Comparative Tai* (Honolulu).

J. A. Matisoff (2003), *Handbook of Proto-Tibeto-Burman: System and Philosophy of Sino-Tibetan Reconstruction*. UC Publications in Linguistics, 135 (Berkeley).

X. L. Meng, R. Rosenthal, and D. B. Rubin (1992), 'Comparing correlated correlation coefficients', *Psychological Bulletin*, 111, (1), 172–175.

National Statistics Department (2003), *Nian renkou pucha Zhongguo minzu renkou ziliao [Information on China's minority population from the 2000 census]* (Beijing).

C. Tang and V. J. van Heuven. (2007), 'Mutual inteligibility and similarity of Chinese dialects: Predicting judgments from objective measures', in B. Los and M. van Koppen, eds, *Linguistics in the Netherlands* (Amsterdam), 223–234.

F. Wang (2005), 'On the genetic position of the Bai language', *Cahiers de Linguistique – Asie Orientale*, 34, 101–127.

F. Wang (2006), *Comparison of languages in contact: the distillation method and the case of Bai*. Language and Linguistics Monograph Series B: Frontiers in Linguistics III (Taipei).

L. Xu and Y. Zhao (1984), *Baiyu Jianzhi [Description of the Bai Language]* (Beijing).

Y. Xu and Q. E. Wang (2001), 'Pitch targets and their realization: Evidence from Chinese', *Speech Communication*, 33, 319–337.

C. Yang (accepted), 'Nisu dialect geography', *SIL Electronic Survey Reports*.

Yunnan Provincial Statistics Department (2004), *Yunnan Statistical Yearbook* (Beijing).

E. Zsiga and R. Nitisaroj (2007), 'Tone features, tone perception, and peak alignment in Thai', *Language and Speech*, 50, (3), 343–383.

THE ROLE OF CONCEPT CHARACTERISTICS IN LEXICAL DIALECTOMETRY

DIRK SPEELMAN AND DIRK GEERAERTS

Abstract *In this paper the role of concept characteristics in lexical dialectometric research is examined in three consecutive logical steps. First, a regression analysis of data taken from a large lexical database of Limburgish dialects in Belgium and The Netherlands is conducted to illustrate that concept characteristics such as concept salience, concept vagueness and negative affect contribute to the lexical heterogeneity in the dialect data. Next, it is shown that the relationship between concept characteristics and lexical heterogeneity influences the results of conventional lexical dialectometric measurements. Finally, a dialectometric procedure is proposed which downplays this undesired influence, thus making it possible to obtain a clearer picture of the 'truly' regional variation. More specifically, a lexical dialectometric method is proposed in which concept characteristics form the basis of a weighting schema that determines to which extent concept specific dissimilarities can contribute to the aggregate dissimilarities between locations.*

I. BACKGROUND AND RESEARCH QUESTIONS

An important assumption underlying most if not all methods of dialectometry is that the automated analysis of the differences in language use between different locations, as they are recorded by dialectologists in large scale surveys, can reveal patterns which directly reflect regional variation. In this paper, in which we focus on lexical variation, we want to address one factor, viz. concept characteristics, which we will claim complicates this picture.

International Journal of Humanities and Arts Computing 2 (1–2) 2008, 221–242
DOI: 10.3366/E1753854809000408

The argumentation which underlies our claim consists of three consecutive logical steps. As a first step, we analyse data taken from a large lexical database of Limburgish dialects in Belgium and The Netherlands, in which we more particularly zoom in on the names for concepts in the field of 'the human body'. Our analysis reveals that concept characteristics such as concept salience, concept vagueness and negative affect contribute to the lexical heterogeneity in the dialect data. We claim that these concept characteristics constitute a second source of variation in the data which needs to be distinguished from the primary source of variation which, for lack of a better term, we will call 'truly' regional variation.

Having established the presence of this second 'layer of variation' which goes back to concept characteristics, we will then demonstrate that this second layer can influence the results of dialectometric measurements.

Finally, we propose and demonstrate an approach which attempts to disentangle (to some extent) both sources of variation, thus making it possible to obtain a clearer picture of the 'truly' regional variation. More specifically, we propose a dialectometric method in which concept characteristics form the basis of a weighting schema that determines to which extent concept specific dissimilarities contribute to the aggregate dissimilarities between locations. We apply this weighting schema to several basic lexical dissimilarity measures known from the literature and we compare the quality of all methods, both with and without weighting.

To sum up, the two following research questions are the main topic of this paper:

1. Can concepts with different concept features show different patterns of variation in the data and can these different patterns influence the results of dialectometric measurements?
2. Can the weighting mechanism proposed in this paper (partially) disentangle the two sources of variation discussed in the paper, viz. concept related variation on the one hand and 'truly' regional variation on the other hand?

A third, less central research question will be:

3. Which of the basic lexical dissimilarity measures inspected in the case study performs best, either with or without the aforementioned weighting schema?

The structure of the paper is as follows. In section 2, we describe the data which are used in the case study. In section 3, we describe the basic lexical dissimilarity measures we will be using. As was already mentioned above, we will consider several measures which are known from the literature. Section 4 then introduces the concept features and discusses their effect on lexical variability. Section 5 describes the core results from the case study. First we describes how a weighting mechanism based on the concept features from section 4 can be attached to the basic lexical dissimilarity measures. Next we propose two criteria to establish the quality of different dialectometric methods and we apply them to the different lexical dissimilarity measures which were introduced in section 3 and to three different weighting schemata based on the concept features from section 4. In section 6, finally we round up with some conclusions.

2. DESCRIPTION OF THE DATASET

The case study described in this paper is based on the section on 'The human body' in the thematically organised 'Dictionary of the Limburgish Dialects' (WLD — Woordenboek van de Limburgse Dialecten).[1] The information in this dictionary is based on materials from several surveys. In the case study we have restricted ourselves to the recent, systematically conducted surveys N10, N106, N107, N108 and N109 (thus excluding older materials as well as materials with a limited geographical scope). We did so in order to maximise the chance that for all the concepts we analyse the surveys were indeed conducted with the same geographical scope). Following this procedure we initially ended up with a dataset of 201 locations, 206 concepts, and 32,591 records of 'naming events' (i.e. in total there were 32,591 records of an informant using a word to name a concept).

However, the data we selected turned out not to be as well-structured as could have been assumed on the basis of the documentation of the surveys. Some locations had materials for only a few concepts and some concepts had materials from only a few locations. Therefore, in order to avoid cases of outspoken data sparseness, we decided to introduce a double threshold for inclusion in the dataset; we only included locations with materials for at least 25 concepts and we only included concepts with materials from at least 25 locations. This way we ended up with a dataset of 172 locations, 179 concepts, and 31,359 records.

3. CHOICE OF BASIC LEXICAL DISSIMILARITY MEASURES

In this section we introduce three lexical dissimilarity measures known from the literature. Two of these three measures are used commonly in dialectometry and can be said to represent contemporary common practice. The third measure actually stems from corpus linguistics, but is applied to survey data based dialectometry here.

In the simple form in which we describe the measures in this section, they express the lexical dissimilarity between two locations for a single concept. We shall refer to this simple version of the measures in terms of 'basic lexical dissimilarity measures'. We illustrate all three basic lexical dissimilarity

Table 1. Frequencies fot the concept NERVE.

Frequencies for the concept NERVE (3 locations shown)			
	Sint-Truiden	Maaseik	Maastricht	...
'zenuw'	0 (0.0)	1 (1.0)	2 (0.67)	...
'peesje'	0 (0.0)	0 (0.0)	1 (0.33)	...
'zeen'	2 (1.0)	0 (0.0)	0 (0.0)	...
...	...	...	...	...

measures on the basis of the data in Table 1. The data in Table 1 are data taken from our dataset.

In Table 1 we see which three words are used for the concept NERVE in three of the locations in the dataset. The columns in the table are the locations and the rows are the words. Actually we use the term 'word' in a rather loose and broad sense; it also covers the multiword answers in the dataset. For instance multiword answers such as *haar wie een stekelvarken* 'hair like a porcupine', *haar wie stro* 'hair like straw', *steil haar* 'flat, straight hair', *stijf haar* 'stiff hair', etc. for the concept BORSTELIG HAAR 'BRUSHY HAIR' are also simply called words. The cells in the table show absolute frequencies, as well as columnwise proportions (shown between parentheses). For instance, for the location Maastricht there are three records related to the concept NERVE. In two of the records the word 'zenuw' is used and in the third record the word 'peesje' is used. Since these are the only three records for NERVE in Maastricht, the proportion of records with 'zenuw' is 0.67 (i.e. 2/3) and the proportion of records with 'peesje' is 0.33 (i.e. 1/3).

Let us start with the most traditional lexical dissimilarity measure, which is the one we call d_{BIN}. It simply states that two locations have a dissimilarity of one with respect to a certain concept if they name it differently and a dissimilarity of zero if they use the same name ('BIN' in d_{BIN} stands for 'binary distinction'). This simple, straightforward measure is used very often, in older as well as more recent lexical dialectometric research, mainly because it is very intuitive and because it is well suited for the common case of databases with exactly one record for each concept in each location.

However, our dataset does not correspond to the common situation of exactly one word for each concept in each location. We typically have one up to five records for each concept in each location, and sometimes even more. Therefore a small adaptation is needed to make d_{BIN} usable for our dataset. The rationale behind the adaptation is that we pick the most frequent word for each location and then apply the measure to these most frequent words (ignoring the other words).

In order to formally describe the technical details of the way we use the measure we introduce some terminology. We will call our set of concepts C and we will refer to individual concepts with a small *c*. Likewise we will use *W* as the notation for our set of words and we will use a small *w* to refer to individual words. Finally, our set of locations will be labeled *L* and individual locations will be indicated with a small *l*. These conventions are summarised in (1).

$$C = \{c_1, c_2, \ldots, c_n\} \qquad \text{the set of concepts} \ (n = 179)$$
$$W = \{w_1, w_2, \ldots, w_m\} \qquad \text{the set of words} \ (m = 3286) \qquad (1)$$
$$L = \{l_1, l_2, \ldots, l_o\} \qquad \text{the set of locations} \ (o = 172)$$

In order to be able to apply d_{BIN} to the dataset we first establish which the top frequency words for each concept are in each location. We use the notation $T(c, l)$ to refer to the set of top frequency words for concept *c* in location *l*. The definition of $T(c, l)$ is given in (2). The notation $f(w, l, c)$ in (2) refers to the number of records in our dataset in which word *w* is used in location *l* to name concept *c*.

$$\text{given concept } c \text{ and location } l, \text{ then:}$$
$$T(c,l) = \{x \in W | \forall y \in W : f(y, l, c) \le f(x, l, c)\} \qquad (2)$$

Now if, given a concept *c* and two locations *l1* and *l2*, we want to calculate the binary dissimilarity $d_{BIN}(c, l1, l2)$, then the easiest case is when both $T(c, l1)$ and $T(c, l2)$ are singleton sets. In that case we can ignore all other words and simply take the unique top frequency words for *l1* and *l2*, which we will call *t1* and *t2* respectively, to best represent the naming preferences for this concept in these locations. We can then apply $d_{BIN}(c, l1, l2)$ in the way it is defined in (3).

$$\text{given concept } c \text{ and locations } l1 \text{ and } l2,$$
$$\text{then for a specific } t1 \in T(c, l1) \text{ and a specific } t2 \in T(c, l2): \qquad (3)$$
$$d_{BIN}(c, l1, l2) = \begin{cases} 0 & \text{if } l1 = l2 \\ 0 & \text{if } l1 \ne l2 \text{ and } t1 = t2 \\ 1 & \text{if } l1 \ne l2 \text{ and } t1 \ne t2 \end{cases}$$

If either $T(c, l1)$ or $T(c, l2)$ or both are not singleton sets, we use the proposal by Nerbonne and Kleiweg (2003: 349) for the calculation of dissimilarities between sets of strings to obtain the overall measure for $d_{BIN}(c, l1, l2)$. In order to do so we first add up *1* for each item which is in $T(c, l1) \cup T(c, l2)$ but not in $T(c, l1) \cap T(c, l2)$, and then we divide this sum by the number of items in $T(c, l1) \cup T(c, l2)$. For instance, if $T(c, l1)$ is {'zenuw', 'peesje', 'zeen'} and $T(c, l2)$ is {'peesje', 'zeen', 'nerv'}, and therefore $T(c, l1) \cap T(c, l2)$ is {'peesje', 'zeen'} and $T(c, l1) \cup T(c, l2)$ is {'zenuw', 'peesje', 'zeen', 'nerv'}, then the overal measure for $d_{BIN}(c, l1, l2)$ is calculated as *(1+1)/4*. The two occurrence of *1* in the numerator represent 'zenuw' and 'nerv'. It should be mentioned however, that in 99 per cent of the cases in our dataset both $T(c, l1)$ and $T(c, l2)$ turned out to be singleton sets.

225

Notice finally that $d_{BIN}(c, l1, l2)$ is not defined if in at least one of the two locations $l1$ and $l2$ there are no records for the concept c. This will be true for all basic measures. The only exception is when $l1 = l2$ in which case the dissimilarity will always be taken to be zero by definition (either with or without data to back this up).

The second measure we introduce is a modification of d_{BIN} which we call d_{GIW}. The subscript 'GIW' stands for 'gewichteter Identitätswert', which is the name for a weighting mechanism that is part of the measure. This measure, introduced by Hans Goebl (1984) is widely accepted to be a state of the art measure for lexical dissimilarity.[2] When two locations use a different word, their dissimilarity will be one, as was the case in d_{BIN}. However, when they use the same word their dissimilarity will not simply be zero, but rather some value between zero and one (this is where the weighting mechanism comes in). The exact value depends on the word. If it is a word used in only a few locations, the dissimilarity will be close to zero. If it is a word used in many locations, the dissimilarity will be higher. The rationale is that the sharing of a word that is used in many locations is not very informative and should not be treated as strong evidence for relatedness/similarity of the locations. The sharing of a rare word on the other hand is informative and must be treated as strong evidence for relatedness/similarity of the locations.

Just like the first measure, the second measure was also designed for the case of one word for each concept in each location. We adapt the measure to our dataset in the same way we adapted the first measure: we pick the most frequent word for each location and then apply the measure to these most frequent words (ignoring the other words).

For our description of the technical details of the measure and of the way we use it we introduce additional notational conventions. Given a concept c and a word w we use $WCcov(w, c)$ as a notation for the coverage of word w for concept c. This coverage is the number of locations in which word w is attested in the dataset as a word for concept c. Additionally, we will use the notation $Ccov(c)$ as a notation for the coverage of a concept c. This coverage is the number of locations for which we have records related to the concept c. With these notations we can define $d_{GIW}(c, l1, l2)$ as is done in (4). The definition in (4) shows exactly how GIW-weighting is applied when two different locations use the same word.

given concept c and locations $l1$ and $l2$
then for a specific $t1 \in T(c, l1)$ and a specific $t2 \in T(c, l2)$:

$$d_{GIW}(c, l1, l2) = \begin{cases} 0 & \text{if } l1 = l2 \\ \frac{WC_{cov}(t1,c)-1}{C_{cov}(c)} & \text{if } l1 \neq l2 \text{ and } t1 = t2 \\ 1 & \text{if } l1 \neq l2 \text{ and } t1 \neq t2 \end{cases} \tag{4}$$

Just like the binary measure in (3) the GIW-weighted measure in (4) is applied to top frequency words only. Therefore all top frequency word related issues

226

raised in the discussion of (3) apply equally well to (4). Most specifically, if either $T(c, l1)$ or $T(c, l2)$ or both are not singleton sets, we once again use the proposal by Nerbonne and Kleiweg (2003: 349) for the calculation of dissimilarities between sets of strings. In order to do so we first add up 1 for each item which is in $T(c, l1) \cup T(c, l2)$ but not in $T(c, l1) \cap T(c, l2)$, we then add to this the result of $d_{GIW}(c, l1, l2)$ for each item in $T(c, l1) \cap T(c, l2)$, and finally we divide the total sum by the number of items in $T(c, l1) \cup T(c, l2)$. For instance, if $T(c, l1)$ is {'zenuw', 'peesje', 'zeen'} and $T(c, l2)$ is {'peesje', 'zeen', 'nerv'}, and suppose that $d_{GIW}(c, l1, l2)$ is 0.43 for 'peesje' and 0.25 for 'zeen', then the overal measure for $d_{GIW}(c, l1, l2)$ is calculated as $(1 + 1 + 0.43 + 0.25)/4$.

Note also that we had to make a choice in the way we interpreted $WCcov(w, c)$. We could either say words only cover a location if they are the top frequency word in this location for the concept at hand. Or we could say it is sufficient for the word to be used in this location for the concept at hand. We chose the latter interpretation.

The third measure, d_{PRO}, is the profile-based calculation of lexical dissimilarity we introduced in earlier corpus based research (Geeraerts et al., 1999; Speelman et al., 2003; Speelman et al., 2006) and which we now apply to survey data. This is not a traditional dialectometric method, but we want to test it here because it is specifically designed to handle multiple responses for one concept in one location, and therefore may turn out to be useful for the type or dataset that is used in this case study. Profile-based lexical dissimilarity uses all information in the dataset, with no a priori privileged position for the top frequency words. Moreover it also uses the frequency information of the attestations of the words. More precisely, it takes into consideration the columnwise relative frequencies of the items (between parentheses in Table 1). It not only expresses whether the same words are used in two locations, but also whether the distributions of the relative frequencies of these words, the so-called profiles, are similar in both locations. This way not only the use of different words counts as evidence for dissimilarity but additionally different preferences (i.e. relative frequencies) for shared words also count as more subtle evidence for dissimilarity.

The usefulness of this measure in the present context is an open question. The dataset at hand is richer than the traditional dialectological case of one word for each location for each concept. However, in corpora, where the profile-based method has been applied successfully, frequency information is typically much richer than here. In the dataset at hand we have records for 17,039 concept-location combinations. However, for 60 per cent of these (9988 combinations) we have only one record. For another 23 per cent (3,860 combinations) we have 2 records. For another 9 per cent (1,618 combinations) we have 3 records. Only for the remaining 9 per cent (1,573 combinations) there are 4 or 5, or in very rare cases, more records (the number of cases per combination going as high as 35 in the most extreme case). So one specific aspect of the third research question of this paper will be how the profile-based method performs in the context of such a modest amount of combination-internal frequency information.

In order to describe the technical details of the measure, we once again introduce notational conventions. We introduce $p(w, l, c)$ as a notation for the columnwise frequency proportions we introduced informally when we first discussed Table 1. The formal definition is given in (5).

given word w, concept c and location l, then:
$$p(w, l, c) = \frac{f(w,l,c)}{\sum_{j=1}^{m} f(w_j,l,c)} \tag{5}$$

Then we can define profile-based dissimilarity as is done in (6).

given concept c and locations $l1$ and $l2$, then:
$$d_{\text{PRO}}(c, l1, l2) = \begin{cases} 0 & \text{if } l1 = l2 \\ 1 - \sum_{j=1}^{m} min(p(w_j, l1, c), p(w_j, l2, c)) & \text{if } l1 \neq l2 \end{cases} \tag{6}$$

As the summation in the formula shows, profile-based similarity is measured as the 'overlap' of word use in naming a concept, where this word use is captured in the proportions (the overlap of two proportions is calculated as the minimum of these two proportion). It expresses the extent to which the same word preferences for naming the concept at hand apply in both locations. Profile based dissimilarity then simply is the opposite, i.e. the lack of overlap, calculated as one minus the similarity.[3]

To conclude this section, we show some examples calculations for the three measures in Table 2.

4. TAKING INTO ACCOUNT CONCEPT CHARACTERISTICS

In the previous section we have introduced three basic dissimilarity measures. They allow us to calculate separate dissimilarities between locations for individual concepts. In section 5, we will come back to those measures and use them as building blocks to calculate global lexical dissimilarities between locations by aggregating over the basic dissimilarities for specific concepts.

The question we want to raise in this section is whether all concepts in the dataset will have to be treated as equally trustworthy contributors to such global dissimilarity measures. Our claim will be that depending on their characteristics, some concepts may disturb the global picture rather than make it clearer. They do so because their characteristics function as a second source of variability in the data, next to the variability which is directly related to genuine regional variation. In this section proper we will not yet arrive at the point of discussing global dissimilarity measures. We first try to establish whether there is an effect

Table 2. Basic lexical dissimilarity measures for the data in Table 1.

d_{BIN} for concept NERVE (3 locations shown)

	Sint-Truiden	Maaseik	Maastricht	
Sint-Truiden	0.0	1.0	1.0	...
Maaseik	1.0	0.0	0.0	...
Maastricht	1.0	0.0	0.0	...
...	...	...	...	...

d_{GIW} for concept NERVE (3 locations shown)

	Sint-Truiden	Maaseik	Maastricht	
Sint-Truiden	0.0	1.0	1.0	...
Maaseik	1.0	0.0	0.51 (79/156)	...
Maastricht	1.0	0.51 (79/156)	0.0	...
...	...	...	...	...

d_{PRO} for concept NERVE (3 locations shown)

	Sint-Truiden	Maaseik	Maastricht	
Sint-Truiden	0.0	1.0	1.0	...
Maaseik	1.0	0.0	0.34	...
Maastricht	1.0	0.34	0.0	...
...	...	....	...	...

of concept characteristics on onomasiological heterogeneity, and we try to do so in a way which is not yet directly related to dialectometry. So in a sense this section actually is a digression from the main dialectometric thread which runs through the article.

The concept characteristics we will inspect are **salience**, **vagueness** and **negative affect**. The hypothesis is that less salient concepts lead to more onomasiological heterogeneity, that vaguer concepts lead to more onomasiological heterogeneity and that concepts with negative affect also lead to more onomasiological heterogeneity. Put differently, the hypothesis is that for some concepts some variability in the naming patterns will show up not because of actual regional differences, but because the nature of these concepts leads to variability.

In order to test this hypothesis, we conduct a multiple linear regression analysis which models the response variable *onomasiological heterogeneity* as a function of a set of predictors which are designed to capture at least some aspects of the *salience*, *vagueness* and *negative affect* of concepts.[4] This regression analysis is explained rather briefly in this section (leaving out some less central technical details), but it is described in more detail in a separate publication, where the reader can find more details and background information (Speelman and Geeraerts, in press).[5]

The hard part of testing the hypothesis is the operationalisation of the variables. We start by discussing our operationalisation(s) of the independent variables. The hypothesis related to the concept characteristic *salience* is that for more salient concepts, i.e. more cognitively entrenched concepts, languages (or language varieties) typically have well known (high frequency) words. For less salient concepts on the other hand there isn't always such a well known (high frequency) word, and this fact by itself may lead to more variation in the answers. The absence of an 'obvious answer' may cause people to give different, diverging answers, for instance because of uncertainty.

We introduce two predictors which operationalise similar but, as it turns out, nevertheless somewhat different aspects of salience. The first is **LACK.FAMIL**, short for 'lack of familiarity'. It is our most direct measure of (lack of) salience. We conducted a small survey in which 7 members of our research unit were asked to score all concepts in the dataset on a five-point scale.[6] The question was how likely they thought people were to be less familiar with the concept (1 = no risk of unfamiliarity; 5 = high risk of unfamiliarity). The averages of these 7 scores were used as the values of LACK.FAMIL. Although admittedly this number of raters is small, their high interrater reliability (Cronbach's alpha of .87) indicates that the reliability of the composite ratings is high. Some examples of concepts with high values for LACK.FAMIL are KNOKKELKUILTJES 'LITTLE DENTS BETWEEN THE KNUCKLES', BLOEDWEI 'BLOOD PLASMA / THE LIQUID COMPONENT OF BLOOD', LEVEND VLEES ONDER DE HUID 'LIVING FLESH UNDERNEATH THE SKIN' and VOORVOET 'FRONT PART OF THE FOOT'.

The predictor **PROP.MULTIWORD**, short for 'proportion of multiword responses', is a second, more indirect variable related to (certain aspects of) salience. It expresses how often multiword responses are given to name a concept. The rationale behind the variable is that several causes of answers being multiword responses boil down to the word being less salient: first, from a cross-linguistic perspective, basic (and thus salient) words tend to have short (single word) names; second, multiword responses may be the result of informants either describing concepts or inventing new names on the spot because their dialect has no specific name for the concept or because they fail to know the name (all of which is more likely to happen in the case of less salient concepts). The variable is operationalised as the number of records in our dataset in which the concept was named with a multiword response divided by the total number of records in which the concept was named. Examples of concepts with a high value for PROP.MULTIWORD are KLEIN VAN GESTALTE 'SMALL IN STATURE', SLUIK HAAR 'STRAIGHT HAIR' and SLECHT GROEIEN 'TO GROW POORLY'.

The predictor **NON.UNIQUENESS** is added to the analysis to capture (at least aspects of) the concept *vagueness*. The hypothesis related to vagueness is that concept vagueness, like lack of salience, can be a source of variation in its own right. If some concepts have fuzzy, overlapping boundaries then names for these overlapping concepts might be used interchangeably, which boosts variation. The predictor NON.UNIQUENESS expresses how often the names for a concept also occur as a name for alternative concepts. The rationale is that the presence of many such cases points to fuzzy boundaries between the concept at hand and other concepts, which in turn point to concept vagueness. Technically speaking, NON.UNIQUENESS is measured as follows: the non uniqueness measure for a concept c is operationalised as the number of different couples (x, y) of a word x and a concept y (different from c) for which it holds true that x is attested in the dataset as a name for both c and y. Examples of concepts which score high for NON.UNIQUENESS are KRUIS 'LOINS', HEUP 'HIP' and BEKKENHOLTE 'PELVIC CAVITY'.

Finally, the predictor **NEG.AFFECT**, short for *'negative affect'*, is a direct measure of negative emotional connotation. The hypothesis for the concept feature *negative affect* is that taboo concepts (as well as other concepts with negative affect) often lead to rich synonymy and therefore can be regarded as a source of lexical variation. For the operationalisation of NEG.AFFECT we conducted a small survey in which 7 members of our research unit were asked to score all concepts in the dataset on a five-points scale. The question was to which degree they expected people to attribute a negative connotation to the concept (1 = no negative affect; 5 = strong negative affect). The averages of these 7 scores were used as the values of NEG.AFFECT. The interrater reliability was sufficiently high (Cronbach's alpha of .93). Examples of concepts with high values for NEG.AFFECT are AARSSPLEET 'ANAL CLEFT', GELUIDLOZE WIND 'NOISELESS FART', KWIJL 'DROOL' and PAPPERIG PERSOON 'FAT, PLUMP PERSON'.

The response variable **HETEROGENEITY** will have to be explained in several steps, because it is a composite variable. The variable is designed to capture a type of lexical variability in concepts which we assume is unlikely to be directly related to 'genuinely' regional patterns. We distinguish two aspects of this variability.

First, there is the lexical DIVERSITY of a concept, which is operationalised as the number of words which are used to name the concept throughout the dataset. The working hypothesis is the following: if there are far more words (word types) for one concept than for another, then this might be caused by lexical uncertainty, triggered by the aforementioned concept characteristics.

Second, there is the geographic fragmentation of the words used to name a concept. This fragmentation, which could informally be described as 'scatter' in the geographic distribution of the words used to name a concept, is itself decomposed in two subcomponents. On the one hand there is what we call LACK.OF.SPREAD at the level of the words that name the concept and on the other hand there is what we call DISPERSION at the level of the individual locations in the dataset. We say there is high LACK.OF.SPREAD if the average geographic range of the individual words used to name a concept is exceptionally

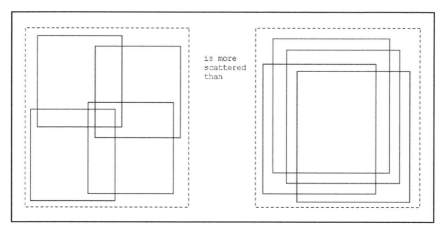

Figure 1. Schematic representation of LACK.OF.SPREAD.

small. Figure 1 is a schematic representation of LACK.OF.SPREAD. The two panels illustrate two possible situations. In each panel the box with dotted lines represents the area of the Limburgish dialects and the four boxes with solid lines represent four words which are used to name some concept. Each box indicates the area in which a specific word is attested. We say there is higher LACK.OF.SPREAD (and therefore higher scatter) in the left panel.

We say there is high DISPERSION if within the geographical range of a particular word used to name a concept there are many 'gaps', i.e. locations in which the word is not attested in the dataset. Figure 2 is a schematic representation of DISPERSION. The two panels illustrates two possible situations. In each panel the box with solid lines represents the area in which a specific word to name some concept is attested. The black circles inside the box are locations where the word is attested. The white circles are locations where the word is not attested for that concept (but others words are). We say there is higher DISPERSION (and therefore higher scatter) in the left panel.

The technical details for our calculation of LACK.OF.SPREAD and DISPERSION are as follows. In order to calculate LACK.OF.SPREAD we first calculate the average[7] relative geographical range of the words used to name the concept (where the relative geographical range of a word is the surface of the region where the word is used for the concept divided by the surface of the whole region for which we have records for the concept) and then we calculate LACK.OF.SPREAD as one divided by this average relative geographical range.

In order to calculate the DISPERSION of a concept we first separately calculate the word-specific dispersion for each word used to name the concept. This word-specific dispersion is a fraction with as its numerator the mean

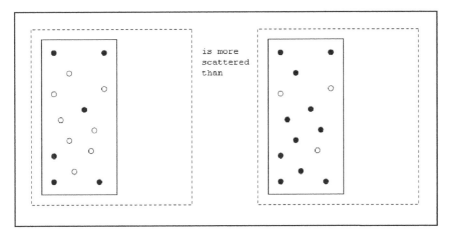

Figure 2. Schematic representation of DISPERSION.

geographical distance from each location where the word is used for the concept to the closest other location where it is also used for the concept, and as its denominator the mean geographical distance from each location where the word is used for the concept to the closest other location with records for the concept, but not necessarily for the word. The global DISPERSION for the concept then is the average[8] of all word-specific dispersion measures.

The composite response variable **HETEROGENEITY** finally is calculated as LOG(DIVERSITY × LACK.OF.SPREAD × DISPERSION). Since diversity as well as both aspects of scatter all three contribute to heterogeneity, we calculate heterogeneity as the product of the three measures. The log-transformation is merely a technical detail.[9]

The regression analysis we conducted on these data (Adjusted R-squared: 60 per cent; p-value for F-test < 0.001) rendered the model which is summarised in (7).

$$\text{HETEROGENEITY} = 0.55 + 0.70 \times \text{LACK.FAMIL}$$
$$+ 2.63 \times \text{PROP.MULTIWORD}$$
$$+ 0.06 \times \text{NON.UNIQUENESS}$$
$$+ 0.46 \times \text{NEG.AFFECT} \qquad (7)$$

In this model all predictors have a significant effect on the response value, and moreover the effect has the direction that was assumed in the hypothesis. Hence the hypothesis formulated at the beginning of this section is confirmed; high values for the predictors significantly increase the lexical heterogeneity of the concept (as it is captured in the variable HETEROGENEITY). In other words, all concept characteristics under scrutiny are shown to have an effect on heterogeneity and thus are shown to be an independent source of variation in the data.

5. RESULTS

Having established that the concept characteristics salience, vagueness and negative affect do have an effect on heterogeneity, we now turn back to the main dialectometric thread of the article to examine whether this effect is outspoken enough to disturb lexical dialectometric measures. In this section, in which we discuss the core of the case study, we compare several ways of calculating aggregate measures. First of all, we compare the three basic measures from section 3 as alternative starting points, viz. d_{BIN}, d_{GIW} and d_{PRO}. Second, we compare three different ways of taking into account the concept characteristics from section 4. This second comparison is given the form of three different weighting schemata; a first, trivial weighting schema (called N, for 'no weighting') does not take concept characteristics into account and gives all concepts the same weight; a second weighting schema (called W, for 'weighting') downplays the contribution of unfamiliar, vague, negatively connoted concepts to the aggregate measure; a third weighting schema (called I, for 'inverted weighting') does the opposite; it downplays the contribution of familiar, non-vague, neutrally or positively connoted concepts to the aggregate measure.

In more formal terms, we calculate all aggregate measures with the generic formula in (8). Note that in (8) we do not sum over all concepts in C, but rather over the concepts in the subset C′ of all concepts c'_1, c'_2, ..., $c'_{n'}$ for which the relevant dissimilarity measure is defined, with $n' \leq n$ (remember that measures may be undefined if data are missing). This subset C′ may be different for different couples of locations.

> given basic dissimilarity measure d and locations $l1$ and $l2$,
> and given concept weighting schema $WEIGHT$,
> then the corresponding aggregate measure is: (8)
> $$d_{agg}(l1, l2) = \frac{\sum_{i=1}^{n'} d(c'_i, l1, l2) \times WEIGHT(c'_i)}{\sum_{i=1}^{n'} WEIGHT(c'_i)}$$

In order to make (8) specific, we fill in a specific basic measure instead of d and we fill in a specific weighting schema instead of *WEIGHT*. In the neutral weighting schema, N, we assign a weight of one to each concept. For the second schema, W, we want to assign to each concept a weight which is low for unfamiliar, vague 'negative affect' concepts and high for other concepts. Technically speaking there are several ways we could use the variables LACK.FAMIL, PROP.MULTIWORD, NON.UNIQUENESS and NEG.AFFECT to build such weights. For instance, we could make separate weights on the basis of each of the variables, or we could combine them in many different ways. We chose to build one global weight on the basis of the four variables, and more specifically to use the formula in the righthand side of equation (7) to combine the values of the four variables.[10]

In more technical terms, we calculate for each concept a 'fitted value' f by using the righthandside of equation (7) and filling in the observed values for LACK.FAMIL, PROP.MULTIWORD, NON.UNIQUENESS and NEG.AFFECT. The resulting value f combines information from all concept characteristics under scrutiny and is high for concepts with 'dangerous concept characteristics' and low for concepts with 'safe concept characteristics'. For our data, this procedure yields values for f ranging from 1.19 to 7.85. Next we introduce the constant m (defined as the highest observed value for f times 1.2) as a basis for normalising the weight. The actual weights we use to downplay the contribution of concepts with high f, is $((m-f)/m)^2$. The weights in the third weighting schema, I, are calculated as $(f/m)^2$. As as result of this, this schema assigns to each concept a weight which is high for unfamiliar, vague 'negative affect' concepts and low for other concept.

Next we introduce two criteria we will use to compare the quality of the different aggregate measures. Both criteria are based on established wisdom in dialectology. The first criterion is based on the assumption that a successful measure should be able to capture dialectologically relevant subdivisions of the area. We look at such subdivisions at three levels of granularity. At a first, very course grained level we test whether the subdivision into 3 provinces is captured by the aggregate measures. Capturing this subdivision roughly boils down to recognising the distinction between Belgian Limburg and Netherlandic Limburg (the third province, the Belgian province Liege, plays only a modest role). At a second and third level we test to which extent the traditional dialectological subdivision of the area into smaller regions (second level) and subregions (third level) is captured by the aggregate measures (we use the traditional subdivisions which are used in the WLD). For our dataset there are 9 regions at the second level (we disregard a tenth region for which we have only one location) and 22 subregions at the third level (we disregard a twenty-third subregion for which we have only one location). The criterion we introduce then is a measure which expresses the 'degree of compatibility' between the aggregate dissimilarity measures on the one hand and the traditional subdivision of the dialect region in dialect areas on the other hand. We will calculate this compatibility measure separately for the three levels of granularity we described above. Given a specific level of granularity, i.e. given a set of dialect areas that are to be distinguished, the calculations are roughly as follows: first the measure that expresses the 'degree of compatibility' is calculated separately for each location. This 'local quality', or *locqual*, formally defined in (9), for a single location is calculated as its mean dissimilarity from other locations inside the same dialect area divided by its mean dissimilarity from locations outside the dialect area. So the lower the value for *locqual* the better the correct dialect area membership of the location is 'captured' by the aggregate dissimilarity measure. Next a global measure 'cluster quality', or *clusterqual*, formally defined in (10), is calculated as the mean 'local quality', averaging over all locations. The lower the value for *clusterqual*, the better the dialect areas are 'captured' by the dissimilarity measure.

More formally speaking, we treat the three levels of subdivisions of the dialect area as three different partitions P of the set of locations L and we introduce a measure *clusterqual*$_P$ (for 'cluster quality') which quantifies how good the blocks (henceforth also somewhat informally called the clusters) of the partition are 'captured' by the aggregate dissimilarity measure. In (10) we define this overall cluster quality *clusterqual*$_P(d_{agg})$ of a dissimilarity measure d_{agg} with respect to a partition P. This definition uses a local cluster quality measure *locqual*$_P(d_{agg}, l)$ for an individual location l, which is defined in (9). The definition in (9) in turn uses the notation *same*$_P(l1, l2)$ and *dif*$_P(l1, l2)$. We define the value of *same*$_P(l1, l2)$ to be one if the locations $l1$ and $l2$ are in the same block (cluster) in P, and zero otherwise. The value of *dif*$_P(l1, l2)$ is one if the locations are in different blocks (clusters) in P, and zero otherwise.

given a location l and a location partition P
and given an aggregate measure d_{agg}, then:

$$locqual_P(l, d_{agg}) = \frac{\left(\frac{\sum_{k=1}^{o} dagg(l,l_k) \times same_P(l,l_k)}{\sum_{k=1}^{o} same_P(l,l_k)}\right)}{\left(\frac{\sum_{k=1}^{o} d_{agg}(l,l_k) \times dif_P(l,l_k)}{\sum_{k=1}^{o} dif_P(l,l_k)}\right)} \qquad (9)$$

given a location partition P
and given an aggregate measure d_{agg}, then: $\qquad (10)$

$$clusterqual_P(d_{agg}) = \frac{\sum_{k=1}^{o} locqual_P(l_k, d_{agg})}{o}$$

Our second criterion for comparing the quality of the aggregate measures is based on the fact that the region of the Limburgish dialects is traditionally considered to be a dialect continuum. From the traditional dialectological assumption that dialect continua are mostly gradual and incremental (Séguy, 1971; Chambers and Trudgill, 1998: 5), we infer that the harder it is to accurately represent the aggregate dissimilarity measures in the form of low-dimensional 'maps of linguistic distances', the less compatible these dissimilarity measures are with the traditional dialectological assumption of a dialect continuum. Therefore we propose to use a measure which expresses how difficult it is to accurately represent the aggregate dissimilarity measures in the form of low-dimensional 'maps of linguistic distances' (using at most three dimensions). More specifically we propose to use a stress value from the technique of multidimensional scaling, which was designed to express exactly this difficulty (see below). The rationale is as follows: not only are solutions (i.e. accurate

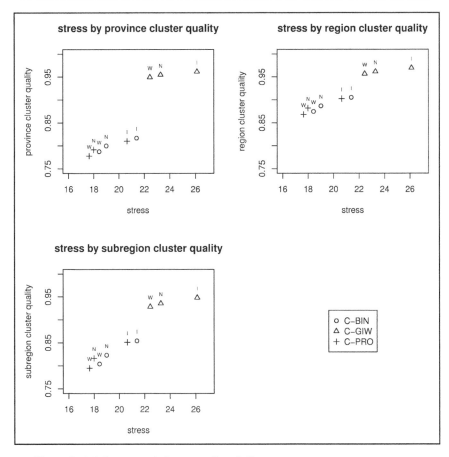

Figure 3. MDS stress and cluster quality of all measures.

'maps of linguistic distances') which need fewer dimensions generally to be preferred over solutions which need more dimensions (because they are clearer and more easily interpretable), the assumption of a dialect continuum can moreover be argued to imply the existence of a two- or three-dimensional solution; the assumption of a dialect continuum implies that the discrepancies between geographic distance and linguistic distance are relatively moderate. If one is to create a low-dimensional 'map of linguistic distances', and the discrepancies between linguistics and geographic distances are indeed relatively modest, then one can start out from a map of geographical distances and then stretch and shrink certain regions to account for the most modest discrepancies between linguistic and geographic distances. If necessary, one can also introduce a third dimension (thus creating 'linguistics mountains and valleys', so to speak) to account for less modest, but still rather moderate discrepancies. If one reasons like this, the need for a fourth or a fifth dimension can be seen as an indication that the discrepancies between linguistic and geographic distance are not moderate and that therefore the aggregate measure under scrutiny is not compatible with the assumption of a dialect continuum.

Formally speaking, we use multidimensional scaling analyses of the aggregate dissimilarities with three dimensions, using Kruskal's Non-metric Multidimensional Scaling (Kruskal, 1964). Our criterion is that the stress value for such an analysis must be low.[11] This stress value expresses to which extent three dimensions are not sufficient to accurately represent the aggregate dissimilarities. Our interpretation, in the context of our dataset, is that the lower this stress value is, the more dialectologically plausible the aggregate dissimilarity measure is.

In Figure 3 the MDS stress values of the different measures are displayed on the x axis (as per cent) and the cluster quality values on the y axis. Different symbols are used for the different basic measures and the characters above the symbols (W, N or I) indicate which weighting schema was applied. Since for both criteria lower is better, the aggregate measures which perform well according to both criteria are in the bottom left part of the plots.

The following conclusions can be drawn. First, when we compare the basic methods, we see that d_{PRO} performs best, immediately followed by d_{BIN} which in turn (surprisingly) outperforms d_{GIW}.[12] Second, when we compare the weighting schemata within each basic method, we see that W is consistently better than N, which in turn is consistently better than I. These findings confirm the hypothesised effect of concept characteristics on dialectometric measurements and show that the weighing schema W can improve the quality of the measurements.

6. CONCLUSIONS

In this article we have first shown that at least in our dataset, and according to our operationalisations, the concept characteristic **salience**, **vagueness** and **negative affect** do indeed affect heterogeneity. The regression analysis described in section 4 confirmed that less salient concepts lead to more onomasiological heterogeneity, that vaguer concepts lead to more onomasiological heterogeneity and that concepts with negative affect also lead to more onomasiological heterogeneity.

After establishing the existence of this effect we have tested in section 5 whether the effect is outspoken enough to disturb traditional lexical dialectometric measures. By varying the extent to which specific concepts contribute to the aggregate dissimilarity measures (using the concept characteristics salience, vagueness and negative affect as weights) we illustrated that decreasing the contribution of concepts with low salience, high vagueness and high negative affect consistently improves the dialectometrical quality of the dissimilarity measures. Conversely, increasing the contribution of concepts with high salience, low vagueness and low negative affect consistently worsens the quality of the dissimilarity measures.

These findings confirm the assumption formulated in the introduction that several sources of variability are at play in our dataset and that indeed there is a 'second layer' of concept characteristics related variability next to the 'first layer' of actual regional variation. They also confirm that this second layer is outspoken enough to affect the results of traditional lexical dialectometric measures. Finally, they also show that a weighting mechanism can effectively be used to mitigate the disturbing effect of this second layer on the dialectometric measures.

If we turn back to the three research questions formulated at the end of the introduction, we can draw the following conclusions:

1. The regression analysis in section 4 has shown that concepts with different concept features do show different patterns of variation in the data. Additionally, the comparison of the weighting schemata in section 5 has shown that these different patterns of variation can indeed influence the results of dialectometric measurements.
2. The superiority of the results of weighting schema W in section 5 supports the hypothesis that this weighting schema can (partially) disentangle the two sources of variation discussed in the paper and can give us a better picture of the 'truly' regional variation in the data.
3. The performance of the profile based measure was the best of the three basic measures we inspected, which is especially remarkable because on average the frequencies in the individual profiles (for one place and one concept) were very low. On the other hand, the GIW-measure (gewichteter Identitätswert) did not do very well in our case study, which amounts to a surprise since it is widely accepted to be a state of the art measure. Further research will be needed to obtain a deeper understanding of the reasons for this poor performance.

The study presented in this article illustrates that concept characteristics are indeed to be taken into account when measuring lexical dissimilarities. It also explores and demonstrates one possible approach to this endeavour. However, it is but a modest first step towards a more encompassing understanding of the effect of concept characteristics on lexical dissimilarity measures. To conclude this article we present a few possible roads for future/related work:

1. Firstly, the concept characteristics and specific effects discussed in this paper may well be typical of the semantic domain under scrutiny (the

human body). It remains to be investigated how general these findings are and/or which other concept characteristics are at play in other semantic domains.

2. Secondly, at several points in this article methodological choices were made for which alternatives exist (and are defendable). We want to mention two points in particular. First, other basic lexical dissimilarity measures should be investigated. Second, other methods for evaluating the quality of the resulting dissimilarity measures should be explored. For instance, the dissimilarity measures could be fed into a robust clustering algorithm (see e.g. Nerbonne, Kleiweg, and Franz Manni, 2008), the result of which could then be compared to the traditional dialect areas by means of measures such as the adjusted Rand index (Rand, 1971; Hubert and Arabie, 1985).[13]

3. Thirdly, we want to mention that many other disciplines throughout (and outside) the humanities also frequently use lexical information in the calculation of (dis)similarities. We believe several of these applications might benefit from the analysis of the effect of concept characteristics on these measurements. Examples are stylometry, register analysis and genre analysis, variationist analyses of standard languages. Additional examples can be found in more computationally oriented disciplines such as computational linguistics and information retrieval (in tasks such as text classification, text retrieval, etc.).

ACKNOWLEDGEMENTS

We would like to thank Ronny Keulen, editor of the WLD chapter on which this study is based, for kindly giving us access to the WLD data.

REFERENCES

J. Chambers and P. Trudgill (1998), *Dialectology*, 2nd ed. (Cambridge).

D. Geeraerts, S. Grondelaers and D. Speelman (1999), *Convergentie en divergentie in de Nederlandse woordenschat. Een onderzoek naar kleding- en voetbaltermen* (Amsterdam).

H. Goebl (1984), *Dialektometrische Studien: Anhand italoromanischer, rätoromanischer und galloromanischer Sprachmaterialien aus AIS und ALF, Vol. 3* (Tübingen).

L. Hubert and P. Arabie (1985), 'Comparing Partitions', *Journal of the Classification 2*, 193–218.

R. Keulen (2004), *Woordenboek van de Limburgse Dialecten (WLD), Deel III, afl. 1.1: Het menselijke lichaam* (Groningen).

J. B. Kruskal (1964), 'Multidimensional scaling by optimizing goodness of fit to a non-metric hypothesis', *Psychometrika* 29 : 1, 1–27.

J. Nerbonne and P. Kleiweg (2003), 'Lexical distance in LAMSAS', *Computers and the Humanities* 37, 339–357.

J. Nerbonne, P. Kleiweg, W. Heeringa and F. Manni (2008), 'Projecting Dialect Differences to Geography: Bootstrap Clustering vs. Noisy Clustering', in C. Preisach, L. Schmidt-Thieme, H. Burkhardt and R. Decker, eds, *Data analysis, machine learning, and applications. Proceedings of the 31st annual meeting of the German Classification Society* (Studies in classification, data analysis, and knowledge organization) (Berlin), 647–654.

W. M. Rand (1971), 'Objective criteria for the evaluation of clustering methods', *Journal of American Statistical Association*, 66(336), 846–850.

J. Séguy (1971), 'La relation entre la distance spatiale et la distance lexicale', *in Revue de linguistique Romane*, 35, 335–357.

D. Speelman, S. Grondelaers and D. Geeraerts (2003), 'Profile-based linguistic uniformity as a generic method for comparing language varieties', *Computers and the Humanities*, 37, 317–337.

D. Speelman, S. Grondelaers and D. Geeraerts (2006), 'A profile-based calculation of region and register variation: the synchronic and diachronic status of the two main national varieties of Dutch', in A. Wilson, P. Rayson and D. Archer, eds., *Corpus Linguistics Around the World* (Amsterdam), 195–202.

D. Speelman and D. Geeraerts, in press. 'Heterodox concept features and onomasiological heterogeneity in dialects', in G. Kristiansen et al., eds, *Advances in cognitive sociolinguistics* (Berlin).

W. N. Venables and B. D. Ripley (2002), *Modern Applied Statistics with S*, 4th edition (New York).

END NOTES

[1] The WLD consists of several volumes. The chapter which cover the materials studied in this paper is Keulen (2004). More information on the WLD can be found online (http://www.ru.nl/dialect/wld/).

[2] Our description of this weighting mechanism is somewhat different from the original description. The mechanism was originally described as a weighting mechanism for the similarity between locations. We describe it as a weighting mechanism for the dissimilarity between locations.

[3] This particular implementation of profile-based dissimilarity is only one of many possible ways to deal with frequency information in multiple responses. More information can be found in Speelman et al. (2003), where several alternative implementations are discussed.

[4] For all calculations and analyses in this paper the freely available tools Python (http://www.python.org/) and R (http://www.r-project.org/) were used.

[5] In this article we only discuss four of the five predictors which are used in Speelman and Geeraerts (in press). The fifth predictor discussed there is MISSING.PLACES, implemented as the number of locations in the dataset for which a concept has no attestations, and intended as an operationalisation of (a type of) *lack of familiarity*. It is not included here because, although it does affect onomasiological heterogeneity, it turns out not to be an appriopriate operationalisation of the concept characteristic *lack of familiarity*.

[6] All raters are native speakers of (Belgian) Dutch. Their dialect background is quite diverse, covering all major Belgian Dutch dialect areas. Only one of the raters has a Limburgish dialect background. The survey was in standard Dutch.

[7] We actually use a weighted average, so that words which quantitatively are more important have a higher influence on the measure than words which quantitatively are less important. We refer to Speelman and Geeraerts (in press) for more details.

[8] Here too we actually use a weighted average (cf. the note on LACK.OF.SPREAD). Once again we refer to Speelman and Geeraerts (in press) for more details.

[9] The log-transformation keeps values for HETEROGENEITY from growing very high in case DIVERSITY, LACK.OF.SPREAD and DISPERSION are all high. It also allows for a more straightforward regression analysis because it renders the relation between predictors and response (almost) linear, which would not be the case without the transformation.

[10] At this point we want to mention that the results reported further on in this section (summarised in Figure 3) do not depend on the specific choice to use the righthandside of equation (7) as the basis for the weights in W and I. Alternative calculations based on LACK.FAMIL,

PROP.MULTIWORD, NON.UNIQUENESS and NEG.AFFECT, using e.g. single variables or using the mean of the normalised variables, yielded very similar results.

[11] We calculated Kruskal's stress by means of the function isoMDS in the R package MASS (Venables and Ripley, 2002).

[12] With respect to the stress value criterion it must be noted that none of the methods perform well in absolute terms. Therefore we must conclude that some of the measurements presented here are more compatible with the 'dialect continuum assumption' than others, but none of the measurements are fully compatible with it.

[13] We thank John Nerbonne for suggesting this validation method.

WHAT ROLE DOES DIALECT KNOWLEDGE PLAY IN THE PERCEPTION OF LINGUISTIC DISTANCES?

WILBERT HEERINGA, CHARLOTTE GOOSKENS AND KOENRAAD DE SMEDT

Abstract *The present paper investigates to what extent subjects base their judgments of linguistic distances on actual dialect data presented in a listening experiment and to what extent they make use of previous knowledge of the dialects when making their judgments. The point of departure for our investigation were distances between 15 Norwegian dialects as perceived by Norwegian listeners. We correlated these perceptual distances with objective phonetic distances measured on the basis of the transcriptions of the recordings used in the perception experiment. In addition, we correlated the perceptual distances with objective distances based on other datasets. On the basis of the correlation results and multiple regression analyses we conclude that the listeners did not base their judgments solely on information that they heard during the experiments but also on their general knowledge of the dialects. This conclusion is confirmed by the fact that the effect is stronger for the group of listeners who recognised the dialects than for listeners who did not recognise the dialects on the tape.*

I. INTRODUCTION

To what extent do subjects base their judgment of linguistic distances between dialects on what they really hear, i.e. on the linguistic phenomena available in the speech signal, and to what degree do they generalise from the knowledge that they have from previous confrontations with the dialects? This is the central question of the investigation described in this paper. The answer to this question is important to scholars who want to understand how dialect speakers perceive

International Journal of Humanities and Arts Computing 2 (1–2) 2008, 243–259
DOI: 10.3366/E175385480900041X

Figure 1. Map of Norway showing the 15 dialects used in the present investigation.

dialect pronunciation differences and may give more insight in the mechanisms behind the way in which linguistic variation is experienced. Our study is of interest to (computational) dialectologists and sociolinguists.

In the spring of 2000, an experiment was performed among Norwegian dialect speakers in order to measure *perceptual linguistic distances* between 15 Norwegian dialects.[1] In each of 15 locations, speakers listened to dialect recordings of the fable 'The North Wind and the Sun' in the 15 dialects and were asked to judge the linguistic distance between these dialects and their own dialect. Henceforth we refer to the recordings as the NOS data or just NOS.[2] The experiment is described in Gooskens and Heeringa (2004). The geographical distribution of the 15 locations is shown in Figure 1. The 15 dialects were classified on the basis of the mean judged distances between the dialects. The classification largely agrees with that of traditional dialect maps (e.g. Skjekkeland 1997).

The perceived distances were correlated with *objective linguistic distances*, measured by means of the Levensthein algorithm, with which distances between different pronunciations of the same concept can be measured. The correlation between perceptual and objective distances appeared to be 0.67 which is a significant, but not perfect correlation. There may be different reasons for this. Firstly, the listeners may have been influenced by *non-linguistic* factors such as familiarity and attitude towards the dialects. They may tend to judge familiar dialects as less deviant from their own dialects or they may judge dialects that they seldom hear as more deviant than could be expected from their objective linguistic distance. A negative attitude towards a dialect may cause the listener to judge a dialect as more deviant from their own dialect than expected from the objective linguistic distances and a positive attitude may have the opposite effect.

Secondly, low correlation may be the result of the fact that the objective distances were based on lexical, phonetic and morphological variation only[3], since prosodic and syntactic variation was not measured, while listeners based their judgments on information at all linguistic levels.

In this paper we want to focus on a possible third explanation. When making their judgments listeners may take into account linguistic information that is based on previous contact with the dialect even when that information does not necessarily relate directly to the recordings. When hearing some characteristic linguistic phenomena (shibboleths), they may be able to identify the dialect and judge the distance on the basis of what they *know* about the dialect rather than on what they *hear* when listening to the recording. We want to test the hypothesis that subjects in a perception experiment do not only use the infor-mation they hear, but also use *extra linguistic* information not available in the speech signal, thus making the perceptual distances more representative for the dialects than the objective measurements based on the recordings. We focus on the pronunciation level only, i.e. we restrict our analysis to phonetic and phonological variation.[4] Gooskens and Heeringa (2006) have shown that pronunciation is a more important predictor of perceived linguistic distance between the 15 Norwegian dialects than lexical distances.

In order to test our hypothesis, we decided to test the degree to which the perceived distances correlate with objective distances based on other data sets from the same dialects as in the NOS data. We expect that other objective distances correlate significantly with the perceptual distances, despite the fact that only the NOS data is the same as the data used for the perception experiment. Furthermore, if listeners do indeed make judgments based on information that is not present in the recording, we expect that distances measured on other data sets will have a significant contribution in a multiple regression model.

In Gooskens (2005) the listeners in the perception experiment were asked to identify the 15 dialects by putting a cross on a map of Norway to indicate where they thought the speakers came from. When excluding the identifications of the dialects spoken by the listeners themselves, Gooskens found that 25 per cent of the crosses were placed in the correct county. In addition to the perceptual measurements based on all data, we also calculated a) distances as perceived by listeners who identified the dialects correctly; and b) distances as perceived by listeners who did not identify the dialects correctly. We hypothesise that listeners who are able to identify the location of a dialect correctly are likely to use their linguistic knowledge about this dialect when judging the linguistic distance. In this case we would therefore expect a lower correlation between perceived distances and objective linguistic distances, since the judgments are not based solely on the linguistic information present in the recordings. On the other hand, the judgments by listeners who were not able to identify a dialect correctly can be expected to show a higher correlation with the objective linguistic distances since the listeners are more likely to base their judgments solely on the recordings.[5]

We start by describing the four different datasets, the NOS, ALE, ALENOR and NOR data. (Section 2). In Section 3 we describe the perception experiment that was set up in order to measure perceptual distances on the basis of the NOS-text and in Section 4 we present Levenshtein distance, which we use to measure objective phonetic distances. In Section 5 phonetic distances that are obtained on the basis of the NOS, ALE, ALENOR and NOR data are correlated with each other and with the perceptual distance measurements. In Section 6, the results of multiple regression analyses are presented. The main conclusions will be presented in Section 7.

2. DATA SETS

We used three datasets in addition to the NOS data, namely the ALE, NOR and ALENOR data. The first one contains material from the *Atlas Linguarum Europae* (ALE) transcribed phonetically according to the ALE guidelines. The second data set contains transcriptions of the *Norwegian dialect atlas* (NOR). The pronunciations in this atlas are transcribed according to the phonetic *Norvegia* transcription system. The third source is also based on the ALE data, but the pronunciations are transcribed according to the *Norvegia* transcription system (ALENOR). By comparing ALE to ALENOR, we are able to measure the influence of different transcription systems on the distance measurements.

In order to be able to carry out objective linguistic distance measurements, we needed digital versions of the four datasets. The NOS data were already available in digital form based on the IPA system and X-SAMPA codes.[6] We converted the phonetic transcriptions of NOR, ALE and ALENOR from the Norvegia and ALE transcription systems into X-SAMPA. Converting the ALE transcriptions to X-SAMPA did not pose a problem, since the phonetic alphabet used in ALE is based on IPA and there is a one-to-one correspondence between IPA symbols and X-SAMPA symbols. The NOR and the ALENOR data are transcribed by means of Norvegia, which is a very detailed phonetic system with more than 100 vowel and consonant symbols. In order to convert the NOR data, we used the information in Nes (1982) where all Norvegia symbols are compared to IPA symbols. Since the NOR transcriptions were very detailed, many symbols representing the diacritics had to be used in the X-SAMPA. In most cases this did not cause any problems. Exceptions are the affricates that we transcribed as two extra short sounds and mediopalatal s, k and g that we transcribed as palatalised s, k and g since there are no symbols for these sounds in X-SAMPA. Norvegia does not make a distinction between tap and alveolar r and between [v] and [ʋ]. We have transcribed these combined sounds with the symbols [r] (X-SAMPA [r]) and [ʋ] (X-SAMPA [P]) respectively.

Most Norwegian dialects distinguish between two tonal patterns on the word level, often referred to as tonemes. Some dialects even have a third toneme, the circumflex. The tonemes are treated differently in the three datasets. In NOS, NOR and ALENOR, the tonemes are marked with ["] for toneme 1, [""] for toneme 2 and [%%] for the circumflex toneme.[7] In ALE main stress and circumflex toneme are indicated along with the X-SAMPA symbols for rising [_R] and falling [_F] tone respectively. The realisation of the tonemes varies considerable across the Norwegian dialects. However, no information was given about the precise realisation of the tonemes in the transcriptions.

Ideally, the datasets should be a random sample of the vocabulary in a dialect since this may be expected to be the best representation of perceived distances. In the case of the NOS-text, we expect the choice of a running text to be a sensible approach to selecting a representative sample of a dialect. The three other datasets are word lists, from which we made random selections of 60 words in order to obtain sets of dialect samples that were comparable in size to the NOS dataset.

2.1 The North Wind and the Sun (NOS)

The fable 'The North Wind and the Sun' consists of 58 different words. The NOS-database at present contains recordings in more than 50 Norwegian dialects. We included the fifteen dialects which were available when we started our investigation in the spring of 2000 (see Figure 1).[8] The dialects are spread over a large part of the Norwegian language area, and cover most major dialect areas as found on the traditional map of Skjekkeland (1997:276). On this map the Norwegian language area is divided into nine dialect areas. In our set of 15 varieties, six areas are represented.

There were 4 male and 11 female speakers with an average age of 30.5 years, ranging between 22 and 35, except for one speaker who was 66. No formal testing of the degree to which the speakers used their own dialect was carried out. However, they had lived at the place where the dialect is spoken until the mean age of 20 (with a minimum of 18) and they all regarded themselves as representative speakers of the dialects in question. All speakers except one had at least one parent speaking the dialect.

The speakers were all given the text in Norwegian beforehand and were allowed time to prepare the recordings in order to be able to read aloud the text in their own dialect. Many speakers had to change some words of the original text in order for the dialect to sound authentic. The word order was changed in three cases.

When reading the text aloud the speakers were asked to imagine that they were reading the text to someone with the same dialectal background as themselves. This was done in order to ensure a reading style which was as natural as possible and to achieve dialectal correctness.

On the basis of the recordings, phonetic transcriptions were made of all 15 dialects in IPA as well as in X-SAMPA. All transcriptions were made by the same trained phonetician, which ensures consistency.

2.2 *Atlas Linguarum Europae with ALE transcription (ALE)*

The Atlas Linguarum Europae (ALE) was an ambitious cooperation between linguists from 51 European countries. The initiative was taken in 1970 with support from UNESCO, resulting in the publication of maps and commentaries from 1975 onward. Lists of 547 words from different onomasiological categories were collected from 2,631 places by means of a questionnaire filled out by hand (Kruijsen 1976). The words were transcribed phonetically with a rather broad phonetic system (Weijnen 1975). In Norway the material was collected from 152 places by linguists in the late 1970s.

For the present investigation it would have been preferable to use ALE material from exactly the same places as those in NOS. However, only two places are covered by both ALE and NOS, so in the other cases we chose material from the neighbouring village instead.[9] The 60 words that we used for the analysis were selected randomly from the ALE word lists. All 15 varieties were transcribed by the same phonetician.

2.3 *Atlas Linguarum Europae with Norvegia transcription (ALENOR)*

In addition to the phonetic transcriptions with ALE symbols of the words in the ALE corpus, most words were also transcribed in Norvegia (see Section 2). This gives us the opportunity to compare the effect of different phonetic transcription systems. We have therefore made a distinction between the dataset transcribed with ALE symbols (ALE) and a dataset with the same words transcribed with Norvegia (ALENOR). Unfortunately, no Norvegia transcription of the Lillehammer dialect was available. We reconstructed the Norvegia transcription ourselves on the basis of regular correspondences between ALE transcriptions and Norvegia transcriptions in the other 14 varieties.

2.4 Norwegian dialect atlas (NOR)

The Norwegian dialect atlas is based on a collection of 1500 words from most villages and parishes in Norway (see Hoff 1960). Most of the material was collected between 1951 and 1970, but it was supplemented with older material that was collected in the 1940s. The 1500 words are everyday words which cover all grammatical and phonetic details that can be expected to be found in the Norwegian dialects. Most of the words are transcribed phonetically in Norvegia by hand. Several field workers were involved in the collection of the material.

As with the ALE material, it was not always possible to use material from the same places as in the NOS material because the material was not complete. In seven cases, material from a neighbouring village was selected.[10]

The words in the NOR-list are divided into 56 sections according to their grammatical or phonetic characteristics. One word was chosen randomly from each section. In addition, a random word was selected from four random sections. In this way we obtained a random list of 60 phonetically transcribed words from 15 dialects to be used for our analysis.

2.5 Comparison of the four data sets

We have taken care to select four datasets that are as similar as possible in a number of respects. Almost the same number of randomly selected words (58 for NOS, 60 for NOR, ALE and ALENOR) were selected and transcribed phonetically in X-SAMPA in the 15 dialects. We aimed to select the same 15 dialects but in a number of cases we had to chose a neighbouring dialect because some dialects were missing in NOR and ALE/ALENOR. Furthermore, it would have been ideal to work with datasets from the same period. However, the NOS material is more recent than the ALE/ALENOR material and the NOR material is oldest. We have also seen that there is a difference in the phonetic details of the transcriptions. The ALE material is transcribed in a rather broad transcription while the NOR and ALENOR transcriptions are very detailed. Also the NOS transcriptions include more diacritics than ALE. Another difference between the datasets is the way in which the words have been selected. The NOS words come from a running text, the NOR words are a random selection of words covering different phonetic and grammatical categories and the ALE/ALENOR words are a random selection from a list of words representing various onomasiological categories.

3. PERCEPTUAL DISTANCE MEASUREMENTS

In order to investigate the linguistic distances between 15 Norwegian dialects as perceived by Norwegian listeners, recordings of the fable 'The North Wind and the Sun' in the 15 dialects were presented to Norwegian listeners in a listening experiment. The listeners were 15 groups of high school pupils (mean age 17.8 years), one group from each of the places where the 15 dialects are spoken (see Figure 1). Each group consisted of 16 to 27 listeners (with a mean of 19) who had lived the major part of their lives (on average 16.7 years) in the place where the dialect is spoken. A majority of the 290 listeners said that they spoke the dialect always (60 per cent) or often (21 per cent), the rest spoke it seldom (16 per cent) or never (3 per cent). A large majority of the listeners (83 per cent) had one or two parents who also spoke the dialect.

The 15 dialects were presented to the listeners in a random order preceded by a practice recording. While listening to the dialects, the listeners were asked to judge each dialect on a scale from 1 (similar to one's own dialect) to 10 (not similar to one's own dialect). In addition to the judgment scores, the listeners were presented with a map of Norway with all counties indicated. They were asked to place a cross in the county where they thought the dialect was spoken. This allowed us to make separate analyses of judgments by listeners who recognised the dialects and by listeners who did not recognise them.

Each group of listeners judged the linguistic distances between their own dialect and the 15 dialects, including their own dialect. In this way we obtain a matrix with 15×15 distances.[11] There are two mean distances between each pair of dialects, depending on the subject's own dialect. For example, the distance which the listeners from Bergen perceived between their own dialect and the dialect of Trondheim (mean 7.8) is different from the distance as perceived by the listeners from Trondheim (mean 8.6). Different explanations can be given for the fact that different groups perceive the same linguistic distances differently. For example, it is likely that the attitude towards or familiarity with a dialect influence the perception of the linguistic distance. Since in the case of the objective linguistic distance measurements there is only one value per dialect pair, the average of the two mean perceptual distances was calculated, e.g. the average of the distance Bergen-Trondheim and Trondheim-Bergen. This makes it possible to correlate the objective and the perceptual linguistic distances (Section 5).

4. OBJECTIVE LINGUISTIC DISTANCE MEASUREMENTS

In this section we describe how pronunciation distances are calculated on the basis of phonetic transcriptions. Since we want to measure pronunciation distances, only cognates (i.e. historically related words) are compared to each other. These cognates may vary both phonetically, phonologically and morphologically. If a particular word corresponds to different lexemes across the 15 Norwegian dialects, we consider variants of the most frequent lexeme only. For example, 'became' is translated by *vart* in some dialects and by *blei* in a majority of the dialects. Since we only wanted one cognate lexeme per item, we fill in missing values for dialects that use *vart*.

Table 1. Changing one pronunciation into another using a minimal set of operations.

Bø	goːɑns	subst. o/ɔ	1
	gɔːɑns	delete ɑ	1
	gɔːns	insert ə	1
	gɔːnəs	delete s	1
Lillehammer	gɔːnə		
			4

Table 2. Alignment which gives the minimal cost.

Bø	g	oː	ɑ	n		s
Lillehammer	g	ɔː		n	ə	
Costs		1	1		1	1

We use the Levenshtein algorithm to compute the distances between pronunciations in each pair of dialects. This algorithm computes the cost of incrementally changing one pronunciation into the other by inserting, deleting or substituting sounds. In the simplest form of the algorithm, each operation has the same cost, e.g. 1. Assume *gåande* (or the variant *gående*) 'going' is pronounced as [²goːɑns] in the dialect of Bø and as [²gɔːnə] in the dialect of Lillehammer. Changing one pronunciation into the other can be performed incrementally as in Table 1 (ignoring suprasegmentals and diacritics for the moment).

It is easy to see that there can be different sequences of operations mapping [²goːɑns] to [²gɔːnə], but the power of the Levenshtein algorithm is that it always finds the cost of the cheapest mapping.

In order to achieve distances which are based on linguistically motivated alignments that respect the syllable structure of a word or the structure within a syllable, the algorithm was adapted so that a vowel may only be substituted by a vowel and a consonant only by a consonant. Exceptions are the semi-vowels [j] and [w] and their vowel counterparts [i] and [u], which may correspond to either vowels or consonants. The central vowel schwa [ə] may correspond to any sonorant. In this way, unlikely matches like [o] and [t] or [s] and [e] are prevented.

In our example, the phonetic symbols are aligned as shown in Table 2.

In a previous study, we divided the sum of the operation costs by the length of the alignment. This normalises scores so that longer words do not count more heavily than shorter ones, reflecting the status of words as linguistic units. However, Heeringa, Kleiweg, Gooskens and Nerbonne (2006) showed that results based on raw Levenshtein distances approximate dialect differences as perceived by the dialect speakers better than results based on normalised Levenshtein distances. Therefore we do not normalise the Levenshtein distances in this paper.

Table 3. Cronbach's alpha values on the basis of the four data sets.

	Cronbach's alpha
ALE	0.89
ALENOR	0.91
NOR	0.89
NOS	0.87

The text 'The North Wind and the Sun' consists of 58 words in most dialects. The distance between two dialects is based on the aggregate distance over at most 58 word pairs. Since we have restricted our analysis to the comparison of cognates only, the number of word pairs per dialect pair will usually be smaller. Therefore the sum of the Levenshtein distances of the available word pairs for a dialect pair is divided by the number of the available word pairs, thus yielding the average Levenshtein distance of the dialect pair.

5. ALE, ALENOR, NOR AND NOS COMPARED TO EACH OTHER AND TO PERCEPTION

5.1 Consistency

In order to test the consistency of the data sets, Cronbach's alpha was calculated as the average inter-correlation among the words in each data set. A widely accepted threshold in social science is 0.70. All alpha values were higher (see Table 3) and the number of words in the four data sets are therefore proven to be a sufficient basis for a reliable Levenshtein analysis (see Heeringa 2004:170–3).

Since our analysis is restricted to the comparison of cognates only, the number of word pairs per dialect pair may vary. Table 4 shows the minimum, average and maximum number of word pairs for each of the four data sources.

5.2 Correlations

Correlations between different distance measurements

We first calculated the correlations between all objective linguistic distance measurements based on the four datasets and the corresponding perceptual distances. The results are shown in Table 5, which shows, for instance, that the correlation between the perceptual measurements (PERC) and the objective measurements on the basis of the NOS data (NOS) is 0.76. As explained in Section 2.1, the correlations are based on half matrices. Furthermore, we exclude the distances of dialects with respect to themselves, i.e. the distance of Bergen to Bergen, of Bjugn to Bjugn etc. In computational matrices these values are always 0, whereas in the perceptual matrix they vary, usually being higher than

Table 4. Minimum, average and maximum number of word pairs taken into account over all pairwise comparisons.

	Minimum	Average	Maximum
ALE	37	43.8	50
ALENOR	37	43.8	50
NOR	22	40.3	55
NOS	41	48.7	55

Table 5. Correlations between the different objective linguistic measurements and the perceptual linguistic distances.

	ALENOR	NOR	NOS	PERC
ALE	0.87	0.75	0.49	0.61
ALENOR		0.81	0.56	0.60
NOR			0.56	0.55
NOS				0.76

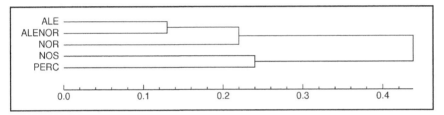

Figure 2. Cluster analysis based on the correlations between the different objective linguistic measurements and the perceptual linguistic distances.

the minimum score. This may be due to the fact that the dialect of the speaker of Bergen, for instance, may differ slightly from that of the listeners from the same location. Since this causes uni-directional distortion of the diagonal distances (they can only be too high, not too low), we exclude them when calculating the correlation coefficient.

From the correlations, distances can be derived by calculating $1-r$. For example, a correlation of $r = 0.75$ can be transformed to a distance of $1 - 0.75 = 0.25$. Using these distances, we classified the five data sources with cluster analysis (UPGMA). On the basis of this clustering, a dendrogram is constructed (Figure 2), which is a hierarchically structured tree where the varieties are the leaves. A dendrogram provides a good visualisation of similarity between (groups of) data sets. The shorter the lines connecting the data sets, the more similar they are. The tree structure shows for example that ALE and

ALENOR measurements correlate strongly, while ALE and NOS measurements do not correlate as strongly.

The highest correlation with the perceptual distances was found for the NOS data ($r = .76$)[12] and these two distance measurements form one cluster. This is to be expected since the perceptual distances and the NOS distances are based on the same data, viz. the recordings of the 'North Wind and the Sun'. The objective linguistic distances based on the other data sets form another cluster. The correlation is highest between ALE and ALENOR ($r = .87$). This does not come as a surprise, since these two distance measurements are based on the same data, but it also shows that these two different transcription systems result in different distance measurements. The NOR distances correlate stronger with the ALE/ALENOR distances ($r = .75$ and $.81$) than with the NOS distances ($r = .56$), which may be explained by the fact that both the ALE/ALENOR and the NOR are based on word lists rather than on running text as in the case of NOS. The NOR in turn correlates more strongly with the ALENOR ($r = .81$) than with the ALE ($r = .75$), since the NOR and the ALENOR share the same transcription system. The fact that NOR, ALE and ALENOR correlate stronger internally than with NOS may also be an effect of the tendency of phonemic transcription in these datasets. The NOS dataset is a more detailed phonetic transcription.

Correlations between objective distance measurements and perceptual distance measurements with and without recognition

Subjects could base their judgment of linguistic distances on the purely linguistic characteristics exhibited by the recordings. They could also use additional information about the dialect that is not directly present in the recordings but which was acquired in previous confrontations with the dialect. However, a prerequisite for such a generalisation is that listeners were able to recognize the dialect. In Table 6, we repeat the correlations between the perceived distances and the objective linguistic distances in the first column. In the second and third column the correlations are given for the judgments by listeners who recognized the dialects correctly and incorrectly, respectively. We see that the perceived distances including all judgments correlate highly with the judgments by listeners who did not recognise the dialects ($r = .99$).[13] The correlations with the objective linguistic distances are therefore very similar for these two sets of judgments.

The correlations between perceived distances and the NOS distance measurements are lower when the dialects are recognised correctly ($r = .58$) than when all judgments are included ($r = .76$). This is probably due to the fact that the listeners include information in their judgments that are not present in the NOS recordings. On the other hand, the judgments by listeners who did

Table 6. Correlations between objective linguistic distances, perceived distances, and perceived distances with and without correct recognition of the dialects.

	PERC	PERC with recognition	PERC without recognition
ALE	0.61	0.61	0.57
ALENOR	0.60	0.59	0.57
NOR	0.55	0.56	0.53
NOS	0.76	0.58	0.78
PERC	–	0.84	0.99

Table 7. Multiple linear regression analysis (stepwise) with perceived distances as dependent variable and different objective linguistic distances as independent variables. All judgments are included.

Input	Correlation	Significant variables
NOS, ALE, ALENOR, NOR	0.81	NOS, ALE
NOS, ALENOR, NOR	0.79	NOS, ALENOR
NOS, NOR	0.77	NOS, NOR
NOS	0.76	NOS

Table 8. Multiple linear regression analysis (stepwise) with perceived distances as dependent variable and different objective linguistic distances as independent variable. The perceived distances are based on the judgments made by listeners who recognised the dialects correctly.

Input	Correlation	Significant variables
NOS, ALE, ALENOR, NOR	0.68	ALE, NOS
NOS, ALENOR, NOR	0.65	ALENOR, NOS
NOS, NOR	0.64	NOS, NOR
NOS	0.58	NOS

not recognise the dialects are slightly higher ($r = .78$). These listeners were not distracted by their knowledge about the dialects but based their judgments on what they heard. This interpretation seems to be confirmed by the fact that the correlation with distances as perceived by listeners who recognised the dialects correctly is slightly higher for the ALE data ($r = .61$) than for the NOS data ($r = .58$). There are apparently some dialect characteristics present in the ALE data that are not present in the NOS data, and the listeners take these characteristics into account when judging the distances.

6. REGRESSION ANALYSES

In Tables 7, 8 and 9 we present the results of multiple linear regression analyses (stepwise) with perceived distances as the dependent variable and the different

Table 9. Multiple linear regression analysis (stepwise) with perceived distances as dependent variable and different objective linguistic distances as independent variable. The perceived distances are based on the judgments made by listeners who recognised the dialects wrongly.

Input	Correlation	Significant variables
NOS, ALE, ALENOR, NOR	0.81	NOS, ALE
NOS, ALENOR, NOR	0.79	NOS, ALENOR
NOS, NOR	0.78	NOS
NOS	0.78	NOS

Table 10. Difference between regression models with NOS data and NOS data combined with ALE data.

	PERC	PERC *with recognition*	PERC *without recognition*
NOS + ALE	0.81	0.68	0.81
NOS	0.76	0.58	0.78
increase	0.05	0.10	0.03

objective distances as independent variables. A model including ALE distances in addition to NOS gives the highest correlation ($r = .81$). For listeners recognising the dialects correctly, ALE (and ALENOR) are better predictors of perceived distance than NOS (see Table 8). When the dialects are not recognised correctly, ALE, ALENOR and NOS add little to the model (Table 9), probably due to the fact that the listeners base their judgments solely on what they hear.

The most important conclusions that can be drawn from the regression analyses are summarised in Table 10. We see that ALE adds most to the model in the case when the dialects are correctly recognised (a difference of 0.1), while ALE adds less to the model when all judgments are included or when only judgments with wrong recognitions are included.

7. CONCLUSIONS

We have shown that it is plausible that listeners do not base their judgments about linguistic distances between dialects solely on what they hear. They seem to generalise their judgments by including information about phonetic dialect characteristics not present in the recordings. This conclusion is based on the fact that in a regression analysis, objective linguistic distances measured on the basis of another data set than the one used for the perception experiment add significantly to the model. This supports the conclusion that listeners take dialect characteristics into account that are not present in the recordings. As could be expected, this effect is stronger for the group of listeners who recognised the dialects on the tape.

An alternative explanation of the impact of recognition on the judgments made may be that the listeners took geographical distances into consideration when making their judgments. In this case, one would expect geographical distances to show a higher correlation with the judgments with recognition than judgments without recognition. This was, however, not the case: the correlation was .53 in both situations.

To a certain degree, our results explain the rather low correlations that we found between perceived linguistic distance and objective linguistic distances in an earlier investigation. However, the best linguistic model in the present investigation results in a correlation of .81 (66 per cent explained variance), which means that 34 per cent of the variance still needs to be explained. It is likely that the other possible factors mentioned in the introduction (attitude, familiarity and other linguistic factors) also play an important role. In future work, we intend to include attitudes in our analysis. A multiple regression analysis with a combination of attitude scores and objective distance measurements will give us an impression of the relative contribution of these two factors to the perceived distances.

As shown in Section 2.5, we have taken care to select four datasets that are as similar as possible in a number of respects. We suspect that a better matching of the four datasets might have further improved the model. The 15 dialects were not exactly the same, the period of data collection differed and there is a difference in the phonetic details of the transcriptions. Finally, the words have been selected according to different criteria. All these differences between the data sets may have contributed to the rather high amount of variance that remains to be explained.

While we think the model could be further improved, we hope that the present work has already contributed to a better understanding of how people judge phonetic distances between their own dialect and other dialects. Judgements differ depending on whether subjects are able to correctly recognise and place a dialect. We interpret this so that people seem to let their previous knowledge of a dialect contribute to their judgement of how close or far it is from their own dialect.

ACKNOWLEDGEMENTS

The NOS recordings were made by Jørn Almberg in co-operation with Kristian Skarbø at the Department of Linguistics, University of Trondheim and made available at http://www.ling.hf.ntnu.no/nos/ along with the phonetic transcriptions (in IPA as well as in SAMPA). We are grateful for their permission to use the material. We thank the University of Oslo for access to the handwritten ALE forms and the handwritten NOR volumes (the latter are now available through the Digital Documentation Unit at http://www.edd.uio.no/). We would furthermore like to thank Benedikte Tobiassen for the digitisation of the ALE, ALENOR and NOR data, which are kept at the Department of Linguistic, Literary and Esthetic Studies at the University of Bergen. Finally we thank three anonymous reviewers for their useful comments.

REFERENCES

C. Gooskens (2005), 'How well can Norwegians identify their dialects?', *Nordic Journal of Linguistics*, 28 (1), 37–60.

C. Gooskens and W. Heeringa (2004), 'Perceptive evaluation of Levenshtein dialect distance measurements using Norwegian dialect data', *Language Variation and Change*, 16(3), 189–207.

C. Gooskens and W. Heeringa (2006), 'The relative contribution of pronunciation, lexical and prosodic differences to the perceived distances between Norwegian dialects', *Literary and Linguistic Computing, special issue on Progress in Dialectometry: Toward Explanation*, 21(4), 477–492.

W. Heeringa, P. Kleiweg, C. Gooskens and J. Nerbonne (2006), 'Evaluation of string distance algorithms for dialectology', in J. Nerbonne and E. Hinrichs, eds, *Linguistic Distances Workshop at the joint conference of International Committee on Computational Linguistics and the Association for Computational Linguistics, Sydney, July, 2006*, 51–62.

W. Heeringa (2004), 'Measuring dialect pronunciation differences using Levenshtein distance' (Ph.D. thesis, University of Groningen).

I. Hoff (1960), 'Norsk dialektatlas. Foredrag i Norsk Forening for Språkvitenskap 3.nov 1959', *Norsk Tidsskrift for Sprogvidenskap*, 595–622.

J. Kruijsen (1976), *Atlas Linguarum Europae (ALE) Premier questionnaire. Onomasiologie, vocabulaire fundamental* (Amsterdam).

O. Nes (1982), *Storms norske lydskriftsystem (med tillegg) definert ved hjelp av IPA's lydskriftsystem* Skriftserie for Institutt for fonetikk og lingvistikk 8, serie B (University of Bergen).

M. Skjekkeland (1997), *Dei norske dialektane: tradisjonelle særdrag i jamføring med skriftmåla* (Kristiansand).

A. Weijnen (1975), *Atlas Linguarum Europae (ALE). Introduction* (Assen).

END NOTES

[1] The term 'dialect' is not used in the strict sense but rather as a variety that is characteristic for some region or place. Variation may be restricted to the phonetic, phonological and morphological level.

[2] In Norwegian 'The North Wind and the Sun' is translated as <u>N</u>ordavinden <u>og</u> <u>S</u>ola, which we abbreviate to NOS.

[3] Gooskens and Heeringa (2004) also processed lexical differences since pronunciations of translationally corresponding words were compared to each other regardless of whether the words were cognates.

[4] The phonetic and the phonological levels are not distinguished in our analysis. Also morphological variation is included, since we base the measurements on whole words from a running text.

[5] Alternatively the profile of the dialect wrongly identified is activated instead of that of the correct accent. In that case the same goes as for the recognized dialect. However, the question may arise to what extent a listener will be able to activate the profile of a dialect variety wrongly identified, since identifying a wrong variety shows that the listener is unfamiliar with both the correct one and the wrongly identified one.

[6] Extended Speech Assessment Methods Phonetic Alphabet. This is a machine readable phonetic alphabet which is still human-readable. Basically, it maps IPA-symbols to the 7 bit printable ASCII/ANSI characters. See http://www.phon.ucl.ac.uk/home/sampa/x-sampa.htm.

[7] Originally, the circumflex toneme was transcribed as [~] in the X-SAMPA transcriptions of NOS.

[8] At the time the perception experiment was carried out, recordings of only 15 varieties were available. Today more than 50 recordings are available, giving much better possibilities to pick a representative selection of varieties.

[9] We replaced Mørkved with Sørfold, Bjugn with Stjørna, Trondheim with Horg, Stjørdal with Leksvik, Verdal with Skogn, Herøy with Vanylven, Elnesvågen with Bud, Lillehammer with Gausdal, Bergen with Lindås, Larvik with Hedrum, Borre with Nøtterøy, Bryne with Klepp, and Halden with Idd. In some cases there were clear differences between the dialects of the NOS-places and the dialects of the replacements.

[10] We replaced Bergen with Loddefjord, Mørkved with Sørfold, Elnesvågen with Bud, Halden with Enningdal, Larvik with Tjølling, Lillehammer with Follebu, and Stjørdal with Leksvik.

[11] The matrix can be found in Gooskens and Heeringa (2004).

[12] Gooskens and Heeringa (2006) found a lower correlation of 0.68 due to the fact they did not average the perceptual distances, e.g. A-B and B-A (cf. Section 3) but copied *objective* distances (e.g. A-B was copied to B-A). If they had calculated the correlation with the two full matrices in the same way as we did (excluding the diagonal A-A, B-B etc.), the correlation would have been equal to 0.73.

[13] The correlation with the judgments by listeners who recognized the dialects is lower (r = .84), probably due to the fact that the proportion of judgements in this category is much smaller (27.5 per cent) than that of the judgments without recognition (72.5 per cent).

QUANTIFYING DIALECT SIMILARITY BY COMPARISON OF THE LEXICAL DISTRIBUTION OF PHONEMES

WARREN MAGUIRE

Abstract   This paper describes a new method for quantifying the similarity of the lexical distribution of phonemes in different varieties of a language (in this case English). In addition to introducing the method, it discusses phonological problems which must be addressed if any comparison of this sort is to be attempted, and applies the method to a limited data set of varieties of English. Since the method assesses their structural similarity, it will be useful for analysing the historical development of varieties of English and the relationships (either as a result of common origin or of contact) that hold between them.

I. INTRODUCTION

In recent years considerable progress has been made in assessing the relationships between linguistic varieties by measuring the similarity between strictly comparable sets of phonetic data. In particular, measurement of Levenshtein Distance (see, for example, Nerbonne, Heeringa, and Kleiweg, 1999; Nerbonne and Heeringa, 2001; Heeringa, 2004) has proved useful for determining the relationships between closely related varieties, and the 'Sound Comparisons' method for assessing the distance between varieties provides a very promising alternative technique for looking into the changing relationships between closely-related and not so closely-related varieties (Heggarty, McMahon and McMahon, 2005; McMahon, Heggarty, McMahon and Maguire, 2007).[1]

Phonetic comparison algorithms of this sort are not, however, without their problems. Firstly, they often depend upon auditory phonetic transcriptions of one degree of fineness or another, with all the associated issues of transcriber

International Journal of Humanities and Arts Computing 2 (1–2) 2008, 261–277
DOI: 10.3366/E1753854809000421
© Edinburgh University Press and the Association for History and Computing 2009

isoglosses, inaccuracies and realism that this method brings (see Milroy and Gordon, 2003: 144–152 for a discussion of the issues). Secondly, it is not at all clear how accurate the algorithms used in these methods for assessing phonetic similarity actually are. Heggarty *et al.* (2005) suggest, for instance, that Levenshtein Distance is not an accurate way of measuring the similarity between phonetic strings, but of course the same might be said for the proposed alternative method, since phonetic symbols do not come with numbers attached. Thirdly, relying on measurements of phonetic similarity is problematic in that historical connections (as a result of common origin or contact) can very quickly become obscured by radical phonetic change.

In the case of Liverpool English, for example, it is a well known fact that this variety is very strikingly different, at the phonetic level, from neighbouring varieties in the north of England (Wells, 1982: 371–3). These differences are the result of the complex history of the variety, but they also help obscure an important point. Despite the existence of numerous phonetic peculiarities, Liverpool English is a rather typical northern English English in terms of the lexical distribution of its phonemes. For example, Liverpool English, like other northern English varieties, lacks the STRUT-FOOT and TRAP-BATH splits, and, despite radical phonetic changes to its voiceless stops, it still has the same lexical distribution of these phonemes as many neighbouring varieties of English. This kind of structural analysis may well give us a deeper insight into the relationships between varieties, since it strips away many of the superficial (phonetic) differences which are of recent origin and which obscure otherwise close relationships between varieties. That is not to say that the phonetic differences are unimportant – rather they are only part of the story which may, in global phonetic comparison, swamp some of the structural similarities.

What is at issue here is the distinction between phonetic realisation, on the one hand, and lexical distribution, on the other (see Wells, 1982: 72–85 for a discussion of this distinction). These two things are not, of course, independent from each other, but if it is possible to examine lexical distribution without examining phonetic realisation we stand a chance not only of avoiding some of the problems identified above, but also of providing another means of assessing the (changing) relationships between varieties of a language, with all the advantages that brings.

Dialectologists have recognised the advantages of studying lexical distribution for some time, although it is not clear that the full potential of this approach has yet been achieved. Structural dialectology (perhaps most well known from Weinreich 1954 and Moulton 1960) attempted to meaningfully compare the lexical distribution of phonemes in different varieties of a language. As Chambers and Trudgill (1980: 38–45) point out, however, this diasystemic approach failed to fully capture the similarities in lexical distribution between varieties, precisely because it did not fully specify the lexical incidence of the phonemes involved. A different approach was adopted by Wells (1982), which involved the setting up of a number of 'lexical sets' based on the lexical distribution of vowel phonemes in two reference accents, British Received Pronunciation (RP) and 'General American' (GenAm). Despite the undoubted usefulness (and consequent popularity) of Wells' system, it suffers from the same problem as structural dialectology – since the precise membership of the lexical sets is not specified, and since different varieties distribute lexical items across these lexical sets in rather different ways, it is impossible to quantify exactly how similar the lexical distributions of different varieties are. I return to this issue in Section 2 below.

Moberg, Gooskens and Nerbonne (2007) also attempt to quantify the similarity in lexical distribution between closely related varieties (the Scandinavian languages). They do so by measuring the conditional entropy of correspondences in lexical distribution in order to determine 'the ease with which a word in one language is understood by speakers of a related language' (pp. 52–3). Their approach is a rather different approach to the one taken here, which assesses the over-all similarity in lexical distribution between pairs of varieties, and does not (as the method employed by Moberg *et al.* does) assess the symmetry (or asymmetry) of the mapping between the varieties. Rather, the approach adopted here is designed to determine the similarity between pairs of varieties, such that the similarity of Variety 1 to Variety 2 is equal to the similarity of Variety 2 to Variety 1. This is an essential requirement of a comparison mechanism if we wish to make comparisons of many varieties at one time and to define the relationships between them in the wider linguistic context.

In the rest of this article, I describe a method for assessing the similarity of lexical distribution of (stressed vowel) phonemes in different varieties of a language (in this case English). This method addresses the concerns raised above, and, at the same time, shares with the phonetic comparison methods a lack of pre-selection of 'interesting features' and the ability to produce percentage similarity scores between any pair-wise comparison so that the relationships between different varieties of a language can be appreciated fully. In Section 2, I introduce the method. In Section 3, I discuss a crucial phonological issue which must be addressed in any analysis of this sort. In Section 4, I provide an example analysis of the method, comparing seven varieties of English as a means of demonstrating its effectiveness.

2. MEASURING THE SIMILARITY OF LEXICAL DISTRIBUTIONS

2.1. Problems with comparing lexical distribution of phonemes

Wells' STRUT, FOOT and GOOSE lexical sets correspond to three vowel phonemes in the Received Pronunciation (RP) variety of English: /ʌ/, /ʊ/ and /uː/

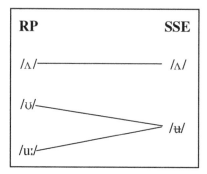

Figure 1. Correspondences in the STRUT, FOOT and GOOSE lexical sets in RP and SSE.

(Wells, 1982 : 131–3, 147–9). In Scottish Standard English (SSE), however, the words defined by Wells as belonging to these three lexical sets have one of two phonemes: /ʌ/ or /ʉ/ (Wells, 1982: 400; Johnson, 2007: 114–5). SSE has /ʌ/ in STRUT words and /ʉ/ in FOOT and GOOSE words, giving the correspondences indicated in Figure 1 between it and RP.

As a simple statement of correspondence, this is a useful summary of the structural relationship, with respect to these vowels, between RP and SSE, and this is of course what Wells' lexical sets are designed to do. There are a number of problems with this approach, however, which mean that it is not ideal for precisely defining the structural relationships between varieties.

Firstly, it assumes that terms such as STRUT, FOOT and GOOSE are meaningful for the varieties being compared. In this instance, this is certainly the case for RP (not surprisingly, since RP is one of the reference accents used by Wells to establish his lexical sets). For SSE they are less meaningful, but given the very straightforward correspondence between /ʌ/ and STRUT, and /ʉ/ and FOOT-GOOSE, these lexical sets are meaningful for the analyst here too. In other cases, things are much more complicated. In Mid-Ulster English, for example, the STRUT lexical set largely corresponds to the phoneme /ʌ/, and GOOSE largely corresponds to /ʉ/ (see Wells, 1982: 438–45; Harris 1985). However, the FOOT lexical set corresponds to both /ʌ/ and /ʉ/, with some words (such as *put* and *foot*) varying between the two phonemes, and others, (such as *book*, *good* and *woman*) invariantly having one or other of these phonemes (/ʉ/ in *book* and *good*, /ʌ/ in *woman*). When we add to this the fact that some STRUT words in Mid-Ulster English may have entirely different phonemes (e.g. *other* and *under* with /ɒ/ and *among* and *oven* with /ɔː/), the result is a rather complex set of correspondences for which the terms STRUT, FOOT and GOOSE are considerably less useful. The problem here is that in using lexical sets, such as those established by Wells (1982), to compare varieties of a language, we are not comparing varieties directly with each other but rather with an externally defined set of lexical categories which may or may not be meaningful for the varieties under analysis. To avoid this problem, it is desirable to develop a comparison mechanism which allows us to compare each pair of varieties directly.

A second problem is that, even in relatively straightforward cases such as STRUT, FOOT and GOOSE in RP and SSE, this kind of comparison does not allow us to quantify how similar varieties are. Since lexical distribution of phonemes involves the occurrence of particular phonemes in particular words, we need to specify exactly which words are involved in order to quantify the similarity of distribution. Although Wells (1982) provides lists of words belonging to each of his lexical sets, they are only example cases, neither exhaustive nor chosen in an entirely systematic way. In order to quantify the similarity in lexical distribution of phonemes between varieties, we need to precisely define a list of words these phonemes occur in, and, in so doing, assign relative importance to particular phonological patterns based on some criteria such as frequency of occurrence or representativeness of historical lexical categories. Once this is done, strict comparison of the lexical distribution of phonemes in different varieties in measurable ways will be considerably more straightforward.

2.2. Strict comparison of the lexical distribution of phonemes in different varieties

In order to avoid the second problem discussed above, a standard wordlist is required. For the purposes of this example, I have used the Thorndike and Lorge top 1,000 most frequent words (Thorndike and Lorge, 1944).[2] Returning to the comparison of STRUT, FOOT and GOOSE in RP and SSE, the Thorndike and Lorge wordlist provides us with the correspondences between RP and SSE given in Table 1.

Unlike the bald set of correspondences revealed in Figure 1, this set of correspondences is precisely defined. Table 1 reveals the following statistics:

1) RP /ʌ/ corresponds to SSE /ʌ/ in 70 words;
2) RP /ʊ/ corresponds to SSE /ʉ/ in 17.5 words (one word, *room*, may have either /ʊ/ or /uː/; in order to account for this, this word is compared twice, but with each comparison only counting as half so that this word does not carry twice the weight in the comparison than it otherwise would);
3) RP /uː/ corresponds to SSE /ʉ/ in 39.5 words (the fraction again because of the variable distribution of *room* in RP).

With this information in hand, it is now possible to quantify the similarity in lexical distribution of phonemes between these two varieties.

265

Table 1. RP and SSE 'STRUT', 'FOOT' and 'GOOSE' in the Thorndike and Lorge wordlist.

RP	SSE
/ʌ/	/ʌ/
above, among, another, become, blood, brother, but, butter, colour, come, coming, company, country, cover, cup, cut, discover, does, done, double, dust, enough, front, government, hundred, hunt, hurry, husband, judge, jump, just, love, money, month, mother, much, must, none, nothing, number, once, one, other, public, run, rush, shut, some, something, sometime, son, study, subject, such, sudden, suffer, summer, sun, thus, tongue, touch, trouble, trust, uncle, under, up, us, wonder, wonderful, young	above, among, another, become, blood, brother, but, butter, colour, come, coming, company, country, cover, cup, cut, discover, does, done, double, dust, enough, front, government, hundred, hunt, hurry, husband, judge, jump, just, love, money, month, mother, much, must, none, nothing, number, once, one, other, public, run, rush, shut, some, something, sometime, son, study, subject, such, sudden, suffer, summer, sun, thus, tongue, touch, trouble, trust, uncle, under, up, us, wonder, wonderful, young
/ʊ/	/ʉ/
book, brook, cook, could, foot, full, good, look, pull, put, room, should, stood, sugar, took, woman, wood, would	book, brook, cook, could, foot, full, good, look, pull, put, room, should, stood, sugar, took, woman, wood, would
/uː/	afternoon, beautiful, beauty, blue, choose, cool, do, duty, few, food, fruit, grew, knew, lose, moon, move, music, new, noon, prove, roof, room, rule, school, shoe, soon, suit, through, to, too, true, truth, two, use, usual, view, who, whom, whose, you
afternoon, beautiful, beauty, blue, choose, cool, do, duty, few, food, fruit, grew, knew, lose, moon, move, music, new, noon, prove, roof, room, rule, school, shoe, soon, suit, through, to, too, true, truth, two, use, usual, view, who, whom, whose, you	

2.3. Quantifying similarity in lexical distribution

Figure 1 reveals that there is a one-to-one correspondence between RP /ʌ/ and SSE /ʌ/ and a two-to-one correspondence between RP /ʊ/ and /uː/ and SSE /ʉ/. As far as Figure 1 is concerned, all of these comparisons are equal. The statistics immediately above reveal that this is not the case, however. Although the correspondence between RP /ʌ/ and SSE /ʌ/ is 100 per cent, such that we can say that the corresponding phoneme in SSE to RP /ʌ/ is /ʌ/, SSE /ʉ/ corresponds to RP /ʊ/ 30.7 per cent of the time and SSE /ʉ/ corresponds to RP /uː/ 69.3 per cent of the time. That is, RP /uː/ corresponds to SSE /ʉ/ in the majority of cases, and vice versa. Another way of putting it might be to say that the correspondence between RP /uː/ and SSE /ʉ/ 'wins out' over the correspondence between RP /ʊ/ and SSE /ʉ/ (which 'loses out'), and that the corresponding phoneme in RP to SSE /ʉ/ is /uː/, but that the correspondence is not perfect. Stating the relationship between these phonemes in this way allows us to quantify how similar the lexical distribution of phonemes in these words is in these two varieties in the following way:

1) RP /ʌ/ = SSE /ʌ/ ('1 point' for each word, total 70);
2) RP /uː/ = SSE /ʉ/ ('1 point' for each word, total 39.5);
3) RP /ʊ/ = SSE /ʉ/, but this loses out to RP /uː/ = SSE /ʉ/ (no score for these words);
4) The over-all percentage similarity of lexical distribution for the vowels in these words in the comparison of RP and SSE is the percentage 'wins' of the total number of comparisons made (127 words), i.e. ((70 + 39.5) / 127) = 0.862 (i.e. 86.2 per cent similar).

Comparing varieties in this way allows us to determine which phonemes in different varieties correspond to each other (at least in the majority of cases) and enables us, as a result, to quantify the similarity in lexical distribution between the varieties directly rather than through some externally defined schema such as Wells' lexical sets. This is despite the fact that the relationships between lexical distribution in different varieties are often complex and the problem that there is nothing in the varieties themselves indicating which phonemes correspond to the phonemes of other varieties of the language.

In order to explore further how this method works, I compare, in Table 2, the distribution of all stressed vowel phonemes in the Thorndike and Lorge wordlist in RP and modern Tyneside English (TE) from the northeast of England.[3] Rather than listing all of the relevant words, I give the total number of occurrences of each correspondence type.[4]

Table 2 reveals that there are 30 correspondences between the stressed vowel phonemes of RP and TE in this wordlist. As was indicated above, these

Table 2. Correspondences between stressed vowel phonemes in the Thorndike and Lorge wordlist in RP and TE.

RP	TE	No.	RP	TE	No.
ɒ	ɒ	56.5	ɛ	ɛ	120
ɒ	ɔː	3	ɜː	ɜː	28
ɑː	a	20.5	ɜː	ɛː	0.5
ɑː	ɑː	27.5	ɛə	ɛː	16
æ	a	61	eɪ	eː	84
aɪ	aɪ	73	əʊ	oː	67
aɪə	aɪə	8	ɪ	ɪ	108
aʊ	aʊ	35	iː	iː	80
aʊə	aʊə	4	ɪə	iə	9
ɔː	ɔː	56.5	ɪə	ɜː	0.5
ɔː	ɒ	0.5	ʊ	ʊ	15.5
ʊə	ɔː	0.5	ʊ	uː	2
ɔː	ʊə	1	uː	uː	40.5
ʊə	ʊə	3	ʌ	ɒ	5
ɔɪ	ɔɪ	9	ʌ	ʊ	65

correspondences are in competition with each other, so that, for example, TE /uː/ corresponds not only to RP /uː/ (in 40.5 cases) but also to RP /ʊ/ (in 2 cases). In cases of competition of this sort, minority cases 'lose' and majority cases 'win'. In Table 2, 'losing' correspondences are greyed out. The competition between correspondences means that 20 out of the 30 'win', and the over-all similarity of lexical distribution of stressed vowels in these two varieties is calculated by taking the scores for these 'wins' as a percentage of the over-all number of comparisons (1,000), giving a similarity score in this case of 95.1 per cent.

It is worth emphasising a number of crucial points which arise out the comparison of RP and TE. Firstly, one phoneme in a variety can only correspond, in the majority at least, to one phoneme in another variety. For example, RP /uː/ = TE /uː/, but RP /ʊ/ ≠ TE /uː/, despite the latter corresponding in two cases. Secondly, the phonetic realisations of the phonemes is not important, only their lexical distributions. Thus, TE /ʊ/ does not correspond to RP /ʊ/ despite the two phonemes being realised in a similar way in the two varieties, and the same symbol being used for both. Rather, TE /ʊ/ corresponds to RP /ʌ/. That is, the method for the comparison of lexical distributions described here is purely structural. This avoids a number of the problems with phonetic comparisons of the type described in Section 1 above, but it does bring with it other complications, as discussed in Section 3.

In advance of this and the example analysis of seven varieties of English in Section 4 which further demonstrates the results of this method of analysis, the comparison mechanism and scoring system may be expressed more formally and generally as follows, in order to further clarify how it works:

1) List all (vowel) phoneme correspondences between the two varieties being compared, with frequencies of occurrence of each for the wordlist under analysis; treat variation within single lexical items as fractions (so that each lexical comparison has the same weight), cross-multiplying as necessary.

2) Identify majority ('winning') correspondences as follows: given two varieties ([1, 2]), a phonemic correspondence, $X^1 = X^2$, between them wins if *neither* X^1 *nor* X^2 occurs more frequently in any other correspondence.

3) In the case of ties, pick one of the tying correspondences at random as the 'winner', assuming the conditions of (2) above are otherwise met. The other tying correspondence 'loses'.

4) Only 'winning' correspondences score – the score each gets is the number of times it occurs in the wordlist under analysis.

5) Express the total 'winning' score as a percentage of the total number of lexical comparisons (in a wordlist of 1,000 words, examining only one stressed vowel per word, the 'wins' would be expressed as a percentage of 1,000). This is the over-all similarity score for the comparison between these two varieties.

6) Repeat for every pair-wise comparison of varieties.

Key to this mechanism is that it ensures *symmetry*; i.e. the similarity of Variety 1 to Variety 2 is the same as the similarity of Variety 2 to Variety 1. This is crucial if we wish to assess the similarities between a range of varieties at the same time in order to better understand the relationships between them, as discussed in Section 1. Additionally, this method for measuring similarity captures the generalisation that speakers of one variety with a single phoneme in a set of words who try to predict the lexical incidence of phonemes in a variety with more than one phoneme in the same words will achieve the highest success if they ignore the phonemic contrast in the target variety and assume their own merger throughout, as indicated in the following (artificial) example.

- Variety 1 has 100 per cent phoneme X in a set of 100 words, corresponding to two phonemes, X (60 per cent) and Y (40 per cent) in Variety 2. I.e. the correspondences between the two varieties for these words are $X = X$ (60) and $X = Y$ (40). If the speaker of 'merged' Variety 1 predicts that all words in Variety 2 have a single phoneme (as Variety 1 does), the speaker will in effect be right in 60 per cent of cases, and wrong in 40 per cent. This is a better result than would be the case if the speaker of Variety 1 attempted to assign a phonemic difference in Variety 2 at random – (s)he would, on average, be right only 50 per cent of the time (i.e. the two groups would consist of equal numbers of words from each actual phonemic group in Variety 2).

Note that this is also true in situations where the 'majority correspondence' is actually a minority of the total number of comparisons, as in a case where Variety 1 has 100 per cent phoneme X, Variety 2 has 40 per cent X, 30 per cent Y and 30 per cent Z. Similarly, it means that a set of correspondences between Variety 1 and Variety 2 such as $X = X$ (60 per cent), $X = Y$ (40 per cent) is no better or worse than a set of correspondences between the two varieties such as $X = X$ (60 per cent), $X = Y$ (20 per cent), $X = Z$ (20 per cent) – if the speaker of the 'merged' variety assumes a single phoneme in the unmerged variety, (s)he will in effect be right the number of times the majority correspondence occurs, which will always be greater than the chances of randomly assigning the correct words to the correct phonemic distinctions in the non-merging variety.

3. PHONOLOGICAL PROBLEMS – RHOTICITY

As was discussed in Section 1 above, phonetic comparison of varieties brings with it a number of assumptions and problems, and this is no less true of comparison of the lexical distribution of phonemes, albeit in different ways. It should be noted at this point that problems of the kind discussed below are not specific to this method (even if they are crucial for it) but, rather, are perennial problems for phonological analysis more generally. The solution suggested here is not necessarily definitive for this comparison method, never mind for models of phonology in general, but without addressing these issues it will be impossible to implement the kind of comparison described in this paper. In what follows, a particularly knotty problem in English phonology is addressed – the phonological analysis of (non-)rhoticity. Note that this is not just a problem of aligning segments in one variety with segments in another – rather it is the result of the limits of phonological analysis.

The examples given thus far exemplifying this method have excluded consonants from the analysis. This was done for a number of reasons, including simplification for demonstration purposes, but also avoidance of the tricky issue discussed below. Additionally, it seems likely that there is considerably less variation in the phonology of consonant systems in varieties of English than there is variation in vowel systems (on rhoticity see below), so that it might be desirable to exclude consonants from the analysis more generally in order to avoid redundant analysis. At this stage in this research programme, this is precisely what has been done, so that much of what follows depends upon the method described thus far being applied only to comparisons of (stressed) vowel systems.

3.1. Rhoticity

The SQUARE lexical set (as defined by Wells, 1982: 155–7) is typically pronounced with the sequence [ɛɚ] in Tyrone English. It seems reasonable to suggest that underlyingly this is /ɛr/, since words like *mess* and *ten* contain the sequence [ɛə], as a positional allophone of /ɛ/ (cf. *tenner*, £10, with [ɛ]). But analysing [ɛɚ] in SQUARE words as /er/ is also not unreasonable, given that /e/ (in FACE words) is pronounced as a monophthong or centring diphthong. This will, to a certain extent, be a subjective choice on the part of the phonologist which affects the outcome of similarity comparisons involving this variety.

Even assuming that the underlying nature of [ɛɚ] can be determined, how might this underlying form (e.g. /ɛr/) be compared with other varieties of English, especially non-rhotic ones such as RP? SQUARE words have [ɛə] in RP, typically phonologised as /ɛə/ (Wells, 1982: 155–7), although other analyses are possible (see below). Should the sequence /ɛr/ in Tyrone be compared directly to RP /ɛə/, or should the /ɛ/ in the Tyrone sequence /ɛr/ be compared with RP /ɛə/? In the first case, there is a good match between Tyrone /ɛr/ and RP /ɛə/ (mostly in SQUARE words) which would be unlikely to 'lose out' to any other correspondence. In the second case, Tyrone /ɛ/ almost always corresponds to RP /ɛ/ and, hence, the correspondence between Tyrone /ɛ/ and RP /ɛə/ would 'lose out'. As before, the choice of analysis affects the similarity in lexical distribution between varieties.

A further problem is the status of things like RP [ɛə], and this also depends upon how (non-)rhoticity is analysed phonologically. This is particularly crucial in cases such as the phonetically identical *saw* [sɔː] and *sore* [sɔː] in RP, where the first cannot be followed by linking-R, but the second can be (Wells, 1982: 225). Where does the phonological difference between these two words lie, and what effect will that difference have on assessing the similarity in lexical distribution of varieties?

The method described in this article is not intended to answer such difficult phonological puzzles, but it must adopt some means of avoiding the subjectivity that they inevitably involve, otherwise meaningful comparisons will remain a pipe-dream. As a working solution, these related problems involving (non-)rhoticity are side-stepped by adopting a polysystemic approach (see Firth, 1948; Lass, 1984) which divides words into two groups: (1) those containing historical coda /r/, and (2) those without historical coda /r/. This is not, however, intended to imply that a polysystemic approach is the 'correct' way of analysing data of this sort. Rather, it is expedient, allowing comparison to proceed without the necessity of determining (or, perhaps more accurately, deciding) the status of rhoticity in any given variety of English. The result of this approach is that words without historical coda /r/ are compared between varieties without reference to the correspondences between words with historical coda /r/. Hence, RP /ɛə/ and

Tyrone /ɛr/ may be compared directly (and 'win out') without worrying about the conflicting majority correspondence between RP /ɛ/ and Tyrone /ɛ/. This approach also removes the problem of determining the exact phonological form underlying RP [ɛə] and Tyrone [ɛɚ] – it is immaterial whether we analyse these as /ɛə/ and /ɛr/ respectively, or as /ɛər/ and /er/, or whatever. The same goes for the problematic pair *saw* and *sore* in RP. The polysystemic approach means that the underlying form of these words can be the same or different without it affecting the comparisons being made.[5]

It is clear that adoption of a polysystemic approach for this analysis brings considerable benefits. It has one other important consequence which ties in with the discussion in Section 1. Since this approach allows us to compare sequences in rhotic and non-rhotic varieties directly without reference to the presence or absence of phonological /r/, this means that (non-)rhoticity is ultimately factored out of the calculation of similarity between varieties. The fact that RP is non-rhotic and Tyrone English is rhotic does not affect the over-all similarity in lexical distribution of phonemes in these two varieties, as calculated by the method described in this paper. As was discussed in Section 1, a feature of comparison at the phonetic level is that phonetic divergence can very quickly obscure close historical relationships between varieties. Loss of rhoticity can, in phonetic comparison, lead to considerable divergence between historically closely related varieties of a language (see Maguire *et al.*, 2008, for example). Although this is an interesting finding in and of itself, it has the inevitable effect of making phonetic comparisons less good at discovering historical connections between varieties. Since the approach adopted here excludes rhoticity from the comparisons, I suggest that it has a better chance of uncovering older relationships between varieties, giving an insight into their historical development in a way that phonetic comparisons may struggle to do.

4. AN EXAMPLE ANALYSIS

In this section, I demonstrate the efficacy of this approach to measuring similarity between varieties of a language in a preliminary analysis of seven varieties of English: RP, Modern Tyneside English, Modern Tyrone English, Traditional Tyneside English, Traditional Tyrone English, SSE, and a variety of Standard American English. The phonological data for RP were derived from the phonetic transcriptions contained in the *Oxford English Dictionary Online*. Those for Tyrone (a variety of Mid-Ulster English) were derived from research on the variety by the author, a native speaker of the dialect, whilst those for Tyneside, SSE and StAm were derived from published descriptions (Viereck, 1966; Rydland, 1998; Wells, 1982; Kretzschmar, 2004) and from research with native speakers of the varieties by the author. Note that the distinction between 'Modern' and 'Traditional' varieties of the same dialect is essentially the one

RP	Modern Tyne	Modern Tyrone	Trad. Tyrone	Trad. Tyne	StAm	SSE	
0.00	0.05	0.14	0.27	0.24	0.05	0.09	**RP**
	0.00	0.12	0.25	0.20	0.05	0.08	**Modern Tyne**
		0.00	0.23	0.25	0.11	0.07	**Modern Tyrone**
			0.00	0.29	0.26	0.24	**Trad. Tyrone**
				0.00	0.23	0.22	**Trad. Tyne**
					0.00	0.05	**StAm**
						0.00	**SSE**

Figure 2. Distance matrix for seven varieties of English.

described in Trudgill (1999) and Kortmann and Upton (2004), and that the 'Traditional' varieties represent the 'broadest', most old-fashioned end of the spectrum of variation still present at the locations concerned.

Comparing all of these varieties against each other using the method described above gives us 21 similarity scores (excluding comparisons of each variety with itself). The distance measurements are derived from these similarity scores by subtracting the similarity scores from 100 per cent (see Goebl, 2006: 413; 2007: 137), giving the distance matrix in Figure 2.

The relationships contained in this distance matrix are best displayed visually in tree and network form – in this case using the phylogenetic software suite *Splitstree* 4 (Huson and Bryant, 2006), which is designed to process distance matrices of this sort using a range of standard algorithms (see also Heggarty *et al.,* 2005; McMahon and McMahon, 2005; and McMahon *et al.,* 2007 for previous application of *Splitstree* to linguistic distance matrices). In this case, the data are visualised as an unrooted tree using the *Neighbor-Joining* algorithm and as a network using the *NeighborNet* algorithm contained within *Splitstree*, as in Figures 3 and 4.

Both the tree and the network reveal a similar picture of the relations between these varieties. In both, there is a major difference between the (very heterogeneous) 'Traditional' varieties on the one hand and the much more homogeneous 'Modern' and standard varieties on the other. In both cases, RP, Tyneside and StAm form a mini cluster within the modern varieties (note that since rhoticity is factored out of the analysis, the rhotic varieties need not group together). The tree and network reveal that Tyrone and SSE are on the other side of this 'split', not surprisingly given that these two varieties share a number of phonological features (e.g., in terms of the lexical sets in Wells (1982), merger of TRAP, BATH and PALM, merger – at least variably in the case of Tyrone – of FOOT and GOOSE, and survival of the NORTH-FORCE distinction). The network, which allows contradictory relationships to be shown

273

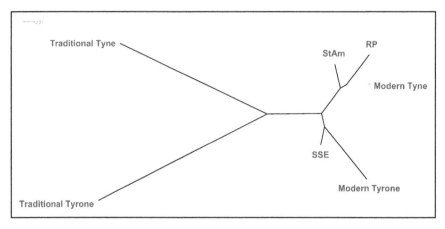

Figure 3. A Neighbor-Joining unrooted tree analysis of the distance matrix.[6]

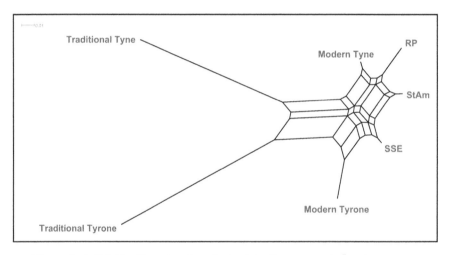

Figure 4. A NeighborNet network analysis of the distance matrix.[7]

(resulting in reticulations in the network) in a way that trees cannot, reveals additional connections between varieties – for example the connections between Modern and Traditional Tyrone and Modern and Traditional Tyneside (despite the larger differences between them), and between StAm and SSE, both of which have merged the LOT and THOUGHT lexical sets for example (Wells, 1982: 402–3, 473–5).

All of these patterns make sense, given what we know about the phonology of these varieties and their historical and geographical relations, suggesting, even with this limited data set, that this method is well suited to determining the relationships between varieties of a language. Although the analysis presented here is only preliminary, it suggests that this approach to the quantification of similarities between varieties of a language may be a profitable way for analysing the synchronic and diachronic relationships between them and the extra-linguistic factors which have played a role in their development. Obvious issues of interest include the relationship between linguistic similarity and geography (and whether this relationship is necessarily the same for different linguistic levels), and whether this method can reach beyond phonetic similarity to reveal deeper structural relationships between varieties. If so, this method may reveal relationships which are indicative of significant historical events such as contact between speakers of different linguistic varieties as a result of migration, resulting in new dialect formation, or language shift and the spread of varieties to new regions, and may help us to identify the input varieties in each case.

In addition to providing an insight into the synchronic relationship between varieties, this method can also be used to investigate the relationship between varieties in 'real' or 'apparent' time, as the comparison between the Traditional and Modern varieties of Tyneside and Tyrone English above indicates. Such a study allows us to determine the changing relationships between varieties as a result of processes such as standardisation and dialect levelling, which may be indicative of wider societal changes and pressures.

5. CONCLUSIONS

This article has presented a new method for assessing the similarity of the lexical distribution of (stressed vowel) phonemes in different varieties of a language. Application of this method provides percentage similarity scores between each pair-wise group of varieties being compared, allowing for a full appreciation of the relationships between varieties in all their complexity. Since this method assesses the structural similarity of varieties rather than their superficial phonetic similarity, it is hoped that it will provide a means of examining historical connections between varieties which are not obvious from surface inspection.

In order for this method (and, I suggest, any method which seeks to compare lexical distribution of phonemes) to produce meaningful result, working solutions to perennial phonological problems are needed. This article suggests a solution to one particularly thorny issue in English phonology, rhoticity, and, in so doing, allows an even deeper insight into the connections between varieties. With its emphasis on assessing deep structural relationships, this method is ideally suited to exploring historical connections between varieties of a language, connections which may be the result of common origin or contact.

Using this method, it is hoped that a range of issues can be explored, such as the relationships between northern Englishes and Scots, the relationship of Standard English (with RP-like lexical distribution) to regional varieties, and the origins of colonial Englishes (such a Tyrone English). In order to do so, data from a wide range of varieties will need to be compared, and work on this has already begun, using data from the *Survey of English Dialects* (Orton, Sanderson and Widdowson, 1962–71) and from the *Linguistic Atlas of Scotland* (Mather and Speitel, 1986), as well as comparable data from RP and Tyrone English (see Maguire 2008 for initial results). It ultimately remains to be seen how the results of this method compare with the results of phonetic comparisons, but it is only through application of a range of complimentary methods that a true picture of the structured complexity of relations between varieties of a language will be revealed.

REFERENCES

J. K. Chambers and P. Trudgill (1980), *Dialectology* (Cambridge).

J. R. Firth (1948), 'Sounds and prosodies', *Transactions of the Philological Society*, 127–152.

H. Goebl (2006), 'Recent advances in Salzburg dialectometry', *Literary and Linguistic Computing*, 21, 411–435.

H. Goebl (2007), 'A bunch of dialectometric flowers: a brief introduction to dialectometry', *Austrian Studies in English*, 95, 133–171.

J. Harris (1985), *Phonological variation and change: studies in Hiberno-English* (Cambridge).

P. Heggarty, A. McMahon and R. McMahon (2005), 'From phonetic similarity to dialect classification: a principled approach', in N. Delbecque, J. van der Auwera and D. Geeraerts, eds, *Perspectives on variation* (Amsterdam), 43–91.

W. Heeringa (2004), 'Measuring dialect pronunciation differences using Levenshtein distance' (Ph.D. thesis, University of Groningen).

D. Huson and D. Bryant (2006), 'Application of phylogenetic networks in evolutionary studies', *Molecular Biology and Evolution*, 23(2), 254–267.

P. Johnston (2007), 'Scottish English and Scots', in D. Britain, ed., *Language in the British Isles* (Cambridge), 105–121.

B. Kortmann and C. Upton (2004), 'Introduction: varieties of English in the British Isles', in B. Kortmann, E. Schneider, K. Burridge, R. Mesthrie and C. Upton, eds, *A handbook of varieties of English: A multimedia reference tool, Volume 1: Phonology* (Berlin and New York), 25–34.

W. Kretzschmar (2004), 'Standard American English pronunciation', in B. Kortmann, E. Schneider, K. Burridge, R. Mesthrie and C. Upton, eds, *A handbook of varieties of English: A multimedia reference tool, Volume 1: Phonology* (Berlin and New York), 257–269.

R. Lass (1984), Phonology: an introduction to the basic concepts (Cambridge).

W. Maguire (2008), 'Quantifying dialect similarity by comparison of the lexical distribution of phonemes'. Paper presented at the Thirteenth International Conference on Methods in Dialectology, University of Leeds, 4–8 August 2008.

W. Maguire, A. McMahon, and P. Heggarty (2008), 'Integrating social and geographical variation by phonetic comparison and network analysis'. Poster presented at the Thirteenth International Conference on Methods in Dialectology, University of Leeds, 4–8 August 2008.

J. Mather and H. Speitel (1986), *The linguistic atlas of Scotland, Scots section, Vol. 3, Phonology* (Beckenham).

A. McMahon, P. Heggarty, R. McMahon and W. Maguire (2007), 'The sound patterns of Englishes: representing phonetic similarity', *English Language and Linguistics*, 11(1), 113–42.

A. McMahon and R. McMahon (2005), *Language classification by numbers* (Oxford).

J. Moberg, C. Gooskens, J. Nerbonne and N. Vaillette (2007) 'Conditional entropy measures intelligibility among related languages', in P. Dirix, I. Schuurman, V. Vandeghinste and F. van Eynde, eds, *Computational linguistics in the Netherlands 2006: selected papers from the 17th CLIN meeting* (Utrecht), 51–66.

L. Milroy and M. Gordon (2003), *Sociolinguistics: methods and interpretation* (Malden, Oxford, Melbourne, Berlin).

W. Moulton (1960), 'The short vowel system of northern Switzerland: a study in structural dialectology', *Word*, 16, 155–83.

J. Nerbonne, W. Heeringa and P. Kleiweg (1999), 'Edit Distance and Dialect Proximity', in D. Sankoff and J. Kruskal, eds, *Time warps, string edits and macromolecules: the theory and practice of sequence comparison* (Stanford), v–xv.

J. Nerbonne and W. Heeringa (2001), 'Computational comparison and classification of dialects', in *Dialectologia et Geolinguistica*, 9, 69–83.

H. Orton, S. Sanderson and J. Widdowson (1962–71), eds, *Survey of English dialects (B): the basic material* (Leeds).

Oxford English Dictionary [online] < URL: http://dictionary.oed.com/ > [28 Sept 2008].

K. Rydland (1998), *The Orton Corpus: A dictionary of Northumbrian pronunciation, 1928–1939* (Oslo).

R. Shackleton (2007), 'Phonetic variation in the traditional English dialects', *Journal of English Linguistics*, 35(1), 30–102.

E. L. Thorndike and I. Lorge (1944), *The teacher's word book of 30,000 words* (New York).

P. Trudgill (1999), *The dialects of England*, 2nd edition. (Oxford).

W. Viereck (1966), *Phonematische Analyse des Dialekts von Gateshead-upon-Tyne, Co. Durham* (Hamburg).

U. Weinreich (1954), 'Is a structural dialectology possible?', *Word*, 10, 388–400.

J. Wells (1982), *Accents of English* (Cambridge).

END NOTES

[1] See also Shackleton (2007) for some alternative phonetic comparison methods.

[2] This wordlist is used here for exemplification purposes only. Although it fulfils the requirement of being an independent wordlist, not compiled to produce 'expected' results, I am not necessarily implying that this wordlist is ideally suited for this kind of analysis.

[3] Data for RP are derived from the *Oxford English Dictionary* (online), and data for Tyneside English are derived from fieldwork with native speakers by the author.

[4] The correspondences involving fractions are the result of variability in the lexical distribution of phonemes in one or other of the varieties, as explained in Section 2.2.

[5] Note also the existence, in Wells (1982), of separate lexical sets for most of the historical sequences of vowel + coda /r/.

[6] Note that distance between varieties is indicated by the length along the lines in the tree.

[7] Note that distance between varieties is indicated by the shortest possible length between varieties *along the lines* in the network.

CORPUS-BASED DIALECTOMETRY: AGGREGATE MORPHOSYNTACTIC VARIABILITY IN BRITISH ENGLISH DIALECTS*

BENEDIKT SZMRECSANYI

Abstract   *The research reported in this paper departs from most previous work in dialectometry in several ways. Empirically, it draws on frequency vectors derived from naturalistic corpus data and not on discrete atlas classifications. Linguistically, it is concerned with morphosyntactic (as opposed to lexical or pronunciational) variability. Methodologically, it marries the careful analysis of dialect phenomena in authentic, naturalistic texts to aggregational-dialectometrical techniques. Two research questions guide the investigation: First, on methodological grounds, is corpus-based dialectometry viable at all? Second, to what extent is morphosyntactic variation in non-standard British dialects patterned geographically? By way of validation, findings will be matched against previous work on the dialect geography of Great Britain.*

I. INTRODUCTION

The overarching aim in this study is to provide a methodological sketch of how to blend philologically responsible corpus-based research with aggregational-dialectometrical analysis techniques. The bulk of previous research in dialectometry has focussed on phonology and lexis (however, for work on Dutch dialect syntax see Spruit 2005, 2006, 2008, Spruit et al. t.a.). Moreover, orthodox dialectometry draws on linguistic atlas classifications as its primary data source. The present study departs from these traditions in several ways. It endeavours, first, to measure aggregate *morphosyntactic* distances and similarities between

International Journal of Humanities and Arts Computing 2 (1–2) 2008, 279–296
DOI: 10.3366/E1753854809000433
© Edinburgh University Press and the Association for History and Computing 2009

traditional dialects in the British Isles. Second, the present study does not rely on atlas data but on frequency information deriving from a careful analysis of language use in authentic, naturalistic texts. This is another way of saying that the aggregate analysis in this paper is *frequency-based*, an approach that contrasts with *atlas-based* dialectometry, which essentially relies on categorical input data. Succinctly put, the difference is that atlas-based approaches typically aggregate observations such as *of two variants X and Y, variant X is the dominant one in dialect Z*, while frequency-based approaches are empirically based on corpus findings along the lines of, say, *in dialect Z, variant X is 3.5 times more frequent in actual speech than variant Y.*

The corpus resource drawn on is FRED, the *Freiburg English Dialect Corpus*, a naturalistic speech corpus sampling interview material from 162 different locations in 38 different counties all over the British Isles, excluding Ireland. The corpus was analyzed to obtain text frequencies of 62 morphosyntactic features, yielding a structured database that provides a 62-dimensional frequency vector per locality. The Euclidean distance measure was subsequently applied to compute aggregate morphosyntactic distances, which then served as the input to dialectometrical analysis.

Two research questions guide the present study's inquiry: first, on the methodological plane we are interested in whether and how corpus-based (that is, frequency-based) dialectometry is viable. Substantially, we will seek to uncover if and to what extent morphosyntactic variation in non-standard British dialects is patterned along geographic lines. By way of validation, findings will be matched against previous work (dialectological, dialectometrical, and perceptual) on the dialect geography of Great Britain.

2. PREVIOUS WORK ON AGGREGATE DIALECT DIFFERENCES IN GREAT BRITAIN

Let us first turn to the literature in order to eclectically review extant scholarship on dialect differences in Great Britain. Trudgill (2000:20–35) is one of the best-known dialectological accounts of accent differences in traditional British dialects. Trudgill studies eight salient accent features to establish a composite map dividing England into 13 traditional dialect areas. These can be grouped into six macro areas: (1) *Scots*, (2) *northern dialects* (Northumberland and the Lower North), (3) *western central (Midlands) dialects* (Lancashire, Staffordshire), (4) *eastern central (Midlands) dialects* (South Yorkshire, Lincolnshire, Leicestershire), (5) *southwestern dialects* (western Southwest, northern Southwest, eastern Southwest), and (6) *southeastern dialects* (central East and eastern Countries).

In the realm of perceptual dialectology, Inoue (1996) conducted an experiment to study the subjective dialect division in Great Britain. 77 students at several universities in Great Britain were asked, among other things, to draw lines on a blank map 'according to the accents or dialects they perceived' (Inoue 1996:146), based on their experience. The result of this exercise can be summarised as follows: dialects of English in Wales and Scotland are perceived as being very different from English English dialects. Within England, the North is differentiated from the Midlands, and the Midlands are differentiated from the South (Inoue 1996:map 3). This division is quite compatible with Trudgill's (1996) classification, except that in Inoues's experiment, Lancashire is part of the North, not of the western Midlands, and the northern Southwest (essentially, Shropshire and Herfordshire) patterns with Midland dialects, not southwestern dialects.

As for atlas-based dialectometry, Goebl (2007) draws on the *Computer Developed Linguistic Atlas of England* (which is based on the *Survey of English Dialects*) to study aggregate linguistic relationships between 314 sites all over England. The aggregate analysis is based on 597 lexical and morphosyntactic features. Among many other things, Goebl (2007) utilises cluster analysis to partition England into discrete dialect areas (Goebl 2007:maps 17–18). It turns out that there is 'a basic opposition between the North [...] and the South of England' (Goebl 2007:145). The dividing line runs south of Lancashire and South Yorkshire, and thus cuts right across what Trudgill (2000) and Inoue (1996) classify as the Midlands dialect area. In southern English dialects, Goebl (2007) finds a major split between southwestern and other southern dialects.

3. METHODS AND DATA

The present study is an exercise in corpus-based dialectometry. Corpus linguistics is a methodology that draws on principled collections of naturalistic texts to explore authentic language usage. A hallmark of the methodology is the 'extensive use of computers for analysis, using both automatic and interactive techniques' and the reliance 'on both quantitative and qualitative analytical techniques' (Biber et al. 1998:4). This section will discuss the corpus as well as the feature frequency portfolio that will serve as the basis for the subsequent aggregate analysis.

3.1 Data source: the Freiburg English Dialect Corpus (FRED)

This study will tap the *Freiburg English Dialect Corpus* (henceforth: FRED) (see Hernández 2006; Szmrecsanyi and Hernández 2007 for manuals) as its primary data source. FRED contains 372 individual texts and spans approximately 2.5 million words of running text, consisting of samples (mainly transcribed so-called 'oral history' material) of dialectal speech from a variety of sources. Most of these samples were recorded between 1970 and 1990; in most cases, a fieldworker interviewed an informant about life, work etc. in former days.

The 431 informants sampled in the corpus are typically elderly people with a working-class background (so-called 'non-mobile old rural males'). The interviews were conducted in 162 different locations (that is, villages and towns) in 38 different pre-1974 counties in Great Britain plus the Isle of Man and the Hebrides. The corpus is annotated with longitude/latitude information for each of the locations sampled. From this annotation, county coordinates can be calculated by computing the arithmetic mean of all the location coordinates associated with a particular county. At present, FRED is neither part-of-speech annotated nor syntactically parsed.

3.2 Feature selection and extraction

Corpus-based dialectometry is essentially frequency-based dialectometry; thus the approach outlined here bears a certain similarity to the method in Hoppenbrouwers and Hoppenbrouwers (2001) (discussed in Heeringa 2004: 16–20). Following a broadly variationist approach in the spirit of, for example, Labov (1966), a catalogue spanning 35 morphosyntactic variables with typically (but not always) two variants each was defined. This catalogue of 35 variables yields a list of $p = 62$ morphosyntactic target variants (henceforth: *features*); the Appendix provides a comprehensive list. In an attempt to aggregate as many variables as possible, the features included in the catalogue are the usual suspects in the dialectological, variationist, and corpus-linguistic literature, regardless of whether a geographic distribution has previously been reported for a particular feature or not. To qualify for inclusion, however, a candidate feature had to fulfill the following criteria:

1. For statistical reasons, the feature had to be relatively frequent, specifically: ≥ 1 occurrence per 10,000 words of running text (this criterion rules out interesting but infrequent phenomena such as resumptive relative pronouns or double modals).
2. For practical purposes, the feature had to be extractable subject to a reasonable input of labour resources by a human coder (ruling out, for example, hard-to-retrieve null phenomena such as zero relativisation, or phenomena where semantics enters heavily into consideration, such as gendered pronouns).

Next, the material in FRED was coded for the features in the catalogue. 26 features for which automatic recall was feasible were extracted automatically using Perl (*Practical Extraction and Report Language*) scripts. 36 features were coded manually after pre-screening the data using Perl scripts, a step which considerably narrowed down the number of phenomena which had to be inspected manually. Even so, the frequency database utilised in the present study is based on 75,124 manual (that is, qualitative) coding decisions. Szmrecsanyi (forthcoming) provides a detailed description of the procedure along with the detailed coding schemes that regimented the coding process.

Once coding was complete, another line of Perl scripts was used to extract vectors of $p_{total} = 62$ feature frequencies per locality. The feature frequencies were subsequently normalised to *frequency per ten thousand words* (because textual coverage in FRED varies across localities) and *log*-transformed[1] to de-emphasise large frequency differentials and to alleviate the effect of frequency outliers. The resulting 38×62 table (on the county level – that is, 38 counties characterised by 62 feature frequencies each for the full dataset) yields a Cronbach's α value of .86, indicating satisfactory reliability.

Finally, the 38×62 table was converted into a 38×38 distance matrix using Euclidean distance – the square root of the sum of all squared frequency differentials – as an interval measure. This distance matrix was subsequently analyzed dialectometrically.[2]

4. RESULTS

We now move on to a discussion of empirical findings. Unless stated otherwise, the level of areal granularity is the county level ($N = 38$).

4.1 On the explanatory power of geography

Let us first consider the role that geographic distance plays in aggregate morphosyntactic variability. First, how much of this variability can be explained by geography? Second, looking at the morphosyntactic dialect landscape in the British Isles, to what extent are we dealing with a continuum such that transitions are gradual and not abrupt?

As for the first question, a Perl script was run on the Euclidean distance matrix based on all $p_{total} = 62$ features and on FRED's geographic longitude/latitude annotation to generate a table specifying pairwise morphosyntactic and geographic distances. This yielded an exhaustive list of all $N \times \frac{N-1}{2} = 703$ possible county pairings, each pairing being annotated for morphosyntactic and geographic distance. On the basis of this list, the scatterplot in Figure 1 illustrates the correlation between morphosyntactic and geographic distance in the database at hand.

Figure 1 highlights two facts. First, while the correlation between morphosyntactic and geographic distance is highly significant ($p = .00$), it is relatively weak (Pearson correlation coefficient: $r = .22$). In other words, geography explains overall only 4.7 per cent of the morphosyntactic variance ($R^2 = .047$). To put this value into perspective, Spruit et al. (to appear: Table 7) – in a study on aggregate linguistic distances in Dutch dialects – report R^2 values of .47 for the correlation between geography and pronunciation, .33 for lexis,

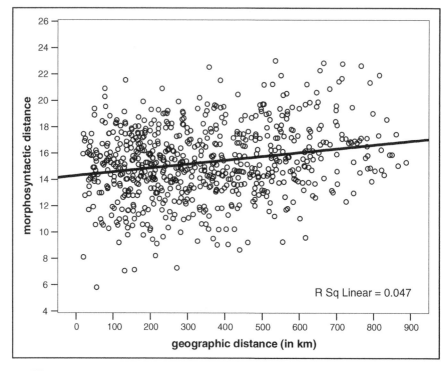

Figure 1. Correlating linguistic and geographic distances, county level ($N = 38$), all features ($p_{total} = 62$), $r = .22$, $p = .00$.

and .45 for syntax. Second, the best curve estimation for the relationship between morphosyntactic and geographic distance in British English dialects is actually linear.[3] Given Séguy (1971) and much of the atlas-based dialectometry literature that has followed Séguy's seminal study, one would actually expect a sublinear or logarithmic relationship. Having said that, we note that Spruit (2008:54–55), in his study of Dutch dialects, finds that the correlation between syntactic and geographic distance is also more linear than logarithmic. Hence, it may simply be the case that (morpho)syntactic variability has a different relationship to geographic distance than lexical or pronunciational variability.

Against this backdrop, it is interesting to note that not all of the 62 features entered into aggregate analysis correlate significantly with geography. In fact, only 23 features do (these are marked with an asterisk in the Appendix).[4] When the aggregate analysis is based on only those $p_{geo} = 23$ features, we obtain the scatterplot in Figure 2. The correlation coefficient between morphosyntactic and geographic distance is now approximately twice as high as in Figure 1 ($r = .41$),

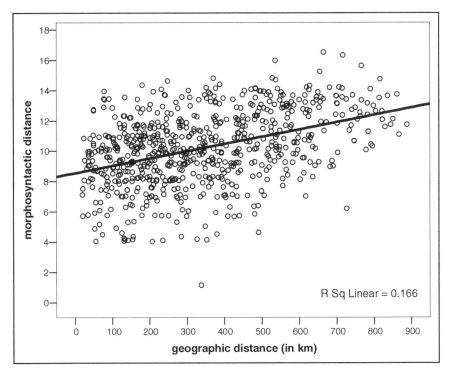

Figure 2. Correlating linguistic and geographic distances, county level ($N = 38$), geographically significant features only ($p_{geo} = 23$), $r = .41$, $p = .00$.

which means that for this particular feature subset geography explains about 16.6 per cent of the morphosyntactic variance ($R^2 = .166$).[5] While these numbers begin to approximate the explanatory potency of geography in atlas-based dialectometry, it still seems that we should base the aggregate analysis on all available data. This is why the subsequent analysis in this paper will be based on the entire feature portfolio ($p_{total} = 62$), despite the weaker geographic signal it provides. Still, we observe that feature selection does matter a great deal, and one is left to wonder to what extent compilers of linguistic atlases – the primary data source for those studies that report high coefficients for geography – really draw on all available features, or rather on those features that seem geographically interesting.

Comparatively weak as the overall correlation between morphosyntactic and geographic distance may be, are we nonetheless dealing with a morphosyntactic dialect continuum? To answer this question, we will now visualise aggregate morphosyntactic variability using cartographic techniques, all relying on Voronoi tesselation (see Goebl 1984) to project linguistic results to geography.

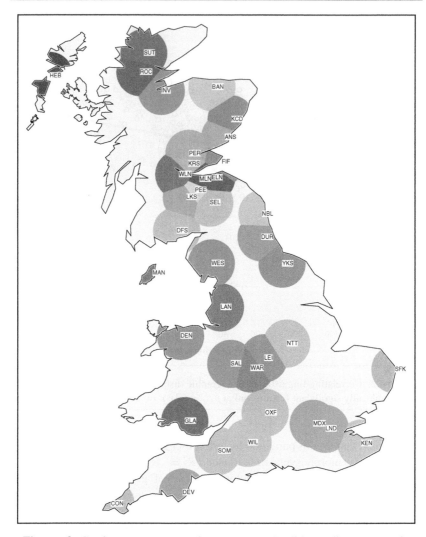

Figure 3. Continuum map: regular MDS on Euclidean distance matrix (county level). Labels are three-letter Chapman county codes (see http://www. genuki.org.uk/big/Regions/Codes.html for a legend). Smooth colour transitions indicate the presence of a dialect continuum. Reddish colours correlate best with increased frequencies of multiple negation, greenish colours correlate best with higher frequencies of non-standard weak past tense and past participle forms, and bluish colours correlate best with increased frequencies of *wh*-relativisation.

Regular multidimensional scaling (henceforth: MDS) (see Kruskal and Wish 1978) was utilised to scale down the original 62-dimensional Euclidean distance matrix to three dimensions; the distances in the three-dimensional MDS solution correlate with the distances in the original distance matrix to a satisfactory degree ($r = .82$). Subsequently, the three MDS dimensions were mapped to the red–green–blue colour components, giving each of the county polygons in Figure 3 a distinct colour.[6] In continuum maps such as Figure 3, smooth (as opposed to abrupt) colour transitions implicate the presence of a dialect continuum. As can be seen, the morphosyntactic dialect landscape in the British Isles is overall not exceedingly continuum-like.[7] While colour transitions in the south of England are fairly smooth (meaning that this is a fairly homogeneous dialect area), the picture is more noisy in the North of England and, especially, in Scotland. To aid interpretation of Figure 3, each of the 62 normalised *log*-transformed feature frequencies was correlated against each of the three MDS dimensions to determine which of the features correlate most strongly with the red–green–blue colour scheme in Figure 3 (see Wieling et al. 2007 for a similar procedure). It turns out that more reddish colours correlate best with increased frequencies of multiple negation (feature [34]) ($r = .79$), greenish colours correlate most strongly with higher frequencies of non-standard weak past tense and past participle forms (feature [23]) ($r = .63$), and bluish colours correlate best with increased frequencies of *wh*-relativisation (feature [49]) ($r = .57$).

By way of an interim summary, the research discussed in this section has two principal findings. Firstly, the explanatory potency of geography is comparatively weak in the data at hand and accounts for only between 4.7 to 16.6 per cent of the observable morphosyntactic variance (depending on whether all available features or only those with a significant geographic distribution are studied). Secondly, the morphosyntactic dialect landscape in Great Britain does not have a very continuum-like structure overall, although transitions appear to be more gradual in England than in Scotland.

4.2 Classification and validation

The task before us now is to examine higher-order patterns and groupings among British English dialects. Is it possible to identify dialect areas on morphosyntactic grounds (and on the empirical basis of frequency data)? If so, do these dialect areas conform to those previously identified in the literature (see section 2)?

To answer these questions, hierarchical agglomerative cluster analysis (see Aldenderfer and Blashfield 1984), a data classification technique used to partition observations into discrete groups, was applied to the dataset. Simple clustering can be unstable, hence a procedure known as 'clustering with noise'

Figure 4. Composite cluster map, county level ($N = 38$), all features ($p_{total} = 62$); input: cophenetic distance matrix (clustering algorithm: WPGMA). Darker borders indicate more robust dialect boundaries.

(Nerbonne et al. 2008) was conducted: the original Euclidean distance matrix was clustered repeatedly, adding some random amount of noise in each run. This exercise yielded a cophenetic distance matrix which details consensus (and thus more stable) cophenetic distances between localities, and which is amenable to various cartographic visualisation techniques. This study uses the clustering parameters described in Nerbonne et al. (2008), setting a noise ceiling of $c = \sigma/2$ and performing 100 clustering runs. There are many different clustering algorithms; in addition to using the – quite customary – *Weighted Pair Group Method using Arithmetic Averages* (WPGMA), we also apply *Ward's Minimum Variance Method* (WARD), as the two algorithms yield interestingly different clustering outcomes.[8]

The resulting higher-order structures can be visualised, for example, via so-called *composite cluster maps* (see Nerbonne et al. 2008 for a discussion). These highlight the fuzzy nature of dialect boundaries such that darker borders between localities represent more robust linguistic oppositions (which, thanks to the clustering-with-noise technique utilized, can be considered statistically significant). Figure 4 presents a composite cluster map that visualises the outcome of WPGMA noisy clustering, which is contrasted with the corresponding WARD outcome in Figure 5. An alternative visualisation, which highlights rough group memberships and fuzzy transition areas, can be attained by applying

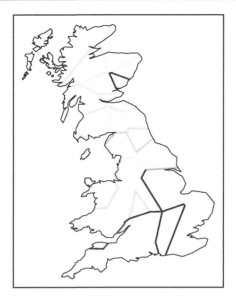

Figure 5. Composite cluster map, county level ($N = 38$), all features ($p_{total} = 62$); input: cophenetic distance matrix (clustering algorithm: WARD). Darker borders indicate more robust dialect boundaries.

MDS to the cophenetic distance matrix (see, for instance, Alewijnse et al. 2007:section 5.3) and subsequently assigning component colours to each of the three resulting MDS dimensions. Such maps – where similar colourings indicate likely membership in the same dialect area – are displayed in Figure 6 (WPGMA) and Figure 7 (WARD). Note, in this context, that the distances in the three-dimensional MDS solution correlate very highly with the distances in the cophenetic distance matrix ($r = .96$ and $r = 1.00$, respectively).

Figures 4 through 7 can be interpreted as follows. Both the WPGMA and WARD algorithms characterise Scotland as heterogeneous and geographically fairly incoherent (more so according to WPGMA than according to WARD). Both algorithms moreover tend to differentiate between English English dialects and non-English English dialects (Scottish English dialects and northern Welsh dialects, in particular Denbighshire [DEN]). This is consonant with the sharp perceptual split between English English dialects and Welsh/Scottish dialects reported in Inoue (1996). As for divisions among English English dialects, however, the two clustering algorithms generate fairly different classifications:

- WPGMA classifies England as a rather homogeneous dialect area vis-à-vis Scotland and Wales. The only outlier in England is the county Warwickshire

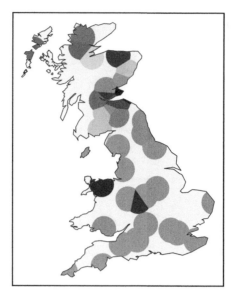

Figure 6. Fuzzy MDS map, county level ($N = 38$), all features ($p_{total} = 62$); input: cophenetic distance matrix (clustering algorithm: WPGMA); felicitousness of the MDS solution: $r = .96$. Similar colours indicate likely membership in the same dialect area.

(WAR; the brownish polygon in Figure 6), which is more similar to Denbighsire (DEN; Welsh English) and some Scottish dialects than to the other English counties.

- WARD broadly distinguishes between southern English dialects (reddish/ pinkish colours in Figure 7) and northern English dialects (brownish/darkish colours). Northumberland (NBL, dark green), Durham (DUR, blue), and Warwickshire (WAR; light blue), albeit English counties, pattern with Scottish dialects. Middlesex (MDS) is grouped with the northern dialects, although the county is located in the geographic Southeast (this fact is responsible for the salient southeastern 'box' in Figure 5). In sum, the WARD algorithm finds a rather robust North–South split in England, which is compatible with all three accounts surveyed in Section 2 (Trudgill 2000; Inoue 1996; Goebl 2007). Figures 5 and 7 can also be seen to reveal a split among northern dialects into Midland dialects (darkish/brownish colours, in particular Leicestershire [LEI], Shropshire [SAL], Lancashire [LAN], Westmorland [WES], and Yorkshire [YKS]) versus northern dialects (Durham [DUR] and Northumberland [NBL]). This opposition would be in accordance with Inoue (1996) as well as Trudgill (2000).

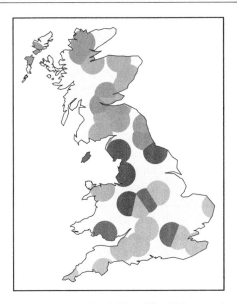

Figure 7. Fuzzy MDS map, county level ($N = 38$), all features ($p_{total} = 62$); input: cophenetic distance matrix (clustering algorithm: WARD); felicitousness of the MDS solution: $r = 1.00$. Similar colours indicate likely membership in the same dialect area.

In summary, we have seen in this section that it seems to be possible – despite a good deal of apparent geographical incoherence – to identify rough dialect areas on morphosyntactic grounds, and that these are not incompatible with previous accounts of dialect differences in Great Britain. For one thing, most English English dialects are rather robustly differentiated from non-English English dialects. Second, the WARD algorithm in particular finds a North–South split among English English dialects that appears meaningful given extant scholarship. At the same time, we note that both algorithms fail to identify meaningful and coherent patterns among Scottish dialects. Also, neither algorithm detects a split between the Southwest of England and other southern dialects, as posited by Trudgill (2000) and Goebl (2007).

5. CONCLUSIONS

This study has demonstrated that frequency vectors derived from naturalistic corpus data – as opposed to, for instance, categorical linguistic atlas classifications – can serve as the empirical basis for aggregate analysis. Focussing on morphosyntactic variability in British English dialects, we have seen that the dataset yields a significant geographic signal which is, however, comparatively weak in comparison to previous atlas-based dialectometrical findings. The analysis has also suggested that overall variability in British English dialects does not seem to have an exceedingly continuum-like structure, and that there is quite a bit of geographical incoherence. Future study will want to investigate whether the comparatively weak explanatory potency of geography is real, or whether it is an artefact of the specific methodology or data type used. Having said that, the results do reveal that British English dialects can be partitioned into rough dialect areas on morphosyntactic grounds. Although the match with the literature is not perfect – as a matter of fact, we should not expect it to be perfect, given that some of the studies cited 'are based on entirely different things and on not very much at all', as one reviewer of this paper noted – the classification suggested here is not incompatible with previous work on dialect divisions in Great Britain. This enhances confidence in the method utilized here. A more detailed discussion of the outlier status of counties such as Warwickshire and Middlesex (including the identification of the features that are responsible for this outlier status), and of the extent to which the methodology presented here uncovers hitherto unknown generalisations is reserved for another occasion.

More generally speaking, though, the present study highlights the fact that a careful and philologically responsible identification and analysis of features occurring in naturalistic, authentic texts (as customary in, for example, variationist sociolinguistics and corpus-based dialectology) advertises itself for aggregation and computational analysis. The point is that the qualitative-philological jeweller's eye perspective and the quantitative-aggregational bird's eye perspective are not mutually exclusive, but can be fruitfully combined to explore large-scale patterns and generalisations. It should be noted in this connection that the line of aggregate analysis sketched out in this paper could easily be extended to other humanities disciplines that rely on naturalistic texts as their primary data source (for instance, literary studies, historical studies, theology, and so on).

The methodology outlined in the present study can and should be refined in many ways. For one thing, work is under way to utilise Standard English text corpora to determine aggregate morphosyntactic distances between British English dialects, on the one hand, and standard English dialects (British and American) on the other hand. Second, the feature-based frequency information on which the present study rests will be supplemented in the near future by part-of-speech frequency information, on the basis of a coding scheme that distinguishes between 73 different part-of-speech categories. Third, given that geography does not seem to play an exceedingly important role in the dataset analyzed here, it will be instructive to draw on network diagrams (in the spirit of, for example, McMahon et al. 2007) as an additional visualisation and interpretation technique.

APPENDIX: THE FEATURE CATALOGUE

Features whose distribution correlates significantly with geography are marked by an asterisk (*).

A. THE PRONOMINAL SYSTEM

[1]* vs. [2]   non-standard vs. standard reflexives
[3] vs. [4]   archaic *thee, thou, thy* vs. standard *you, yours, you*

B. THE NOUN PHRASE

[5]* vs. [6]   synthetic vs. analytic adjective comparison
[7] vs. [8]   the *of*-genitive vs. the *s*-genitive
[9] vs. [10]*   preposition stranding vs. preposition/particle frequencies

C. PRIMARY VERBS

[11] vs. [12]*   the primary verb TO DO vs. the primary verbs
                 TO BE/HAVE
                 NOTE: this includes both main verb and auxiliary verb
                 usages

D. TENSE, MOOD, AND ASPECT

[13] vs. [14]   the future marker BE GOING TO vs. WILL/SHALL
[15] vs. [16]*   *would* vs. *used to* as markers of habitual past
[17]* vs. [18]   progressive vs. unmarked verb forms
[19]* vs. [20]   the present perfect with auxiliary BE vs. the present perfect
                 with auxiliary HAVE

E. VERB MORPHOLOGY

[21] vs. [22]   *a*-prefixing on *-ing*-forms vs. bare *-ing*-forms
[23] vs. [24]   non-standard weak past tense and past participle forms vs.
                 standard strong forms
[25]* vs. [26]   non-standard 'Bybee' verbs vs. corresponding standard
                 forms
                 NOTE: 'Bybee' verbs (see Anderwald 2009) have a three-
                 way paradigm – e.g. *begin/began/begun* – in Standard
                 English but can be reduced to a two-way paradigm – e.g.
                 begin/begun/begun – in dialect speech
[27]   non-standard verbal *-s*
[28]* vs. [29]   non-standard past tense *done* vs. standard *did*
[30] vs. [31]   non-standard past tense *come* vs. standard *came*

F. NEGATION

[32]* vs. [33]	invariant *ain't* vs. *not*/*n't*/*nae*-negation
[34]* vs. [35]	multiple negation vs. simple negation
[36]* vs. [37]	negative contraction vs. auxiliary contraction
[38]* vs. [39]*	*don't* with 3rd person singular subjects vs. standard agreement
[40] vs. [41]	*never* as a preverbal past tense negator vs. standard negation

G. AGREEMENT

[42]	existential/presentational *there is* vs. *was* with plural subjects
[43]* vs. [44]	deletion of auxiliary BE in progressive constructions vs. auxiliary BE present
[45]* vs. [46]*	non-standard WAS vs. standard WAS
[47] vs. [48]*	non-standard WERE vs. standard WERE

H. RELATIVISATION

[49]	*wh*-relativisation
[50]*	relative particle *what*
[51]	relative particle *that*
[52]	relative particle *as*

I. COMPLEMENTATION

[53]*	*as what* or *than what* in comparative clauses
[54] vs. [55]*	unsplit *for* to vs. *to*-infinitives
[56] vs. [57]	infinitival vs. gerundial complementation after TO BEGIN, TO START, TO CONTINUE, TO HATE, TO LOVE
[58] vs. [59]	zero vs. *that* complementation after TO THINK, TO SAY, and TO KNOW

J. WORD ORDER PHENOMENA

[60]	lack of inversion and/or of auxiliaries in *wh*-questions and in main clause *yes/no*-questions
[61]* vs. [62]*	prepositional dative vs. double object structures after the verb TO GIVE

REFERENCES

M. S. Aldenderfer and R. K. Blashfield (1984), *Cluster Analysis*, Quantitative Applications in the Social Sciences (Newbury Park, London, New Delhi).

B. Alewijnse, J. Nerbonne, L. van der Veen and F. Manni (2007), 'A Computational Analysis of Gabon Varieties', in P. Osenova, ed., *Proceedings of the RANLP Workshop on Computational Phonology*. 3–12.

L. Anderwald (2009), *The Morphology of English Dialects* (Cambridge).

D. Biber, S. Conrad and R. Reppen (1998), *Corpus Linguistics: Investigating Language Structure and Use* (Cambridge).

H. Goebl (1984), *Dialektometrische Studien: Anhand italoromanischer, rätroromanischer und galloromanischer Sprachmaterialien aus AIS und ALF* (Tübingen).

H. Goebl (2007), 'A bunch of dialectometric flowers: a brief introduction to dialectometry', in U. Smit, S. Dollinger, J. Hüttner, G. Kaltenböck, and U. Lutzky, eds, *Tracing English through time: Explorations in language variation* (Wien), 133–172.

W. Heeringa (2004), *Measuring dialect pronunciation differences using Levenshtein distance* (Ph.D. thesis, University of Groningen).

N. Hernández (2006), *User's Guide to FRED*. http://www.freidok.uni-freiburg.de/volltexte/2489/ (Freiburg).

C. Hoppenbrouwers and G. Hoppenbrouwers (2001), *De indeling van de Nederlandse streektalen. Dialecten van 156 steden en dorpen geklasseerd volgens de FFM* (Assen).

F. Inoue (1996), 'Subjective Dialect Division in Great Britain', *American Speech*, 71(2), 142–161.

J. B. Kruskal and M. Wish (1978), *Multidimensional Scaling*, Volume 11 of *Quantitative Applications in the Social Sciences* (Newbury Park, London, New Delhi).

W. Labov (1966), 'The linguistic variable as a structural unit', *Washington Linguistics Review* 3, 4–22.

A. McMahon P. Heggarty, R. McMahon and W. Maguire (2007), 'The sound patterns of Englishes: representing phonetic similarity', *English Language and Linguistics*, 11(1), 113–142.

J. Nerbonne, P. Kleiweg and F. Manni (2008), 'Projecting dialect differences to geography: bootstrapping clustering vs. clustering with noise', in C. Preisach, L. Schmidt-Thieme, H. Burkhardt and R. Decker, eds, *Data Analysis, Machine Learning, and Applications. Proceedings of the 31st Annual Meeting of the German Classification Society* (Berlin), 647–654.

J. Séguy (1971), 'La relation entre la distance spatiale et la distance lexicale', *Revue de Linguistique Romane*, 35, 335–357.

M. R. Spruit (2005), 'Classifying Dutch dialects using a syntactic measure: the perceptual Daan and Blok dialect map revisited', *Linguistics in the Netherlands*, 22(1), 179–190.

M. R. Spruit (2006), 'Measuring syntactic variation in Dutch dialects', *Literary and Linguistic Computing*, 21(4), 493–506.

M. R. Spruit (2008), *Quantitative perspectives on syntactic variation in Dutch dialects* (Ph.D. thesis, University of Amsterdam).

M. R. Spruit, W. Heeringa and J. Nerbonne (to appear), 'Associations among Linguistic Levels', *Lingua*.

B. Szmrecsanyi (forthcoming), *Woods, trees, and morphosyntactic distances: traditional British dialects in a frequency based dialectometrical view*.

B. Szmrecsanyi and N. Hernández (2007), *Manual of Information to accompany the Freiburg Corpus of English Dialects Sampler ("FRED-S")*. http://www.freidok.uni-freiburg.de/volltexte/2859/ (Freiburg).

P. Trudgill (2000), *The dialects of England*, 2nd ed. (Cambridge, MA, Oxford).

M. Wieling, W. Heeringa and J. Nerbonne (2007), 'An aggregate analysis of pronunciation in the Goeman-Taeldeman-van Reenen-Project data', *Taal en Tongval*, 59(1), 84–116.

END NOTES

[*] I am grateful to John Nerbonne, Wilbert Heeringa, and Bart Alewijnse for having me over in Groningen in spring 2007 to explain dialectometry to me. I also wish to thank Peter Kleiweg for creating and maintaining the *RuG/L04* package. The audience at the Workshop on 'Measuring linguistic relations between closely related varieties' at the MethodsXIII conference in Leeds (August 2008) provided very helpful and valuable feedback on an earlier version of this paper, as did four anonymous reviewers. The usual disclaimers apply.

[1] Zero frequencies were rendered as .0001, which yields a *log* frequency of −4.

[2] The analysis was conducted using some custom-made Perl scripts, standard statistical software (SPSS), and Peter Kleiweg's *RuG/L04* package (available online at http://www.let.rug.nl/ ~kleiweg/L04/) as well as the L04 web interface maintained by Bart Alewijnse (http://l04.knobs-dials.com/).

[3] $R^2_{linear} = .0469$, $R^2_{logarithmic} = .0439$.

[4] In order to test individual features for significant geographic distributions, dialect distances were also calculated on the basis of individual features (using one-dimensional Euclidean distance as interval measure) and correlated with geographical distance. If the ensuing correlation coefficient was significant, a given feature was classified as having a significant geographic distribution.

[5] Still, the relationship is more linear ($R^2_{linear} = .0166$) than logarithmic ($R^2_{logarithmic} = .134$).

[6] To do justice to FRED's areal coverage – which is unparalleled in the corpus-linguistic realm, but certainly not perfect – the polygons in Figure 3 have a maximum radius of ca. 40 km. This yields a 'patchy' but arguably more realistic geographic projection.

[7] Having said that, it should be made explicit that the present study is based on an aggregate analysis of features that are known to display variation (though not necessarily geographic variation). As one reviewer noted, the inclusion of more invariable features – say, basic word order or the like – would yield smoother dialect transitions. This is of course true, yet we note that linguistic atlases, and thus atlas-based dialectometry, also of course have a bias towards variable features.

[8] Notice that given the present study's dataset, the *Unweighted Pair Group Method using Arithmetic Averages* (UPGMA), another popular algorithm used in, for instance, Nerbonne et al. (2008), yields almost exactly the same classification as WPGMA.